ALSO BY LAURENCE LEAMER

Madness Under the Royal Palms:
Love and Death Behind the Gates of Palm Beach

Fantastic: The Life of Arnold Schwarzenegger

Sons of Camelot: The Fate of an American Dynasty

The Kennedy Men, 1902–1963: The Laws of the Father

Three Chords and the Truth:
Hope and Heartbreak and the Changing Fortunes in Nashville

The Kennedy Women: The Saga of an American Family

King of the Night: The Life of Johnny Carson

As Time Goes By: The Life of Ingrid Bergman

Make-Believe: The Story of Nancy and Ronald Reagan

Ascent: The Spiritual and Physical Quest of Willi Unsoeld

Assignment: A Novel

Playing for Keeps: In Washington

The Paper Revolutionaries: The Rise of the Underground Press

THE PRICE OF JUSTICE

THE PRICE
OF
JUSTICE

A TRUE STORY OF
GREED AND CORRUPTION

LAURENCE LEAMER

TIMES BOOKS   HENRY HOLT AND COMPANY   NEW YORK

Times Books
Henry Holt and Company, LLC
Publishers since 1866
175 Fifth Avenue
New York, New York 10010
www.henryholt.com

Library of Congress Cataloging-in-Publication Data
Leamer, Laurence.
The price of justice : a true story of greed and corruption / Laurence Leamer.
   pages cm
Includes bibliographical references and index.
ISBN 978-0-8050-9471-8
   1. Caperton, Hugh—Trials, litigation, etc.   2. Massey Energy (Firm)—Trials,
litigation, etc.   3. Judges—Recusal—United States.   4. Fair trial—United
States.   5. Coal trade—Corrupt practices—West Virginia.   I. Title.
   KF229.C37.L43 2013
   346.7302'2—dc23   2012041537

First Edition 2013

Designed by Kelly S. Too
Map by Jeffrey L. Ward

Printed in the United States of America
1   3   5   7   9   10   8   6   4   2

In Memory of David B. Fawcett Jr.,
1927–2012

CONTENTS

CAST OF CHARACTERS

Tarek F. Abdalla: A Pittsburgh attorney who worked on *Caperton v. Massey* in association with Bruce Stanley and David Fawcett.

Tony D. Arbaugh Jr.: A troubled young man drawn into Don Blankenship's political battle to change the Supreme Court of Appeals of West Virginia.

Brent D. Benjamin: A justice of the Supreme Court of Appeals of West Virginia.

Robert V. Berthold Jr.: A Charleston, West Virginia, plaintiffs' attorney in *Caperton v. Massey*.

Donald Blankenship: The chairman and CEO of Massey Energy, the biggest coal company in Appalachia.

James G. Bradley: The former CEO of Wheeling-Pitt, one of the last major steelmakers in the Northeast.

Delorice Bragg: Her husband, Don "Rizzle" Bragg, died in a fire at the Aracoma mine, operated by a Massey subsidiary.

Hugh Mason Caperton: The owner of Harman Mining Company, whose lawsuit against Massey Energy set off a more than decadelong fight against the company and its CEO, Don Blankenship.

Robin Jean Davis: A justice of the Supreme Court of Appeals of West Virginia.

David B. Fawcett: A third-generation Pittsburgh attorney who, with Bruce Stanley, fought Don Blankenship and Massey Energy for more than a decade.

Thomas V. Flaherty: A Charleston, West Virginia, attorney who attempted to mediate *Caperton v. Massey* and was Don Blankenship's defense attorney in *Bragg and Hatfield v. Aracoma, Massey and Blankenship*.

Freda Hatfield: Her husband, Ellery "Elvis" Hatfield, died in a fire at the Massey-run Aracoma mine.

Tonya Hatfield: A West Virginia lawyer who represented Freda Hatfield, whose husband, Elvis Hatfield, died in a fire in the Aracoma mine.

Jay M. Hoke: A West Virginia circuit court judge who oversaw the *Caperton v. Massey* civil trial in the Boone County Courthouse and was one of three judges assigned to the Massey coal slurry case.

Anthony Kennedy: A justice of the United States Supreme Court.

Elliot "Spike" Maynard: A justice of the Supreme Court of Appeals of West Virginia.

Warren McGraw: A justice of the Supreme Court of Appeals of West Virginia.

Theodore B. Olson: America's leading conservative appellate attorney.

Ancil G. Ramey: A Charleston, West Virginia, defense attorney in *Caperton v. Massey.*

John Roberts: The chief justice of the United States Supreme Court.

James Sample: A professor at Hofstra University and an attorney at the Brennan Center for Justice at New York University School of Law.

Antonin Scalia: A justice of the United States Supreme Court.

Scott Segal: A prominent trial lawyer and the husband of Robin Jean Davis, a justice of the Supreme Court of Appeals of West Virginia.

Bruce E. Stanley: Raised in southern West Virginia and now a Pittsburgh attorney who, with David Fawcett, fought Don Blankenship and Massey Energy for more than a decade.

Larry V. Starcher: A justice of the Supreme Court of Appeals of West Virginia.

Amir C. Tayrani: Theodore Olson's associate at the Washington law firm of Gibson, Dunn & Crutcher.

Kevin Thompson: A plaintiffs' attorney in the Massey coal slurry case.

Jeff A. Woods: A Massey defense attorney in *Caperton v. Massey.*

Margaret L. Workman: A justice of the Supreme Court of Appeals of West Virginia.

THE PRICE OF JUSTICE

© 2013 Jeffrey L. Ward

Prologue

When I was a young man, I worked in a coal mine in southern West Virginia. It was 1971, and I had read *Night Comes to the Cumberlands,* Harry Caudill's classic account of the deprived, exploited people of the Appalachian highlands in eastern Kentucky. I realized that amid the poverty and pain, there was something gritty and real in those lives that was absent from my own. So I gave up my apartment on the West Side of Manhattan and drove down to West Virginia, hoping to write about the region and its people.

In the coal fields, it was a time of turmoil. In 1969, Joseph "Jock" Yablonski, the defeated reform candidate for the presidency of the United Mine Workers (UMW), had been shot to death in his bed along with his wife, Margaret, as had their twenty-five-year-old daughter, Charlotte. The fear and paranoia in the industry did not lessen until four years later, when Anthony "Tony" Boyle, the president of the United Mine Workers, was convicted for having ordered Yablonski's murder.

When I arrived in southern West Virginia, the reformist Miners for Democracy was campaigning to take over the corrupt union. The coal companies, meanwhile, were nervous about what they considered outside agitators trying to stir up the miners. The only contact I had was a friend of a friend who ran a furniture store in Beckley, population 16,000—the largest town in south-central West Virginia. He said that if

I truly wanted to learn about this world, the best way to do it was to become a coal miner.

The UMW and the Westmoreland Coal Company agreed that I could work in a mine as long as I didn't tell anyone else I was a journalist and wrote only about the job and its particulars, not union politics. And so the next day I went to work on the "hoot owl" shift, from midnight to 8:00 A.M., in the mine outside Beckley known as Eccles No. 6.

That first night, I showed up in the bathhouse, where the men changed before their shift and where they showered off the coal dust afterward. I arrived just as the second shift was leaving the mine. In my new work pants, long-sleeved green shirt, and unblemished black helmet, I looked like the greenhorn I was. Taking the elevator 150 feet down the shaft with the other men on the shift, I was nervous. In a seam 300 feet beneath the one in which I would be working, 186 miners had died in a 1914 blast, the second-largest disaster in the state's mine history. A decade later, nineteen men had died in another explosion.

There hadn't been another accident of that magnitude since, but every time a man went down in the mines he put a tin tab with his name on it on a board in the bathhouse; he took it off when he came back up after finishing his shift. If he was trapped or dead, the octagonal medal would tell the tale.

During a lifetime in the mines, a worker averaged three or four accidents serious enough to require time off. And when miners retired, they often wheezed with black lung disease—a debilitating affliction that came from inhaling too much coal dust for too long—or had other life-shortening ailments.

Despite the risks, the mines were the one place a man without much of an education could make a decent living. At that time, there was one other way the men could earn good money—by leaving the mountain land they loved to work on the auto assembly line in Detroit.

That was why the miners believed me when I told them that I was a garage mechanic from upstate New York and had come down because I needed work. It made sense to them that a man might have to leave everything he cared about to go to a strange place to make a living. Almost from my first night, the miners accepted me as one of them. That was important, for if the men didn't like you, you probably wouldn't last.

These days, before a man goes down in the mine for the first time, he must sit through a week of safety classes. Back in the 1970s, there was no such preparation. A trainee depended on his fellow miners to show him ways to protect himself: how to avoid the overhanging open wires, which would electrocute him, and how to tie his bootlaces so they would not catch in the conveyer belt and drag him down to be mangled or killed.

For the first few nights, I worked resupplying the mine for the daytime shifts, and then I became a member of an eight-man mining crew. One miner in our group worked the continuous mining machine, which clawed out the coal with its whirling, sawlike blades. Two shuttle-car drivers scooped up about five tons of the newly mined coal at a time and carried it back to the conveyer belt. The shuttle-car drivers were expert at their job, but they always spilled some coal on the ground next to the belt. I stood at the belt and shoveled that coal onto it. If I didn't keep up, the belt might go down or the shuttle cars wouldn't be able to deliver their coal properly. I had to be constantly alert for the shuttle cars as they groaned through the tunnel like mammoth centipedes, their headlights breaking through the blackness. On one of my first nights, I broke my finger in two places.

During the lunch break and when the equipment was down, we had plenty of time to talk. I soon realized that most of the miners, unless they'd served in the military, had been no more than fifty miles from Beckley their entire lives and could not really talk about the world much beyond the mine and these mountains. In some ways, these men were almost as isolated from the rest of America as their ancestors had been a hundred years ago, when they had lived off the land in these mountain hollows. Some of them had worked thirty years in the mines and could remember the days before the mechanization of the industry, when they had mined with picks and shovels.

At the end of the shift, heading out, we squeezed past car after car of the coal we had just mined. On a good night, there might be eighty cars or more. Many people feel sorry for coal miners, but the men I worked with were proud of their jobs. And for good reason: they knew they had done something of measurable value, and each morning they saw precisely what they had accomplished. The miners did not talk about what those coal cars symbolized, but without coal there would have been no Industrial Revolution. We now know how coal-powered electric plants pollute the air, and we are slowly moving away from their use. But even at the end of the industrial age, without coal the lights of America would grow dim and there would be no coke to make the steel that constructs the buildings in our cities and towns.

I worked in the mine for only a few months, and when I left, I wrote a third-person account about a miner's life that ran in *Harper's* in December 1971. The story was a big deal in West Virginia and was featured in several papers, including the Beckley *Register-Herald*.

A year later I went back to Beckley, while writing a piece for the *New York Times Magazine* about the strife in the union. One evening I attended a union rally and met two of the men with whom I had worked. "Where ya bin, buddy?" one of the men asked. "You just done one day quit 'n' left us." They knew nothing about my article, and I felt that in some way I had betrayed them. I had arrived under false pretenses, and I had left without telling them anything about who I was and why I'd worked among them.

I thought about my experience in coal country many times in the years that followed. Then, in November 2010, I saw the dateline "Beckley" on a *New York Times* article. It reported how Donald Leon Blankenship, the chairman of the largest coal producer in Appalachia, Massey Energy, had driven a small coal mine into bankruptcy in 1998. That mine's owner, Hugh Mason Caperton, together with his company, had won $50 million in a lawsuit fighting Massey's actions, but Blankenship had fought back. It was a baroque saga of envy, revenge, and corruption that had wound its way from the remote hills of West Virginia all the way to the United States Supreme Court and back. And it was still evolving.

"The machinations in Mr. Caperton's case resembled a plot line in John Grisham's courtroom drama *The Appeal*," the *Times* said of the epic legal struggle. I thought that the story had the makings of a powerful book of narrative nonfiction. I took the train from my Washington, D.C., home to southern West Virginia. I had forgotten the beauty of the state's mountains—and how they tend to isolate people, carving the region into small towns and villages, with people living in distant hollows. The train passed any number of half-deserted coal camps, mobile homes, and modest houses before arriving at a tiny station in Prince, eleven miles from Beckley.

Caperton was there to meet me. His family had run the Slab Fork mine outside Beckley for four generations, and he took me to the coal camp where he had grown up. As we drove the twisting mountain road, I told him how after I'd quit Eccles No. 6, I had gotten to know ninety-year-old Major W. P. Tams Jr., the last of the old-time coal barons, and had written an article for *Playboy* about him. Tams lived in the half-deserted coal camp named after him just over the mountain from Slab Fork, in the cabin he had hauled over the mountain in 1909, when he'd opened his mine. Caperton said that as a little boy he would sit on Tams's lap listening to his stories of the pioneer years. Like Tams, the Capertons had run one of the best operations in the state, and the cabins in which the miners lived had been clean and well painted. But since the mine had gone bankrupt, Slab Fork had become a jumble of boarded-up buildings and ill-kept homes.

West Virginia is the second-poorest state in the country, but when I was living there people were proud of their state and culture and had a sense that things were getting better. Then Beckley had vitality, and I liked to go downtown and walk the streets. But when I returned four decades later, downtown Beckley was like most of coal country: full of empty stores and dirty windows.

The union I'd thought would last forever was a forlorn institution that serviced mainly retirees and the disabled. Back in the 1970s, there had been a big fight over strip-mining. Few could have imagined that not only would its opponents lose but there would be massive mountaintop-removal operations, leveling the mountains into high-altitude parking lots.

Blankenship's footprint was everywhere. He had broken one of the most militant unions in America. He was promoting politics that would end or limit the social welfare programs that kept many West Virginians out of desperate circumstance—programs that Blankenship believed sapped resolve and daring. He was the most vociferous defender of mountaintop removal in the state.

I traveled next to Pittsburgh to meet with Caperton's two lawyers, Bruce Stanley and David Fawcett III, who are the central characters in this book. They are partners at Pittsburgh-based Reed Smith, one of the largest law firms in the world, and I met them in their offices on the seventh floor of the firm's imposing building.

I talked with Stanley first. He is short and plump and has a warm, unassuming manner that makes him instantly likable. He seems a gentle

soul who has somehow wandered into the wrong profession, but the
bold, powerful words he spoke that day suggested that it could be a fatal
mistake to underestimate him. Stanley grew up dirt-poor in southern
West Virginia, an hour and a half northwest of Beckley. Despite his two
decades in Pittsburgh, he has never tried to hide his Appalachian roots.

Stanley had other important cases pending against Massey and Blankenship, involving wrongful death and the poisoning of the water of
hundreds of citizens. The lawyer explained to me how Blankenship's
company and its disregard for safety was so outrageous that he believed
Massey had been responsible for the deaths of scores of miners. Blankenship fostered vendettas against anyone who dared challenge his sovereignty over coal country.

I sensed that this story was far larger and more socially significant
than I had first realized. It wasn't just about one lawsuit; there were half
a dozen. And it wasn't just about West Virginia. It was about the nature
of justice in America.

I then walked over to David Fawcett's office. Fawcett, who dresses
elegantly, is a precisely spoken third-generation Pittsburgh lawyer, the
least likely person to have been Stanley's partner in a decade-long struggle against Blankenship and Massey Energy. The tall, lean attorney is
cautious and circumspect, and it took me a long while to win his confidence. Fawcett didn't feel the harm Blankenship was doing in the same
visceral way West Virginia–born Stanley did, but he, too, had been
brought up with a concern for justice. He, too, had taken on other cases
against Massey, and he was just as determined to go to any length necessary to bring Blankenship down.

Blankenship, the most powerful coal baron in the history of the industry, had risen up just as the industry began what in Appalachia is probably
a terminal decline, when West Virginia desperately needed leaders to help
the state look elsewhere for a future. The worse the future appeared, the
more Blankenship's power tightened. For over a decade, just about the
only significant things that stood in the way of Blankenship's control
over a state and an industry seemed to be these two Pittsburgh attorneys,
who had undertaken a relentless legal quest to bring justice to this corner of America.

Many people view West Virginians as another people, remote and
distant, unworthy of concern. When Spike TV did a series on a West

Virginia coal mine, the program's editors added subtitles beneath the images, as if the miners spoke in an incomprehensible foreign tongue.

I had never had any trouble understanding that language. And so I headed down to West Virginia and reentered a world I had known long ago. As I drove those mountain roads, I kept thinking of the miners I had worked with so many years ago. To me, the most troubling aspect of their lives had been their fatalism. They'd often done unsafe things and taken chances they should not have. They'd figured that if bad things were going to happen, they were going to happen, no matter what you did or what precautions you took, so you might as well do pretty much as you pleased.

Stanley's father and brother had been miners, and he was as much a son of West Virginia as any of the men with whom I had worked. But he had not one iota of that mountain fatalism, and neither did Fawcett. They fought Blankenship with every ounce of their energy and ability. No matter how desperate and forlorn their chances, they refused to give up. Theirs was the story I would tell this time.

PART ONE

———————•◆•———————

MARCH 3, 2009

"General, if you come out of this horror and misery alive, I want you to do something for these mountain people who have been shut out of the world all these years. I know them. If I live, I will do all I can to aid, and between us perhaps we can do the justice they deserve."

—Abraham Lincoln to General O. O. Howard, 1863

1

In the predawn hours of March 3, 2009, Tonya Hatfield huddled outside the darkened home of the United States Supreme Court. A late-winter storm had fallen on Washington, D.C., dropping eight inches of snow on a city expecting cherry blossoms. Crews had shoveled snow from around the court, and Hatfield climbed the forty-four steps to the main entrance, where three others were already in line, hoping to attend the court's morning session.

Forty-year-old Hatfield wore a heavy coat and leather gloves but nothing to protect her feet from the temperature, which hovered near zero. In her haste to drive north from her home in southern West Virginia before the snow made the roads impassable, she had forgotten her winter boots, and her toes went numb in her shoes.

Hatfield had traveled to Washington only once before, as an eleventh-grader with an exalted vision of American democracy. She was a coal miner's daughter who had been raised to believe that when everything else failed, a courtroom was the one place where the poorest could find justice against the richest and the most powerful. That belief had driven Hatfield from her home in Gilbert, West Virginia (population 417), to study at the University of Kentucky College of Law. Degree in hand, she'd returned home to set up her law practice in Gilbert. For the most part, she handled small personal injury cases, real estate closings, lots of wills, and other legal issues.

Hatfield wanted to use the law to help those who needed help most and to bring them true justice. But every time one of her cases brushed against the powerful and the well placed, she saw that in Mingo County the coal companies so effectively controlled the political system that overwhelming injustice and corruption were inevitable. For the young lawyer, it was one futile fight after another, and Hatfield had been thinking of giving up the law. That was when she'd met Pittsburgh attorney Bruce E. Stanley, who became her co-counsel in a case involving the death of two miners in a mine run by the Massey Energy Company, the largest and most powerful coal company in Appalachia.

The West Virginia–born Stanley had so inspired Hatfield that she had not only kept her practice but, this morning, had driven 360 miles through a snowstorm to hear another of his cases involving Massey. It was Stanley's first visit to the court, too, but as a counsel of record, he would breeze through the building's mammoth doors. Hatfield, however, had not wanted to bother Stanley for a pass to the hearing, scheduled for 10:00 A.M. She would take her chances in line with the others.

As dawn arrived, Hatfield looked up at the Vermont-marble façade of the four-story court and saw the inscription "EQUAL JUSTICE UNDER LAW." She could hardly believe that, if she were lucky enough to get in, she would watch the justices apply those words to her friend's case. It could redefine judicial conduct not only in West Virginia's often coal-beholden legal system but in every court in the land.

Two miles from the shivering Hatfield, Theodore B. Olson drove through the city's empty streets. As his vehicle moved through the corridors of power, the sixty-eight-year-old lawyer sat in his thick wool coat reviewing yet again the case he would be arguing before the Supreme Court in a few hours.

Olson's mane of chestnut hair had a Reaganesque fullness, without a spot of gray. His face was that of the common man writ large. To a jury, it would have proved seductive. This morning, however, it wouldn't help him; the only jurors Olson would be facing were the court's nine justices. Olson was a man of great public modesty, but he had the fierce ego of a lawyer who practiced the most unforgiving kind of law: at the

Supreme Court, lawyers were given precisely a half hour to make their case. Olson, and his clients, lived and died in those few minutes.

Ted Olson not only ranked among the top six attorneys in Supreme Court appearances; he had won forty-three of those fifty-four cases. A lifelong conservative, he had etched his place in legal history in the aftermath of the disputed 2000 presidential election. The Berkeley Law graduate had argued before the Supreme Court on behalf of George W. Bush in *Bush v. Gore.* The decision seating Bush as president made Olson nationally prominent, lionized by Republicans and despised by Democrats. Bush rewarded Olson by naming him solicitor general, the government's top lawyer, whereupon he won eight consecutive victories for the administration in the Supreme Court. If Olson had not been so disliked by Democrats, Bush would likely have nominated him to the Supreme Court.

On the morning of September 11, 2001, Olson's wife, Barbara Olson, a lawyer and a prominent conservative commentator on Fox News, boarded American Airlines flight 77 from Washington's Dulles Airport to Los Angeles. The plane had just taken off when Olson's wife called him, saying that hijackers had commandeered the plane. A few minutes later the jet flew into the Pentagon, killing her and everyone else on board, as well as 125 on the ground there. To many who loathed Olson's politics, her death made him seem vulnerably human, even a tragic figure.

Olson was now six months away from his sixty-ninth birthday. At many firms he would have become the hoary, revered senior partner, his picture displayed in the boardroom, his duties relegated to winning new business and placating unhappy clients. Yet he remained at the very center of the firm's operations, and he often squared off against lawyers a quarter century or more his junior.

As he turned onto stately Connecticut Avenue, Olson kept thinking about what faced him this morning. The case Olson would be arguing today, *Caperton v. Massey Coal Company,* had been brought to him by two Pittsburgh attorneys, David Fawcett III and Bruce Stanley, who would be sitting next to him as he addressed the justices. Olson preferred cases of historic significance, and this one offered a potentially precedent-setting result. In the preceding eleven years, it had worked its way through two states and three courtrooms, including the Supreme Court of Appeals of West Virginia. It had devastated the life of the primary plaintiff and emboldened the ultimate defendant, the most powerful coal baron in the industry's 130-year history in the region.

The plaintiff, Hugh Mason Caperton, was the operator of a small coal mine in southwestern Virginia. His business had been driven into bankruptcy by Donald Leon Blankenship, the chairman of Massey Energy, the fourth-largest coal company in America, which in 2008 had recorded coal revenues of $2 billion.

The Massey chairman was the unchallenged voice of the industry. There was no coal Blankenship did not covet. As his nearly six thousand workers and their machines chewed up the earth, producing some forty million tons of coal annually, he chewed up his competitors, buying up their bankrupt operations, picking up mines at fire-sale prices, busting the United Mine Workers, and opening scores of nonunion underground and surface mines. Over twenty-eight years at Massey, Blankenship had risen from office manager to autocrat, building the greatest realm of coal Appalachia had ever seen and controlling more than a third of the region's remaining seams of the mineral. At Massey, he says, he "learned about, and struggled against, the ignorance and evilness of the United Mine Workers, much of the media, the 'greeniacs,' and much of corporate America."

Amid the 1984–85 UMW strike against his company, Blankenship had declared, "What you have to accept in a capitalist society generally is that it's like a jungle where it's the survival of the fittest.... From a business standpoint, it's survival of the most productive, and in the long term the most productive people who benefit."

Blankenship considered Hugh Caperton's small mine, in Harman, Virginia, to be the kind of debt-ridden union operation that needed to adapt to Massey's ways—or die. Massey companies were known for doing anything to advance their position: using financial leverage with customers, sabotaging competitors, and fighting the union.

One of Massey's newly acquired subsidiaries, United, had a subcompany, Wellmore, that had a long-term contract to buy Harman's coal, but Blankenship decided the price was too expensive. So when he saw an opportunity to nullify the contract, he jumped. His meddling destroyed Caperton's company—a small sacrifice in Massey's inexorable advance in a free-market, capitalist society where any economic advantage must be exploited.

Blankenship warned Caperton that if he were so foolish as to sue Massey, the company had the money and the power to destroy him. But Caperton filed a suit anyway and, with Fawcett and Stanley as his attorneys, won a $50 million jury judgment in Boone County, West Virginia.

Blankenship called the verdict "a frightening result" and appealed to the Supreme Court of Appeals of West Virginia. Three of the court's five members were avowed progressives, and Blankenship, a conservative Republican, had reason to believe that he and his company stood little chance among them. West Virginia, however, is one of thirty-nine states that elect judges, and before Massey's *Caperton* appeal could be heard, Blankenship had spent more than $3 million to defeat an incumbent liberal Democratic West Virginia supreme court justice who would have likely ruled against him. His money helped elect Brent D. Benjamin, the first Republican to the court in seventy-six years.

Despite Blankenship's massive donations, which would indicate a certain conflict of interest, the newly elected judge refused to recuse himself from *Caperton*. Benjamin joined the court's 3–2 majority overturning *Caperton*'s lower-court victory on a narrow technicality, voiding a jury verdict that, with interest, had reached $75 million.

The United States is one of the very few countries, including Japan and Switzerland, that elect judges to office. In the eight years before this Supreme Court proceeding, contributions to judicial elections across America had doubled. The money had grown so fast and so large that some experts felt the integrity of the entire American court system might be at stake. The contributions had reached such a magnitude that critics believed they risked breaching the "impenetrable bulwark" of an independent judiciary, as described by James Madison when he introduced the Bill of Rights in Congress in 1789.

The donations had been monitored by the progressive nonprofit Justice at Stake, which works to ensure fair and impartial courts. The organization followed twenty-nine contested elections in the first decade of the twenty-first century. In these contests, 144 groups contributed an average of $473,000 apiece in elections across America. Large donations accounted for more than 40 percent of all judicial campaign funding during the decade. Blankenship had given more money, by far, than any other group or individual in any one judicial contest. Most likely, no individual in American history had ever contributed as much money to one judicial campaign as Blankenship had.

Critics argued that these contributors typically did not open their checkbooks to elect thoughtful, independent jurists who would deeply and deliberatively contemplate each decision. Rather, they spent their money to elect judges who thought the way they thought and would vote the way their money dictated. The way Blankenship saw it, he had done no more than what any other freeborn American citizen could have done and had backed up his beliefs with his money.

In *Caperton,* the questions were clearly and vividly defined, and the case would be zealously argued this morning. Was a citizen's constitutional right to due process and a fair trial violated when one side made large contributions to a judge considering the case? Did an ordinary citizen have the right to force a judge to step aside from a case where, because of massive donations to his election, a reasonable person would assume that the judge would likely favor one side?

Due process, as established in the Fifth and Fourteenth Amendments to the Constitution, is a fundamental right of every American. It holds that the government has an absolute obligation to afford every citizen legal rights, no matter how rich or poor, no matter their race or religion, no matter how heinous the crime of which they stand accused, and no matter their ability to contribute to a judge's election campaign.

If the court ruled that what Blankenship had done was constitutionally permissible, critics of unfettered campaign contributions argued, there would be no stopping him and other wealthy individuals, organizations, and unions from essentially buying elections in states without campaign finance laws. If the Supreme Court ruled that Blankenship had spent too much, people like him would still have their say, but they would not be able to overwhelm other voices. In West Virginia, the impact would be unprecedented if the highest court in the United States rebuked both the Supreme Court of Appeals of West Virginia and Blankenship, the most powerful private citizen in Appalachia.

Olson knew that he would be making the kind of argument before the court that he had rarely made before. Olson's conservative soul mates argued that you could not regulate free speech; if you started tinkering with people's rights to express their views through financial contributions, you were heading down a dark road.

Olson's opponent today would be Andrew L. Frey, a New York attorney who had his own stellar record in front of the court. Massey's attorney argued that the West Virginia judge whose integrity was being challenged had not asked Blankenship for money, although he most certainly had, according to an interview Blankenship gave to the *New York Times* as well as a second witness. The appellate attorney argued, further, that to agree to the petitioner's " 'vague and malleable standard' would almost certainly 'open the gates for a flood of litigation.' "

Olson's closest personal friends on the court, Antonin Scalia and Chief Justice John Roberts, would almost certainly agree and were the most likely votes against him. The three men had marched politically and intellectually together for three decades, and now here was Olson wandering off to the left.

Many in Washington found it unthinkable that Olson had decided to argue *Caperton* simply because of its legal merits. Some felt that Olson had softened ideologically since his wife's death, and that was why he would even consider advocating the progressive arguments in the case. Others credited the attorney's fourth wife, Lady Booth, a tax attorney and liberal Democrat, for his having taken the case. A few opined that Olson, an adept user of the media, had agreed to argue *Caperton* to cloak himself in a new, more moderate image.

But Olson truly saw in Blankenship's and the other disproportionate special-interest contributions to judicial candidates a challenge to the very notion of American justice. In such situations, he did not believe that the decision to recuse could rest simply on the judgment and honor of the individual judge.

Olson knew that the odds today in front of the court were not as favorable as they usually were for him. The majority of the justices had been reluctant to hear the case, and he feared that no matter how well he honed his arguments and how eloquently he spoke he might walk away a loser.

Olson kept thinking about his strategy until he arrived at the building on Connecticut Avenue housing Gibson, Dunn & Crutcher. It was a little after five in the morning when the attorney took the elevator up to his office at the Washington law firm.

Amir C. Tayrani was not a morning person, and Olson's youthful associate did not arrive until seven. The lawyer was crucial to Olson's appearances before the Supreme Court and he had worked alongside the senior lawyer in the months of preparation. Tayrani knew that at this moment *Caperton* rested within Olson's head and there was little more that he could do but leave Olson to spend the next few hours going over his argument for a final time.

Olson was like a novelist obsessed with the first sentence of a manuscript. He worked and reworked the opening words, playing with phrases, toying with new ideas. "A fair trial in a fair tribunal is a fundamental constitutional right"—that, he had decided, was how he would begin, keeping it short and simple. "That means not only the absence of actual bias, but a guarantee against even the probability of an unfair tribunal." There, as he saw it, in two neat sentences, sat everything that was at stake—for himself, for Hugh Caperton, for Don Blankenship, for the citizens of West Virginia, and for all Americans.

2

For this morning's hearing, Bruce Stanley and Dave Fawcett had driven from Pittsburgh with their families. The two lawyers were a legal version of *The Odd Couple,* with the fifty-year-old Fawcett playing the compulsively neat Felix and the forty-nine-year-old Stanley as the sloppy Oscar. This morning Stanley had dressed in a dark suit and tie, but he was far outdone by Fawcett, who wore a tailored blue suit, pants pressed as sharply as a West Point cadet's, a white shirt as bright as premium paper, and a conservative designer tie.

What bound the two men in this and other cases against Massey was an obsession to bring Blankenship to justice. The two lawyers were like a laminated piece of wood, with a strength that neither one of them had alone. They had taken the *Caperton* case on a contingent-fee basis, and their firms had not seen a cent from the initial $50 million verdict, which the West Virginia supreme court had erased. In this pursuit, they had sacrificed other lucrative clients, but they were as determined as ever. They were so possessed that they risked destroying whatever peace of mind they still had, and even their health.

Two years earlier, sitting together at a bar, Stanley had said to Fawcett, "Blankenship may have a ton of money, but he ain't happy. He can't be happy. You know why?"

"Why?" Fawcett asked.

"Because he's got a big oozing boil on his ass that he can't get rid of, no matter what. That's us."

Stanley may have thought that, but for all the times he and Fawcett had been in Blankenship's presence in depositions and courtrooms, the Massey chairman had hardly acknowledged them. They were just another two of his pesky, petty detractors.

Fifty-eight-year-old Blankenship was as pure a product of southwestern West Virginia as a lump of coal on a freight train traveling north. Stanley was nine years younger than Blankenship, close enough to be of the same generation. Both men had grown up in homes without indoor plumbing, about thirty miles from each other, in two of the toughest communities in the state; they even looked like brothers. And both were daring men who had taken radically different lessons from their impoverished childhoods.

Appalachia shared little in the billions of dollars that had been shorn from its hills. Blankenship blamed his neighbors' impoverishment on their lack of get-up-and-go and the oppressive, corrupt forces of government and the unions, which tamped down individual initiative. He had not picked up these ideas from reading books. He boasted that he hardly ever read a book. His book was the world as he knew it.

Stanley believed that people must help others and stand together against the economic and political establishment, which dominated the state and held them down. To Blankenship, such thinking was sentimental hogwash. Blankenship saw himself as a fighter of injustice, only his targets were the tyranny of the United Mine Workers, the government bureaucracy, and politicians' pitiful compromises. Once these shackles were removed, he was sure, Appalachia would finally become a world where men like him ruled free and true.

Stanley, like Blankenship, had never forgotten his West Virginia roots. He had not attempted to diminish his West Virginia accent, which some in the North deemed the language of ignorance. Stanley was five and a half feet tall, with a stocky build. His primary exercise, he liked to say, was riding his lawn mower. He had a rubbery, expressive face suited more for comedic roles than tragedies. His little mustache seemed like a halfhearted attempt at vanity, and even when he wore a fancy lawyer's suit he looked as if he would be more comfortable in jeans.

Stanley had obtained a pass for his wife, Debbie, to get into the Supreme

Court. He could not secure passes for his two daughters, so he'd decided that Laura, twenty-one, and Emily, fifteen, had better get in line early. The court was only three blocks away from their hotel, but after five minutes of forging through the frigid streets he realized that they should have taken a cab.

It was so cold that Stanley did not think he could ask his daughters to stand outside. They saw a line running down the steps; near the front stood Tonya Hatfield. She had said she was thinking of coming, but that was before the storm, and he was astounded to find his friend there.

"Tonya! I can't believe you're standing here in this frigging weather," Stanley said, locking her in a bear hug.

"It's nothin', Bruce," Hatfield said with a shrug. At five feet nine inches, Hatfield hovered over Stanley. The two of them shared a stoicism that was a natural quality in West Virginians. No matter how bad things got, you did not complain. You went on.

Just as the Stanleys arrived at the court, one of the guards took pity on the line of freezing hopefuls. He passed out numbers for seating in the hearing and allowed them into the Supreme Court Building's entry hall to warm up before marching them out to line up again to enter in proper order.

Hatfield shepherded the two Stanley daughters through security and into the building, where they met Bruce and Debbie in the cafeteria for hot chocolate and coffee.

"I'm so glad you're here, Tonya," Stanley said. "It means a lot."

"Ah, come on, Bruce," Hatfield said. "I would have driven across the country to see you, Bruce Stanley of Breeden, West Virginia, arguing before the Supreme Court."

"But I'm not arguing, not saying anything," Stanley said. "We got a big-time Washington lawyer doing all the talking."

"I'll be damned," Hatfield said.

"Me, too," Stanley said. He and Fawcett felt they knew the case better than Olson did. The two lawyers would have loved to have presented it to the nine justices. But if Caperton's legal team had not hired someone of Olson's expertise and record who was part of the Supreme Court fraternity, *Caperton* most likely would not have gotten a hearing.

"Ah, don't worry about that; you'll have your chance another time,"

Hatfield said. She was a passionate woman from whom words came in a ceaseless torrent.

"I want you to know, girls," Hatfield told Laura and Emily, "how important what your dad is doing is for the state, even for people who have no idea or appreciation. You understand?

"If he was in school," Hatfield continued, laughing, "he'd be the boy on the playground standing up to the class bully, no matter how big and tough he was."

Stanley had fought another suit against Massey with Hatfield as his co-counsel. In 2006, she'd agreed to share with him her representation of Freda Hatfield, whose husband, Ellery "Elvis" Hatfield, had died in a fire at the Massey-run Aracoma mine. And later she had been instrumental in Stanley's being retained by Delorice Bragg, whose husband, Don "Rizzle" Bragg, had also died in the blaze.

As Stanley looked at Tonya, he felt the widows' presence, even though they were back in southern West Virginia.

"You know it's all the same fight, Tonya," Stanley said.

"I know," Tonya said.

Stanley saw that it was time to head back to the lawyers' lounge, and after kissing his wife he hurried out into the corridor. There his co-counsel in *Caperton* was waiting. Although Fawcett hated to be defined as such, he was a third-generation Pittsburgh attorney. He was tall, as lean as a matador, and had perfectly coiffed brown hair with an off-center part. Fawcett's searching, judgmental eyes looked out on the world and found much that was wanting. He had attended a leading prep school in the years when Stanley was being bused to a small-town high school, where the young West Virginian was viewed as a troublemaker. Fawcett had graduated from the well-regarded University of Pittsburgh School of Law, as had his father and grandfather before him. Stanley had attended the second-tier West Virginia University College of Law.

In August 1989, Stanley arrived in Pittsburgh. For his first two and a half years in the city, he worked beside Fawcett at the law firm of Buchanan Ingersoll. When the two men walked down the corridor at the respected firm, the six-foot-one Fawcett glided down the middle on his long legs as if he were the managing partner. As Stanley hurried to keep up, he kept to the side and looked more like the guy who fixed the computers than one of the junior associates.

Stanley was a progressive Democrat who felt that the Republican Party was a genteel conspiracy bent on helping the well-off stay well-off. Fawcett was a moderate Republican, as much an endangered species in Pennsylvania as the orange-footed pimpleback mussel.

The two men were just as different in the way they approached their profession. Fawcett was methodical; Stanley was intuitive. Fawcett was controlled and controlling; Stanley wrestled to contain an almost manic energy. Fawcett wanted every motion, every document in perfect place; Stanley moved at his own pace, often doing his best work in the middle of the night, sometimes seemingly disorganized, squandering time and opportunity, yet usually, out of somewhere, producing a unique contribution.

Everything Fawcett did took time. One of Fawcett's law professors at Pitt told him he thought "more like a whale than a dolphin." Whales are slow, but they're the unchallenged leviathans of the deep, and Fawcett liked the description. He *was* ponderous. He did not often flash with quick brilliance. He would rather be deliberate and right than fast and wrong.

Fawcett prepared for his trials with a rabid diligence. Obsessed with honesty, he could hardly believe that people could be dishonest on the witness stand. When he faced a dissembler there, Fawcett was sometimes so abruptly caught off guard that he froze with surprise.

On occasion, Fawcett displayed such an imperious attitude that Caperton's nickname for his lawyer was "King Dave." Fawcett may have seemed perfectly self-assured, but he constantly worried that he had not done enough and was not good enough. His underlying fear of imperfection was the great engine of his life. When one of his cases received a verdict that he did not think was fair or just, he blamed himself.

Stanley, meanwhile, conveyed a welter of insecurities that hid his supreme confidence, at times overconfidence. That got him into trouble sometimes, thinking he could never lose.

For Fawcett, justice was the foremost ideal of his profession, and he was as happy defending the strong as the weak, as long as he believed that they had been wronged. When Stanley saw injustice, he usually found it wrapped around inequality. He believed that to have legal justice, you also had to have economic and social justice.

Fawcett had been coolly driven to take Blankenship down for even longer than his more emotive friend. He had embarked on this fight more than a decade ago, and he'd had to wear a face of invincibility for a long time, even when all in his life was not well.

Like Stanley with the mine widows, Fawcett also had his own separate case against Massey. In 2004, Massey had reneged on its contract to deliver large amounts of metallurgical coal to Wheeling-Pittsburgh Steel. Massey's conduct risked destroying Wheeling-Pitt and putting several thousand union steel workers in the unemployment lines.

Fawcett's eighty-one-year-old attorney father, David B. Fawcett Jr., had driven down with him from Pittsburgh to attend the Supreme Court arguments this morning. Fawcett's father was one of the most well liked and prominent trial lawyers in Pittsburgh. He believed that you took whatever came in the door. You were honest and clear to your client and your opponent alike. You charged fairly, you did your best, and then you moved on, win or lose. His son was a different kind of lawyer, and he wasn't quite sure what to make of Dave. Somehow he had raised a son who was "a cause kind of fellow." Dave became crazily obsessed with winning his cases when he thought his client was right.

Fawcett had never in his professional life believed in any case as strongly as he did in the struggle against Massey and Blankenship. He could not abide the idea that after ten years of fighting *Caperton*, their earlier victory might well be erased forever here this morning, and if that happened he surely would find some way to blame himself. He gave off an aura of impenetrable cool. Almost no one knew how deep and debilitating his inner anxieties could be. For years he had dulled them with evening whiskey. Now he had largely given that up and relaxed by going for long runs, but the angst remained, often arising at the worst of times as he stood in a courtroom.

When Fawcett had checked into the Washington hotel with his father, wife, Kathleen, and nineteen-year-old daughter, Claire, the night before the Supreme Court hearings, he'd picked up a copy of the *Washington Post* at the front desk. Right there on the front page—above the fold, even—he saw a headline about the Supreme Court hearing: "Case May Define When a Judge Must Recuse Self: W. Va. Justice Ruled for a Man Who Spent Millions to Elect Him."

"Hugh Caperton was born into the coal business, but for more than a decade he has spent more time in a courthouse than a mine," the story, by Robert Barnes, began. "The complex, intrigue-filled legal tale he will present to the Supreme Court this week was literally enough to spawn a suspense novel. The facts are so compelling that John Grisham used them as a basis for his best-seller *The Appeal.*"

Fawcett had become a bit of a connoisseur of journalism on the case, and it was as good a piece as he had seen. The best part of it was that, most likely, each morning a copy of the *Washington Post* landed on the front steps of each of the Supreme Court justices.

3

At around 8:30 A.M., Olson and Tayrani took the elevator down from their offices and walked out to the sedan, which drove them to Capitol Hill. As many times as Olson had been to the court, he still felt that it was a thrill just to be here, a double thrill "to have the honor of being allowed in there handling a case. There's just nothing to match it. It's impossible to express, but it's a very, very significant and important experience."

Olson and Tayrani entered by a side door, a guard checking their names on his clipboard. They went to the lawyers' lounge, where Fawcett, Stanley, and the attorneys involved in the second case to be heard this morning were waiting.

Shortly afterward, another car arrived, this one carrying fifty-three-year-old Hugh Caperton, his forty-eight-year-old wife, Kathy, and their eleven-year-old daughter, Preston. Caperton, six feet two, had thick eyelashes, a large aquiline nose, and tightly pursed lips. Kathy, with her blue pants suit and pearl necklace, looked very much the wife of a successful executive.

When the Capertons walked into the courtroom, it was already full of spectators. A half hour before the hearing, there was a churchlike quiet. Caperton whispered with the woman seated next to him, a Washington federal judge who wanted to hear the arguments in *Caperton*.

Olson, meanwhile, walked down the aisle with his co-counsels, Tayrani,

Fawcett, and Stanley. They sat at a table directly in front of the long, high bench from which the nine justices oversaw the courtroom. Hatfield's predawn arrival had paid off, and she'd gotten a seat, though one far in the back of the auditorium. On the other side of the room sat Fawcett's father and daughter.

At about ten minutes before ten, a large contingent of reporters filed in to sit along the side. Stanley recognized several of the most famous names in journalism. He took out his yellow legal pad and wrote, "Caperton v. Massey, U.S. Supreme Court, March 3, 2009." Then he leaned toward Fawcett, pointed to the pad, and winked. "Not every day you get to write that," he said.

Fawcett seemed strangely unimpressed. Though he had never before entered the United States Supreme Court, it all looked familiar. The courtroom had been designed by the architect Cass Gilbert, who'd modeled the building after the courtroom he had created for the Supreme Court of Appeals of West Virginia, where Fawcett had spent several disillusioning, spirit-sapping days. Most of the people here this morning were in such awe that they treated the court like a secular cathedral. Fawcett, however, had not come to worship.

"I've been screwed in buildings with marble walls before," Fawcett thought. It was no victory just to present their case today. He cared nothing about a neat little addition to his résumé. A wrong had to be righted, and if it was not righted none of this would mean anything. At his fancy prep school and in the big law firms, people tended to think themselves as of a higher moral standing because of their surroundings—conveniently ignoring the obligations that accompany power and money.

Fawcett knew that they were here largely because of Olson and Tayrani's petition. In it, the Washington attorneys had crafted a narrow, technical argument. They'd focused on whether a judge who had received large contributions from an interested party in a case should have recused himself. Fawcett believed that the issue was far larger, what he called "the beginning of the end of our court system, the crumbling of our country's pillars of justice." He had had the considerable gumption to tell Olson how to present the case: he should stand before the justices and argue *Caperton* in the broadest, most truthful way. He should expose Blankenship's contemptible schemes and how he had perverted justice. That was what Fawcett would have done if he'd been arguing the case this morning.

For a last time before the hearing, Stanley craned his neck to look back out on the courtroom. Lots of people had assumed that Blankenship would show up, but Stanley was convinced otherwise. Blankenship, Stanley thought, was perfectly willing to spend millions of dollars electing a justice to his liking, but that did not mean that he respected the courts and what he considered their intrusion into the private lives and liberties of Americans.

Stanley could usually sense Blankenship's presence even before he saw him; he understood Blankenship the way Caperton or Fawcett never could. In other circumstances, Blankenship could have been a friend, not the man he despised above all others. Stanley kept scanning the rows of spectators, but Blankenship and his ever-present entourage weren't there. Stanley turned his head back and saw his own wife and daughters. They were watching him with pride in a way he had never seen before.

Then the spectators rustled. Retired justice Sandra Day O'Connor had entered and was walking to a seat at the front of the courtroom. O'Connor was here because she had taken on the cause of judicial reform, championing it in public forums and making her opinion known in her writings. The seventy-eight-year-old O'Connor spoke with a boldness that she would have found unseemly as a sitting justice. She wrote that "in too many states, judicial elections are becoming political prizefights where partisans and special interests seek to install judges who will answer to them instead of the law and the constitution." Her presence here this morning signaled that she thought this issue important to the future of American democracy.

The nine justices appeared from behind the tall scarlet curtain. At precisely 10:00 A.M., the gavel sounded and the clerk cried, "Oyez! Oyez! Oyez!"

That evening after the Supreme Court hearing, Fawcett, his wife, and his father grabbed a taxi to take them to an early dinner hosted by Stanley. The driver was listening to National Public Radio's *All Things Considered*. When Fawcett heard legal-affairs correspondent Nina Totenberg talking about the hearing, he yelled with excitement, "Turn it up!" The reporter gave a concise and telling recap of everything that had gone on a few hours earlier and gave background on the case.

"When Benjamin won, he three times refused requests that he disqualify himself from ruling on the case," Totenberg said. "Today, on the steps of the U.S. Supreme Court, Hugh Caperton recalled how he felt back then."

Fawcett was stunned to hear his client's voice coming out of the taxi's radio.

"Well, you know, I obviously was wondering how it was going to be a fair trial when I saw a judge that had received three million dollars," Caperton said.

"I want to tell you something," the cabbie said as he turned down the sound at the end of the report. "I came to this country eight years ago. I am from Nigeria. And I love this country."

The driver paused for a moment. Then he raised his voice: "But I have been following this case, and, you know, this kind of thing should not happen in America! If justice can be bought, there is no justice! In America, this should not be!"

Fawcett gave the cabbie a generous tip and walked into the restaurant where the Stanleys and Capertons had gathered. Fawcett let himself go, drinking, hugging, and laughing. He and his friend Bruce had, indeed, fought a long, hard battle, and, for once, he rejoiced in the sheer duration and intensity of the fight.

Fawcett hugged Debbie Stanley and told the Stanley girls how much he loved their dad. That was the kind of thing he never said, but he said it this evening. He made a toast to Hugh. "None of us would be here without the courage and the optimism of Hugh Caperton," he said. "Here's to standing up to power and injustice."

For a decade now, Fawcett and Stanley had been fighting Blankenship and Massey, locked in a struggle of drama and challenge that they believed was finally ending. They could not possibly imagine that the road ahead would be as arduous as the road they had already traveled.

PART TWO

APRIL 7, 1998

4

D ave Fawcett's involvement with the case that would consume him began in early April 1998. Fawcett got a call from Bruce Americus, a colleague at Buchanan Ingersoll, to discuss a potential new client. The man's name was Hugh Caperton. He was a West Virginia businessman claiming that the A. T. Massey Coal Company had driven his small Virginia coal mine into bankruptcy. Caperton's company had been drained of its resources, and Caperton had no money to pay the Buchanan Ingersoll's high hourly rates. So he was looking for a firm to handle the case on a contingency basis.

Buchanan Ingersoll seldom took commercial cases without charging a hefty hourly fee and insisting on an up-front retainer. Fawcett was surprised that Americus would even talk to Caperton. For the most part, Fawcett's fellow attorneys at the firm looked down on the sort of plaintiffs' trial lawyers who peddled their wares on television and billboards, earning their living taking a cut of any settlement or verdict, regardless of the issue. Such law firms rarely had more than twenty hungry, hustling lawyers, who spent most of their time fighting scrappy insurance defense firms. Most at Fawcett's firm preferred the more sedate, gentlemanly business of million-dollar corporate retainers, billing $500 an hour win, lose, or draw. But Americus thought the case had enough potential to merit a seventy-mile drive to Morgantown, West Virginia, to meet with Caperton and his lawyer.

Americus was one of the law firm's premier rainmakers. The rotund, gregarious senior partner had perfected schmoozing into a fine art. Fawcett would have been terrible at that, but then, Americus would have been terrible at actually litigating the case. Americus's role ended once he had reeled in the client. Thus it would be largely Fawcett's decision whether the firm took the case. If it did, he would be the one representing Caperton.

On the morning of April 7, 1998, Fawcett left his home in the quaint little town of Oakmont, Pennsylvania, to drive to Morgantown. There he would meet with Americus before their get-together with the potential client and his attorney.

Fawcett was heading south to discuss a case involving two warring coal companies, yet like most residents of the Pittsburgh area he rarely if ever reflected upon how much his city depended on the men who dug deep into the earth for the fuel that had stoked the Industrial Revolution. As early as the 1820s, enormous plumes of dark coal smoke had risen above the growing town, while other cities across the Eastern Seaboard still warmed themselves with wood and used water to power their machinery. As America's steel capital, Pittsburgh became the sootiest, smokiest city in the Western Hemisphere.

In the midafternoons in the 1920s, when Fawcett's ancestors were already established in the city, it was sometimes as dark as night and residents moved through the streets guided by electric lights fueled with coal. In the slums, children walked on brittle, thin legs deformed by rickets, likely caused by the lack of light. In 1913, a psychologist investigating the effects of the smoke found "chronic ennui." That was not an emotion felt by the Carnegies and Mellons, who lived on estates above the river valleys of the dark city and filled Pittsburgh with ornate buildings celebrating their business acumen.

When Fawcett was growing up, the city's steel furnaces were shutting down, and the sun was becoming visible once again above a diminishing city in which the skyline had heights and grandeur worthy of a city several times Pittsburgh's dwindling population. An orange sulfur dioxide glow still emanated from the river valleys at dusk, but the few steel mills that remained were cutting back and being superseded by such enterprises as health care, law, insurance, and technology. Still, coal remained the largest source of the city's electrical energy, and that coal came mainly from West Virginia. As Pittsburgh shrank, most of what was memorable and worthy was preserved, and much that was fresh and inspired was built. This new Pittsburgh had a panache that the industrial city of old had not.

The West Virginia state line was less than an hour south of Pittsburgh, but Fawcett had seldom crossed it. He was comfortable in places he knew and understood. He was entering a world that was as foreign to him, and to most Americans, as Bhutan or Belize would have been.

When, at the turn of the twentieth century, pioneering industrials arrived to mine the black treasure, the Appalachian highlands were one of the most remote places in America. Up in its hollows lived a breed of mountain men who were the least likely to become subjected to the ordered life in a coal camp, yet they came down to join poor immigrants from Europe in the darkness of the mines.

By the 1920s, around 80 percent of West Virginia miners lived in coal camps, regimented communities where families survived at the will and whim of the mine owners. In 1922, the U.S. Coal Commission found dismal conditions in most of the 708 company towns it surveyed, noting that "in the worst of the company-controlled communities, the state of disrepair at times runs beyond the power of verbal description or even photographic illustration, since neither words nor pictures can portray the atmosphere of abandoned dejection or reproduce the smells."

The towns of southern West Virginia were extensions of the coal camps, overseen by political leaders beholden to the coal industry. Throughout that decade, the companies pushed their control even further in the coal-dominated courts, seeking injunctions that prevented miners from marching in protests on the street or meeting in public halls or even churches to indulge in what others called free speech.

Over one hundred thousand American miners have died in the pursuit of coal, a death toll higher than the combined losses in the Korean and Vietnam Wars. At its peak in 1940, when the camps were still full, there were 130,457 miners in the state, producing 126,619,825 tons of coal. By 1997 there were only 20,542 miners left in the heavily mechanized industry, producing a record 181,914,000 tons of the mineral. Coal was still the anchor of the state's economy, dominating every political and economic fiber of the second-poorest state. A man was judged—be he a politician, a lawyer, a minister, or a teacher—by his fidelity to the industry.

In 1998 coal produced about half of the nation's electricity, but it produced 98 percent of the state's. That was a mark of how West Virginia's industrial and political leaders aggressively guarded the role of coal in the economy against attack from what they viewed disdainfully as liberal do-gooders, environmental elitists, and misguided federal bureaucrats. Coal was the linchpin of the state economy, and protecting it became an industry of its own.

As Fawcett drove south, he could tell that West Virginia did not have the economic vitality of much of his native Pennsylvania. The state had always been a place of small towns and rural living (1998 population: 1,811,688). In the 1940s and '50s, the towns still had a certain commercial energy and often a picturesque charm. But in the past half century, the state had suffered an exodus of, on average, 15,940 citizens each year. And many of these towns were depressed hollows of vanished people and shuttered businesses.

Morgantown, the home of West Virginia University, is spread out over a large area without a true center, bisected by two interstate highways. It takes a native or at least a WVU sophomore to master the directions. No wonder, then, that Fawcett missed a turn and arrived uncharacteristically late to the meeting in the restaurant at the Morgantown Quality Inn, where his colleague was already waiting, along with Caperton and his local lawyer.

After greeting both Pittsburgh lawyers, Caperton directed almost all his attention to Americus. The senior lawyer came highly recommended; Caperton assumed that Americus would be handling the case and that Fawcett was little more than a briefcase-carrying aide. Fawcett did not know why he was being studiously ignored, but it didn't bother him. He had a job to do, and he could do it better by sitting back and observing.

Five years earlier, in 1993, Caperton had bought the closed Harman coal mine along a narrow, meandering road outside Grundy, Virginia. The facility had operated since the 1930s, when a thousand miners worked the seam, living in company homes set up along the hollow. Next to the mine stood what had once been the company store, which Caperton turned into offices to service the operation and its 125 union miners.

Caperton's second cousin Gaston was governor of West Virginia from 1989 to 1997. Although people figured that with his last name Hugh had lots of money, he had little, and he bought the shut-down mine without investing a penny of his own savings. Instead, he personally guaranteed a $2.5 million note. He also agreed that the Harman Mining Company would, over the years, pay down the long-term obligations saddling the former owner. The previous owner was delighted to give the mine away to someone who might be able to make a go of it and reduce its millions of dollars of obligations to miners' health and retirement benefits and to mine reclamation.

Caperton brought in a mining engineer, Henry Eugene Cook Jr., to run the operation. It turned out to be the most inspired choice of Caperton's many decisions. Cook was a big, burly miner's son. A highly resourceful individual, he had previously worked at Harman, where he'd developed a plan to upgrade the old mine to dramatically increase its working life, production, and profits. At the time, Harman's management had thought his proposal too expensive, and Cook had resigned, taking his plan with him. Now it was Caperton's blueprint.

Caperton plowed revenues back into the business, but the Harman Mining Company needed more money to undertake capital improvements under Cook's plan. And so while Cook ran the mine during the day, Caperton scurried around trying to find money. In retrospect, it might seem that Caperton was running around mindlessly, setting up other small companies, financing outlandish business schemes, but he was in a terrible bind. He had no capital, and he had to use every bit of his creative energies to find a way to get the money to do what Cook believed had to be done.

At one point, instead of borrowing funds from a bank, Caperton came up with the innovative but risky idea of selling the underlying coal to a land company, then leasing back the coal, paying a premium on every ton mined. In its first years Harman had lost money, but Caperton and Cook were convinced that the investment would pay off. They believed that once costly refurbishments and improvements were in place, Harman would start making big profits in 1998 and continue to do so well into the future.

In the summer of 1997, Massey purchased United Coal, the company to whose Wellmore subsidiary Caperton sold all his coal under a long-term contract. In turn, Wellmore sold the coal to a coke plant in Pittsburgh. "We mined about seven hundred thousand tons a year, and we sold every ton of it to Wellmore," Caperton told the Pittsburgh lawyers. "We had a ten-year contract. We mined coal. They agreed to buy it—all of it. We were totally dependent on them but never thought about it."

Caperton assumed that associating with the biggest coal company in the region would prove an enormous plus. "When we found out Massey was buying Wellmore, we were happy as hell," Caperton said. "We knew Massey was big. We were putting our heart and soul into a long-term mining plan. So now, we thought, we'd always be sure of getting paid, and we knew Massey could afford to pay what the coal was worth."

But in early August 1997, just a few days after the purchase, the new, Massey-installed president of Wellmore told Caperton that the aging coke plant might be shutting down, and that as of 1998 Wellmore might be taking only about a third of its contracted order of Harman coal: from a minimum of 573,000 tons to only 200,000 tons.

Massey would do this within the terms of the contract by directing Wellmore to claim force majeure, a maneuver common in business contracts. It is invoked when a calamitous, unexpected event occurs: A fire burns down an automobile parts manufacturer and the company cannot possibly ship a crucial item to Detroit. A frost destroys the oranges in a grove in South Florida, preventing a farmer from sending his fruit to an orange juice producer. A strike shuts down a steel plant and the superintendent is unable to produce girders on time for a San Francisco bridge.

In contracts, force majeure must be carefully and narrowly defined. If not, businesses would use it whenever they want to escape an agreement that is merely inconvenient. Harman's contract with Wellmore defined force majeure as "acts of God, acts of the public enemy, epidemics," and other "causes reasonably beyond the control of the parties."

Caperton believed that the coke plant's possible closing did not qualify. Harman's contract was with Wellmore, not the coke plant. The declaration should have had nothing to do with Caperton's company. What's more, summer was the time when coal companies signed their contracts to sell next year's coal, and if they needed to, it was the perfect time for Massey to find other buyers for Harman's product.

When Caperton inquired of the Wellmore management about the likelihood of Massey's invoking force majeure, Caperton said he was told by the subsidiary's president not to worry, that the note was merely "a cover-your-ass memo."

Caperton always looked at life in the most positive way. He was not about to spend his days worrying about something he'd been told was not going to happen, and so he went back to running his mine. In the fall he started hearing rumors that Massey had lost its business with the steel company that owned the Pittsburgh coke plant. That made him nervous.

Caperton decided that he better get together with Blankenship. At their meeting, on the day before Thanksgiving 1997 at Harman's office in Beckley, West Virginia, Blankenship said that he had lost the business with the steel company and the Pittsburgh coke plant was shutting down. Massey would be invoking force majeure.

It was too late in the year for Caperton to find buyers for next year's coal. Caperton said that he might have to sue. The Massey chairman replied that if Caperton was so foolish, Blankenship would bury him. "You don't want to sue Massey," Blankenship said. "We spend a million dollars a month on attorneys." And then Blankenship said that perhaps the best thing was for Massey to buy the mine.

Caperton had no other options, and that afternoon he confided all kinds of confidential business information to Blankenship. He told him of a large seam of coal adjacent to the Harman mine that he intended to buy or lease, dramatically increasing the coal his company could mine.

Caperton believed that, even with its long-term obligations, Harman was worth $17 million, and a few days later he presented an offer to Blankenship. The Massey chairman said no and kept negotiating a lower price until all that was left on the table was $6 million, a sum that included paying off some bonds and $2.5 million in cash. Caperton felt he had no choice but to accept. Then, after dragging Caperton through months of the most tedious negotiations, Blankenship walked away from the purchase, leaving Caperton no option but bankruptcy. That left Massey the likely prospect of picking Harman up for almost nothing, without having to rehire the union miners.

It wasn't just Caperton who was hurt. There were 125 Harman miners and 25 support staff out of work, many of them with unpaid medical bills and health insurance premiums as well as retirement benefits that had not been funded. Harman owed hundreds of thousands of dollars to creditors, many of them small, vulnerable businesses that could not afford such a loss. For Caperton, the worst of it—worse than his realization that he had been deceived, worse than failing the Harman miners and suppliers, worse than the impending corporate bankruptcy—was Harman's defaulting on the reclamation bonds that the federal government had imposed so that one day the mine property would be returned to a pristine state. That meant his name landed on the federal government's Applicant/Violator System list, effectively banning him from ever again running a mine or being a top executive.

While the May 1998 bankruptcy would erase all of Caperton's hard work and achievements, the federal listing erased his future. He would never again be the proud owner of a mine or walk with the men who managed the industry. For Caperton, as for Blankenship, coal was all he knew, all he'd ever wanted to know. Beneath his veneer of civility, Caperton was in some respects a desperate man. And so he decided he had little to lose by suing Massey, even though most of any money awarded would go to the miners and the creditors and not personally to him.

As Caperton pitched his case in Morgantown that April day, Fawcett spent most of the time listening and observing. He was trying to determine if Buchanan Ingersoll should risk taking a contingency case, charging 40 percent of any settlement or verdict plus expenses. He was an apt judge, for despite his relative youth he had a deep grounding in breach-of-contract law, as well as extensive court experience.

A natural skeptic, Fawcett had come into the room looking for reasons to say no. He'd listened to all kinds of people pitch their potential cases. It was almost always the same: they had been so wronged and their case was such an outrage that there was no way Fawcett could lose.

Caperton was different. He did not push too far. He undersold, purposely letting the Buchanan Ingersoll attorneys think that they were the ones figuring everything out. He told his story in a simple, straightforward manner. Caperton looked his listener in the eye and connected emotionally. He seemed to speak from the heart, without pretense.

Fawcett decided he liked this man, but he wasn't in search of a college-fraternity brother. The stakes were enormous, and he needed to assess Caperton's story. The facts might be complicated, but to win over a jury the story needed to be told in a way that fit a time-honored theme. When Fawcett heard Caperton describe the superior qualities of the Splashdam seam of metallurgical coal and how in the end Blankenship wanted Massey to gain both Harman's customers and the Harman mine through menacing tactics and subterfuge, the themes came to him in bold terms. This was a story of greed and arrogance and abuse of power.

Fawcett had only a couple of hours to decide whether Caperton had the stuff. He kept his eyes focused on his potential client, but his mind zoomed in and out of the conversation. Fawcett asked himself a series of crucial questions: Is this a man I can trust and a jury will trust? How will he handle brutal questions in a trial? If it gets tough, will he bail?

If Caperton were paying by the hour, Fawcett would have taken the case immediately. But this was a contingency suit, and he had to rigorously assess the risks. He could not have a client who might give up and settle for pennies, leaving Buchanan Ingersoll with less than nothing. Fawcett concluded that this man would not go down easily. Something told him that Caperton had the guts to fight it out.

As Fawcett listened, he realized that neither Caperton nor his local lawyer had any inkling that there might be two different claims here. It was one thing to breach a contract. If everything Caperton said held up, then Wellmore could be sued for breach of contract with limited damages. But if Blankenship had set out with will and calculation to destroy Harman for Massey's financial gain, that made it a tort with a potentially far larger damage claim against Massey. In that case, a good part of that money would go not to his company but directly to Caperton.

As Fawcett listened, he became more and more excited. He suspected that Americus had no idea what they might have stumbled upon and how much these two cases might be worth. It could be tens of millions of dollars.

Fawcett mulled over how he should advise Buchanan Ingersoll. He had gone against some difficult opponents before, but nothing quite like Massey. Its lawyers would throw everything at them, from fighting over the venue to peppering the plaintiffs with disclosure demands. Massey ruled coal country and, if the case ever reached court, Fawcett would have to come down here and challenge the company on its own turf, in front of a jury that would likely think of the coal giant as a hometown benefactor.

Fawcett estimated that his legal team would incur some $2 million in expenses in fighting this case, with no guarantee that the firm would get any of it back. Yet there was injustice here, and he had been asked to right it. *Caperton* was a cause in which Fawcett could believe, one he could fight with all his energy and ability. Hugh Caperton needed his help. He had a problem and Fawcett believed that he could fix it, and fixing it might fix something in himself too, letting him reassert the lawyer he had always intended to be.

Fawcett took Caperton's story back to Pittsburgh with him, weighing the challenges and pondering the approach. When a box arrived from Caperton, full of Harman documents, he reviewed every item with care. Everything supported Caperton's recounting of events. Ultimately, he decided that the case was worth his firm's risk.

Fawcett was one of the up-and-coming stars at Buchanan Ingersoll. When he went in to present the potential client to the senior partners, they said yes as much because they believed in him as because they believed in the case.

The lawyer called Caperton to tell him the news.

"Well, Dave, how long do you think it will take?" asked Caperton, trying to hide his disappointment that Fawcett, not Americus, would be his lawyer.

"I don't want to overpromise you, Hugh," Fawcett said. "It could take two years."

"Two years?" Caperton asked.

"That's how long it sometimes takes to get justice," Fawcett said.

Harman's contract with Wellmore specified that any contract dispute had to be settled in the Virginia courts where the mine resided. That was a crucial legal reality, and thus Fawcett filed the contract suit in May 1998 in Grundy, Virginia, a few miles from the closed Harman mine.

As Fawcett did more research, and as he reviewed documents he had subpoenaed from Massey, he became convinced that this was not simply that the Massey subsidiary had violated a contract. He concluded that Blankenship had set out in a calculated manner to squeeze Harman and, if necessary, destroy it without any concern for the miners and their families. Massey had used the closing of the Pittsburgh coke plant as a bogus excuse.

Fawcett ordered exhaustive research to confirm that Harman could file a separate, much bigger suit against Massey in West Virginia. This action would not involve Wellmore but would be an attempt to prove that as Massey's CEO Don Blankenship had directed a series of actions to defraud Harman with the intent of creating such financial havoc that Harman would have no choice but to bend to Massey's will. Fawcett would have to prove, with clear and convincing evidence, not some breach of a business contract but that Massey had purposely interfered with Harman to inflict harm to suit its own purposes.

Fawcett believed that the law clearly dictated that the second suit could be filed separately from the narrow breach of contract case in Virginia because it involved different parties, different damages, and much different evidence.

And so while Fawcett pressed on with the Virginia contract suit, he filed a second suit, in October 1998, charging that Massey had tortiously interfered with Harman and defrauded it, destroying the company in the process. He filed the suit in West Virginia, where Massey had about 82 percent of its coal reserves, where Caperton lived, where Harman's corporate office was, and where Blankenship had made his ominous threats.

Fawcett would have to build his evidence mainly from Massey's internal documents, to prove that this wasn't just some contract dispute between Harman and Wellmore but that Massey—in the person of Don Blankenship—had come in from the outside and interfered for the purpose of damaging Harman as well as Caperton personally.

Fawcett liked neatness, clarity, and certainty, but these cases were messy, convoluted, and uncertain. He had to prepare for both cases simultaneously, knowing that if he lost the first trial in Virginia, he would have neither the money nor the momentum to continue on to West Virginia. And even if he won in Virginia, that was just a preliminary skirmish before he'd one day face Massey and Blankenship in a West Virginia courtroom.

Fawcett gave off an aura of superiority, yet it rankled him that he was known as "David B. Fawcett III, a third-generation Pittsburgh lawyer," as though he had grown up eating with golden cutlery. He rarely used that "III," which he thought pretentious, and when naming his son he rejected any suggestion that he might pass along the name yet again. Every man defined himself, he believed. He was not a scion of some knighted race of lawyers. Maybe he had not grown up poor, but life had many kinds of struggles.

Fawcett's father set the highest standards for his son. Whenever Dave's father thought his son had not played fairly or had diminished the family reputation, he shunned him with a silence far worse than any verbal condemnation. That was the way Dave's father had been treated by his father, the Fawcett tradition, a thoroughly WASP ethos.

Young Dave chafed at the whole hoary business, and felt that his father was obsessed with impressing people. And yet he could not walk away from these standards. He wanted and needed desperately to win, to be the best at whatever he did. And he strove to do so while exhibiting the highest moral standards and being honored for doing so.

Fawcett was a fine athlete, and when he caught passes on his undefeated prep school football team the crowd cheered. His father, however, didn't, fearing that the young man might develop an inflated view of himself. After the game, his father challenged him for arguing a referee's call. "You don't ever want to do that," his father said, as if that mattered more than the outcome of the game.

Beyond that, Dave's father felt his son did not understand that the name of the game was not football. He was going to school with kids from rich families who could do him good. But Dave did not befriend them. He was a loner.

While some of Fawcett's high school classmates were playing Motown and the Beach Boys, Fawcett found himself listening to an English band, Ten Years After, whose few hits included a bluesy ballad titled "I'd Love to Change the World." The singer laments how he'd like to make a difference, but he can't figure out what to do and decides he'll just leave it up to others. That was precisely the attitude Fawcett saw in the people around him.

Fawcett had gone from college into a profession where he thought he could change the world. One of only five people in his class at Carnegie Mellon to earn a teaching degree, he'd initially taken a job as an English teacher in a public high school in upstate New York. But he'd quickly become frustrated by how the school's attention went to the best students and most of those with less than stellar intellects were taught that they did not much matter. As he saw it, this was symptomatic of what had become the American way.

Fawcett left teaching after only two years to go to law school. Practicing law, it turned out, was stressful and hadn't proved to be a way to change the world, either, sentiments he shared with Bruce Stanley, his Buchanan Ingersoll colleague. "They wouldn't pay you if it wasn't work," Stanley reminded Fawcett. In Stanley, Fawcett found a friend who understood precisely what he was going through at the firm. People who thought civil law was more refined and genteel than criminal law hadn't a clue.

"Nobody is nastier than people fighting over money," Fawcett would say. That made it difficult enough, but the two young lawyers felt they were fighting on two fronts. They had no problem with tough competition in the courtroom; what troubled them was the form competition took at their law firm. When they sat in bars drinking and talking about books and politics, most of their contemporaries were back in the office billing time, with few outside interests to distract them.

Fawcett had been friendly with Bruce Stanley since their days as young associates at Buchanan Ingersoll. Both men had sought something at the firm that they had not found. Fawcett had fancied the lawyers would get together for serious philosophical discussions about the law, but all he saw were scores of dronelike creatures with their heads bowed before their computers. Stanley, too, craved those discussions, and like his friend he'd entered the law as a way to do good.

The two lawyers admired each other's work, and each thought that the other had integrity. There was a subtle competitiveness between them, and they sometimes measured themselves against each other. When they worked together, Fawcett assumed that he was the senior associate gently mentoring his slightly younger colleague. Stanley thought they were equals and did not defer to Fawcett.

Fawcett rarely talked about his marriage or his life at home. He had met his wife when he was a senior at Carnegie Mellon. The beautiful, statuesque blonde from the Midwest had been anointed with the nickname "Perfect." Fawcett was so consumed with doing everything right that he could have been nicknamed "Perfect Dave." They seemed an ideal match. When they married, Dave took care of his career, and his wife took care of their children, the girls Claire and Amelia born two years apart and little Daniel six years younger. Fawcett thought the obligations had been neatly divvied up. He focused on one thing at a time with absolute zealous devotion, and it was rarely his wife. Nonetheless, he thought of himself as a caring husband who was there when it was important to be there.

Fawcett and Stanley became close enough that when Stanley left Buchanan Ingersoll and moved to another Pittsburgh firm, they stayed friends. In 1996, when Fawcett ran for Congress as a Republican in a suburban Pittsburgh district, Democrat Stanley and his wife virtually became part of the candidate's staff, working devotedly in the unsuccessful campaign.

As good friends as the two men were, Fawcett had a certain closed-off quality. He wasn't going to confide in Stanley or anybody else that his perfect marriage wasn't so perfect, or that when he went home to his wife and three children he was met by simmering tensions.

With all the pressures of their jobs, Fawcett and Stanley loved to go out on occasion to vent about their profession and have another of their engaging, unpredictable conversations. Fawcett would throw out topics and listen with utter amusement as Stanley, his eyes bulging and his drawl growing more pronounced, spoke with outlandish confidence about everything from the policies of the Federal Reserve to his favorite World War I poet. Stanley was a fountain of opinion and information, spouting animated analysis on whatever the topic might be, while Fawcett needed to think things through and study the issues before coming to conclusions.

Fawcett and Stanley always managed to get out to Pittsburgh's old Three Rivers Stadium to see a few baseball games each season. The stadium looked like an enormous concrete mixer and would have been a perfect subject for a painting by that Pittsburgh-born icon of pop art, Andy Warhol.

In September 1998, the two friends drove to the park for the last time that season. Back in his college days, Fawcett had played shortstop for the Carnegie Mellon Tartans. After graduating, he'd played on a Mexican-American team in a winter league in Arizona. As a young boy, Stanley had been too sickly to play much baseball. He had picked up his love of the sport by following the Cincinnati Reds on the radio with his dad.

As they watched the Pirates take on the streaking Chicago Cubs, Fawcett talked about a book he had been reading on the history of work and unionization in West Virginia. He expressed surprise that in the early years, miners hated the thought of unions and saw cities like Pittsburgh and Detroit as nothing more than enslaving factories. What the men in the hills of West Virginia wanted above all was independence.

"A man wants to make a living," Stanley said. "And blacks and whites worked alongside one another. No one thought anybody was better than anyone else, or deserved anything different. A man was worth what he hauled out of the mine that day and asked for nothing else."

When the two men were not talking about mining history or the wretched Pirates, who were nursing an eight-game losing streak, they had time to discuss their law practices. Fawcett told Stanley about Caperton, his new client. As soon as Fawcett mentioned Blankenship, Stanley shook his head in disbelief: Fawcett was taking on the man fast becoming the most powerful coal baron in American history. When Fawcett said that one day there might be a role for Stanley in the case, he laughed at the idea. He knew Blankenship, and he knew West Virginia. He wanted no more of either one. Beyond that, though Stanley admired Fawcett, he could hardly imagine working with him again.

Stanley was stunned that Fawcett had engaged with such an important, problematic case in his home state. Stanley was the kind of person who almost always reached out to help or to offer suggestions, be it with the law or anything else. This time, he felt he shouldn't say anything. He wasn't about to stir Fawcett up and tell him that he was likely in for the struggle of his life. But it was incredible to him that his upscale Pittsburgh friend would be headed down to the courtrooms of West Virginia to learn about a world he could hardly envision.

"You've picked yourself one this time," Stanley said.

5

On September 30, 1998, a few weeks after the ball game, Fawcett flew down to Richmond to depose Blankenship. Fawcett had been representing Caperton for six months, and this was his first meeting with his main adversary. Unlike Stanley, Fawcett did not relish gladiatorial confrontations. As he waited in a law-firm conference room, he tightly gripped the handle of his briefcase, which held the documents he intended to use in the deposition. He was so nervous that when Blankenship and his attorneys walked into the room he broke into a cold sweat.

Though Blankenship was six foot three, he had a slouching, unprepossessing manner that made him seem shorter. He was a good thirty pounds overweight and looked more like a roofing salesman than the chairman of a Fortune 1000 company. His face was expressionless, and he spoke quietly, barely moving his mouth, as though he wanted his listener to strain to understand him. He had small, brown, hooded eyes so deeply set that they appeared hidden in the shadows, and a complexion as swarthy as an old baseball glove. His mustache was a triangular swatch that set off his jowly face, his lips so thin that they were little more than a line. Whenever he got nervous, he would flick his long, serpentine tongue in and out of his mouth, wetting his lips.

Blankenship was disdainful of most top executives in American companies, considering them "figureheads involved in peripheral things around the business." He proudly called himself a "bean counter" with "a willingness to focus in on the details." He'd cut down expenses at Massey in a way that would soon become common in American companies as they faced a brutally competitive world economy. When he'd taken over as Massey CEO, in 1991, he'd dismissed 12.8 percent of the employees, pared the benefits in the company-sponsored drug plan, and ended retirement medical care for new employees. He ran the company from a modular double-wide trailer just across the West Virginia state line in Belfry, Kentucky. The structure suggested an auto parts store or a middling real estate office, not one of the headquarters of the biggest coal company in Appalachia.

Massey Energy had most of its mines in southern West Virginia, but it also operated in southwestern Virginia and eastern Kentucky. The three regions, which make up the central Appalachian highlands, share a unique mountain culture and an economy dependent on the coal industry.

Whereas the region's other top coal company executives resided outside West Virginia, the state that delivered most of their fortunes, Blankenship proudly lived within the state in which he'd been raised. The Massey chairman was born in Stopover, Kentucky, in 1950 and grew up poor in the nearby village of Delorme, West Virginia, along the Tug Fork River, a meandering stream that marked the state line.

Blankenship's mother, Nancy, had an affair while her husband was in the army. When he returned and discovered that she had borne a child, Donald, who was not his son, he wanted nothing to do with either of them. There was little stigma in being on welfare, and Nancy Blankenship could have brought up her three sons and one daughter on the dole. Instead, she made a living for her family by running a little store with two gas pumps in Delorme. The establishment, like half a dozen other little stores along the road, offered a jumble of Wonder bread, spiced ham, baloney, and Twinkies. Working sixteen hours a day, this proud, determined woman earned just about enough to keep her family clothed and fed.

From his mother, Don learned to be a stern, suspicious judge of character and motives. Businesses like Nancy's gave credit to their cash-strapped customers. She knew who she could trust to pay for a tank of gas when they got their coal company wages or monthly welfare check—and she could tell who would stiff her and then move on down the road to stiff somebody else. She knew which teenager would pilfer a Hershey bar while buying a loaf of bread for his family's table. She told her children which customers measured up, those children they could play with and those they could not.

Rails ran behind the house, and when the Norfolk and Western coal trains thundered past, the earth shook for several minutes and you had to shout to be heard. There was an outhouse behind their unfinished cinder-block home. Blankenship recalled years later, that "you could only use two perforations of toilet paper." After a bracing jaunt in a winter storm, Blankenship washed his hands in well water so red from iron that it sometimes looked bloody.

A group of taverns lined the road, filled with drinkers—some of whom had ridden in on horseback—from dry Kentucky. Blankenship's favorite entertainment was to climb atop the roof of a neighboring barbershop long after he should have been in bed and wait until the drunken miners came staggering out into the street for a brawl.

Blankenship's three older half siblings had a Korean War veteran father whom they often visited, the one diversion in their young lives. Don was not invited. In that era, Blankenship had the curse of a bastard son and was in some respects an outcast.

Nancy Blankenship became both father and mother to Don. Like her son, she spoke sparingly, as if words were a treasure not to be squandered. She totaled up customers' bills in her head and almost never made a mistake. Don learned to do figures in his head, too, and as he became adept at math he saw a moral dimension in addition and subtraction.

In high school, the tall, sinewy Blankenship was not so much shy as self-contained. Donnie, as everyone called him, was a popular young man who was voted president of his senior class. He did not care much about politics or economics or the world beyond his native Mingo County, except when it concerned major league baseball and his hero, Willie Mays of the San Francisco Giants. Mays was fast, strong, slammed the hide off the ball, and ran out every hit, all qualities Donnie admired.

Donnie's other pleasure was driving fast. A kid could earn enough money in the summer to buy a car, and many high school students had one. Blankenship would drive his over the Kentucky line to the one straight strip of macadam within twenty-five miles, then get the car up to 110 miles an hour before throttling it down.

In 1968, Blankenship enrolled at Marshall University, in Huntington, West Virginia, one of the best schools in the state. In the summer,
he came home and worked as a union miner. His foreman, Darrell
Ratliff, had him firing blasting caps to dislodge coal, a dangerous job for
a new man.

Blankenship had no money or time for a college student's easy life.
He took off one year to make money working the mines and did so well
in school that he graduated in 1972 with an accounting degree in only
three years. He passed his CPA exam the first time he took it. To get a
decent job, he moved to Chattanooga, Tennessee, and from there to
working for the cookie giant Keebler in Macon, Georgia, followed by
Chicago and Denver. He married a pretty homebody, Mary Gant, in
Colorado, and they soon had two children, Jennifer and John. Blankenship kept up an itinerant life, taking a job at another baking company,
Flowers Industries, back in Georgia. But a true son of West Virginia is
comfortable only down its country roads. In 1980, he got the chance to
return to a few miles from where he'd been raised. He became the office
manager at Rawl Sales, a subsidiary of the A. T. Massey Coal Company.

When Blankenship assumed the presidency of Rawl, in 1984, he moved
into the former mine superintendent's house, which had been built in
1904. He had coveted the residence since he'd been a young boy.

The house sat high on a hill in Sprigg, above everyone and everything. Sprigg was a dispiriting little place, with squalid trailers, junk-filled
businesses, and low-end modular homes. From his own home, Blankenship looked out upon the epicenter of a tragic, bloodstained history. Not
six miles to the east sat the town of Matewan, where he'd gone to high
school. It was here in May 1920 that gunfire had erupted between pro-
union townspeople and a dozen agents from the Baldwin-Felts Detective
Agency hired by the coal companies as a private militia. When it was
over, seven of the agents and three townspeople, including the mayor,
lay dead in the street, fatalities of what became known as the Matewan
Massacre. The following year, as many as one hundred miners died on
Blair Mountain in what is often described as the largest civil insurrec-
tion since the Civil War.

Two miles north of Sprigg sat another tiny village, Lobata, where in
1984 and 1985 a Massey subsidiary was at the center of one of the defining strikes of the modern era. The members of the union locals along the

Tug Fork were among the most militant in America. But Blankenship, the new, young president of Rawl Sales, won the strike and set the UMW on a diminishing course that continues to this day.

In 2000, the Fluor Corporation, which had owned the former family business since 1981, spun off Massey as a separate company, renamed the Massey Energy Company. That gave Blankenship no one to oversee him but a complacent board.

"I don't know anyone who's more hated," Blankenship said during the 1984–85 strike. "It doesn't matter whether you're hated or not, all that matters is that you do the right thing." It was one of his favorite themes. Blankenship believed he had won his enemies honestly by fighting to change the corrupting social and political system. He believed that you had to stand up to your enemies and confront them. You could not let them surround you and taunt you. You could never give in. You could never compromise. You could never settle. You stood head to head with your foes, and sooner or later they flinched and walked away.

That was what Blankenship did at Massey every day. And that was precisely what he intended to do here in Richmond with Dave Fawcett, during what he considered an onerous, unnecessary deposition.

Fawcett thought there was no way the Massey attorneys would let him depose Blankenship for five hours, but they seemed not to care. It was as if the lawyers were saying, You can throw whatever you want at us, hit us with your hardest punch, but if anything is hurt it will be your clenched fist.

The deposition was Fawcett's favorite part of the legal process. Depositions took place mainly before a trial, when lawyers from both sides questioned potential witnesses and others. For the most part, depositions were long, laborious, exhaustingly tedious examinations of a subject. The more easeful and natural a deposition seems, the more elaborate and exhaustive was the preparatory work.

There was no jury here, no judge, and Fawcett sought no devastating moments of revelation, just subtle admissions. He pursued clarity and specificity. As Fawcett explained later, he was "closing down doors so that at trial the witness can't say something like 'I was confused or I really didn't understand your question.'"

Blankenship's voice rarely rose more than a few decibels above a whisper, but it was a controlling voice that was used to being obeyed. At times one had to lean forward to hear him, which made his hushed words off-putting and imposing.

But this wasn't a corporate meeting in which Blankenship could chastise his subordinates for their failings and dismiss them. Fawcett had internal Massey documents that appeared to show a calculated decision to put Harman up against the wall. Document by document, line by line, he was intent on getting Blankenship to admit what the documents showed.

Whatever strategy the Massey lawyers might have had in mind in allowing this lengthy deposition, as the hours went by it became clear that Blankenship and Fawcett were evenly matched antagonists: meticulous, detail-oriented, obsessive. Fawcett went after Blankenship subtly but systematically. It was unlikely that anybody had ever questioned Blankenship so repetitiously or relentlessly.

"You'll have a real problem getting me bothered because I did exactly what I think was appropriate as fair as I could do it," Blankenship said at one point. That told Fawcett just how bothered the Massey chairman truly was. But Fawcett knew that this was only the beginning. One day he would likely be confronting Blankenship in a courtroom, and the Massey chairman would be the most formidable, unyielding of witnesses.

6

On February 4, 1999, Fawcett and his legal assistant Rob Devine drove from Pittsburgh to meet with Circuit Judge Jay M. Hoke in Hamlin, West Virginia. Fawcett was spending much of his time preparing for the contract trial in Virginia, but he had to work to push the West Virginia case ahead as well. If the Massey lawyers had their way, the West Virginia trial would never take place, and this meeting at the judge's office in the Lincoln County Courthouse was their attempt to bury it once and for all.

Fawcett's drive was slowed a few times by trucks hauling oversized loads consisting of one half of a double-wide modular home. People in the state used to hire local builders to construct their homes, but now a great many of them bought prefabricated houses built anywhere but West Virginia. They were cheap but costly, too, for they were purchased on credit at high interest, they amassed no equity, and they did not last long. These modular homes dotted the narrow roads and hollows where most people lived.

As Fawcett cut off the interstate, onto a state road, his vehicle moved through a tunnel of foliage, the green hills rising on both sides. Reaching Hamlin, Fawcett parked in the lot next to the new courthouse, which looked more like a power plant than a building to which one went seeking justice.

Hoke, balding, with long tufts of hair over his ears and a walrus mustache, enthusiastically greeted the Pittsburgh contingent and Massey's defense attorney Jeff A. Woods. Fawcett felt immediately at a disadvantage, his natural reserve in stark contrast to the friendly, backslapping manners of these Appalachian hills. Woods's law firm, Wyatt, Tarrant & Combs, was in Lexington, Kentucky, and the defense attorney was familiar with the region's customs and spouted its idioms.

Woods and Hoke carried on like good old buddies. It was not until much later that Fawcett learned that the meticulously dressed Woods was from Michigan. He was no more a scion of these Appalachian hills than Fawcett was. But Fawcett did not know that yet, and watching the two men jawing like hunting buddies, he worried that Hoke might view him as a slick city lawyer and in the courtroom tell him to keep everything short. Fawcett always seemed to need more time than other lawyers, and here that could be disastrous.

Hoke would largely determine if the jury trial went forward, and both lawyers knew that this meeting might end the West Virginia case for good. But no meeting with Hoke could begin until he shared some uproarious tale.

"So you fellows came through that metal detector, right?" Hoke said, leaning back in his chair. "It should have my name on it. I started as a prosecutor right here. I was a just-arrived idiot from the Public Service Commission. My first murder trial was a rape-murder. The daughter was raped, and the mother was murdered. And so the grandmother was testifying. And when I said I had no further questions and the defense lawyer said he had no questions, she bent down and pulled a thirty-eight snub-nose out of her purse."

Hoke recited the oft-told tale as if for the first time, bobbing and feinting as if dodging bullets. His mustache was so massive that it seemed to weigh him down.

Fawcett could hardly believe this scene, even though Stanley had warned him that it was a different world down here. Never in his days had he appeared before a judge like this one. Hoke was like some guy you might meet in a bar, his patter growing more extravagant as the night went on. Fawcett smiled more at the bizarre situation in which he found himself than at the story Hoke continued to tell.

"Now, the defendant is sitting behind law books, and a bullet literally ricocheted off one of the two big volumes of a law treatise—the famous

Handbook on Evidence for West Virginia Lawyers, by Professor Franklin D. Cleckley, and lodged in the door," Hoke said. "Everybody in the courtroom was down on the floor. I was the only one standing. The judge was yelling for the bailiff to get that gun away from that woman. And the bailiff was screaming, 'Pearl, give me that gun. Pearl, give me that gun.' That was her name. Pearl."

Hoke's eyes teared up with laughter. "And so the next time I saw Judge Cleckley, he asked, 'Aren't you from Lincoln?' I said, 'Yeah.' He said, 'Were you in the room during the shooting?' 'Yeah.' And he asked, 'Well, what do you think about all that?' I said, 'Justice Cleckley, it's the only time that damn book of yours ever saved any lives.'"

Fawcett saw Woods doing his best to laugh hard. But Hoke did not appear to notice or care. Fawcett had a wry, subtle sense of humor, but his ironic asides rarely resulted in knee-thumping, throat-clearing laughter. That hardly mattered, for Hoke's belly laugh overwhelmed everything as he exercised a judge's prerogative to laugh loudest at his own joke. Even as he guffawed with his mouth open, Hoke's enormous mustache obscured his teeth. Listening to the languid, amusing way Hoke was handling this initial meeting, Fawcett was put at ease, feeling that the judge would give him the time he needed and everything would be okay.

"I just didn't get no satisfaction from sending that poor fellow to prison for the rest of his life," Hoke said. "I just wasn't cut out to be a prosecutor." He decided that if he was going to be part of the judicial system, he would prefer to do it sitting up above, dispensing justice as a judge, and let others spend their days putting people away or defending them.

Hoke felt some connection with almost everyone who walked into his courtroom. His father was a Baptist minister who lived off the meager Sunday offerings, supplemented by his mother's work running a fourth-class post office. He was twelve before his family moved into a house with indoor plumbing and he had his first bath in a real bathtub.

Hoke could have taken his degree from the West Virginia University College of Law and gone anywhere and done well, but he chose to stay in Lincoln County, one of the poorest parts of the state. He lectured young people that they should go and get their educations and then come back to the county and help other people advance. Hoke thought the most useful thing he could do was to make sure that people in Lincoln and Boone Counties got fair trials.

Hoke broke up this long session with several more stories, but Fawcett quickly realized that he was dealing with a serious, sophisticated jurist. It was clear that Hoke loved the law in all its subtlety and understood its every nuance. He believed in the jury system and he was nobody's fool. Over time Fawcett realized that Hoke's humor was not only a mark of his nature but an effective device to calm combative opponents, as well as to temper courtroom tedium while pushing the proceedings ahead.

Fawcett knew that lawyers from Washington and New York often referred to West Virginia as the Wild West, a dangerous place where erratic judges practiced frontier justice and corporations risked legal lynching. What they were actually condemning was a theory of justice largely developed piecemeal, opinion by opinion, over the years by the liberal state supreme court, which gave the individual judges and juries great power.

Hoke liked to think that the broad discretion the juries in the state had was rooted deeply in history. "It's the way it was done in England after the Magna Carta," he says. "A man was brought in front of a jury and the people who were accusing him said their piece and the accused said his piece, and the jury decided who was lying and who was telling the truth. West Virginia still thinks that's the best way to approach the problem."

Hoke was perfectly aware that this new commercial case was of a consequence and complexity beyond anything he had ever adjudicated. The defendant, Massey, was the biggest employer in Boone County and one of the most powerful political forces in the state. The plaintiff was from one of the most celebrated families in the state. Big-firm lawyers from outside the state were involved on both sides. That meant that whatever the verdict, the loser would inevitably appeal to the Supreme Court of Appeals of West Virginia, where the judge's conduct would be given a scrutiny it had rarely received before.

Hoke divided his time between courtrooms in Hamlin, the seat of Lincoln County, and Madison, the seat of Boone County, where *Caperton* was scheduled for trial. He had grown up in Lincoln County, and he had overseen most of his cases there. There were only three coal mines in that county, unlike next-door Boone, where there were ninety-two. In all his years on the bench, Hoke had never before overseen a case involving coal companies. He knew little about the coal industry other than what he had learned in a couple of classes at law school. He also had no familiarity with business tort cases and the massive discovery involved, in which each side asked the other for thousands of pages of documents and other material.

This might have made many judges nervous, but Hoke welcomed the challenge. He looked forward to refereeing what he assumed would be the most daunting case of his career.

During the session in the judge's chambers, Woods took nearly an hour calmly presenting a number of reasons to have the case thrown out. He argued that the venue was wrong. The Harman mine was in Virginia, and the contract between the two companies specified that any legal proceedings must take place in Virginia. If Hoke wrongly let the case go to trial, Woods said, he wanted limits put on the amount of money the jury could award.

Popping his glasses up and down on his forehead, Hoke listened closely. When the session ended, Fawcett felt that Hoke had asked the right questions in the right way and that he would be fair in his decisions.

Fawcett had certain rituals that did not vary. One of them was to scope out the courtroom months before a trial. That way he could meet the courthouse staff and have a clear image of where he would be examining witnesses. He would spend months thinking ahead about the questions he would ask, and he wanted to picture it all: what a witness might say, how he would react, where he would stand. He had learned that if he wanted to be quick and think on his feet, he needed to know all he could and do his best to avoid any surprises.

Although it would be months before Hoke ruled on whether the trial could take place, Fawcett and Devine drove the thirty miles to Madison to get a feel for the town and the courthouse. From a distance, the golden dome of the 1921 neoclassical limestone building rose far above Madison like the spire of a cathedral. Out front stood a statue of an old-time coal miner with a helmet on his head and a pickax in his hand. It was the closest Fawcett had come to a working miner.

Fawcett and Devine walked into the building, up to the second floor, and into the courtroom. The large, beautifully wrought auditorium would be an exquisite setting for the trial. Fawcett tried to visualize Hoke presiding from above, a jury in their box, and a row of Massey defense attorneys at a table on one side with himself and his colleagues on the other.

Fawcett and Devine walked around the town a little, though there was almost nothing to see. The short, narrow main street had only a few businesses and a bunch of boarded-up stores. The loaded coal cars sitting on a siding were about the only vital thing Fawcett noticed.

Fawcett thought about how, in Pittsburgh, the captains of steel, however you might view them, had at least built museums and libraries—monuments to themselves and the prosperity they'd created. Here, the parking lots were gravel, and even the few sidewalks in town were crumbling.

Fawcett was a Republican perfectly comfortable with what he viewed as the natural inequalities among men, but this was different. Billions of dollars had been taken out of these hills, but what had the people gotten except gravel? As he walked these coarse streets, he recognized that the *Caperton* case was not really just about Hugh Caperton and the Harman mine. It was about this region and what had gone wrong.

7

A year later, in March 2000, Fawcett called Stanley and asked if he'd like to catch some lunch. Fawcett suggested that they meet at the 130-year-old Original Oyster House in Market Square. Fawcett's favorite was the oyster sandwich, which he ate as meticulously and slowly as if it were a plate of beluga caviar. Stanley devoured his with the gusto of a man who fancied food one of life's honest pleasures and believed that french fries tasted better if you ate them with your fingers.

Fawcett told his friend that he had won the liability phase of the breach of contract trial in Virginia. The second phase, which would determine damages, would not begin until August 2000. Although Fawcett's professional life was going well, Stanley sensed that something was not right with Dave. His friend didn't say anything, but Stanley just knew.

Fawcett, however, didn't. He shrugged it off when just before he and his wife were going out to a dinner party, she would say she wasn't feeling well. Then, about a month after Fawcett's lunch with Stanley, one of his relatives confronted him, saying that things could not go on like this any longer.

Fawcett could no longer shield himself from the truth that his wife had a serious health issue. He had thought of himself as a caring husband who was there when it was vital to be there. Learning that he had been so obsessed with his own life and career that he had been oblivious to his wife's situation shocked him, shattering his sense of what was important. He had been going where his work and his dreams took him—traveling the country to try cases, taking time off to wage a political campaign, drinking with his friend Bruce—and had missed the growing problem at home. By the time his denial was pierced, his wife had trouble caring for herself, let alone the kids.

Fawcett hadn't understood what his father meant when he'd said that Fawcett and his wife were "like ships passing in the night"; now it was clear. While his wife was in and out of treatment centers, he found a part-time housekeeper to help with his ten- and twelve-year-old girls and four-year-old son, but that did not make him feel less guilty. Nor did it relieve him from the layers of additional work at home. He needed to get the children to school, help them with their homework, and comfort them.

Fawcett had always viewed those who sought solace in religion and feel-good psychology as weak, self-indulgent, and self-involved. Now he found himself spending time in the self-help section of Barnes & Noble. He had never been ashamed of anything he had done in his life, but he was ashamed now. He treated this family crisis like one of his cases, thinking that if he worked at it hard enough he could make it right. He read books. He took his young daughters to counseling sessions and family therapy. But the girls were angry with him and resented that they could no longer have a normal life. He moved from pain to pain. His wife would be out of their home for much of the next eighteen months.

With his new role, Fawcett realized for the first time in his life what many women and single parents faced. He also learned to appreciate the fact that there were so many caring, committed people out there—preschool teachers, family counselors, social workers, nurses, and therapists—who made less money than he but did work that was so much more important. He set his sights on working hard to be a more caring and humble person. He enrolled his son in day care and had to get him there before work and pick him up. He took the girls to buy clothes and reassured them that everything would be all right. He shopped for groceries. Meanwhile, he had to keep putting in full days at the firm. He saw that he was part of the ravage inflicted by his wife's condition and that his ideal marriage was so distressed that it could not be salvaged.

In July 2000, Fawcett called Stanley to say that a judge had warned him that he had a conflict of interest in representing both the Harman Mining Company and Caperton personally. That did not matter in the corporate Virginia trial, but from what Hoke had ruled it looked as if the West Virginia trial would be going ahead. Fawcett asked if Stanley and his new firm, Reed Smith, would be interested in joining the case representing Caperton.

Stanley was floored, and though he usually followed his gut, he had much to consider here. Bruce loved Dave like a brother, but a brother he understood almost too well. Stanley knew that Fawcett thought of *Caperton* as his. He had to control every last aspect of a case. If the judge had not insisted, Fawcett never would have brought in another lawyer.

Like almost any other successful trial lawyer, Stanley had his own full measure of self-esteem, though he disguised it under an ample coating of affability. If he could not steel himself to defer to Dave, he might win the case but lose a friend.

What was more, Stanley didn't know if he wanted to go back to West Virginia. "Do I want to jump back into that fucking Mingo County cesspool?" he asked himself. "Do I want to swim in that water?"

Stanley was, after all, a Pittsburgh lawyer now, a proud and honorable appellation for a poor boy from southern West Virginia. And as he contemplated joining this fight, it all came back to him: so much that he had hated, so much that he had escaped.

Stanley was born in 1959 and grew up in the tiny, isolated community of Breeden, in Mingo County, bordering Kentucky. Breeden, West Virginia, was only a scattering of houses hidden high up in the hollows and along a narrow road built on the old Norfolk and Western railroad bed, which represented the first effort to open up the southern West Virginia fields. This part of the county had a reputation as a lawless place where, in the first two decades of the twentieth century, seventeen deputies had died seeking out the draft dodgers, outlaws, and bootleggers who lived in these hills. When Bruce was growing up, it was still a place that hardly anyone went uninvited.

Bruce was the youngest of seven children. Since his next-oldest brother was five years older, he was practically an only child, a circumstance exacerbated by his poor health. Diagnosed with a diseased lung that was likely the result of a congenital defect, he was in the hospital nearly every year of his young life. Before the sickly little boy was old enough to go to school, he spent hours with his father, napping on the canvas mail sacks of the fourth-class post office he ran, and learning to read by puzzling out the FBI's Most Wanted posters. His mother worked as a school cook, and when Bruce took the bus to elementary school she rode along with him.

The Stanleys did not have indoor plumbing until Bruce was eight years old. The family grew much of their own food on their bottomland farm, including potatoes, tomatoes, pumpkins, and green beans. They raised geese, turkeys, and chickens and had up to a dozen head of cattle, with at least a couple milking cows. They hunted rabbit and squirrel. The Stanleys were generous to those who did not work as hard as they did and were hungry.

Bruce's two older brothers often trudged up the steep mountain pathway above bottomland so thick with foliage that sunlight hardly reached the forest floor. Bruce was too ill to join them in their foraging for blackberries, huckleberries, and ginseng to sell for pocket money. His mother watched over him with tenderness but could shoot the head off a rattlesnake, and when people caused her grief, she was not above pointing a shotgun at them and telling them to get off her property.

When Stanley was in the third grade, he spent thirty-two days straight in Miners Memorial Hospital, in South Williamson, Kentucky. The doctors gave him penicillin shots until his backside was callused. But he never seemed to get better.

His two strongest memories of that stay in the hospital helped to shape his morality: the glimpse of a young boy about his own age with third-degree burns over most of his body, an image accompanied by echoing shrieks of pain, which Stanley tried to erase from his mind but never could. "No matter how bad it is, somebody always has it worse," he thought. The other was the assassination of Martin Luther King Jr. He learned about it when the nurses started gathering in his room because his mother had rented a small black-and-white television to help keep him company. They came in and out, listening to the bulletins and reports, and Stanley struggled to understand who this man was and why his death was so important.

When Stanley was fourteen, surgeons in Charleston cut away the lower lobe of his left lung. In the hospital, his wound became infected and he nearly died. Once he made it home, though, for the first time in his life he felt truly healthy.

Stanley attended Lenore High School, where students from Breeden were branded dumb roughnecks capable of little but sitting in the back of the classrooms measuring out the days until they could end their halfhearted education. That irked Stanley, who believed that his friends and neighbors were as capable as the students from Lenore. One of the smartest students in his class, and one of the most popular, he was elected student body president.

Stanley took on the school administrators, who, he believed, judged students by their family backgrounds. He fought for a young woman who was cheated out of becoming a school queen because of her less than stellar outsider upbringing. The fact that he was right only made the school authorities even angrier and their attempts at revenge more mean-spirited. At the end of Stanley's senior year, the whole school was told over the PA system that because of Bruce's "misconduct," the 1977 senior class trip had been canceled. Only when he agreed not to take part did the other seniors head off to Myrtle Beach, South Carolina.

The best thing Stanley got out of his four years in high school was Debbie Bartram, whom he had known since the seventh grade. Like Stanley, she had an unbridled intelligence and an adventurous sense of life and its possibilities. People married young in the Appalachian hills, and when the eighteen-year-old Stanley drove north to attend his sophomore year at West Virginia University, the sixteen-year-old Debbie traveled with him as his bride. She finished high school in Morgantown and went on to study at WVU.

Bruce was too young and too happy with Debbie to think that their circumstances were hard. He was the first one in his family to go to college. His parents had no money to give him, but a Pell Grant helped pay his expenses, as did the school's work-study program. He ran the pool tables in the student union and cleaned up after pigeons in the psychology department. He also went out on his own to paint houses.

Stanley succeeded in both studying and working, and he learned that a poor boy with nothing could do as well as rich boy with everything. It was the seminal lesson of his life. He became an example of what was possible when people were given a chance.

Blankenship had also gone off to college with nothing and, with great diligence and discipline, worked his way through. He learned a different lesson, however: that a few could rise out of the primeval ooze, but only a few, and for the most part the downtrodden deserved to stay where they belonged.

Stanley wanted to write, and he wanted his writing to make a difference. In late 1984, after a couple of years of studying literature in graduate school, Stanley and his young wife went back to Mingo County, where Stanley got a job as a reporter for the *Williamson Daily News*. He found himself in the midst of one of the most consequential strikes in American labor history.

In the early 1980s, the new president of the United Mine Workers, Richard Trumka, had vowed to create a new union for a new age, one in which wildcat strikes, rock-throwing pickets, violent marauders, and blustering confrontations had no place. Trumka was an educated man with a law degree. In 1984, for the first time in decades, the UMW negotiated a strong new contract without a nationwide strike. The only problem was that the then sixth-largest coal company in America, A. T. Massey, refused to sign. Don Blankenship, the bold young president of Rawl Sales, the crucial Massey subsidiary, vowed to fight the union no matter how long it took or how high the price.

Stanley was assigned to work out of the *News'* bureau in Pike County, Kentucky, covering events not just in the Bluegrass State but over the border in West Virginia. While growing up, Stanley had often heard the famous protest song "Which Side Are You On?" by Florence Reece, written during a bitter 1931 UMW strike in Harlan County, Kentucky. And that's the way it was around Williamson. Either you were for the union or you were for the company. But as a journalist, he was supposed to be neutral, and he drove those twisting mountain roads not knowing from which side danger would come.

Stanley's reporting often pleased neither side. The Massey people thought he was pro-union. The strikers marked him as little more than a scab. Wherever he went, he felt unwanted. He decided to spend time around family members, but he had kin on both sides of the strike, and even they were not talking to each other.

Stanley was warned to be careful about what he wrote. One evening Debbie got a call from a high school classmate who was married to a union miner. The woman said the picketers had been talking about killing Stanley and that her husband wanted to warn him. Another time, a nonunion mine manager walked into the newspaper bureau office in Pikeville and, laying his sidearm on the desk, told Stanley, "Let's talk about your coverage."

Over the many months of the strike, Blankenship became the figure around which the conflict coalesced. Blankenship had worked at Massey for only four years, as office manager of Rawl Sales, when, at the age of thirty-four, he was named its president. Even the most seasoned coal executives would have been apprehensive taking on one of the most powerful unions at the center of its strength. Blankenship embraced the challenge, reveling in the danger and controversy.

Trumka, the UMW president, was young and new, too, and he set out to avoid the irresistible pattern to these strikes, one that had held for more than eighty years. They started with peaceful demonstrations and picketing, but sooner or later the violence began. The striking miners were taking home up to $200 a week from the UMW strike fund and could hold out for many weeks. But among the miners were a number of uncontrollable men ready for a fight. Blankenship knew that once the violence began it would be hard to stop. If the union was blamed, the UMW would almost certainly lose the strike.

Rawl had its headquarters in Lobata, two miles from the house in Sprigg where Blankenship lived. Early on in the strike, one night somebody fired seventeen shots from a high-powered rifle into Blankenship's office. Blankenship kept the bullet-shattered Zenith television in his office for years.

One day in February 1985, more than a thousand protesters marched in front of Rawl Sales. They held placards and shouted Blankenship's name. He heard them from his office, in which he was protected by a high chain-link fence, guards with rifles, and an armored personnel carrier, its turret hidden under a tarp. He had planted video cameras to record the strikers' every action.

The protesters shouted louder and louder, and finally Blankenship walked out nonchalantly, telling the guards to unlock the gate. He asked the protesters, "What do you want?" He could have been assaulted; whatever Blankenship was, he was not a physical coward. That moment meant so much to him that he recounts it in the opening of his unpublished autobiography, "Give People Hell."

During the strike Blankenship told a reporter that the UMW had "gotten too powerful and it's time they [miners] don't have to be slaves of the union any longer." He acted as if destiny had delivered him to bring the union down. He had worked in the mines, and he understood that the UMW was far more vulnerable than its leaders realized. The younger miners had only a vague sense of the union's history and the struggles. For some of them, the UMW was little better than an expensive club to which they were forced to belong.

Blankenship had a powerful need to control the world around him and a cunning awareness of the foibles of lesser beings. But his head and heart seemed to be disconnected. In the Appalachian world in which he and Stanley had been raised, that would have made him an outcast. That world, however, was dying, and Blankenship believed he had been anointed to introduce his mountain kin to a new society—one in which the powerful and the strong ruled with a fierce and steady hand, and such dangerous anachronisms as the UMW were ground into the dust.

Stanley also covered stories for the paper involving Elliot "Spike" Maynard, a young circuit judge in Mingo County. Like almost anyone else in a position of legal authority in the state, Maynard had graduated from the West Virginia University College of Law. He had served for five years as a prosecuting attorney before running for judge in 1981. Maynard had a prosecutor's zeal and, although a Democrat, was more conservative than many people who called themselves Republicans. In the most crucial decisions of his young career on the bench, Maynard made rulings that made him seem like Blankenship's virtual partner in destroying the strike. The two men forged a lifelong friendship. They helped each other as Blankenship grew to be the most powerful business figure in the region, and in 1996 Maynard was elected to a twelve-year term in the Supreme Court of Appeals of West Virginia.

As Mingo County's circuit judge, Maynard hit the union with huge fines and injunctions, hurting the UMW in ways Blankenship could not. After Maynard's limits on marches and pickets, the miners had no way to protest legitimately, and the violence ramped up. A few strikers took up guns and torches. They did most of their damage not to their enemy but to the union itself. Although the UMW disavowed the actions, nobody much listened. And then a young, strike-breaking truck driver was shot and killed and another driver was wounded.

After fifteen months, the violence forced the union to settle the longest strike in its history. The UMW pretended it had won, but the result was an overwhelming victory for Massey and, personally, for Blankenship. He'd proved prophetic: the strike was indeed the beginning of the end of the UMW as the unchallenged voice of the miner. In partial payment for the victory, five years later Massey named Blankenship the first company president who was not a family member.

Stanley, meanwhile, hadn't changed the world with his reporting—he had managed only to chronicle bits and pieces of a tragic tale. Beyond that, he saw the county where he'd been born emptying out of almost anyone with initiative and daring, leaving primarily the elderly, the weak, and the vulnerable.

Stanley wanted to get away and never come back. He hoped to reach a place where he could do good things and see tangible results. He decided the way to do that was to become a lawyer. He graduated near the top of his class at the West Virginia University College of Law and was the editor of the *West Virginia Law Review*. As strong a student as he was, one of his professors, Patrick C. McGinley, reflected years later that he "wouldn't have expected that Bruce would have the energy and the strength of character to go toe-to-toe in high-powered litigation against some of the country's top lawyers."

Stanley was recruited at Buchanan Ingersoll, one of Pittsburgh's premier corporate law firms. For a century, West Virginians had been trudging north to the Pennsylvania city, mainly to work in the steel mills, and Stanley was part of that migration.

Stanley was so glad he had escaped. Every time he went back to Breeden, the roads were worse, ruined by the coal trucks lumbering down the narrow lanes. And above the farm on the steep hillsides where his brothers had picked berries and walnuts, the surface miners had come and removed the mountaintops, and the trees of his youth were no more.

When coal companies finished stripping the mountaintops, they sprayed a mix of seed and fertilizer that would grow grass on rock, and they planted exotic trees that thrived in denatured soil. In the spring, when the rains came, so did the flooding. In the river valley and up the hollows, prescription painkillers had become the drug of choice. Stanley's mother and father loved their home and their neighbors, but their son and his siblings got them out and moved them elsewhere. He knew there had to be a better life for them in Prichard, an hour and a half away from their lifelong home.

Stanley despised this world, where, he thought, justice was rarely found and corruption a fact of life. He felt his people deserved better. He had not been able to help deliver justice to them as a reporter. He did not know if he was the one to try to deliver it to them as a lawyer. But there was a craving within his soul to do something worthwhile, something more than fighting for corporate clients, bringing even more money into their coffers.

Stanley was not like most of his colleagues. He knew things and had experienced life in ways they scarcely imagined. He had escaped Breeden, but part of his soul was still back there in those hills, and he knew that he might have an opportunity to do something that could begin to change the land of his birth. Maybe it was crazy to enter this fray and challenge Blankenship and Massey, but maybe it took somebody a little crazy to stand up to them—or somebody like Fawcett, who had no idea what he was up against.

8

In August 2000, before deciding whether he should accept Fawcett's invitation and present the Caperton case to Reed Smith's managing partner, Stanley decided he better first meet Caperton. Two years before, when Fawcett had first met Caperton in Morgantown, he had been concerned about the strength of the case and how well his potential client would hold up in extended litigation. Stanley cared about that, but he had other matters to discuss as well.

Despite what Fawcett had told him, Stanley was worried that the bankrupt mine owner might be just another wealthy operator and the case little more than your rich guy against my rich guy. Moreover, Stanley knew that the defense attorneys would go after whatever personal weaknesses they could find, and most of that would have to do with Caperton's lifestyle, family background, and supposed wealth. These were all matters that Stanley would have to resolve in his mind before agreeing to take the case. And so he drove down to Charleston to meet his potential client.

Charleston (population 50,000) is the biggest city in the state, but except for the glorious Italian Renaissance–style capitol building it felt more like a provincial town than a state capital. Its businesses largely served people who did not have much money. The Charleston Town Center Mall, where Stanley met Caperton for lunch, had none of the upscale retailers, like Saks or Neiman Marcus, that graced most affluent suburbs, and there was not a Starbucks or an Apple store in the entire city.

Stanley was no fan of sons of wealth and privilege. For four generations the Capertons had run the Slab Fork mine, which gave the family four generations in which to develop an overweening sense of self-importance. Stanley expected Caperton to be just another "egocentric coal-country asshole." But he found that he liked this friendly, modest man immensely. In southern West Virginia, there was no sin worse than pretension, no one more disliked than a show-off. A man learned to act no better than anyone else. "Don't get above your raisin'," Flatt and Scruggs sing in their bluegrass classic.

The two men exchanged stories of their childhoods. As a Pittsburgh attorney, Stanley talked to all kinds of prominent people, but he had never met anyone who was part of the coal-country aristocracy. Almost everybody in West Virginia knew the Caperton name and treated the family with respect.

"I was raised in a house on a hill in the coal camp at Slab Fork, where my father ran the mine," Caperton recalled, loving to talk about those years. "It was the same house my grandfather lived in and my great-grandfather when they ran the mine. Below were the miners' cabins, laid out like on a grid, and the four-room brick school that I attended. And there were the mine portal and the tipple, where the coal was loaded onto railroad cars, and across the bridge was 'Colored Town,' where the African-American miners lived with their families. They had the same cabins, a school and church."

Stanley had never been to Slab Fork, but as grim as things were for many West Virginians now, he was convinced that they'd been worse before, when miners lived at the whim of the bosses in these sad little coal camps, which were often industrial tyrannies.

"I know what people say about these camps," Caperton said, as if reading Stanley's mind, "but my father was like a father to everyone at Slab Fork, honest and fair and generous. People stayed for generations, sometimes moving up to management or working in the company store. I was treated no different than anyone else. I went to the same school and played with the sons of miners, and it was just the greatest place to grow up."

Stanley knew that these were Caperton's honest recollections. But in

Slab Fork, Hugh was the president's son. He couldn't possibly have been treated the same as the other children. When Hugh's friends went to high school, he attended Greenbrier Military School, and after graduation, when many of them went to work in the mines, he went off to West Virginia Wesleyan, where he earned a degree in business.

Hugh was proud of his family and the way they had run Slab Fork. They could have become absentee landlords, but they had lived there generation after generation. It took the most assiduous, determined efforts to keep Slab Fork the pristine, orderly, neat little town that it was. His family had taken care of the place and its people. The Capertons made it a safe, loving community to grow up in, even if your name was not Caperton. Hugh was a part of that tradition, and he had tried to run Harman the same way.

Caperton talked about the joy and excitement of building the Harman operation into something worthwhile, how much he cared for the miners, and how he was convinced that without Blankenship's intrusion he would have turned Harman into a highly profitable, long-term venture. Caperton described how he and Henry Eugene Cook Jr., the mining engineer who ran the mine, had built an apartment at the mine where Henry lived much of the time, both of them working to turn Harman into a company that would provide jobs and income well beyond their working lives. Caperton's description of how Blankenship had destroyed his company and his life was devastating, and Stanley could hear it playing before a jury to brilliant effect.

Stanley knew that if he felt Caperton was spoiled and overprivileged, the jury would likely think so too, and the Massey attorneys would probably successfully mock Caperton and his losses. Growing up in coal country, people like the Capertons usually had nothing to do with folks like the Stanleys. Stanley asked himself if he wanted to spend his time and energy seeking justice for this man. Could he believe in Hugh Caperton and his case the way he could get behind some poor miner Blankenship had abused?

Stanley knew that when Caperton walked into the courtroom, the jury would hear his name and assume that he was a wealthy inheritor, when he had, in fact, started Harman without a cent from his family. Stanley would make this clear to the jury, but Fawcett had laid out for Stanley another sensitive issue: Caperton was living in a million-dollar house, which his wife had decorated in a manner that could have been featured in *Southern Living*. Hugh loved that house beyond reason as the symbol of what he had become, and he was not going to leave it willingly, certainly not because of Massey's intrusion into his world.

Caperton was banned from a top job in the coal industry, but he was not about to move away from his beloved home in the only world he had ever known and take a job somewhere else doing work in some other industry. He never would have done any of that if not for Don Blankenship, and he wasn't going to start now.

Stanley grasped that while Caperton's attitude might have been unrealistic and pigheaded, it had given him the stamina to fight on. Few men driven into bankruptcy by Blankenship would have had the guts, even foolhardiness, to take on the man and the company. But Caperton had. You could not parse him into pieces, choosing the parts you admired and discarding those you did not. Caperton was devoting everything he had to bring Blankenship to justice.

Stanley knew that on the witness stand, only the bits and pieces of Caperton that served the plaintiffs and the defense would appear. The lawyer reminded himself that *Caperton* was not about Caperton personally and his choice of residence or job; it was about what Massey and Blankenship had done to destroy Caperton's mine and his life. As long as Fawcett and Stanley could keep the focus there, they would be fine.

"You know, I had the strangest experience with Don," Hugh said, half-laughing. "It was soon after Harman declared bankruptcy. I'm in my Beckley office, cleaning up stuff, and who comes in unannounced but Blankenship, and he slumps down on my sofa and starts talking."

"No lawyer with him?" Stanley asked.

"No, and, of course, I shouldn't have been talking to him without Dave sitting beside me, but I figure something good may come out of this—maybe he's wanting to settle. But he starts talking to me like I'm his shrink. He says, 'I'll never get married again. It was the biggest mistake of my life.'"

"Well, he's not the first guy to say that," Stanley said.

"No," chuckled Caperton. "But then he goes on and says, 'I used to have friends, Hugh; I had all kinds of friends when I was in high school.' And then he looks at me like he's about to cry."

The contrast between Blankenship and Caperton was devastating.

Hugh had a father he had admired beyond all men, a mother he adored, a wife he loved, a young daughter who delighted him, and many friends. Blankenship had an unknown father, a wife he'd divorced, an estranged daughter, and people who feared him.

"I could have given Don a long list of why many people despised him, but that's not me," Caperton said. "I was about to say something that would make him feel a little better, but then just as suddenly as he arrived, he jumps up and walks out of the office. That's the last time I ever saw him."

As Stanley listened to this story, he realized this case was not about power and money. It was about class. It was about a Don Blankenship who had grown up hating sons of privilege. Stanley understood, because he had grown up with those same feelings.

Blankenship had first gotten to know the Capertons in the 1980s, when Hugh's brother Austin had been an executive at Massey, vying to become president. Austin had a prestigious name, a law degree, gracious manners, and matchless political and business connections. Blankenship had none of that, but he won the presidency, and Austin left Massey. Now Blankenship had bested Hugh Caperton, too. And it infuriated Blankenship that despite losing his mine Caperton was living in a fancy house without a job while wringing his hands at how mean Blankenship had been to him.

On the drive back to Pittsburgh, Stanley mulled over the meeting. He had thought he would dislike Caperton, but he had hit it off with him and felt a commonality. Stanley saw that Fawcett was right: here was egregious wrongdoing. Caperton deserved justice the way anyone else did. There was a real chance of winning, too. The victory would teach Blankenship that he could not run over the lives of West Virginians the way Massey's overweight coal trucks rumbled over the country roads. Stanley was convinced that *Caperton* was a case he wanted to take. Now he had to persuade his firm.

Reed Smith had once served the Mellons and stood at the center of economic and political power in western Pennsylvania. The 220 lawyers in the Pittsburgh office spent most of their time advancing the economic interests of some of the richest, most powerful people in America. Its managing partner Gregory Jordan was attempting to transform Reed Smith into a top international law firm.

Stanley knew that picking a fight with the most aggressive and most powerful coal company in Appalachia would not help Jordan advance his goal. Yet he felt no trepidation going in and pitching *Caperton* to Jordan. The idealistic Stanley had succeeded in a calculating corporate world—and become highly regarded at Reed Smith—partly because he shrewdly assessed others' motivations. He understood what he had to deliver to get what he wanted.

Stanley explained to Jordan the excellent odds he thought they had in this case and how winning it might help the firm's bottom line. But he did not stop there. The managing partner was also a West Virginian and, Stanley knew, would understand the damage Blankenship and Massey were wreaking in their native state. Jordan listened but, as he often said to his colleagues, he did not have to be sold by the lawyers at the firm. He had to be intrigued, and by the time Stanley got through talking, Jordan was intrigued. He said yes.

In late August 2000, in the damages half of the Virginia trial, the jury found that the Wellmore Coal Corporation had violated the contract and done irreparable harm to Harman Mining. They awarded Harman $6 million, the maximum amount.

Massey would, of course, appeal to the Supreme Court of Virginia. It could be a year or more before Caperton's bankrupt company would see any of the money, of which Buchanan Ingersoll would take 40 percent plus expenses. Meanwhile, Caperton and his lawyers had to convince the company's creditors that when the Virginia verdict money arrived, they should not take their cut, which would amount to a fraction of what they were owed. Instead, he asked them to agree to let them use the money to pay for expert witnesses and other expenses in the second trial, in West Virginia, in the hope that it would deliver a verdict large enough to resolve the entire debt.

All the creditors agreed except for the most important business contact, the Grundy National Bank, in Grundy, Virginia, which had made significant profits lending to Harman over the years. Grundy asked for a place at the front of the line when a settlement or verdict was reached, to pay the $1.2 million outstanding on its $2 million loan to Harman. Beyond that, the bank demanded that Caperton sign a personal note for more than $400,000 to cover legal fees, late fees, and interest.

"Look, Hugh, you sign this and you're on the hook for good," Stanley said, knowing that Caperton already owed around $400,000 to the IRS in back taxes. "No way can you wiggle off."

"Yeah, and if I don't sign it, what happens?" Caperton asked, knowing the answer.

"The cases go away. It's all over."

It was simple. If Caperton signed and the plaintiffs did not win big in the Boone County trial, he would be destroyed. But if he did not sign, his fight against Massey and Blankenship would be finished. Caperton signed.

9

For Caperton, waiting for the trial to take place was torture. Fawcett had said it would take two years to bring him justice, but it was already December 2001, three and a half years since Fawcett had told him that, and they were still several months away from calling the first witness in West Virginia. The Massey lawyers had tried every legal maneuver possible to prevent the suit from going forward. They'd attempted to move it to federal courts. They'd meddled in the corporate bankruptcy, asking the bankruptcy judge to take the case out of Boone County and to remove Caperton as the trustee in charge of Harman's affairs. They'd used their money to buy time and aggravation, causing the plaintiffs all kinds of legal expenses before they reached the courtroom. But none of that had worked, and the trial was scheduled for March 2002.

Caperton vowed to make Christmas 2001 a memorable one for four-year-old Preston and for Kathy, hoping it would take his wife's mind off the impending trial. Then, a week before Christmas, their house caught on fire. The blaze started in the crawl space under the house and worked its way up inside the walls to the second floor. It took volunteer firefighters five hours to extinguish the flames, leaving an uninhabitable shell. Caperton could not prepare for the trial while, with insurance money, he was working to rebuild their house, and the court date was postponed until May 2002.

A few weeks before the trial the Caperton family moved back into their rebuilt house, and Hugh drove up to Pittsburgh for preparation. Helping Caperton was the legal team's newest addition, Reed Smith partner Tarek F. Abdalla. His Egyptian-born father was a radiologist who had practiced in Elkins, West Virginia. Abdalla had been a year behind Stanley at law school, and the two men were close friends.

Abdalla viewed the case with an objective detachment that Fawcett and Stanley had long since lost. Fawcett and Stanley had become so impassioned that they might have regarded Abdalla's dispassion as disloyalty, but they realized that Abdalla could step back and spot holes they might have missed.

The most vulnerable part of the case was Caperton's financial condition. That was irrelevant to what Massey had done to destroy Harman. Nevertheless, Caperton's finances would surely be questioned at trial.

During the five years Caperton ran Harman, he had created a number of small companies, some of which had nothing to do with mining. He had borrowed hundreds of thousands of dollars from the Harman operation, to fund other ventures, including the purchase of a radio station. Several of these investments failed. Getting involved in these businesses may have been foolish, but it was not illegal, and Caperton had accounted for every cent he had borrowed. A shrewd attorney, however, could make it sound as if Caperton had been stealing from Harman.

In 1997, Caperton had started building his house in the upscale, gated community of Glade Springs, built by his father before he declared bankruptcy. Hugh was projecting a substantial profit for his mine the next year, and he wanted a dream house for his bride and baby. He took a $400,000 construction loan for an $850,000 house. The house was nearly finished when Harman was pushed toward bankruptcy, and since no bank would lend him more money he had to use his savings to finish the job. That meant he no longer had the money to pay his taxes.

Five years later, in the spring of 2002, Caperton was in dire financial straits. He was supposed to be earning $60,000 a year handling the onerous, unpleasant job of closing down Harman, but Massey continued to put off paying the $6 million Virginia verdict, and Caperton hadn't received a cent of that money. Cook, who had run the Harman operation, had gone on to other successful jobs, and he had hired Caperton as a consultant, but that money had run out, too. At this point, Caperton couldn't pay many of his bills, and when the phone rang it was bound to be one bill collector or another, or perhaps the IRS.

In a few weeks, Caperton would be going before a jury of West Virginians. He'd be claiming poverty while living in Glade Springs, so far beyond the lives of most of the jurors that they had probably never even visited such a place. None of this mattered in a purely legal sense, but it might matter to jurors who wouldn't understand why Caperton lived beyond his means.

Abdalla set out to ask Caperton the questions about his finances the defense attorneys would likely pose. The attorney took professional satisfaction in stinging Caperton again and again with his probing queries. As he kept hammering away with tough, menacing questions about Caperton's fancy house and his failed businesses, Hugh grew livid. It was beyond embarrassing. Beyond that, it was irrelevant to what Blankenship had done to him.

Even if this was just a moot session, Caperton was not about to allow anybody to caricature him as having spent his way into financial disaster. He became so enraged that he stomped out of the office. When he returned, Abdalla asked some more rude queries. Once again Caperton jumped up and left, only to return again for more questioning.

During this tough grilling, a package arrived at the office containing the exhibits that the defense intended to use in the trial. As Abdalla and Caperton went through the material, Caperton was stunned to see photos of his house, one taken from the corner of his garage. Anyone who had shot those pictures would have had to get past Glade Springs' security before trespassing on Caperton's property.

Caperton was outraged that his privacy had been violated, but Abdalla saw another problem. The photos proved that he'd been right in preparing Caperton for questions about the house and his business dealings. The defense was not only going to ask about the residence but in all likelihood would show pictures of the home on a courtroom screen.

Stanley was supposed to be helping with the preparation but, as usual, he was late. When he finally walked into the office, Caperton shoved the photos at him. "I want to call the judge right now!" Caperton said. "I'm not taking this! You understand, Bruce?"

Stanley had seen Caperton distraught, but never like this. Hugh's face was ashen. The lawyer looked at the photos, slowly turning them over, one after another. And then, inexplicably, he began to laugh. "We'll use this against them so badly, Hugh," Stanley said. "You just wait."

Stanley viewed those pictures as a gift. He'd needed something to illustrate that Caperton was a bleeding victim. This case, after all, could not be just about money. Stanley had to make Caperton's loss seem personal, and this trespass was personal. When Stanley was through countering these pictures in court, the jury would understand precisely how far Massey, Blankenship, and their lawyers would go to destroy Hugh Caperton.

10

W hen all of Massey's attempts to kill the case failed and the May 2002 trial date approached, both sides agreed to mediation. Judges love mediation as a cheap, expedient way to clear their calendars. Defendants, too, often love mediation. They first extend the plaintiffs' pretrial work as long as they can, then settle just before a trial that would cost them far more and involve great uncertainty. In this instance, the lawyers were trying to resolve both the impending West Virginia trial and the $6 million Virginia verdict, which Massey had not paid during its ongoing appeal; that money would figure into any agreement.

Fawcett and Stanley did not drive down to Charleston in April 2002 for the mediation to bluff. They had spent hundreds of hours in discovery, asking for crucial documents, and, each time a box arrived, using whatever they found to ask for even more material. They had spent hundreds of hours, too, finding and preparing their expert witnesses. Their plan was in place, and if they couldn't win what they considered a fair settlement today, they would confidently proceed to trial.

Fawcett, Stanley, and Caperton walked into the Charleston law firm of Flaherty Sensabaugh Bonasso for settlement discussion. Robert V. Berthold Jr., a Charleston attorney, sat next to them in the conference room. Fawcett had invited Berthold to join the corporate plaintiffs' legal team largely because he had what were presumed to be strong local political and legal connections. The mediator, who would try to bring the warring sides together, was Thomas V. Flaherty, a Charleston business defense attorney. Berthold admired Flaherty's work and thought a settlement was possible.

As soon as they walked into the meeting, Fawcett and Stanley decided that nothing good would come out of the mediation. Lead defense attorney Woods and his co-counsel were there but no Massey executives. The absence of Blankenship, let alone one or two of his top lieutenants, indicated that Massey was not ready to make a deal. Caperton was more hopeful. Here in this room, for the first time in four years, his personal claims would be addressed. He might well walk out this afternoon a whole man, his life and fortunes renewed.

Flaherty was an adept mediator. He did not begin by talking about money. He let each side do its war dance. He then had the attorneys sit down and begin talking, sometimes together, sometimes in separate rooms. Finally, alone with the plaintiffs, Flaherty asked Fawcett what they were seeking. Fawcett said $50 million. Flaherty went off to talk to the Massey attorneys alone. The negotiator had spent hours reviewing legal documents for the case. He told the defense team that he thought the case should settle for around $25 million.

When the two sides got back together, no firm figures were mentioned, but by the way the Massey lawyers ran in and out of the room for private discussions there was reason to believe that they would make a decent offer. This was the first time Fawcett and Stanley had been together in a legal meeting in this case, but they were like an old married couple who could convey their meaning with a glance or a nod.

The two lawyers did not have visions of Dom Pérignon champagne and Kobe beef in their heads; they felt a continued sense of foreboding. Fawcett's worry was that Caperton was in such desperate financial straits that he would cave. In their discussions about a settlement with the mediator, Stanley kept talking about $20 million. Flaherty did not flinch, and it seemed Massey might be close to that figure. Fawcett did not think that was nearly enough. Had Massey not put Harman out of business, Fawcett believed, the mining company would have prospered for years.

Had Fawcett and Stanley been thinking primarily about their firms' take, they would have been salivating at the prospect of settling for anything close to $20 million. That amount would mean $8 million in contingent fees, plus full reimbursement of expenses for the two firms. As Fawcett saw it, $20 million wasn't enough to send the message that he believed had to be sent. But he sensed that Caperton was becoming emotionally vulnerable and that Harman's creditors, who had already likely written off their losses, might agree to go away for as little as $10 million.

As Caperton sat there, he thought differently. He had spent hours doing the math, calculating just how much he needed to take care of the Harman creditors and his personal debts. He wanted to put this behind him. He was tired of picking up the phone and hearing some bill collector speak to him with disdain. He wanted his life back. And he wanted it now.

Late in the afternoon, when it appeared that both sides were deadlocked, Massey attorney Woods revealed that he was privately discussing a settlement with Blankenship. For the first time, Caperton, Fawcett, and Stanley grew excited, believing that this might get resolved today.

The Massey lawyers returned to the conference room yet another time and finally announced their total offer: $1 million, so long as it resolved both suits. Given that Massey already owed Harman $6 million plus interest on the Virginia verdict, the figure was clearly meant to convey what was in store for Caperton in the courtroom rather than any real attempt at settlement.

Caperton and his lawyers had no time to express their outrage, for the Massey lawyers kept running in and out of the room, saying they were having discussions with Blankenship about a second offer. Thirty minutes later, the Massey lawyers returned to the conference room. They carried not a new offer but a further stipulation: not one cent of the $1 million could go to Hugh Caperton personally.

As Stanley heard the proviso, he knew he had been right in sensing that Blankenship had a personal vendetta against Caperton. It seemed that Blankenship saw Caperton as nothing but a spoiled son of wealth and privilege who needed to be taught a lesson.

Stunned, Caperton and his legal team said nothing. They put their papers away and walked out of the office.

"I don't understand what that was about in there," Caperton said as they left. "Why would they do that?"

"It was all about sending us a message, Hugh," Stanley said. "The message is 'Fuck you, Hugh Caperton.'"

"Look, Hugh, I've been in lots of mediations," Fawcett said. "But I've never seen anything like this. What they did in there insults the whole legal process. It's a disgrace. Their lawyers should have had to guts to say to Blankenship, 'They have a good case. You can't play the game like this.'"

"But I don't get why they did this," Caperton said. "How does it benefit them?"

"It drives up our costs," Fawcett said. "It upsets us. They still think they can be tough with us."

"It's something else, too," Stanley said. "This isn't just about the courtroom any longer, or just about money. This is about Don Blankenship seeing someone he hates. He doesn't just want to win. He wants to destroy you, Hugh. He wants to salt the earth with you."

"You know we're fighters, Hugh," Fawcett said, seeing Caperton's anguish. "Bruce and I, we're not going away."

Fawcett and Stanley drove back to Pittsburgh together that evening. They were silent. They did not have to say anything. They were thinking the same things. It wasn't the failure to settle that bothered them. It was Blankenship's mocking attempt to waste their time. They were sure that on their own accord, the Massey lawyers would have made some sort of real offer but that they dared not stray from Blankenship's direction. The Massey chairman had turned the law into a vehicle for leverage and revenge.

"You know, Bruce, these guys are total assholes," Fawcett said finally. "Their only intention was to jerk us around."

"Yeah, but they're through pushing that bullshit on us," Stanley said. Fawcett had heard his friend's temper before. When he turned his righteous anger on you, it was frightening.

Fawcett was glad that he had brought Stanley onto the team. In the first months, his friend had made strong intellectual efforts, but he was now as emotionally bonded to *Caperton* as Fawcett was.

"I wish I had a fuckin' knife," Fawcett said.

"Ah, it's not that bad," Stanley laughed, pushing the car to eighty miles an hour up I-79.

"No, Bruce, we need to take a blood oath. I'm serious. All we want is justice."

Justice meant something different to these two men now than it had this morning. Massey's name was on the legal documents, but Blankenship stood behind everything. They believed that the Massey chairman must be called to account, and that what they saw as his malevolent dominance over coal country had to end. They had no vehicle to do that, but Blankenship needed to feel the lash of justice.

"Until we have justice, we never settle, we never stop," Fawcett said, putting his hand out to his partner.

"Blood oath," Stanley said. They had no knife, so Stanley settled for shaking Fawcett's outstretched hand and repeating his words. "We never settle. We never stop. Until we have justice, we never stop."

PART THREE

MAY 30, 2002

11

Fawcett and Stanley felt energized as they and their legal team drove down to Madison, West Virginia, for the trial, which had finally been set to begin on May 30, 2002. The two lawyers had won important cases before, but they had never entered a courtroom with such determination and resolve. The key would be not letting those emotions overwhelm them in front of the judge and jurors.

Massey had touched so many lives in southern West Virginia that in the Boone County courtroom one potential juror after another in *Caperton* was dismissed during jury selection. Hoke led the sorting out himself. The judge knew that he would be scrutinized during *Caperton* as he had never been before, and he questioned the would-be jurors extensively. He was not, however, about to shelve his sense of humor or his folksy analogies.

"This is what we refer to as individual voir dire," Hoke told the jury pool as he began the interviews. "*Voir dire* comes from a French word. It means to speak the truth. We've had it around for about . . . oh, it will soon be a thousand years since that bunch of idiots from France came over and took over England. We've been talking some French ever since then, including petit juries and grand juries."

Hoke went on to quiz the candidates, one of whom was named Denver Ramey. "Now, there is one of the lawyers for the defendants named Ancil Ramey," Hoke said. "Is he any relative of yours that you know of?"

"All of my kin people are over in Kentucky," Ramey replied.

"All of my kin people are in penitentiaries," Hoke said. "So I am limited from them, too."

There were plenty of people out there—especially Massey employees and their families—who thought of Blankenship as a generous benefactor of West Virginia and its people, someone who used his power to create jobs and better their lives. It took three days to find six women and men and two alternate jurors who did not have strong opinions pro or con about Blankenship and would render justice in a trial they were told would last two weeks.

Fawcett and Stanley got what they thought was a decent jury. The jury, an eclectic group, included four women (a medical assistant, a retiree, a construction manager, and a government employee) and two men (an inspector for the West Virginia Office of Miners' Health, Safety and Training and an unemployed, self-styled jack-of-all-trades). After their selection, the jurors had two and a half weeks before they were to show up in the courthouse for the beginning of *Caperton*.

On June 17, 2002, Hoke sat in his elevated seat gazing out on the auditorium paneled in dark wood and its deep balcony. He was looking forward to this trial, though he knew it would reveal all the physical deficiencies of the courtroom. The summer promised to be a hot one, and the decrepit air-conditioning system would turn the packed hall into a steam bath. It was already hot, and there were so many people in the courtroom for the opening statements that some of them were fanning themselves. It reminded Hoke of the old-time revival meetings he had known as a boy. Beyond that, there was all the noise from the coal trains that rumbled by across the street. Every time that happened during a trial, it reminded him, Hoke said, of a "Charlie Chan movie where Charlie goes, 'And the killer is . . .' and all you hear is, 'WAAAAAAAAUGGGHHH.'"

Hoke gladly put up with the heat and the noise to work in a splendid setting that, he thought, recalled the courtroom in *To Kill a Mockingbird*. The second floor had a balcony like the "colored section" in the novel and the movie. The proceedings, typically, were not so dramatic. Hoke dealt mostly with personal injury and other routine civil actions, along with a steady parade of petty drug dealers, small-time criminals, welfare cheats, and other lowlife ne'er-do-wells, their fates monitored in the court-room only by their lawyers and relatives.

As Hoke looked out on the jury, he believed that six average West Virginians would come up with a better rendering of justice than even the most erudite and seasoned of judges. The judge felt that if he did his job correctly, justice would prevail. Thus, he spent his days on the bench watching out for the jurors, trying to make sure they were not bored or needlessly frustrated. He wanted them to know everything relevant before arriving at their decision.

On the plaintiffs' side, Hoke knew Charleston-based Berthold. He had met the Buchanan Ingersoll team, Fawcett and his legal assistant Devine, as well as Reed Smith's Stanley and Abdalla. Hugh Caperton, who sat at the plaintiffs' table, distinguished by his quietly diffident manner, was the central plaintiff. The judge knew about him because his cousin Gaston Caperton had been governor during the 1990s. Hoke expected that before the trial was over, the former governor would be sitting for a few hours in clear view of the jury, but that never happened.

On the defense team, Hoke was well acquainted with George Daniel Blizzard, who practiced in Madison. Hoke also knew the Charleston counsel and the premier West Virginia lawyer on the defense team, Ancil G. Ramey, because the two men had gone to college and law school together. The judge had had extensive pretrial dealings on *Caperton* with Woods but not with the elderly Richard Ward, the other senior member of the team, or their associate Penny R. Warren.

Hoke had rarely seen so many spectators in the courtroom. One of the most striking stood well over six feet tall and was outfitted from head to foot in black: dark hair, dark eyes, black mustache, black blazer, black knit shirt, black belt, black pants, black socks, and black shoes. A hush fell over the crowd as the man walked across the courtroom to take a seat at the defense table. As he passed in front of the bench, the judge's clerk cupped his hands and said, "Whaa whoo" in a worthy imitation of Darth Vader, the dark knight of *Star Wars*.

"What's the matter with you?" asked an irritated Hoke as the black-garbed figure passed out of his line of vision.

"Don't you know who that is?" the clerk asked.

"No," the judge said.

"That's Don Blankenship."

12

As Fawcett stood in his designer suit to make the plaintiffs' opening statement, everyone in the courtroom could tell he was an outsider. Of all the senior lawyers in the courtroom, Fawcett was the only one who could not play up any Appalachian country roots, real or invented. He looked and sounded like exactly what he was: a sophisticated, big-city lawyer.

Fawcett and Stanley had divided up the trial in a manner that worked off their personalities. Fawcett was a forceful, truthful man who kept his distance from almost everyone and everything, and so he was in the courtroom. He typically made little attempt to connect emotionally with the jury. He saw himself as a teacher, and he believed that the power of the evidence, if carefully presented, would carry the day. "Even the most complicated case is simple," he liked to say, "once you understand it."

In representing the corporate interests of Harman, Fawcett dealt with documents and facts. He was less interested in the well-being of the jury than in making a technical case that would not be overturned by the Supreme Court of Appeals of West Virginia.

Stanley's focus on Caperton's personal losses emphasized the intimate emotional cost. Of course, he was concerned with the facts of the case, but he sensed that the jury would not be persuaded merely by a bloodless recitation of those facts. Stanley was from southern West Virginia, and he spoke the emotional language of the jurors. They needed to feel as much as to think. If emotions and ideas could ride in tandem in this courtroom, he believed, the plaintiffs would win a stellar verdict. Stanley needed the jury not merely to understand the case but to empathize with Caperton's plight.

This was the first time Fawcett and Stanley had ever stood before the same jury. They offered the jury ideas and thought, emotion and feeling. Fawcett was here to help the jury understand what Caperton had lost. Stanley was here to help them feel what Caperton had suffered.

Fawcett began by asserting that this was not simply a business dispute between a large company and a small one, but a story about corporate greed, precisely what he had realized when he'd first met Caperton. To Fawcett, Blankenship epitomized everything that was wrong with corporate America, and he said so. It was a daring strategy: some jurors might consider this an attack on American business and local jobs, preferring to judge the case on its specific merits.

Fawcett set out to try Massey not only for its misconduct against Hugh Caperton and Harman but for its general iniquity. "The first part of the story is about people coming together trying to build something," he said, looking toward the jury. "The second part of the story is about another part of life in America today, and that part of America is as ugly as it is real. It is about corporate greed."

The jury listened intently to this first presentation. Stanley could read juries with an eerie prescience. In this instance, he saw nothing in these alert faces that betrayed their reactions to Fawcett's statements. "Ladies and gentlemen," Fawcett said, "corporate greed is when the people who run big corporations, the people who make big money, start to believe that they can use enormous power and enormous resources at their disposal to overpower people or to threaten people, and the evidence will show that is exactly what occurred here."

As Fawcett told his story of how Harman had been taken down, he kept mentioning Blankenship. And every time he did, he looked over at the black-garbed Massey chairman, who sat as motionless as a statue. Fawcett remembered that in his Richmond deposition nearly four years earlier, Blankenship had said, basically, "You can't bother me." He wanted Blankenship to see how wrong he'd been.

Fawcett saw the trial as *Caperton v. Blankenship*. From his first words on this first day, the attorney wanted the jury to understand that every Massey decision led back to Blankenship.

To illustrate this, Fawcett quoted a memo Blankenship had written just before Massey purchased Wellmore/United: "This is the coal that we have coveted for some time." Blankenship coveted whatever he did not have, and Fawcett believed that Blankenship was willing to do whatever had to be done to stop buying and instead start controlling Harman's rich seam of Splashdam coal.

Fawcett had spent enough time with the Massey attorneys to presume that they would attack Caperton's honor and integrity. To minimize that threat, he set out, as he said later, "to inoculate the jury" by injecting them with a gentle version of Massey's case, so that when they heard the defense attorney's full version, they would resist it.

"Massey has spent four years trying to dig up dirt on Harman and Hugh Caperton," Fawcett said, looking directly at the jury. "And Massey will try to do everything possible to persuade you that these people are dishonorable."

Stanley's opening statement on behalf of Caperton marked the first time in his legal career that he'd addressed a West Virginia jury. He, too, had worn his best go-to-court blue suit, but the heat had already begun to take out the creases in his pants, and he was only an hour or two away from looking his familiar rumpled self.

Stanley stood before what he believed was a jury of *his* peers. He spoke in a confidential tone, barely above a whisper. The jurors could understand, but the spectators and even the other lawyers had to strain to hear him over the whine of the malfunctioning air conditioner and the occasional clatter of the long coal trains. That was perfectly fine with Stanley. He fancied himself having an intimate conversation here with his fellow West Virginians. Stanley was taking the jury on a private journey. He was attempting to present himself not as an advocate but as a guide.

"So, what is Mr. Caperton's case about?" Stanley asked. He was bringing the courtroom drama down to an intimate, emotive level. "Hugh was trying to build something to make a future for himself and for his family, his wife, Kathy. Kathy, would you stand up?"

Kathy Caperton rose from her seat behind the plaintiffs' table. She had dressed in an expensive, upscale manner not because she wanted to show off but to send a message that Blankenship could not force her to wear the sackcloth of failure. Stanley and Fawcett understood what Kathy was trying to say, but they wondered whether she'd dressed so well that the jury might doubt that her husband could be in such financial trouble.

Stanley told the jury how Massey had driven Harman out of business and how Blankenship had then had Massey walk away from its agreement to buy the company. "Massey crushed the deal," Stanley said as he concluded his opening statement. "Harman declared bankruptcy, and Hugh Caperton was ruined, of course. And Massey just walked away. And there was one common denominator, one common fact, and one common player in every step of that ruination, and that was Massey."

Stanley said "Massey," but everyone in the courtroom knew he meant "Blankenship." The Massey chairman remained quietly seated, his face devoid of emotion.

For the defense's opening statement, Ancil Ramey stepped forward. He was a prominent Charleston appellate attorney who for more than a decade had been the clerk of the Supreme Court of Appeals of West Virginia. Ramey made much of his living speaking in the state supreme court in technical, legal language that the average jury would have a hard time following. He had neither Ward's grandfatherly persona nor Michigan-born Woods's edginess. Ramey's presence suggested that the defense would appeal any loss to the state's high court. To do that, as they fought to win in Boone County, the defense would be preparing a legal dossier to take to Charleston. They would record anything and everything that could possibly indicate that the trial was flawed—especially the conduct of Ramey's personal friend Hoke.

A jury in Virginia had found that Massey had broken its contract with Harman and awarded the plaintiffs the maximum amount allowed by the judge. That should have given the defense attorneys pause, made them contemplate settlement or at least a different strategy. They could have employed a more philosophical approach, suggesting that Harman was the victim of the natural workings of capitalism, and that Caperton had tried his best to run the mine but had bought into an impossible situation. That kind of argument might not have won, but it could have minimized the damages. Blankenship, however, had a personal vendetta against Caperton, and his lawyers were the Massey chairman's surrogates, presenting what was essentially his case.

"I represent Massey and its West Virginia family of companies in this action," Ramey began. "I want to introduce some folks that are here from Massey today and will be in attendance while this case is at trial."

Ramey immediately began playing the down-home country lawyer. He described Massey not as a Fortune 1000 company but as a "family," neighbors you could invite for dinner. Nor were its leaders pretentious, distant business executives. They were "folks." It was obvious, Ramey implied, that they were nothing like the starched and lean, long-haired Pittsburgh lawyer.

"Mr. Don Blankenship, he's the president and CEO of Massey," Ramey said, gesturing toward Blankenship, who barely nodded. "He's here in the courtroom today. Stan Suboleski, chief operating officer of Massey, he's in the courtroom today."

Ramey was speaking not only to the jury but to Blankenship himself. The Massey chairman was a one-person jury, monitoring how the defense lawyers handled themselves and his case. Blankenship believed that in his dealings with Caperton, he had done nothing wrong. He had merely applied the cleansing powers of capitalism to level a soft, indulgent inheritor and brush aside a prince of privilege, allowing history to move boldly forward.

Ramey set out to portray Caperton as a spoiled, selfish son of wealth who had mismanaged Harman as he had mismanaged everything else in his life. "No company that Mr. Caperton has ever owned or operated has done anything but failed," Ramey said. "He also took money out of Harman and spent it on himself and built a million-dollar house. And he bought his fancy cars. He leads a very nice lifestyle. Now, why is this important? Because it weakened Harman to the point where it couldn't survive any downward business such as the closing of the Pittsburgh plant."

Caperton glared at Ramey. He wanted the jury to see that he would never flinch. He had been brought up to look a man in the eye, and he would never gaze away.

"So how do they hope to convince you that somehow they can turn things around?" Ramey continued. "They want to convince you that they can take a sow's ear and turn it into a silk purse. I call this the Silk Purse, Incorporated. Now, even though this silk purse ought to pay its bills, even though this silk purse has diverted all its money off to other companies, somehow it was going to turn itself around."

Caperton's lawyers had prepared their client for personal attacks, but even Abdalla's most savage questions had not toughened him enough for these initial blows. Caperton couldn't believe the things Ramey was saying. He had so much wanted Kathy to be here in the courtroom, but it pained him to have his wife listening to this. He had been thinking of asking his seventy-four-year-old mother to come down from her Richmond home, but now he was glad that she wouldn't have to listen to this abuse. He thought he had been ready for the trial and anything that might happen, but it was just beginning and it was already too much, too painful, too humiliating.

Fawcett and Stanley could tell that Ramey's opening had devastated their client, and they knew it would get worse, far worse. They could not allow the defense to break him down emotionally or he would fail on the witness stand, and so would their case.

13

In his opening, Ramey was not about to talk, even for a minute, about the crucial question in the case: whether or not Massey had set out to destroy the Harman mine. Ramey preferred to focus on Caperton's lifestyle, a matter that could more easily sway the jury. As Fawcett and Stanley listened, they knew that the defense still had those photographs of Caperton's home, and even if the plaintiffs were able to get them thrown out of the case, the defense would portray Hugh as an Appalachian pasha.

"Caperton knew from the beginning that Harman was old, inefficient, and idle from the very time it was purchased," Ramey continued. "He then received the diverted revenue from Harman and then he's got all these other enterprises and then his million-dollar home." There was the defense's entire argument.

Caperton didn't dispute that Harman was "old, inefficient, and idle." That was why he'd been able to buy it for no money up front. That he'd "diverted revenue" made it sound as if he'd been a thief stealing from his own company, when in reality he'd put Harman revenues back into the business in the form of needed capital improvements and had borrowed money from the mining operation to start other small businesses.

"Now, I'm sure you've all heard that many successful businesspeople, especially on the start of business, say how they succeeded," Ramey said. "'I plowed money back into the company in the early years; I took less for myself.' That's how you build a business. Here there was taking money from this company and giving it to other companies, giving it to himself.

"We believe, unfortunately, that with Mr. Caperton's name he believes he is entitled to a certain lifestyle. He's entitled to success. Unfortunately, unlike most of his other successful relatives, all of his business ventures have gone sour."

As Ramey told the tale, the real defendant was not Massey but Caperton. He had failed upward in life until he'd had no way to continue his extravagant ways except by suing his betters. Nothing offended an Appalachian highlander more than a man pretending to be something he was not, and Caperton was living beyond his means.

The uglier it got, the less Stanley worried—and the more he thought that Massey was giving his side a gift. Stanley had feared that this case would amount to little more than a couple of coal companies fighting over money and business technicalities. To win, Stanley believed, he would have to make *Caperton* a highly personal struggle between two men. He thought Ramey was making what he later called a "fundamental strategic mistake" by doing the job for him.

For his part, Fawcett was upset by what he believed was a wildly exaggerated attack, much of which was immaterial or flatly untrue. He felt that he and his colleagues could educate the jury as to what was right and true, but their job would be far more difficult if Massey's lawyers were given wide latitude to raise irrelevant points. Fawcett rushed forward and asked for a private lawyers' sidebar with the judge.

"The opening by Mr. Ramey contained numerous statements that are prejudicial, that are matters that are totally irrelevant," Fawcett said as the two sets of lawyers huddled beneath Hoke. "A perfect example is the party wanting to build a million-dollar house, [which] is only being said to inflame the jury, and it has no relevance to this case. I would urge the court to give a cautionary instruction to this jury."

As Hoke looked down from the bench, he realized that it was time for him to educate both teams of lawyers as to how cases were tried in his court. He did that not by lecturing them privately but by having them step back to allow him to tell the jury how they should handle what they were hearing. "Ladies and gentlemen, a couple of things," he began, looking at the panel. "In regard to what the lawyers tell you they think the facts are going to be, that's a subject to be proved, because what the lawyers say ain't evidence. One of your jobs at the conclusion of the case is to judge what was proposed to you to be the evidence in the case and what the evidence actually was, and what was proved."

There, simply put, was Hoke's theory of jurisprudence. It was up to those six men and women in the jury to parse through whatever the lawyers and witnesses said and decide where the truth lay. He was not going to try to sort that out for them by limiting what the lawyers could do in the courtroom. Fawcett would have been happier if Hoke had stopped the attorneys from making intemperate, irrelevant assertions, but this was just how Stanley liked to play the game.

14

Fawcett had given much thought to who should be his first witness, defining the case for the jury. He'd decided on forty-seven-year-old Henry Cook Jr., the mining engineer who had run Harman's day-to-day operations. The problem was that the engineer possessed a sometimes maddening amiability, convinced that he could make a friend of anyone. When he'd given his deposition, he'd answered the defense attorney's questions in meandering soliloquies, as if he and the lawyer were out on the back porch, chatting away over a tumbler of Jack Daniel's. Fawcett had called a break and pulled Cook out into the hall. "What are you doing, Henry?" he'd asked. "These Massey lawyers aren't your fucking friends. You can't just agree with them. Answer yes or no."

For the trial, Fawcett had spent hours prepping Cook. When he called him as the plaintiffs' first witness on the morning of the second day of the trial, he was convinced that the engineer would do well. Fawcett knew that the jurors had grown up around the coal industry, but he wanted them to understand in detail what had gone on in the Harman mine. He believed that Cook could make all of this vivid and hold the jury's interest. The engineer looked the part. He was wearing jeans and a brown work shirt, as if he had stepped out of his mine office.

Cook told how he had implemented his plan for restoring the old mine. "I was laying this mine out for the long term," he said, adding that he had purchased top-quality equipment. "I mean, I was laying it out to be there until I retired." What Cook said was clear and telling, and Fawcett kept at him, having him repeat in slightly different iterations many of the same points.

In these first hours of examining his first witness, Fawcett signaled how he was going to handle the entire trial. His intention was to create a record of every single aspect in such detail and authority that an appeals court would understand what had gone on and would not challenge it. That may have been a sound legal strategy, but it did not lead to the most scintillating discourse. Cook was a talker, but as the hours passed, even he thought this was going on too long.

As Stanley sat listening to the testimony, he could hardly believe the number of times Fawcett asked the same question in a different way. If Stanley was about to scream, what did the jury want to do? Stanley looked over at the jury and saw some of those once alert faces turning wooden, doing their best to disguise their boredom. He would have liked to grab Fawcett by the back of his suit jacket and sit him back down.

Fawcett spent the whole day examining Cook, and he seemed to be only beginning. The next morning, Cook returned to the witness stand. Fawcett led him on an account of the last months of the Harman mine. Cook was a proud man. It pained him to revisit those long, humiliating days and his walking away from Harman and Hugh.

If Cook had stayed on as an officer in a company that was reneging on its pension and reclamation obligations, his name would have been placed on the federal government's Applicant/Violator System list. "A person that gets on the list can no longer have a responsible job in the coal industry," Cook said. "You can't be an owner. You can't be an operator. You're basically blackballed from the coal industry. I mean, this is my profession. I'm a professional engineer, and I won't be able to work. So I told Hugh that I thought I should resign, and he concurred."

Fawcett asked Cook one last question. "In his opening statement, Counsel Ramey said that there was no sacrifice," Fawcett noted, referring to Ramey's portrayal of Caperton as living an extravagant life as the Harman mine slowly sank into bankruptcy.

Cook recoiled. "No sacrifice from me?" the mining engineer said. "I take exception to that. I mean, I left the security of a large company and took a chance. It was five years, and it was the hardest work I'd ever done. At the same time, it was the most satisfying. But I can be insulted by Mr. Ramey's comment."

When defense attorney Woods cross-examined Cook, he used him to cast aspersions on Caperton's business practices. In order to get much-needed cash, Caperton sold the Harman coal reserves to Penn Virginia and from then on paid a royalty to the land-holding company on every ton of coal mined.

"The question, Mr. Cook, was, shortly after this transaction, did Mr. Caperton begin construction of a big new home?" Woods asked. He was suggesting that Caperton had sold the coal reserves so that he could build his dream house.

Stanley immediately objected: "This goes to the argument of this con-spiracy that they're attempting to allege."

"But, Your Honor, I—" Woods began, but Hoke cut him off.

"I understand your objection, and I understand your responses," the judge said, looking down at Stanley. "But what's sauce for the goose is completely sauce for the gander."

"Oh, God, it's SG squared again," Stanley whispered to Fawcett as he sat back down at the plaintiffs' table, his objection overruled. Hoke invoked the sauce-for-the-goose dictum so often that the two lawyers had developed their own code for it. Translated, it basically held that what-ever one side did, the other side could do, and therefore complaining was childish and futile. It suggested that if Hoke had been a teacher and a student had whined that someone had pulled his hair during recess, he would have told the pupil to dry his tears, go out on the playground, and pull his tormenter's hair right back.

Woods forged ahead, suggesting the profligate Caperton pilfered from his own company, which Fawcett and Stanley contended was utterly false. But Woods laid out a compelling scenario, and Stanley kept look-ing at the jury, trying to puzzle out their feelings, which were still a mys-tery to him. The defense was trying to exploit the deep populist strain in the West Virginia psyche. These people would have no use for a lowlife inheritor exploiting everyone—even the miners who worked for him—so he could have his fancy house and his fancy life.

Caperton, who sat at the plaintiffs' table with his lawyers, found it maddening that Fawcett and Stanley were not allowed to stand up and protest what he considered slanderous attacks. As he listened to what he viewed as one false assertion after another, anger built up in him until it was close to erupting. He knew he would have his day to tell his story, but after all these accusations, he asked himself, who would the jury believe? And even if they did believe him, what kind of price was he having to pay to seek what was called justice?

15

At the close of every day during the trial, Caperton's legal team drove thirty miles north to the Hampton Inn in South Charleston. The lawyers had taken over half a floor of the hotel, which included their bedrooms and a conference chamber they had dubbed the war room.

In the evenings, the group marched into the war room to prepare for the next day's proceedings. Their main arguments were about what role each lawyer would play in the courtroom. Fawcett favored a painstaking, encyclopedic approach, burying the defense with carefully presented evidence that would preempt any appeal. Stanley seemed truly ready for war, prepared to overwhelm the enemy in a blitzkrieg of emotion. Berthold, for the most part, wanted to get on with it and end this business before the jury fell, exhausted. As for Abdalla, he stood back, testing the others' arguments with intelligence and logic. Once the team reached a consensus on an issue, however, they returned to court the next morning as a solid front.

Caperton spent most of his evenings in the war room. He sometimes prepped for his upcoming testimony, which his lawyers kept delaying, calling an array of other witnesses. He hid his nervousness, but he was overwrought. Caperton had abundant time to worry about what might go wrong on the stand, and he took full advantage of it. He worried how he might not remember crucial facts. He pictured the defense attorneys savaging him over some minor date or name he had forgotten. He sensed that his attorneys were also apprehensive about his testimony.

  And he was right. Fawcett feared that Caperton would behave as he had when Abdalla had grilled him or, even worse, as he had during one of the early depositions at Harman's office. That day Caperton had exploded at Woods's unremitting requests for data and his suggestion that Caperton had hidden crucial documents. Caperton had run into the next room and returned with a carton, which he'd held up, then slammed down on the table, screaming, "There's the fucking box!"

  Fawcett and Stanley spent hours preparing Caperton for what he would face: a battery of allegations that would address his competence and his very honor. How would he perform on this dangerous stage? How would he act when Woods tried to provoke him? Would he be able to control himself, knowing that during just a few minutes on the witness stand he could destroy his own case?

On June 24, the fifth day of the trial, the plaintiffs called as their witness Harman's CPA, William Shortridge. He was there not simply to boast of Harman's good financial aspects but to disclose the bad. It might seem a bizarre strategy to expose the weakest part of one's case so early, but Fawcett and Stanley figured it was better for them to put it out there themselves than to let Woods and his cohorts spin it for them.

  Stanley had the unenviable task of leading Shortridge through an examination of Harman's finances. He was extremely well versed in everything he was about to ask Shortridge, but he began with cunning self-deprecation.

  "This is an old English major talking," Stanley said. "I don't even get control of the checkbook, so we've got to go slowly here."

  Shortridge was a fussy Dickensian character more comfortable with figures than with the nuances of the courtroom. He detailed how the company had fallen from a profit of $600,000 in 1993 to succeeding losses thereafter: $1 million in 1994, $1.5 million in 1995, $2.3 million in 1996, and $8 million in 1997. The accountant explained how these paper losses were primarily for tax purposes. These were the kinds of losses that do not constitute a bottom-line hemorrhaging and that many companies, including Massey, take as they go through periods of restructuring. But that might be difficult for a lay jury to understand—a group of people who did not have the luxury of paper losses.

The accountant listed the various other ventures Caperton had attempted while running Harman. Despite Harman's rising losses, Shortridge testified, Caperton had taken mine money to start other businesses. Some of his investments succeeded and some failed. In documents submitted to the court and in testimony, Shortridge accounted for every dollar. He said that despite all the business problems, Caperton had never discussed bankruptcy nor was he ever less than optimistic about Harman's future.

Stanley asked the accountant to assess the estimated $3 million to $4 million of personal liability Caperton had incurred to keep Harman running by agreeing to personally pay corporate bank loans if Harman failed. These were liabilities that most business executives would never have accepted.

"Given those obligations," Stanley asked, "does it make sense to you that Mr. Caperton would take money out of the companies to the point of causing them to crash?"

"No, sir, it doesn't," Shortridge said.

"Why not?"

"He's taking less money out of the company than he's going to have to come up with somewhere," the accountant said. Shortridge was pointing out the obvious. Caperton would have been crazy to steal from Harman, for if the company failed he was personally on the hook for several million dollars. And with that thought, Stanley concluded his questioning, moving aside for Fawcett.

Fawcett was concerned with a chart that he believed the defense would use to show that Harman was inevitably headed to bankruptcy without even a gentle nudge from Massey.

"Suppose," Fawcett asked Shortridge, holding up the chart, "a certified public accounting firm rendered the opinion that this chart proved that Harman is going out of business?"

"Personally, I think that's hogwash," Shortridge said.

"Did you use the word 'hogwash'?" Fawcett asked.

"Personally, I think that's what it would be," Shortridge said.

"I wonder if opposing counsel would mind us referring to [the CPA firm that had prepared the defense's chart] as Hogwash, Inc.?" Fawcett asked, looking at the Massey attorneys.

Fawcett had ridiculed the defense, and when Woods rose to begin cross-examining Shortridge, he was revved up to destroy much of what the accountant had said. The defense attorney suggested that Caperton had withheld information from Shortridge that would have made Harman's quarterly financial statements even worse. Woods's hectoring wore down the small-town accountant, and he only tepidly challenged Woods's assertions that the company was doomed regardless.

Woods and his associates had combed through the thousands of pages of financial documents, just as Devine had for the plaintiffs. The defense had found small mistakes the accountant had made: financial documents Shortridge had misfiled or not filed at all and financial transactions he had overlooked. The accountant pallidly countered what seemed a litany of mistakes. Woods made Shortridge look like a perfect match for the equally inept Caperton.

This was the most vulnerable part of Caperton's case, and Woods had prevailed. Once the accountant stepped off the witness stand, Fawcett and Stanley wanted to hurry on, hoping that the jury would forget the stumbling Shortridge.

16

Caperton had begun to feel that his day on the stand would never arrive. Then, on the ninth day of trial, Fawcett told him that the time had come. Fawcett had planned Caperton's testimony to fall on the last Friday in June. Fawcett would question Caperton for several hours, and then the jury would leave for an extended weekend; because of Hoke's other responsibilities, there would be no session on Monday. The jurors would thus have three days to ponder the misery that Massey had caused Caperton, with the defense unable to counter the evidence until the following week.

As Caperton and his attorneys filed into the courtroom, ready for the testimony that day, Ramey sat alone at the defense table with his head down, sobbing. Eventually, he composed himself and told the plaintiff attorneys, through red-rimmed eyes, that a secretary at his co-counsel's Kentucky firm had died after a long struggle with cancer. Ramey said that the inconsolable Woods, Ward, and Warren had driven back to Kentucky for the viewing and to serve as pallbearers at the funeral on Monday. Ramey said he was praying for them just as they had prayed for her each night. He had never met the woman, but he grieved as if she had been a close relative.

At such a moment, Fawcett hated to play the professional cynic, but he wondered why the defense attorneys hadn't given him the courtesy of a call the previous evening, alerting his team to the secretary's passing and their decision to depart. If they had, today's court session could have been canceled and Caperton would not have been strung along. But a call would not have allowed Ramey the opportunity to show how heartfelt he and his fellow attorneys were.

"I'm so pissed," Fawcett told his team. "We're going to say something to Hoke about them not calling last night, throwing us off, and screwing up Hugh again."

"No, Dave, you're not saying anything," remonstrated Berthold, the plaintiffs' expert on all things West Virginian. "You can't do that down here. My God, death is sacred."

"It *is* sacred; that's why I want to say something."

"I'm telling you, Dave," Berthold said, grabbing Fawcett's arm, "you must be quiet."

Fawcett walked over to Ramey, who had managed to compose himself. He truly was profoundly upset. Working with the Kentucky legal team, Ramey had heard them speaking about the woman for days, and he felt that he knew her and this was his loss too.

The two attorneys heatedly discussed a piece of evidence Fawcett wanted to submit. Ramey's response was, to Fawcett's way of thinking, overly combative. Fawcett was fed up with Ramey constantly accusing the plaintiff attorneys of ill will and unprofessionalism. Ramey set him off so badly that he decided to stick it to the Charleston attorney.

"Do you have proof that this secretary died?" Fawcett asked.

Ramey slammed down his yellow pad, sending thick binder clips exploding around the courtroom. He charged out the door and down the stairs. Fawcett went to the window and looked down at Ramey stomping around the block.

Ramey returned finally, and when Hoke entered the courtroom, he knew nothing of the altercation that had escalated the tension inside. Ramey could have complained to the judge about Fawcett's comment, but it probably would not have done him any good; besides, he would have plenty of opportunities to get even before the jury. As for the incident itself, several years later Ramey still fumed at the idea that he had used the poor woman's death to advance his case. He said that if he was crying it was only because he had just learned of her passing.

Hoke and the lawyers agreed that it would not do to have Caperton—he and Blankenship were the trial's key witnesses—testify in the absence of most of the defense lawyers. Instead, the plaintiffs would fill the day reading one deposition from the former head of purchasing for the LTV Steel Company and screening a video deposition of an executive of the Penn Virginia Land Company.

"I know that you guys are already talking about exchanging names for Christmas, because you've been here so long," Hoke told the jury. "Given the circumstances here, I want you to understand that the lawyers very much appreciate the fact that time is passing, and so we're trying to reach an accommodation of interests."

The plaintiffs had planned to present the two depositions after Caperton had testified, helping to validate part of what he had said. But to move the proceedings along, Fawcett and Stanley agreed to use them today. If they had had a few more days, they might have further edited out some of the depositions' more tedious, irrelevant exchanges; now they had no choice but to subject the jury to two hours in the morning and a half hour after lunch.

After Hoke dismissed the jury early for the long weekend, he asked the lawyers if they had any last issues before everyone left the overheated courtroom.

"Your Honor, we would ask for a mistrial at this time," Ramey said. "We understand that all references [to the Virginia trial] had been taken out, but one came up this morning with respect to the reading of the deposition transcript. I don't believe it was intentional, but the unfortunate fact remains that the reference was made."

Hoke had strongly admonished the lawyers not to bring up the Virginia case in front of the jury. If the jurors learned that men and women like them had already found a Massey subsidiary guilty and awarded Harman $6 million, it could have a dramatic impact. Previously in the proceedings, the defense had also inadvertently mentioned the Virginia trial, though not its result, but that had gone largely unnoticed and unmentioned. Today's mention during the plaintiffs' deposition was equally trivial and also omitted the verdict, but the Massey attorney still pounced.

"If I may, Your Honor," Fawcett said. "It certainly was unintentional. Most importantly, I don't think that registered with this jury."

"So, under the word of Your Honor, what is sauce for the goose is sauce for the gander," Stanley said. "They were the first one to mention

Virginia, and this was accidental and I just can't see a reason for a mistrial."

"I don't know what they do in Boone County, but in Lincoln County we call this pissing in the punch bowl," Hoke said, recognizing a matter that could either end the trial or create a strong cause for appeal. "I mean, we did our best to keep this from happening, but it happened."

Hoke said that he would spend the extended weekend thinking about whether he should call a mistrial. Fawcett and Stanley agreed that it was highly unlikely that the judge would end the trial, but they had both painfully learned that you could never gauge a judge's thinking with any certainty, especially a jurist like Hoke, who was predictable only in his unpredictability. And so the two attorneys spent a long, tedious three days in which they prepared for the following week—knowing that their failure to double-check the text references in the deposition might mean the trial would start over with a new jury. For Caperton, it was even worse; he once again prepared to testify while fearing that everything might have to be rebooted.

On Tuesday morning, Hoke did not decide immediately but, outside the presence of the jury, he heard arguments from both sides. Ramey escalated the issue as best he could. Pointing to Blizzard, the local Madison lawyer, he said, "My co-counsel, who was watching the jury at the time the reference was made, noticed one juror shoot a glance at another juror as they visibly reacted when this language that we object to was played for the jury."

Most jurors' greatest achievement during the reading of long transcripts is to not appear comatose. That the two jurors had been so startled by the passing mention suggested a remarkable sensitivity to the nuances of the case. Hoke knew that his old friend Ramey was trolling for a mistrial. If he did not give it to him and the defense lost, Ramey would use that fact in an appeal. West Virginia's system was unlike most states' in that there was no intermediate superior court. That appeal would therefore be directly to the Supreme Court of Appeals of West Virginia, the highest court in the state.

To appease the defense attorney, Hoke asked the bailiff to confiscate the jurors' notebooks to see if any of them had written even a bare mention of Virginia. When Hoke found not a word about the previous proceedings, he declared that the trial could continue.

The mourning Kentucky lawyers were absent for the second day in a row, so Hoke proceeded with matters that could be addressed without them. The plaintiff attorneys played more video depositions, which they made doubly sure had no more inadvertent references to the Virginia trial, while Caperton sat trying to contain his restlessness.

17

When Caperton walked up to the witness stand the next morning, July 3, with the full defense team seated in the courtroom, he was relieved that his moment had finally come. He believed that if he could have the jury relate to his story, the jurors would see that he was telling the truth and that he had been terribly wronged. Caperton knew that Fawcett would steer him around any issue with which the defense attorneys could bludgeon him during cross-examination.

As Caperton settled into the witness chair, Fawcett did not know how well Hugh would do. For days, Fawcett had been lecturing his client: "Hugh, you got to take your time. You got to give them the details. You got to give the jury the nitty-gritty. You have to talk to the jury, Hugh. You have to explain it, so they can picture it." Fawcett worried that in preaching and prepping Caperton, he had made him so nervous that he would sputter and lose control.

Fawcett began in the simplest way imaginable: "Would you state your full name for the record?"

"Yes, my name is Hugh Mason Caperton."

Hearing Caperton's calm, authoritative tone, Fawcett believed that Hugh would be okay.

As they proceeded, it was not so much questions and answers as a deeply felt dialogue. Fawcett set Caperton up to say what he wanted him to say.

"Your Honor, I feel like we're getting started off wrong here," Woods objected just as Fawcett was finding a natural rhythm with Caperton. "He's obviously talked to his witness, and he's already doing the testifying, and it seems like we need to have some nonleading questions."

"I'm going to allow him to do that, to get us to where we need to go," Hoke said. Then he faced Fawcett. "But I expect you to get that done and then turn him loose."

"Sure," Fawcett replied.

Fawcett had Caperton narrate the tale of his rise from birth in a coal camp (albeit the son of the mine's owner) to the ownership of Harman Mining. Caperton's life story had little to do with the issues at stake in the trial, but it was information that the jury members could readily understand and that would likely affect their verdict. In some measure, this had become a trial of two counternarratives. In Fawcett's telling, Caperton's life was a steady, magnificent journey upward. In the defense's version, it was one inept failure after another.

"I wanted to be in the coal business," Caperton said proudly. "I had grown up in the coal business, so my objective was to be in the coal business, and to ultimately be an operator."

Fawcett moved on from Caperton's early life and career to his management of Harman. He got Caperton to explain to the jury just how tough a situation he faced when he purchased the mining company, how monumental the financial obligations, and how much he had overcome.

The primary reason Caperton could pursue his dream of owning his own mine was that nobody else wanted to purchase Harman. He could not have bought a car without a down payment, but he bought a mine. He did so by taking on all kinds of financial obligations. Harman was a union mine, and Caperton was responsible for UMW medical and retirement benefits. The mine also came encumbered with millions of dollars of obligations, primarily to retirement, medical, and reclamation liabilities that would go on for years.

Fawcett wanted the jury to understand that Caperton was not some fly-by-nighter out to make a quick killing and leave the state. He was a Caperton, and coal was his life. "Our objective was to retire from it," Caperton said. "I mean, this is what I dreamed of a long time, was to have a coal operation of my own. One that I could build up, so, I mean, that's the dream."

In early 1997, Caperton had finessed a new million-dollar loan from his main banker, the Grundy National Bank, and renegotiated the Harman contract with Wellmore, netting three dollars more a ton. With all that in place, Caperton believed the future of Harman looked great.

"Was there anything that occurred in 1997 that caused you to miss these last payments?" Fawcett asked, referring to the Grundy National Bank loan.

"Massey claimed a force majeure on our contract and we lost all of our tonnage on our contract and we couldn't operate anymore," Caperton said.

After most of the day, Fawcett had reached one of the crucial subjects in the trial. The attorney knew that "force majeure" was an esoteric term likely unknown to the jury. He intended to hit it again and again and again. He wanted the members of the jury, in their deliberations, to speak knowingly about force majeure and to conclude that it had been misused by Massey and Blankenship.

"And how is the term used?" Fawcett asked.

"Force majeure in the industry generally means an act of God," Caperton said, "something that is beyond your control and something that happens suddenly that prevents one party or the other from performing on their contract."

"And give us some examples," Fawcett said. "What about for the buyer? What would be a force majeure event?"

"Well, in the case of Wellmore, maybe they had an electrical fire, something goes wrong, something breaks down, if the rails wash out, or a barge-loading facility goes down for an extended period of time," Caperton said. "Something like that is beyond their control."

Fawcett offered a litany of events and asked if each would qualify as force majeure: Insurrections. Epidemics. Labor Disputes. For each, Caperton said yes, that would be a force majeure event. Fawcett went on, with Caperton agreeing each time: Strikes. Government closures. Boycotts. Fires. Explosions. Floods.

It was late in the afternoon at the beginning of the four-day Fourth of July weekend, and almost everyone in the courtroom wanted to go home. But Fawcett would not be deterred. When he finally finished and the jury was dismissed, everyone in that courtroom understood force majeure and when it could legitimately be declared. That was the concept the jury members would hold vividly in their minds until they returned, five days later.

Everyone on the plaintiffs' team went home for the long holiday weekend, the only major break in the lengthy trial, except for Fawcett, who remained at the Hampton Inn. He had driven back to Pittsburgh other times to see his children, but the following week was a crucial one in the trial, and he had to be ready. He found time to go for a run on an Appalachian trail and swim in a nearby creek. But he still rose at six and worked until midnight.

Developers were blasting into the ground behind the Hampton Inn to build a strip mall, and the motel sat next to a virtual moonscape. A Toys "R" Us outside Fawcett's room lit up the parking lot all night long, so he kept his curtains tightly shut. The store reminded him of his kids, and he tried to block that out, too. Thirteen-year-old Claire, eleven-year-old Amelia, and five-year-old Daniel were only four hours away in Pittsburgh. He longed to see them, but they were staying with his wife, from whom he was now separated, and he felt they would be safe.

The year before, Fawcett had taken Claire to a birthday party for one of her friends. There he'd met Kathleen Trow, a divorced mother of two, and they'd begun dating. She had been in television news and had moved from there to corporate communications. Trow was full of good advice and suggestions, and not just about parenting. During the trial he missed her profoundly. But he was still the man he had always been, a man who could do only one thing at a time well, and the challenge before him was *Caperton*.

One of the ways Fawcett's anxiety and anguish exhibited itself was in a stomach so sensitive that sometimes he could not eat a proper meal, and when he did he often washed his food down with buttermilk. When his stomach was rumbling for dinner, he would have nothing but a cocktail of regular and chocolate milk. But most of the time, he kept on working, ensuring that he'd be ready to continue his examination of Caperton when the trial resumed.

18

As the court reconvened on Monday, July 8, Hoke announced, "The clerk is out washing her car. And as a result of that, can't call the roll this morning, but when she gets here I'll have her call the roll."

Caperton had tried to enjoy the Fourth with Kathy and Preston, but all he could think about was the testimony and what would happen when the Massey lawyers confronted him. Like Fawcett, he could not eat. His stomach churned, marking the onset of chronic gastrointestinal trouble.

When Caperton got back up on the witness stand for the second day of Fawcett's questioning, he knew that his attorney was going to ask him about the day before Thanksgiving 1997, when Blankenship came to Harman's Beckley office to discuss the future of the mining company. That summer Stanley C. Suboleski, the president of Massey-owned Wellmore/United, had told Caperton not to worry about a letter Suboleski had sent him in early August, saying that the company might stop buying most of Harman's contracted coal, which Wellmore/United sold to LTV Steel, where it was made into coke. Suboleski said that the note was only a "cover-your-ass memo," a legal formality that meant nothing. But Caperton had been hearing rumors that Massey had lost its LTV Steel business. So he decided to confront Blankenship with his concerns. That's why he'd set up a meeting with the Massey chairman, who arrived accompanied by Massey chief operating officer Ben Hatfield.

"Do you know how they got there?" Fawcett asked.

"They flew in on their plane, because I picked them up at the airport," Caperton said.

Caperton told the court that the Massey chairman spent the early minutes of the meeting spouting off about the good fortunes of his company. "So finally I looked at Don Blankenship, and I said, 'You've lost the LTV business,'" Caperton told the jury. "He looked at me, and he said, 'Yes, we lost the LTV business.'"

"Okay, then continue on with the meeting," Fawcett said. "After you said, 'You lost all the business,' what turn did the meeting take?"

"Well, you know, we had gotten these letters about a potential force majeure," Caperton said. "I looked at him, and I said, 'Don, this is not force majeure.' And his response to me was 'Look, for every expert you find that says it's not force majeure, I'll find three experts that say it *is* force majeure.' Then he said, 'We spend a million dollars a month on attorneys. We can tie this up in court for years.'"

"Now, in delivering what you took to be a threat, what was Mr. Blankenship's demeanor like?" Fawcett asked. "Was he threatening with you? Did he raise his voice?"

"His demeanor never changed," Caperton said. "He was calm and calculated and never, never raised his voice and never changed his expression."

Fawcett had feared that his client would become overly emotional or would go off on a tangent. But today Caperton had a diamond-edged focus and spoke compellingly, holding the attention of everyone in the courtroom. He did not like to be called a salesman, but he was trying to make the most important sale of his life.

"So after the discussion of force majeure, what took the rest of the time of the meeting?" asked Fawcett.

"Basically, the rest of the meeting was focused on [Blankenship's saying] 'You know, maybe we ought to just buy your companies,'" Caperton recalled. "At that point, I don't have much choice. I'm in a pretty difficult position. I've got very little sales for the next year, and I've got this wave of expenses coming that's going to hit me from behind. So I've got to see what my best options are here."

The last thing Caperton wanted to do was to sell the company that was his life's dream. But it was too late in the year to find a buyer for next year's coal. Selling the mine might be the only way to pay his vendors, the miners' medical bills, and other obligations while avoiding bankruptcy. He and Cook and a friend and fellow mine owner, Tom Deskins, went into the next room to discuss what he should do.

Caperton told the court how the three men gathered mining maps, financial statements, and everything else they could about the company and walked back into the other room to start giving Blankenship the information that would allow him to evaluate the mine. Cook was proud of the work he had done over the past five years. He showed the Massey chairman the mine plan, with the new ventilation system that would allow the company to mine coal more quickly but still safely. Caperton was equally proud of his work. He pointed out the thick band of reserves abutting the Harman mine. He was waiting until they mined right up to the boundary. Then he expected to lease those reserves from Pittston Coal and mine several million more tons of coal.

Caperton and Cook had one other worry beyond the price Massey would pay for the company. Blankenship was notoriously anti-union. The two men feared what might await their 125 employees, who were members of the UMW.

"Was there any discussion at all regarding obligations of Harman to the union and what Massey intended to do?" Fawcett asked.

"Blankenship said they have done union operations in the past," Caperton said. "He kind of paused for a minute, and I thought we were going on to something else, and he said, 'But, if we bought this property, we would drive up the hollow, and we would bring about three Ryder trucks up the hollow full of SWAT-team people. They'd get out of that truck in full SWAT-team gear, and we would take over the property that way.'

"And he said, 'You know, if they pick a fight with us, by golly, we've got an injunction against them or a restraining order against them. It's been in place since back in the eighties, and if they came in here and caused any problems, then we'll have that restraining order slapped against them. That way we would get out of the contract. That would void their contract, and then we can go nonunion.' That's exactly what he told me."

———

After a lunch break, Caperton returned to the witness stand. The jury seemed riveted, in a way they had not for any other witness so far in the trial.

"Generally, what was it that Massey was willing to give you for Harman?" Fawcett asked.

"Well, they were going to pay off our bank note," Caperton said. "They were going to assume the bonds. And they were going to give us $2.5 million to pay everything else."

"Do you have any idea of what the value of that was?" Fawcett asked.

"Oh, probably around $6 million."

"Was that a fair price in your mind?" Fawcett asked.

"Well, it's a fair price for a *broke* company," Caperton said. "I mean, no, it's not. It's certainly not what I thought our company was worth. Massey had me backed into a corner."

Caperton thought he had a deal that would close at the end of January 1998. He was getting calls from Harman's creditors almost every day, and he wanted to pay them whatever he could. But Blankenship, Caperton said, seemed to take pleasure in drawing the deal out, making one excuse after another. Caperton told the court that while this was going on, Massey, unbeknownst to him, was negotiating with Pittston to buy a wall of coal around Harman. That was part of the reserves that Caperton and Cook had told Blankenship about in their November meeting. By buying the narrow seam of coal, Blankenship blocked Caperton's dreams of expansion or even long-term survival.

Blankenship kept procrastinating. It was not until the second week in March 1998 that Massey was ready to close the deal.

"Tell the jury what happened on the day that this closing was to take place," Fawcett said.

"Well, we were in his office at a big conference table, and we had each of the documents set up," Caperton said. "Each document had to be signed by three or four different parties. So we had them all in line and all ready to go. We had worked all day on that. It must have been three o'clock in the afternoon; we got a phone call that said the deal wasn't going through."

Caperton told the jury how all those months, he had been working with Blankenship, giving up almost everything he had of value in Harman to salvage something. And now he had nothing except the devastating revelation that Blankenship had played him for a fool. Caperton had no choice but to declare corporate bankruptcy.

Caperton believed that if not for the lawsuit, Blankenship likely would have picked up Harman for almost nothing in bankruptcy court. Caperton was proud of always paying his obligations. He was left facing seventy-seven creditors claiming that Harman owed them over $25 million, most of it in long-term obligations to the retirement and pension funds.

After a day and a half of examining Caperton, Fawcett asked as his final question before turning him over to Stanley: "And in their bankruptcy maneuvers and then the litigation that's occurred, do you believe that Mr. Blankenship has been a man of his word that he would tie you up in court for years?"

"He's lived up to every word he said," Caperton said. "We've been tied up for four years now."

"And in your dealings with Mr. Blankenship, in your conversations with him, what was his manner in dealing with you?"

"Same as it always was. He was very cool and calm and collected, never changed his emotion, never was high and never was low. It was the same every time."

19

It was midafternoon by the time Stanley began asking questions. The attorney had a folksy, unpretentious manner that connected well with juries, but a different Stanley stood there today. He did not ask the deeply human questions typical of him. Instead he probed, in unbearable detail, into bank loans and sales and lease agreements. That would have been sufficient torture, but the air-conditioning was still not working properly, and it was close to eighty degrees in the courtroom.

After a few hours of this, the jury's primary task was maintaining consciousness, and still Stanley droned on. Fawcett felt sick. He knew that Stanley sometimes criticized him for going on too long, boring a jury with technical minutiae. But in his examination of Caperton, Fawcett had worked hard to make even the most esoteric financial matters compelling. Now Stanley was ruining everything.

Fawcett admired his co-counsel enormously and would not think to criticize, but he could not believe how miserably Stanley was questioning Caperton. Hoke had already told the lawyers that because of the judge's other cases, they would have the next day off, and for a whole day the jurors would have this numbing material stuck in their heads.

Hoke kept looking over at the spent jurors, and when the clock struck five he called a blessed stop to the proceedings.

"All right. Mr. Caperton, the witness, is in the box in the middle of the creek, and we haven't switched mules yet," Hoke lectured the jury.

"You've got to keep on course. So I don't want you discussing your testimony with anybody else."

After the jury left, Berthold turned to Fawcett, angry at and bewildered by Stanley. "Does this guy have any idea what he's doing?" Berthold asked. "He put that jury to sleep up there. What does he expect?"

Stanley overheard but said nothing. Later, back at the Hampton Inn, Fawcett sidled up to Stanley and delicately prodded him about what had happened in the courtroom. Stanley said nothing and walked away.

Stanley could not tolerate anyone challenging his courtroom acumen. He was so irritated at his co-counsels that he kept largely to himself. He told them nothing of his strategy. When he had examined Caperton, he'd known there would be no trial the next day. He could have ended with something riveting. But that would have meant that after a day off, the defense would start cross-examining Caperton, while the jury would have only fading memories of the testimony Fawcett and Stanley had so carefully evoked. Instead, he'd wanted to eat up enough time so that when the jurors returned they would hear him examining Caperton for another half day before the defense had its first opportunity with the witness. So Stanley had called up every bit of the most tedious material he could find and had dragged it out hour after hour, boring himself as much as he'd bored the jury.

When the trial resumed, Stanley began with what came close to an apology to the court. "After that scintillating afternoon on Monday going through all those documents, maybe we can move things along here a little bit for the jury," he told Caperton, as the jury listened. "I will try to get a few wrap-up questions with you and then move on."

Stanley might have apologized to his co-counsels as well. If he had let them in on what he'd planned to do, they would have appreciated every last dreary moment of his examination. But Stanley had his peevish prima donna moments too, and he'd chosen not to tell them. Of course, they figured it out as soon as a very different and very familiar Bruce Stanley began examining Caperton.

As Fawcett watched his co-counsel, he thought, "Thank God he had the balls to drag that out in the afternoon. Nothing harder than wasting time like that. And here I am, his close friend, contributing to the insecurity." Fawcett did not blame Stanley for keeping what he was doing secret, creating all sorts of unnecessary anxieties for the rest of the legal team.

Stanley began by trying to evoke just how positive Caperton had been about the future until Massey drove Harman into bankruptcy. "In 1997, before Massey got involved, did your personal financial future look bright?" Stanley asked.

"The year 1997 was by far the best financial situation I had ever been in [in] my entire life," Caperton said, gazing at the jury. "I never expected it to be that good."

"What kind of future did you envision for your family in '97?"

"Well, you know, everybody wants to have a solid foundation, and that's what I was trying to build, a solid foundation for my family and for generations to come. That's what I hoped I could do, leave something behind for my family. We just want to live a comfortable life and have some normalcy."

These were simple questions, and they reinvigorated the courtroom. Caperton's testimony this morning remolded the case into a human drama. And once Stanley got Caperton to describe his life at its peak, as the proud owner of Harman, he steered him into an intimate, painful evocation of the decline.

Stanley showed Caperton his hefty Applicant/Violator System evaluation. It listed Caperton's twenty-five violations of the AVS, which monitors things such as how well a mine owner reclaims property he's finished mining.

"What's your understanding of what it means?" Stanley asked.

"I can't be an officer or a director of a company," Caperton said. "I can't own a company. My whole dream in life has been to be an independent operator, to own my own business, and I can't do that in the coal business. I can't go open a coal mine."

"Are you current on your income taxes?" Stanley asked.

"No, I'm not current on my taxes now," Caperton said.

"Why not?" Stanley asked.

"Because I haven't been able to pay my . . ." Caperton stopped. "I just haven't been able to afford to pay my taxes because of my personal situation."

Stanley was pushing Caperton to expose his financial vulnerabilities in a manner that devastated him.

"Tell the jury why you're not current on your taxes," Stanley said.

"One of the things that happened to me was in the middle of all this,

I was building my home, and I couldn't borrow any more money on that home," Caperton said. "I went to borrow money to pay my taxes when taxes came due, and I couldn't borrow any money against my home because I had all these liens and judgments against me personally. So I owe the IRS now, and they have a judgment and a lien against me at this time."

"Do you have any savings?" Stanley asked.

"I don't have any savings," Caperton said. "I'm just living month to month."

Stanley paused. "What's it like to walk into your office today?" he asked.

"Well, it's a shell of what it used to be. I mean, my office now is just me. There's no one else there. The desks are there, but it's nothing—there's nothing else in the office but myself, and it's quiet."

Stanley led Caperton to explore the psychological costs of these past four and a half years.

"Massey's lawyers, in their opening statement, called you a failure," Stanley said. "What do you think about that characterization?"

"Well, first of all, the person that made those statements, Mr. Ramey, over there, doesn't know me," Caperton said, looking directly at the lawyer. "I bet he hasn't said three words to me in the year he's been involved in this case, never spoken to me. How would he know? Has he talked to my family? Has he talked to my friends? Has he talked to people in the industry about me? You know, I'm not a failure. I have never been a failure. You know, ask all the people that worked for me if I was a failure."

"You testified previously about a lot of the things that you've gone through in this litigation, depositions and everything else that's been involved, but there's one thing you didn't touch on," Stanley said. "Did you recently become aware that Massey has pictures of your home?"

Stanley had understood the value of the photos to the plaintiffs' case before anyone else. He knew that this had nothing to do with the fundamental issues at stake in *Caperton,* but it showed what kind of adversaries Massey and Blankenship were. Stanley sensed that to these jurors listening day after day to details about business and mining, this violation of Caperton's privacy could outrage them so severely that it would spill over onto whatever else they thought about the case.

"Yes, I did become aware," Caperton said.

"Have you seen those pictures?"

"Yes, I have," Caperton said. "They trespassed on my property. They came onto my property to take pictures of my home. They stood two feet from my house and took pictures of my home. Nobody asked my permission to come on my property to take pictures."

"Have you had to deal with your family about this invasion of your privacy?" Stanley asked.

"There have been days my wife hasn't been here," Caperton said, adding Kathy to the story. "My wife is now afraid to leave our daughter home with a babysitter because she's afraid who's going to come on our property."

"How long have you been doing battle with Massey?" Stanley asked.

"Five years."

"After what they've put you through, put your family through, why do you continue to fight Massey?" Stanley asked.

"I'll fight them as long as I need to fight them. What they've done to me, they can do to anyone, and I'll stop them. They're not going to do this to anybody else. I'll fight it as long as they want to fight it. I'll go to my last dollar, I'll do whatever it takes, but they're not going to do this to anyone else if I have anything to do with it."

"That's all, Your Honor," Stanley concluded.

20

Stanley had spent several hours portraying Caperton as a humane, beleaguered man who had been wronged and had suffered for it. Woods got up to cross-examine Caperton—and to tear that portrayal apart. He began by focusing on the violations federal and state audits had revealed in Harman's mining operations, including Harman's failure to pay certain fees. Caperton's lawyers had warned him that whatever the provocations, if he lost his temper and confronted the defense attorneys, he might hurt his case. It was one thing to preach that, Caperton realized, but the lawyers weren't the ones sitting up here facing taunting, badgering questions.

Woods was trying to suggest that Caperton was running not only an inept but possibly a dangerous operation. Caperton was not going to allow that to go unchallenged. "Mr. Woods, everybody in the coal industry, including A. T. Massey, goes through audit violations," Caperton said angrily. "Every one of them, okay?"

Caperton's livid rebuttal showed an aspect of him the jury had not seen before, but he wanted the jurors to realize that he wasn't backing down.

"Tell you what, let's perform this process," Hoke said, looking at Caperton. "Let's carefully listen to the question that's asked, and then if you can give a yes or no answer, let's do that. If you can't give a yes or no answer, well, explain that, and then I'll let you go ahead and explain your answer."

"Thank you, Your Honor," said Woods as Caperton digested the judge's instructions.

The defense was trying to center the case on the question of whether Caperton had been a successful manager. By casting aspersions on almost everything Caperton had done in his life, which had culminated in his allegedly miserable mismanagement of Harman, the defense lawyers hoped not only to prevail but, even if they lost, to minimize the jury's award.

Caperton's adult life was in many respects an attempted journey back to the warmth and security of his Slab Fork childhood, and he had viewed Harman as a rebirth of his life in the coal camp. Though he had alluded to that in court, it had seemed a human aside that had nothing to do with the intricacies of *Caperton*. But Woods saw a connection in the jumble of the personal and professional.

"And Slab Fork closed down after going into bankruptcy, didn't it?" Woods said.

"I had nothing to do with it," Caperton said. "I don't know what Slab Fork did when they filed bankruptcy."

"That wasn't Massey's fault, was it?" Woods said.

"It wasn't my fault, either," Caperton replied. "But no, it wasn't Massey's fault."

"And I think the next job you had, you said you worked for Massey," Woods said. "Then after that, your next job was with a company called Raleigh Coal Sales. Is that right?"

"Yes, that's correct," Caperton said.

"And you worked in that company with your father. Is that right?"

"That's correct."

"But Raleigh Coal Sales went into bankruptcy, didn't it?" Woods asked.

"Yes, Raleigh Coal Sales went into bankruptcy," Caperton answered softly.

"Okay. And eventually liquidated?"

"I believe so," Caperton said.

Woods cast aspersions on almost every financial deal in which

Caperton had been involved, suggesting that the man had spent his life hopscotching from failure to failure.

Just before lunch, Hoke told the jury members that they would have an hour-and-a-half recess.

"The reason I'm doing this," Hoke informed the lawyers and the spectators once the jurors had left, "is that I've got a young couple out in the hall who are going to get married. You're welcome to sit and watch."

Although the Massey chairman had not been in the courtroom since the opening day, he was the overwhelming presence in the trial. He was not going to squander time here when he found the whole business an irritating irrelevance that kept him from his central task of having his company mine more and more coal. But Massey's team of lawyers and the company's acting chief operating officer, Suboleski, who was in the courtroom daily, kept Blankenship informed of everything that happened.

"Now, I believe," said Woods when he resumed his cross-examination of Caperton, "you testified on a number of occasions in response to Mr. Fawcett's and Mr. Stanley's questions that Harman was going to be successful in the future, that despite the growing losses and the mounting debts, you always thought that things were going to get better. Is that right?"

"Harman *was* successful," Caperton said. "I wasn't hoping it was going to be successful. Harman *was* successful."

Then Woods asked Caperton to revisit that day before Thanksgiving 1997. "The fact of the matter is that prior to that meeting, you had threatened litigation, hadn't you?" Woods said. "You said that if Wellmore fails to accept or pay for our coal, Harman intends to seek consequential damages for economic loss or business failure, as the case may be. Is that right?"

"Yes, that's what I said," Caperton replied.

On the third day of cross-examination, July 12, 2002, Woods explored a new area of vulnerability. In 1996, Caperton had sold Harman's underlying reserves to Penn Virginia for $7 million in a lease-back deal in which the land company paid a royalty on every ton mined. Caperton gave about half of that money to his sometime business partner Tom

Deskins, in exchange for what he said was Deskins's taking over the less lucrative of the reserves. Caperton described it as "pruning a tree." The following year, 1997, Caperton received a $1 million check from Deskins as his cut of a timber deal that had been brewing for several years.

"Isn't it a fact that you got a million dollars under the table out of that deal?" Woods said.

"I am so tired of you talking about me getting things under the table in this deal," Caperton said. "I got nothing under the table in this deal, Mr. Woods, and you know it, but you worked four years to try to figure out how you can do this to me."

"Documents don't lie, do they?" Woods said, though he had no documents to prove his assertion.

"No, they don't," Caperton said. Woods's vigorous cross-examination could not refute what Stanley and the accountant Shortridge had established. Caperton was personally responsible for several million dollars of Harman's debts. If he'd pilfered the company into destruction, he'd have been destroying himself.

"In March of 1997, a month after the million dollars came in from Mr. Deskins's company, you undertook to build a big house, didn't you?" Woods asked.

"Yes, I did. I . . . I started building my dream house in . . . I think it was April of '97."

"And that house cost you how much to build?" Woods asked.

"Well, I believe it was about $850,000," Caperton said. Stanley had known that the defense would bring up the house, but he still cringed. The people in the jury likely thought of $850,000 as a fortune beyond imagination. All this talk of money risked losing their sympathy. Stanley was worried that even if the jury bought Caperton's story, they might award only $1 million, thinking that a sufficiently massive sum.

"Is this the house?" Woods asked, holding up one of the surreptitiously taken photos.

"It sure is," Caperton said. "You don't have to hold it up. I know my house."

"And this house was built, was it not, through 1997 and into 1998?" Woods asked. "Is that right?"

"Yes," Caperton said.

"And this is at the same time when, back at the mine, the employees and their families were not getting their health-care benefits paid for and were not getting their medications, and vendors such as Mountain Supply weren't getting paid for what they furnished the mine. Is that right?"

"No," Caperton said. "They're not getting paid because of what A. T. Massey did to me, not because of what I did to them."

Woods finished up his cross-examination by detailing all the monies Caperton had made, starting with the estimated $1 million in consulting fees that Cook had paid his former boss since the bankruptcy.

In 1998, the year Harman had declared bankruptcy, Caperton had netted $789,000. He'd earned $351,000 in 1999 and $212,000 in 2000, the last year for which he had submitted his tax returns. In three years, Caperton had earned more money than the retired jurors had probably made in their entire lives.

"My recollection is that before you got started with Harman, your income had been in the neighborhood of thirty thousand dollars to forty thousand dollars a year," Woods said.

"That's correct, yes," Caperton said.

"Would it be fair to say that you're leading a substantially more comfortable life than you did before Harman came along?" Woods asked.

"No," Caperton answered. He was living far better than before he'd purchased Harman, but he was living far beyond his means. With bill collectors on the phone and dunning letters from the IRS in the mailbox, Caperton said he hardly had "a substantially more comfortable life."

"That's all the questions I have at this time, Your Honor," Wood said, ending Caperton's five days on the witness stand.

Woods had spent two and a half days cross-examining Caperton without once directly addressing the central issues in the case: whether Blankenship had purposefully made misrepresentations and executed a scheme to make Caperton and Harman as vulnerable as possible and whether Massey had then willfully destroyed Harman. The defense lawyer's questioning was a masterpiece of irrelevance and non sequiturs, with the goal that Caperton would end up so diminished that the jury would find it unthinkable to give him anything for his troubles.

The plaintiffs called another witness, and the defense soon asked for a mistrial based on another small technicality. Hoke had grown tired of Massey's attorneys running around the courtroom cackling for a mistrial at every opportunity. Usually understated, Hoke could not contain himself. "Let everybody understand," the judge said, "that, with all the dancing that's been done around here, somebody's going to have to wave a flag or shoot off a cannon before I declare a mistrial. Is everybody understanding me?"

21

As Hoke saw it, his job was to ensure that the jurors received the widest possible range of information—and that they maintained enough interest and focus—to reach a fair verdict. That was why no one in the courtroom watched the jury more carefully than the judge. He scanned their faces from morning until night, and he did not like what he was seeing. Much of Caperton's testimony had been riveting, but as other witnesses came forward, he felt that some of the jurors were growing lethargic.

Hoke was not blameless. After talking to the attorneys, he had told the jurors, during the selection process, that the trial would likely last two weeks. That was time enough to ask most people to postpone their summer vacations or take time away from their jobs or families.

The trial had entered its fifth week, with no end in sight. That didn't bother the lawyers: each side had its reasons for extending the affair. For the plaintiffs, Fawcett in particular wanted an almost encyclopedic rendering of every issue, examining each witness to the point of exhaustion, while the defense wanted time and space to pursue every topic that might lead to a mistrial or a reversed verdict in the Supreme Court of Appeals of West Virginia. Several of the jurors were growing visibly restless and irritated. Hoke was convinced that terminally bored jurors had difficulty delivering justice. Beyond that, the trial was backing up other legal proceedings and risked impinging on the rights of others.

Before the trial proceeded any further, Hoke announced a dramatic means of expediting the proceedings. "Subject to exceptions that I might determine, the time limit for direct shall be the time limit for cross," Hoke told the lawyers. That meant that the precise time one side spent directly examining a witness would be granted to the other side for its cross-examination.

The unusual restriction had been employed in a few other legal proceedings, including General William Westmoreland's 1980s libel suit against CBS. Ramey thought the move unprecedented and likely unconstitutional, a splendid argument for the defense in any appeal to the Supreme Court of Appeals of West Virginia.

The judge's rule would keep Fawcett and Stanley to a brisk, compelling pace, since every minute they unnecessarily prolonged the questioning of a witness would give the defense more time to savage that person in cross-examination.

Fawcett and Stanley quickly ran through the next set of witnesses, who provided evidence of Harman's financial condition, before playing for the jury Fawcett's video deposition of Blankenship, taped in Richmond, Virginia, in September 1998.

The previous trial witnesses had all attempted to ingratiate themselves with the jury, but the Massey chairman was different. Although he spoke to the camera in a soft, emotionless tone, he was antagonistic and forceful.

Blankenship described how Massey had purchased Wellmore/United with the idea of transferring its business to his large-scale, highly profitable operation at Massey's mine at Marfork, in southern West Virginia. He listed a number of places where he could have sold the Harman coal, but he said he was not in the business of selling at no profit.

Blankenship said that he had initially had some interest in purchasing Harman but had soon changed his mind because it didn't have enough coal and was a union mine. In his assessment, Harman failed not because of Caperton's incompetence but because Caperton did not have a big enough seam of coal to mine or enough capital to overcome the liability of being a union operation.

In the video, Blankenship said that when he was negotiating with Caperton, he'd concluded that "absent a reorganization, which would consist of somehow shedding liabilities, . . . it was not going to make it."

Harman, he thought, was doomed. Blankenship then laid out precisely what Massey would have to do to get Harman running at a profit.

"You can avoid liabilities by not having to hire the people that they have on their payroll, particularly union people, because one day of employment earns you the obligation of the retired medical," Blankenship said. "You can avoid employing them for three years, because three years gives you the black lung liability."

Following the Blankenship video, the plaintiffs called Mark Gleason, a CPA from Pittsburgh, who had an MBA in finance and accounting from the University of Pittsburgh. He was testifying as an expert witness paid to analyze Harman's financial condition—its viability and the damages it had suffered when Massey had allegedly put it out of business.

As the accountant described Harman in July 1997, just before Massey raised the specter of force majeure, Harman had $17,839,000 in assets but $29,000,103 in liabilities, a negative value of more than $11,000,000. As devastating as that might sound, it was not actually quite so bad, since as much as $22,000,000 of the liabilities constituted long-term retirement benefits to miners who weren't yet owed them. Gleason believed that the company could "continue to operate and to work out of their problems."

After Massey forced Harman to declare bankruptcy, a year later, Harman had about $500,000 in assets and $33,810,000 in liabilities, including the long-term liabilities. After adding other factors, Gleason concluded that Massey had caused Harman $29,696,000 in damages. The plaintiffs put into evidence a memo Massey had prepared as it had contemplated buying Harman. The document predicted profits of $48,148,000 over an eleven-year period. Although Gleason admitted that the figure included the reserves around Harman that Caperton was hoping to lease or buy, and other reserves as well, it was an extraordinary sum for a mine that the defense was now arguing was worthless.

To testify about Caperton's personal losses, Stanley called Daniel Selby, an accountant who spent most of his time testifying as an expert witness in cases such as this. As a young man, he had worked for the prominent accounting firm today known as Ernst & Young and bore other significant credentials. Selby displayed a chart that projected that if Harman had not gone bankrupt, Caperton would have earned a total of $4,783,098 before he retired at age sixty-five, in 2020.

Stanley wanted to ask questions that would help the jury understand the magnitude of Massey's wealth. No matter how much the jury might award the plaintiffs, Massey was so wealthy that even the largest jury verdict was little more than pocket change and would not affect the jobs of West Virginians working for the coal giant. Hoke, however, ruled that Massey's past financial record was irrelevant and could not be brought into the record. So Stanley's final question was how much stockholders' equity Massey had documented in its most recent filing before the SEC.

"That comes to $866,350,000," Selby said.

"I'm sorry, would you say that number again, please?" Stanley asked. Selby repeated the figure.

"Very good." Stanley turned to sit down. "That's all I have, Your Honor."

The next morning, July 17, the eighteenth day of the trial, Ramey would have to rebut Selby's often arcane, technical testimony. He would have to do so quickly—taking no longer than the plaintiffs' presentation. Ramey was barely warming up when Hoke reminded him: "Two minutes."

Ignoring the judge, Ramey forged onward. After about fifteen minutes, Hoke spoke again, asking him to finish up: "Let's close the door over there, Mr. Ramey."

And still Ramey continued. After ten more minutes, Stanley jumped up to protest Ramey's going so far over his allotted time, but Hoke motioned for him to sit down. The lawyer watched incredulously as for several minutes more Ramey prolonged the repetitious cross-examination.

Stanley could tolerate this no further. He rose again and said, "Your Honor, I think we're beyond the scope, beyond the time limits, and beyond everybody's patience here, and I would object."

"I'm going to allow Mr. Ramey to continue," Hoke replied, "I have a remedy to this."

When Ramey finally concluded his questioning, Hoke sent the jury out of the courtroom. Hoke then announced that, as a sanction, he would allow the plaintiffs' attorneys to ask Selby questions about Massey's past financial condition.

"When you said two minutes, I thought you were referring to two minutes left on the tape," Ramey said, indicating the court reporter's transcribing machine. "I was looking at the court reporter during the remainder of my cross-examination and seeing if we were running out of tape."

Stanley would have jumped up to mock Ramey for his the-dog-ate-my-homework excuse, but Hoke was so irritated at Ramey's apparent dissembling that he didn't need Stanley to complain. "I wouldn't have imposed this remedy, but I gave a second thing about closing the door on the barn," Hoke said, reminding Ramey that he had twice asked the defense attorney to end his cross-examination and the lawyer had twice ignored him. "Now, I may be shooting myself in the foot by allowing additional inquiry here, but I want everybody to understand that there's going to be a sanction."

Because of Hoke's sanction, if the defense lost and took the case to the Supreme Court of Appeals of West Virginia, the appellate attorneys could argue that Hoke's unconstitutional limits had prevented the defense from fully presenting its case. Ramey says that although that may have been the result, he was totally blameless and had no other motive than making his case as fully as possible.

While the defense was exploiting every opportunity for a mistrial and documenting multiple grounds for an appeal, the plaintiffs were trying to stop them by keeping the trial narrowly focused. Stanley, now permitted to examine Massey's financial history, kept his questions to Selby short. Stanley merely wanted the record to show that despite losing the LTV business in 1997, the following year Massey's profits rose from $126 million to $142 million, and the shareholders' equity rose from $1.2 billion to $1.3 billion. It was clear that whatever the jury awarded the plaintiffs, Massey's financial condition would be essentially unchanged.

After Ramey's short recross, the judge excused the witness.

"Your Honor, on this seventeenth day of July, in the year of our Lord 2002, the plaintiffs rest," Fawcett said.

Fawcett felt that he and Stanley had done a good job, but he feared what awaited them when the defense presented its case. Massey's lawyers would have a full slate of powerful rebuttal witnesses, including the one everybody was waiting to hear: Don Blankenship.

22

Caperton could not help thinking about Blankenship, because every day in the courtroom he had to look at his surrogate sitting there observing everything. Caperton had known Stanley C. Suboleski, the acting Massey chief operating officer and former president of Wellmore/United, since Suboleski, a mining engineer, was a young executive and Caperton was a Massey coal salesman. Then, Suboleski had had an agreeable, unassuming manner, and Caperton had liked him. But now Caperton deemed him smug and self-satisfied.

On August 1, 1997, Caperton had figured it an immense advantage when Suboleski, a man he had known most of his business life, became president of Wellmore/United, then the newest Massey subsidiary. Caperton thought Suboleski a man of integrity, but he had helped to manage what Caperton viewed as a fraudulent assault on Harman. At the end of the year, as Harman sank into bankruptcy and Caperton was financially destroyed, Suboleski retired to become chairman of the highly regarded Department of Mining and Minerals Engineering at Virginia Tech before once again returning to Massey as interim COO, the second-highest position in the company.

Suboleski was scheduled to be a defense witness. But it was a measure of how important Blankenship thought this trial that he had sent his number two man to spend his days in the courtroom tracking the defense lawyers' performance and sending messages to the chairman.

As the mining engineer sat there day after day, he smiled at Caperton, waving occasionally. Caperton thought he was doing this to make the jury think the two men were friends. Caperton responded with frigid stares, but Suboleski kept smiling. Caperton did not warn his lawyers, but he was not going to tolerate Suboleski's behavior any longer.

When Caperton walked up to the courthouse the following morning, there was Suboleski, prancing up the sidewalk, waving at Caperton, and shouting a warm hello. Jurors were making their way along the sidewalk too, and Caperton figured that Suboleski was up to his usual self-serving tricks.

"Hey, let me talk to you for a second, Stan," Caperton said, motioning Suboleski toward a private conversation.

"I want you to wipe that fucking smile off your face!" said Caperton, who rarely swore. "I'm sick and tired of it. You're not my fucking friend. You're here to testify against me. You're here to ruin my life, and I don't want you to acknowledge my existence anymore."

"Oh, ah, okay," Suboleski sputtered before scurrying into the courtroom to tell his lawyers. When Hoke was apprised of the incident, he directed Caperton to avoid the Massey executive. And from then on Suboleski refrained from smiling.

In the afternoon, the defense called Suboleski as its first witness. Suboleski had been a professor at Penn State and Virginia Tech and had shuttled back and forth between academia and long stints at Massey. A timid man, he saw in Blankenship qualities he himself lacked. He had done whatever he'd had to do to nestle ever closer to the Massey chairman, and he had been handsomely rewarded for it.

As the president of Wellmore/United in the second half of 1997, during Harman's last months, Suboleski had implemented Blankenship's plan to stop buying coal from Harman. He knew more about the details of Wellmore's dealings with Harman than did anyone else. The gently disheveled professor was used to speaking before appreciative young students, but he was painfully uncomfortable in a public setting like this courtroom. It was immensely difficult for him to say what he was expected to say here.

The stakes would have been high even if Suboleski had gone later in the trial. As the defense's first witness, he would set the tone for its entire case. Everything was larger and the pressure greater. This morning, the elderly Ward questioned Suboleski. A few years before, Ward would have been the lead defense attorney here, but that role had been assumed by the younger Woods, his aggressive, uncompromising partner. Ward was more amiable, and his forte, like Stanley's, was connecting with a jury.

"There's been some discussion about Mr. Blankenship," Ward said. "Tell the jury the kind of person Mr. Blankenship is to work for."

"Don is probably the smartest businessman I've ever met," said Suboleski. "He picks up on issues real quickly, probably a lot more quickly than I do, and I think sometimes he gets a little frustrated with me. He's probably the toughest guy I've ever worked for as well. He's real demanding and wants to see things get done, and I think sometimes the . . . his impatience and his demands sometimes come across as being almost arrogant." Ward was trying to have Suboleski inoculate the jury about Blankenship the same way Stanley had earlier tried to prepare the jury for Harman's tenuous financial position.

If Suboleski disappointed Blankenship on the witness stand, the chairman, in his own testimony, scheduled for later that day, could do what he often did at the company: rush in to save Suboleski from his mistakes and failure of nerve.

Suboleski wanted to return the discussion to Blankenship's greatness and leave it there. "On the other hand, Don is the most safety-conscious person I've worked for," he said. "He's never turned me down on capital for safety in the company, and Don has high ethics. Massey's motto is 'Doing the right thing with energy,' and Don always stresses doing the right thing."

Suboleski neglected to mention that the most safety-conscious person Suboleski had ever worked for headed a company that had one of the worst safety records in the industry.

As Fawcett began his cross-examination, he had before him several memos and other documents without which there would have been no case. That was due largely to his own obsession with documents during the lengthy discovery process. It was the paralegal Rob Devine, however, who had spent more than twenty-five hundred hours scouring box after box of Massey documents, which filled much of one large storage room at Buchanan Ingersoll.

Devine had an engineering degree, but he had been working as a legal assistant for close to two decades. He would gather memos, letters, and faxes and analyze each page before giving annotated versions to Fawcett. The lawyer would then build his case from these documents, setting them out in precise, calculated order for their day in court or at a deposition.

Devine knew as much about the law as many lawyers, but he was too reticent to be comfortable with even the minimum public role of an attorney, and he had found a profession that utilized his abilities to the maximum. He read each page again and again, trying to puzzle out the context and decode the obscure mining jargon.

Blankenship was not a computer person. The Massey chairman's staff members communicated to him mainly by fax. He read their messages and often scribbled a note on the page before having his secretary fax it back. That left a physical record of a sort rare in contemporary corporations, where top executives communicate largely by e-mail.

In one of the boxes, Devine found a memo from Suboleski to Blankenship dated August 1, 1997. It revealed that Suboleski, the newly appointed president of Wellmore/United, had confirmed his intention of having Wellmore take the full complement of 720,000 tons of Harman coal in 1998. A firm contract existed between the two companies. As he took office, Suboleski was merely noting his intent to abide by a contractual obligation.

Devine kept trying to decipher the words Blankenship had scribbled in the upper right-hand corner. Finally, he got it: "No. We'll indicate minimum tons and caution (with legal department approval) of a force majeure possibility because of Pitts." Devine realized that he was looking at what could become the most crucial document in the entire case.

It showed that Blankenship, with calculation and forethought, had planned to dump the expensive Harman coal. Devine ran to tell Fawcett what he had found. Then he quickly returned to the boxes of documents. He discovered that in the weeks following that August 1997 memo, a series of legal memos had gone back and forth between Blankenship and Massey's lawyers. Devine knew the dates of the memos, but because of lawyer-client privilege, he did not know the content of the communications. Nevertheless, it was obvious that Blankenship had decided to declare force majeure without even reading the Wellmore contract with Harman or requesting legal advice. It was apparent that only later had he asked his lawyers to clean up after him and build legal justifications for actions he had already planned.

When it was Fawcett's turn to cross-examine Suboleski, he stood and looked at the COO before speaking. As a teacher at an esteemed university, Suboleski was presumed to possess the integrity and credibility that a salesperson or an executive was often thought to lack. From Fawcett's previous experiences cross-examining the professor during the Virginia trial, he'd deduced that Suboleski was not comfortable saying what he had been rehearsed to say in defense of Massey and Blankenship.

"I had examined him before, so I had other statements by him under oath," Fawcett reflected later. "So I had to be like a dog trainer. I had to let him know who's in control. If he speaks right, you give the dog a treat."

"Now, tell the jury who first came up with the idea, who first raised the idea of force majeure," Fawcett said.

"Well, the . . . I sent this letter off again because Dave Fortner had . . . I asked for Dave's advice . . ." Suboleski said, mentioning another Wellmore/United executive. Everyone in the courtroom knew from previous testimony that Blankenship had been the one to declare force majeure. Suboleski's attempt to avoid saying so outright seemed little more than an ineptly told lie.

"Excuse me, Mr. Suboleski!" Fawcett said, his voice reverberating through the courtroom. For most of his questioning, the attorney had kept his voice low, so that any increase in volume was all the more powerful.

"Yes, sir," Suboleski said meekly.

"Why don't you try answering my question? Will you tell the jury who first raised the idea of force majeure?"

"The letter—" the chastened Suboleski began.

Fawcett interrupted him: "Who first had that idea?"

"The reply from my memo came back from Don Blankenship," Suboleski said. "This copy shows that. Don said, 'We'll indicate minimum tons and caution of a force majeure possibility.' So, it was Don Blankenship."

"So, it was Don Blankenship who had the idea of force majeure," Fawcett repeated, relishing the answer. "He raised the idea. Is that correct?"

"He . . . Yes, sir," Suboleski said.

This teacher of the next generation of mining engineers was acknowledging that he had gone ahead and sent out a memo that had ended up destroying a company, putting 150 people out of work, without inquiring whether what he was about to do was legal or ethical.

Prompted by Fawcett, Suboleski said that if Blankenship had asked him to do so, he would have purchased the Harman coal. And if Caperton had lowered his price, Suboleski added, "we could probably move it more places, yes sir."

Suboleski admitted that in his entire career he had seen only one other declaration of force majeure. That was in 1977, when there had been widespread floods.

"Don Blankenship had asked you to be the president of United and Wellmore?" Fawcett asked.

"He did, yes, sir," Suboleski said.

"And what was your response?" the lawyer asked.

"I told him I would do whatever he wanted me to do."

"And Don Blankenship asked you to come back to Massey full-time?" Fawcett asked.

"Don called me and told me that [COO] Ben [Hatfield] was leaving and asked if I would fill in on an interim basis," said Suboleski.

"And what did you say?"

"Pardon?"

"And what did you say?"

"I said yes."

23

Blankenship was not in the courtroom for Suboleski's testimony. The Massey chairman walked into the courthouse on Thursday afternoon, July 18, 2002, on the nineteenth day of the trial, just as Suboleski stepped down. Blankenship arrived with a team of Massey executives. He seemed always to be surrounded with a Praetorian guard of tall, muscular men.

As the group entered the court, Devine overheard the Massey chairman lecturing the defense lawyers. "You guys have been outlawyered from day one," Blankenship said. "Now I'm gonna have to go in there and save your butts."

For the first few days, the courtroom had been largely empty of Massey supporters, but now the seats were full of miners with black-rimmed eyes; they had just come from work. "Why are you here?" Caperton heard one of the miners ask another in the parking lot. "Got no idea. They told us to get down here after my shift."

Woods began his examination of Don Blankenship by asking him about his childhood. Blankenship enjoyed discussing his modest upbringing, which gave him a commonality with many of the jurors that Caperton lacked. Blankenship had labored in the mines just as several of them and their family members had, in both small "dog hole" truck mines and union operations.

"What was it like growing up in Mingo County?" Woods asked.

"Your Honor, may we approach, please?" Berthold interrupted, walking forward to talk to Hoke and the other lawyers. "There's absolutely no reason to get into that he grew up on a dirt floor and had chickens running through the backyard."

Berthold was mocking Woods's attempt to portray the Massey chairman's humble beginnings, but Hoke had let Caperton's attorneys spin the tale of his own early years in detail, and he ruled that Blankenship deserved the same opportunity. "I'm going to allow you to put the icing on the cake here," Hoke said. "But let's not break the bakery down."

Woods decided to question Blankenship with an almost manic haste, knowing that the sooner he finished, the less time the plaintiffs would have to try to tear the chairman apart. Blankenship, however, was not about to edit his words.

"What was life like for you growing up in Mingo County?" Woods asked, resuming his examination.

"I grew up in a town of about four hundred people and seven beer joints," Blankenship said, reveling in the moral lessons of his childhood. "I think you could characterize our family as poor at the time but didn't know it. We did okay, but I was raised in a single-parent home, and it was difficult at times, but I can't complain. Mother, she did fine. It was a good childhood."

"Did you go to school there, in Mingo County?" Woods asked.

"Yeah, I graduated second in [an elementary school] class of six in Delorme, West Virginia."

When asked about his rise to the presidency of Rawl Sales, in 1984, he answered, "I guess they couldn't find anyone else."

Blankenship said that he called Massey employees "members" because he wanted "to create a feeling of membership like you might in other organizations." He added that about 60 percent, or three thousand, of these members lived in West Virginia, along with their nine to ten thousand dependents. In Boone County, Massey was by far the biggest private employer. The roughly fifteen hundred employees there constituted some 30 percent of the county's private payroll.

Blankenship said that in early August 1997, his company had alerted Caperton that Wellmore might declare force majeure, radically diminishing the amount of coal they would buy from Harman the following year. Blankenship pointed out that legally he did not have to warn Caperton of the prospect but that he did so anyway, as "a business courtesy." Blankenship said that in the ensuing months, Massey tried to sell Harman coal to many steelmakers and other potential buyers, but no one was interested.

Blankenship added that it was his duty "to deliver bad news or concerning news in person." That was why, he said, he set up a meeting with Caperton on the day before Thanksgiving 1997. Blankenship said that he told Caperton then that he had no choice but to declare force majeure formally and that he'd decided that the best solution for both of them might be for Massey to buy the mining company.

When questioned about Caperton's testimony that Blankenship had threatened to sue him and that Blankenship had talked about unleashing SWAT teams to fight union militants, he said, "We don't go around threatening people. . . . We know that our size and so forth means that we cannot threaten people or threaten companies. We have to be quite gentle and professional in the way we deal. The purpose of the meeting was to say that we have this issue, and we have different things we can do, and actually, as evidenced by the lawsuit, we were the ones being threatened."

Woods asked, "Have you ever had any dealings with Hugh Caperton or his family prior to the events that have been discussed in this trial?"

"Well, I had a few opportunities to meet his father," Blankenship said. "A few times he rode on the plane. I would drop him in Beckley on my way back from Richmond when he was ill, and I knew [Hugh Caperton's brother] Austin Caperton pretty well, because he worked for quite a while at Massey and, at one time, was a candidate, I believe, to be president of Massey, back in the eighties."

"Don, do you have some ill will or bad feelings toward Mr. Caperton and Harman?" Woods asked.

"Not during this entire time, but it has generated some in the last year or so with the behavior and the accusations," Blankenship said. "It's been disappointing to see the extent that they're willing to go to fabricate stories that are simply not true."

"Just to clarify, were you trying to put Harman out of business?" Woods asked.

"Absolutely not," Blankenship said. "It never crossed my mind to try to put Harman out of business."

"I believe that's all, Your Honor," Woods said.

A break was called, and among the spectators trooping out of the courtroom was a group of half a dozen women from Sylvester, a tiny community a few miles from the courthouse. They and their neighbors were fighting Massey in a different case. For years Massey had run a coal-preparation plant on the outskirts of their town. Between Sylvester and the plant stood a high bluff, and the people hardly even noticed the operation. But then Massey removed the bluff to disgorge the coal that lay beneath. From then on, coal dust drifted over the town. It covered not just the outside of the homes but entered inside and coated people's lungs as well. The Sylvester residents had sued, charging that the coal dust caused all kinds of health problems and changed the life of the community.

This morning the women had been attending a hearing with a different judge in this courtroom. When they'd learned that Blankenship would be testifying they had stayed on, glowering at him from their seats.

Blankenship left the courtroom, too, and the women confronted him in the corridor.

"You're destroying our community with all the dust!" one woman shouted.

"We can't live like this!" another yelled.

"It's not our fault," Blankenship said softly, without emotion. "We always do our best for people."

Kathy Caperton had come out into the corridor, too. When she saw the women surrounding Blankenship, she hurried over. "You're a liar, Don Blankenship!" she shouted. "You're nothing but a liar!"

The Sylvester women were so impressed with Kathy that they decided to attend the trial and sit every day near their new ally.

When the trial resumed, the defense lawyers told Hoke about Kathy Caperton's altercation with Blankenship. As he had done so many times before, Hoke ordered everyone involved to control their emotions.

Fawcett would typically have cross-examined Blankenship first, but Caperton's team had decided that Stanley, raised in these coal fields, should take the lead. The previous year, when Stanley had deposed Blankenship for this trial, the two men had chatted about what it was like growing up poor in Mingo County.

Stanley could not understand how a man who had experienced such inequality and social abuse as a child could turn away from his people and become a right-wing apologist. Blankenship, meanwhile, could not understand how an intelligent person could believe liberal ideas that, Blankenship thought, had been so thoroughly disproven.

In his deposition as well as at the trial, Blankenship referred to Caperton as "Hugh." There was a patronizing quality to this, as if Blankenship's adversary was not even worthy of a last name. Yet in the deposition, Stanley had addressed Blankenship deferentially. He'd asked the most fawning questions, and Blankenship might easily have concluded that his fellow West Virginian was an unctuous wannabe overwhelmed by being in the presence of greatness. What Blankenship surely had not realized was that Stanley had been using the deposition as a learning tool, trying to understand the man and figure out what might break him in a cross-examination.

Today Stanley began in the same obsequious tone he had employed so lavishly in the deposition. It was so extreme that it seemed a shameful betrayal of Caperton and his team. Even Fawcett was shocked at how his friend seemed to have melted into a pathetic Massey sycophant.

The windows of the courtroom were open, but there seemed to be no air. Fawcett, who trusted his friend deeply, now blamed himself for not having reviewed Stanley's plan of attack ahead of time.

"You described how you grew up in Mingo County," the lawyer said.

"That's correct," Blankenship replied, as if already bored.

"We both know a little something about that," Stanley said. He sounded as if he was trying to ingratiate himself with one of his betters. But as with his mysteriously tedious examination of Caperton earlier in the trial, Stanley had a strategy. He was trying to suggest to the jury that anyone who grew up in Mingo County knew how corrupt it was—and that this had been Blankenship's greatest childhood lesson.

"I don't know your background," Blankenship said.

"Oh, you don't remember our prior conversation [during the deposition], when we shared a little bit of our common background about being from Mingo County?" Stanley asked.

"No," said Blankenship, dismissing Stanley, as he had every time he'd seen him.

"There were some pretty emotional and tough times at Rawl while you were there, weren't there?" Stanley asked.

"I think you could characterize it that way, yes," Blankenship said.

"Mass protests by the union?" Stanley asked.

"Mass violence would be a better description," Blankenship said.

As Stanley asked about those days, he mentally traveled back to 1984 and 1985, to driving those twisting mountain roads and trying to report and write fairly about the UMW strike. Although it may have seemed a personal indulgence to relive those days here in court, it had been during the strike that the formidable, uncompromising Blankenship had come into being, and Stanley wanted the jury to understand how Blankenship had behaved during that time.

"Do you recollect sit-down strikes in the middle of the highway and state police officers asking civil-disobedient union workers who were sitting in the middle of the road to vacate and they wouldn't, and they hauled them away in buses?" Stanley asked.

"It's not my most vivid recollection," Blankenship said. "But I do recollect that, yes."

"Well, did you consider that portion of the protest to be violent?" Stanley asked.

"Some of it was violent. It normally wasn't reported correctly in the press," Blankenship said, subtly criticizing Stanley. "You wouldn't want to walk through a UMW nonviolent protest. You might find yourself ailing."

The strike had been the defining moment of both Blankenship's and Stanley's adult lives, and the lawyer could not let it go. Stanley might have gone on too long, but he hoped the jury remembered enough of those days to know that the blame for the agony lay on both sides. If Blankenship could not see that clearly, then the jury should question everything else he said. Beyond that, this was a man who'd suffered no challenges to his sovereignty over the coal fields, whether from the UMW or a small-mine owner like Caperton.

Stanley discarded his obsequious tone. He again sounded like a prosecuting attorney. His sentences might have had question marks at the end, but they were more accusations than queries. This irritated Blankenship. And when Hoke tried to make the CEO answer yes or no, Blankenship argued that he couldn't give such simple answers to questions that were so full of misstatements.

"Mr. Blankenship, I have a copy here in my hands of the deposition that we took in Richmond, Virginia, on October 25, 2001," Stanley said. "And do you remember we talked about your recollection of the November 26 meeting?"

"Actually," Blankenship said, "I don't recollect much of anything about the meeting." He had not only given three depositions where he had talked about the gathering, but the jury had just heard him speaking extensively with defense attorney Woods about the meeting on the day before Thanksgiving 1997.

"I don't suppose it was a threat that someone hired by your attorneys sneaked up to Hugh and Kathy Caperton's home and took pictures of it," Stanley said. "That wasn't a threat, was it?"

"I would not consider it a threat considering what I've been through for a long time," Blankenship replied.

"Just a business reaction?" Stanley asked.

"No, you know Hugh is trying to pretend that he has been devastated," Blankenship said. "His future is destroyed. His life is destroyed, and I think the house that we put in evidence as well as his background shows that's not the case. You know, he has lived at Glade Springs and had money most of his life. So I think we were trying to make sure that the jury didn't misunderstand Hugh's background."

There it was for the court and jury to see, if only Stanley could help them grasp it: Stanley felt that Blankenship envied people like Caperton— who, Blankenship believed, had gotten everything without working. Growing up, Blankenship had viewed the Capertons and their ilk from a distance, and now he had risen far above them and he wanted everyone to know that he had gotten there on his own.

Blankenship did not like it when people stood up to him, and Stanley wanted to show that Blankenship took on all who dared challenge him and made them suffer, even the people of West Virginia. "I have a May 2002 quote attributed to you," Stanley said. "It says, 'We are moving the equipment we can to east Kentucky. The future plans for growth will be east Kentucky.' Would you deny making that statement?"

"No, I wouldn't deny making that. I don't have a whole lot of choice, given the permit situation [for mountaintop removal] and all that's going on to do that."

"Well, so, it doesn't have anything to do with the fact that you don't consider West Virginia to be family?"

Of all the many questions Stanley had asked Blankenship, this was the cruelest of all, as it suggested that Blankenship was not truly a loyal son of West Virginia. "I think that if there's any CEO in the coal business or any other business that's in favor of West Virginia, it is me," Blankenship said, never raising his voice. "I'm the only Fortune 1000 CEO living in West Virginia, and while I could live anywhere in the world, I choose to live in the same house I've lived in for twenty-two years and within eight miles of where I have always lived and take the abuse of these types of cases and of reporters and everything that gets said. So I don't think that anyone could say they're more dedicated to West Virginia than I am."

When Blankenship stepped off the witness stand late that Thursday afternoon, Stanley felt good about his cross-examination but there was no clear-cut victor. Blankenship could feel that he had gone a considerable way toward saving the case that he believed his lawyers were losing.

24

When Blankenship returned the next morning, Friday, July 19, 2002, the skies were dark and a storm was falling on the Appalachian high country. It was so hot that steam rose off the macadam, and damp warmth filled the courtroom.

Stanley resumed questioning Blankenship, but the rain beat so loudly on the windows that their voices were hard to hear. The lawyer returned to Blankenship's testimony from the previous afternoon. Stanley considered Blankenship's admission that Massey intended to end further investments in West Virginia devastating. He wanted the jury to hear this man, the biggest employer in their county, say those words once again.

"We're unable to continue to invest in West Virginia because of shareholder interest," Blankenship said. "We will invest in Kentucky."

Blankenship's subtext: If the jury was so brazen as to award damages to Caperton, it would exacerbate the state's poisonous business climate. Massey would leave, and the jury would have to explain to their friends and neighbors why they had no work.

Stanley then read a devastating list of the environmental disasters Massey had caused. In October 2000, Massey had spilled 230 million gallons of coal slurry—the black muck left from cleaning coal with a mixture of water and chemicals—into the streams of eastern Kentucky. This contaminated water typically contains elevated levels of chlorides, sulfates, arsenic, lead, mercury, and selenium. In the past eight months alone, there had been three other spills. But Blankenship said that most of these were "small spills" and had happened in the past.

The courtroom darkened. The storm outside had intensified, dropping as much as three inches of rain in three hours on a wide region including the small community of Winding Shoals Hollow forty miles south of the courthouse.

In 2000, a Massey subsidiary had sliced off the top of the mountain above the town, stripping out 870,000 tons of coal. The mining had ended two years ago, and Massey had not worked so quickly to clean up afterward or to reclaim the diminished mountain. All the townspeople saw as they craned their necks upward was a massive dirt dam holding back the water that had once flowed past their homes in a mountain stream. As the storm raged and Blankenship testified about Massey's problems with small spills in the past, the sediment dam overflowed and a ten-foot-tall wave of black water roared down the hollow, destroying two homes and damaging most of the others, carrying televisions and refrigerators like paper boats, picking up cars and trucks and tossing them like twigs.

Neither Blankenship nor anyone else in the courtroom had any idea of what had occurred at Winding Shoals Hollow. Stanley continued, now raising the complaints of the Sylvester women who had confronted Blankenship and were sitting in the courtroom.

"Our nonunion operation has less dust in the community than there is in the Charleston [Public] Library," Blankenship said, his voice hardly audible. "But we have been required to build a dome over part of the operation."

Stanley held up Massey's latest 10-K financial statement. The company that was condemning Caperton for not making a profit had watched its earnings fall from $203.4 million in 1999 to a loss of $1.1 million in 2001. That was the kind of paper loss that happened to many expanding companies and had nothing to do with the underlying value of Massey and its massive coal reserves.

The company had incurred such costs as $6.9 million for premiums never paid by Massey contract mines to the West Virginia Workers' Compensation Fund; $2.5 million awarded by a Mingo jury for a spill; $225,000 in fines for a Kentucky spill; and $41.5 million in other cleanup costs, most paid by insurance.

Despite the large losses, fines, and verdicts, Blankenship had signed a new contract that, with potential bonuses, could raise his income to $15 million a year.

"Are you well compensated?" Stanley asked as the rain poured down.

"I believe most people would think so, yes," Blankenship said. "Pretty good for a boy from Mingo County—"

At that moment lightning struck near the courthouse, blowing out the lights and knocking out court reporter Jennifer Meadows's transcription machine. The courtroom fell silent as Meadows struggled to restart her equipment. Blankenship leaned over toward the jury and said, "It must have been all them numbers."

After an interlude in which Meadows tried unsuccessfully to evaluate the damage to the transcript, Stanley resumed questioning Blankenship. "I don't necessarily want to burden the court reporter's computer with some more big numbers that might cause it to break down," Stanley said. "But suffice it to say, the new employment contract you signed with Massey significantly increases your base, bonus, and other compensation with that company, doesn't it?"

"Yes, by about ten percent over what it was in the previous contract I had," Blankenship said.

It had been a long, difficult day, but Stanley had one more area he wanted to discuss. "And on December 1, 2001, if Massey had learned that 64 percent of its 2002 contract sales had been canceled, that would have had a material impact on the company, wouldn't it?" Stanley asked, replicating what Harman had experienced in 1997.

"Yes, it would," Blankenship said, speaking, as always, with not an iota of emotion.

"And, in fact, it would have threatened Massey's very existence, wouldn't it?" Stanley asked.

"It could," Blankenship said.

"That's all I have, Your Honor," Stanley said.

In the corridor, Blankenship ran into the *Charleston Gazette*'s Paul Nyden, the Massey chairman's least favorite reporter. When Nyden asked him for an interview, Blankenship said no, adding "You're one of the two biggest assholes in West Virginia." Nyden asked who the other one was, and Blankenship said it was Cecil Roberts, the president of the UMW.

25

Blankenship returned on Monday morning to resume his testimony. Before the bailiff showed the jury into the courtroom, Woods stood before Hoke, shaking his head over the weekend's wide media coverage of the flood at Winding Shoals Hollow, of another Massey spill, which had flooded into a popular recreational lake, and of Blankenship's testimony.

"Your Honor, we are very concerned about the violent news coverage pertaining to Massey this and Massey that," Wood said while the other defense lawyers and the plaintiffs' team stood around the judge.

In the *Charleston Gazette,* a well-researched article by Ken Ward Jr., one of the journalists Blankenship had marked as a dangerous radical, traced how the flood at Winding Shoals Hollow had likely arisen from the Massey subsidiary's many safety violations. No one was injured in the incident, but the people living there had been terrified and had suffered considerable damage. The *Gazette*'s front-page story included photos of toppled trailers and cars.

Over the weekend, as Massey had tried to deflect the bad publicity by immediately reaching out to help the Winding Shoals victims, the coal company had faced another problem. A few miles from Madison, at another Massey operation, a bulldozer operator appeared to have cut through the wall in a pond holding mucky black residue left from a coal-cleaning operation. Here rock and sulfur had been removed from the coal by running the coal through screens and "washing" it in large cylinders of dense liquid; the rock drops to the bottom and the coal floats to the top, leaving a mucky liquid known as slurry. Twenty thousand gallons of this watery mixture full of chemicals and minute pieces of coal had flowed into Laurel Creek and from there into the state-owned Laurel Lake. It was summer, and no one wanted to fish in polluted water.

On July 27, Blankenship would write a letter to Massey employees stating that although water had flowed over the dam at Winding Shoals, the dam had not broken and that the Laurel Creek spill could have been "sabotage." The day after the spill, he had driven along Laurel Creek and "observed children swimming in the water reaching the lake. . . . The water wasn't black. The water was somewhat discolored in some areas."

Woods asked Hoke to warn the jurors about not reading newspapers or watching television news. "I don't want to point a bright light at anything and cause further trouble," the judge said.

Woods persisted while Blankenship listened intently, and Stanley and Fawcett watched the defense lawyer's discomfort with delight. "It seems awfully coincidental to us that the press coverage shows up at the times in the case that the plaintiffs would hope to have press coverage," Woods said. "Those facts obviously cause me concern that the plaintiffs are cooperating with the press to let them know when to be here so as to be able to report the parts of the case that they would like for the jurors to hear twice. So that is of great concern. It seems awfully coincidental."

A former reporter himself, Stanley empathized with journalists and understood how they did their jobs. He was more amused by than angry at the defense attorney's accusations, and doubly amused by Hoke's response.

"Well," said Hoke, "I take that and note that for the record. If there is any credence to that, particularly I would like to know how you arranged the rain, if you can explain that to me."

"Your Honor, there is one other matter," Berthold said for the plaintiffs. "Unfortunately, we just found out this weekend, there was a break-in at Mr. Caperton's personal office. The only things taken were the two items that would have memory, a fax machine and a personal computer of the secretary. The laser printers and other valuable things were left. The file drawer was open on a subject of this litigation, and additionally, Your Honor, there was a note with a vulgarity directed at Mr. Caperton lying on his desk with his reading glasses, broken in half, setting on top of it." The thief had taken from Caperton's bulletin board a caricature of a man urinating on a Massey sign, placed it on the desk, and scrawled "FUCK YOU" on top of the picture.

"So there are more issues going on in this case," Berthold said, not making the obvious point that the fax and computer would have contained Caperton's communications with his lawyers, potentially useful to Massey's defense. "Given the personalization of Mr. Woods's comments, we felt the court should be aware of that matter as well."

"Oh, my," Hoke said, dropping the matter for good.

As Fawcett prepared for what would likely be the most important day in a courtroom in his life, he kept thinking about his father. He had never asked his father to come to see him in court, but now he did. That typified their dynamic since Dave had been a little boy. He'd asked his father for little and had told him nothing—while his younger brother, Danny, had sat on his father's knee, sharing everything and asking for advice.

Their father was so proud that Dan Fawcett had attended his alma mater, the University of Pittsburgh School of Law, and been a wildly successful young associate at Reed Smith before heading out to Hollywood for a top job in the entertainment industry. When Dave won admission to the same law school as his brother, he did not even mention it to his father.

"I didn't see your grades," the elder Fawcett told Dave after the second semester.

"It's none of your business," Dave said.

"I pay your tuition," his father said.

A few weeks later, Dave's father invited him to breakfast to discuss his future.

"If you want to work for a law firm, you should intern in the summer and make application early," his father advised.

"I would never work for a big firm like yours," Dave said. "I'm interested in the environment. I want to do good, and I'm not sure that what you're doing is so good." Dave's father never forgot that remark, especially after his son joined a law firm that was far bigger and fancier than his.

Fawcett had never asked his father to attend one of his trials, but he figured his dad knew how important this case was to him. And so on the day before his crucial cross-examination of Blankenship, Fawcett had called his father and invited him down to the Boone County courtroom.

"How long of a drive is it?" the elder Fawcett had asked before declining. And so Dave, in the hours before one of the most important days of his professional life, felt a deep disappointment.

That evening Dave's father told Janet Fawcett about the invitation. Dave's mother did not insist on many things in life, but she insisted that her husband get up early the next morning and drive down to Madison. And so, as Fawcett stood up to begin his cross-examination, he saw his father sitting in the courtroom.

"Good morning, Mr. Blankenship," Fawcett said.

"Do you really mean that?" Blankenship replied.

"That is the way I start most days, but we will see."

Stanley had already questioned Blankenship extensively about his childhood, but Fawcett began with the same material.

"Do you have a wall or a fence around your home?" Fawcett asked.

"I have a fence," Blankenship said.

"And did you bring any pictures of your home with you today?" Fawcett continued.

"No, I didn't bring any pictures."

Though Fawcett was trying to remind the jurors of Massey's photographing of Caperton's home, the question gave Blankenship an opportunity to contrast his home with Hugh's, a distinction he was delighted to make.

"The home is ninety-eight years old," Blankenship said. "It is probably worth a hundred fifty, two hundred thousand dollars. It is sort of an old relic. It's about two miles from the Rawl Sales office, and it has been known as the superintendent's house, and I have been living there for twenty-two years. I reared my children there. So I have just stayed there."

"Where are your offices?" Fawcett asked, posing yet another question whose answer was already numbingly familiar.

"Well, I have two," Blankenship said. "One is in Belfry, Kentucky. It is just a double-wide trailer, and then I have one in Richmond, Virginia, that I don't frequent very often."

On this initial exchange, Blankenship was the clear winner, appearing uninterested in the highfalutin life that enamored outsiders. Not only did he live in a house far less expensive than Caperton's, but he worked in an office that had not a speck of pretension or show. He did not talk about the helicopter that often whisked him from his home, taking him on occasion to one of his two luxury cabins in the Kentucky hills; nor did he mention that he flew around the coal fields in a corporate jet. And Fawcett did not ask him.

Fawcett set out to establish Blankenship's autocratic rule. Blankenship had no problem acknowledging that. "You could save the jury a lot of time if you are looking for who made the decisions," Blankenship said nonchalantly, "because I made nearly all of them throughout this case."

Fawcett moved on to the August 1, 1997, faxed memo on which Blankenship had scribbled his note stating that Massey should declare potential force majeure. "At the time, I had not read the contract, but I knew that the event had occurred outside of our control," Blankenship said.

Fawcett pretended that he had not heard or did not understand the answer. That way he could get Blankenship to repeat it, imprinting the answer on the jurors' minds.

"But you did not read the contract before putting that note on his [Suboleski's] August 1 memo?" Fawcett asked.

"As you know, the legal profession works slow," Blankenship said. "Had I waited for a legal opinion on the contract, it would have taken me a while to get the letter out. So the courtesy would have been lost by going through a lot of trouble."

Blankenship was not known for his business courtesy, and the Massey lawyers would have taken no more than a day or two to read the contract and reply, but to nonlawyers his response would have sounded plausible.

When Massey was contemplating declaring force majeure, Blankenship admitted, he had done the numbers in his head, figuring out how much it would likely cost the company if Caperton sued. "I take it from your comment or mannerism that you think it is odd for a corporation to evaluate whether to take a force majeure or to cause it litigation and so forth, but I can assure you it is a necessary part of doing business," Blankenship said.

Fawcett forged forward: "Is it a practice of Massey?"

"It is a practice of any company to evaluate frivolous lawsuits and the problems it brings," Blankenship said.

During the discovery process, Devine had come upon a May 15, 1997, memo that Blankenship had signed, acknowledging that he had read it. The document showed that, on that day, Wellmore/United already knew that the LTV coke plant was shutting down and management was planning in 1998 to sell the Harman coal to different buyers. Here was irrefutable evidence that nearly three months before Suboleski notified Harman, the Massey chairman had been aware that the coke plant was closing. He'd also known that Wellmore/United executives were not planning to invoke force majeure but had gone out to find other buyers for the high-grade coal.

Faced with this document, Blankenship admitted that it "probably" showed what the Wellmore/United sales executives were planning; he was "not a hundred percent sure, but probably, yes." Despite the memo confirming the closing of the plant, Blankenship said, "I never know what one of those steel companies is going to do"; he said he could not remember when he had received the information about the closing of the plant.

Fawcett had learned during discovery that Wellmore/United had become a disaster for Blankenship in which Massey stood to lose millions of dollars. It was only then, as Fawcett saw it, that Blankenship had found the idea of declaring force majeure irresistible.

"Really, Mr. Blankenship, when you are talking about your business experience or your business sense, you are talking about your sense of how to extract benefits from those who are weaker than Massey?" Fawcett asked.

"I am disappointed that type of question is allowed, but no, it is not," Blankenship said.

"What you meant by your business experience is really how to put people in a bind? What you really meant was your business experience of squeezing people and companies?"

"I would say it is clear I am being more squeezed today than others," Blankenship said. "We were a little surprised that this case got in here," he added, a touch of self-pity in his voice. "This case is here because we tried to create jobs at a time when not many places were trying to create jobs in that county."

"No further questions, Your Honor," Fawcett said, leaving the jury to wonder how shutting down Harman created jobs.

26

The struggling air conditioner was throbbing so loudly it was like another witness in the courtroom, and it was almost as hot inside as out. On July 29, day twenty-six of the trial, the proper Woods asked Hoke if the lawyers could take off their suit coats. The judge said yes. "Oh, man, I wish I could let you go down to tank tops," Hoke added, squinting in amusement.

The heat was so oppressive that it threatened court decorum. The jurors had become boisterous in the jury room and could be overheard discussing everything but the case. A juror presented a note from her doctor saying that she was close to a nervous breakdown. One juror had already left due to a personal matter, and only one alternate juror remained. If a second juror departed, driven away by the drawn-out proceedings and the oppressive heat, there would likely be a mistrial. Fortunately, the distressed juror pulled herself together and was able to continue.

Hugh and Kathy Caperton had also become irritable. For Kathy, the tension of the past four years had been overwhelming: the fire, the photos, the creditors, the lawsuit, and ocular histoplasmosis, an eye disease exacerbated by tension that had left her blind in her left eye. Kathy worried not only about Hugh but their four-year-old daughter. Kathy had left Preston with friends and relatives but felt she had no right to be away from her for even an hour. The girl had been sick with pneumonia the previous winter and had experienced other infections and difficulties.

And as Kathy sat in the courtroom day after day, she grew angrier and angrier at what she saw less as a trial than a harangue, in which the Massey attorneys abused her husband with impunity.

After the proceedings ended that day, Hugh and Kathy headed out for dinner. Their SUV had scarcely left Madison when they saw a Mercedes bearing a Massey banner, the lead car for a racing event the company was sponsoring. As Caperton passed the vehicle, Kathy looked at the car jammed with hulking Massey men. She could not tell if they were some of what she called the "Massey thugs" who sat in the courtroom, but she glared at them and put her hand out the window. She made a gesture that she rarely made, but she found it wonderfully liberating. She had told these people what she thought of them in a language they would understand.

The couple stopped at a popular steakhouse and were managing to enjoy their meal when twenty Massey employees, including those Kathy had saluted, marched in. They surrounded the Capertons, menacing Hugh. "Did you give us the bird?" one asked.

"That wasn't my husband," Kathy said, tucking her right hand into her lap. "That was me."

The restaurant manager intervened, escorting the Massey group to their cars.

In the courtroom the next morning, the defense called Roger Osborne, an accountant hired by Massey's attorneys. Osborne was there to bolster the case that Harman would have failed even without Massey's having declared force majeure. A white-haired, modest man likely to connect with the jury, Osborne was unfailingly civil as he deemed the 1997 Harman mining company worthless. To help the jurors understand the numbers, he employed a down-home analogy.

"Let's assume that an individual, let me call him Sam," Osborne said. "Sam buys a house in 1993 and pays $50,000 for that house. He finds a friendly lender who lends him that entire purchase price, and he lives in the house for several years until, let's say, 1997. During that period, he doesn't maintain the house, and, in fact, he abuses it, and as a result, the value of that house deteriorates from $50,000 to $30,000. If something adverse were to happen to Sam, if his employer were, for example, cutting him back to three days a week for work, then he might have trouble making his mortgage payments, and he might have to consider and perhaps file bankruptcy. I think that analogy is similar to the situation that existed with respect to Harman in July of 1997."

This well-rehearsed comparison was something every juror would understand and remember. It was a respite from the bewildering figures to which they had been subjected. Fawcett could tell that the story resonated with the jury, and when he got up to cross-examine Osborne he returned the accountant to Sam's house.

In Osborne's telling, good ol' Sam had neglected his house. The truth was that Caperton and Cook had not neglected Harman. The mine was in far better shape when Harman went bankrupt than when Caperton had purchased the closed mine. Fawcett got Osborne to acknowledge that, yes, if Sam had taken care of his house, the comparison wouldn't hold.

The lawyers discussed Sam's saga in such detail that the jurors might well have begun calling Caperton by a different first name. Hoke, who liked folksy analogies, had seen the jurors' eyes gleam over Sam. So far in the trial, the judge had rarely posed a question to a witness, and whenever he had, he'd kept it short and pointed. But he thought Sam the perfect device to help the jurors understand the central issue in the trial, so he decided to weigh in.

"Since we are on that analogy, while you are talking about a number of these things, you really didn't talk in that scenario about the measure of damages," Hoke said, leaning toward Osborne. "Let me talk about Sam here again. Sam purchased this $50,000 house. Upon moving into the house, he realizes it doesn't meet his needs. He starts making alterations. He even borrows money to make those alterations. In order to upgrade his home, he has substantially changed it, and also taking into account the fact that he has borrowed more money to do that.

"Let's say he has a new neighbor come in. The new neighbor is a construction company with a crane with a wrecking ball on it, and one day while doing their work, they hit his house and tear it down, destroy his home.

"What is the measure of damages, and how does it take into account the way Sam handled himself under the first set of circumstances and the measure of damages and how Sam handled himself in the second example?"

Osborne answered, "That is an interesting question," looking like he wished it had been asked of someone else and quickly dropping his country charm. "I offered my analogy for the limited purpose of illustrating what I believe was the hole Harman had itself in in '97. So I didn't offer it for the purposes of discussing the damage issue in general."

Hoke said, "That is the one reason I did it, because that is what you are an expert on." For several minutes, the judge then continued talking about Sam's house and the wrecking ball.

Hoke did not say that Massey had used a wrecking ball on the Harman mine; he said only that the plaintiffs were making that argument. The defense attorneys were, nonetheless, upset by the comparison. Away from the jury, Woods expressed to Hoke the defense's "concern with regard to the court's questioning of witnesses. My best recollection is the court did not question any of the plaintiffs' witnesses but has been questioning the defendants' expert witnesses."

Up until this point, Hoke had asked judicious, informational questions to four of the plaintiffs' witnesses and seven of the defense's witnesses. The judge's only major insertion into the trial was the wrecking ball analogy, and Woods was arguing that it characterized Hoke's conduct during the entire proceedings. For the plaintiffs, the wrecking ball was the trial's most vivid and most favorable image, but Stanley and Fawcett feared that their opponents would use that fact in an appeal, so they never mentioned it again.

The next day, the last Saturday in July, Massey staged its annual get-together for employees at Magic Island, a park in Charleston along the Kanawha River. The park was the only large public venue on the west side of the capital. On summer weekends it hosted bikers, joggers, rollerbladers, dog walkers, couples pushing strollers, seniors sitting on blankets and benches, and the occasional paraglider. Corporations and other institutions often rented the park, but their events had always been open to the public. This all-day event was limited to Massey employees and their families.

While most of the legal team had headed out for the weekend, Stanley had decided to remain at the Hampton Inn to work on his closing statement in the trial that would wrap up the following week. He walked out of his room on Saturday morning to see dozens of people swarming throughout the hotel and the surrounding properties wearing yellow T-shirts emblazoned with the Massey Energy logo. "They're goddamn everywhere," he thought. With images of Hugh and Kathy's steakhouse encounter still fresh, and concerned that some of the Massey "members" might confront him, Stanley kept to himself.

Three weeks earlier Massey had started building a stage at Magic Island and hauling in fences and Porta Potties. Although Saturday was rainy, about fifteen thousand people arrived for food, games, and entertainment, including country artists Shenandoah, Billy Dean, and Exile.

The event was free, but attendees bore a hidden cost: they first had to listen to Blankenship speak. He was their boss, and they had little choice but to murmur their approval. "Today I respectfully ask and plead with the media, and yes even the UMW, to stop the bashing," Blankenship said. "Stop the exaggeration. Stop the negativism. Stop the untruths. Join with us to make West Virginia a better place."

"Bashing" was Blankenship's code word for any negative comment about Massey, even what most would consider objective news stories about a spill or mine accident. He was particularly upset about articles that suggested that Massey was less than concerned with the environment and that the company often did a miserable job of restoring the land after mountaintop removal.

Massey faced more bashing when, on the morning following the company event, Magic Island had become a muddy quagmire resembling a Massey strip-mining site. The Porta Potties' stench rose up into the homes that lined the park. Massey promised quick restoration, but weeks later much of Magic Island was an empty lot with pigeons feasting on the grass seed.

27

The following week, on the morning of Wednesday, July 31, 2002, the defense called Franklin Dover McGuire, a mining engineer, to the stand. McGuire had been recalled to rebut testimony on behalf of the plaintiffs concerning the costs of mining and production at Harman. When he finished, shortly before noon, the defense rested its case, and Ramey argued, out of the jurors' earshot, that the plaintiffs' lawyers had made so many mistakes that Hoke should grant the defense a directed verdict. In essence, he was asking the judge to rule summarily against the plaintiffs instead of sending the case to the jury.

Hoke was such a boisterous jokester that sometimes lawyers who appeared before him did not understand how serious he was about what he did and how passionately he cared about the jury system. And so this morning he lectured the courtroom on how important it was, in order for justice was to be done, for the jurors to have their say. His was a complicated, subtle argument, in places hard to understand, and it was unlike anything that had yet happened during the trial.

"I have sat through all the evidence in this case, and I did not come with the handicap of knowing more than what I heard in the courtroom," Hoke said. "Many times the lawyers, the wonderful advocates though they may be, they are not ignorant enough. As a result of what I have heard in the courtroom, I believe that the weight of the evidence and the credibility of the witnesses' testimony and other evidence adduced are clearly the issues to be decided by this jury. I believe that there are dichotomies that have been distinctly underscored in support of the plaintiff versus the defendant in this case. If ever there was a case that had jury issues in it, it is this one."

Before the closing arguments, Hoke gave the jury its instructions, which fill thirty-four pages in the official transcript. Many were directives applicable to any trial, but he had worked to make sure that what he said was fair and fully rendered.

"Nothing that I have said or done at any time during this trial shall be considered by you as evidence of any fact, or as an indication that I have any opinion concerning any fact, the credibility of the witnesses, or the weight of the evidence," Hoke cautioned the jury. "As jurors sworn to try this case and to render a true verdict on the law and the evidence, you can act only upon the evidence which has been properly introduced to you at this trial."

For their closing arguments, the plaintiffs and the defense each had two and a half hours to address the jury. The plaintiffs would speak first, and their time would be split into two segments. After the defense's response, Fawcett and Stanley would have the last word.

In their closing arguments, lawyers generally return to what they promised in their opening statements and show how they have proved their case. As he began the plaintiffs' closing statement, Fawcett did not batter the jury with assertions but led them through a summary of the crucial evidence in the lengthy trial, reminding them of what they had heard and seen. He talked about the great theme of his professional and personal life: the truth. And then he revisited the testimony of a number of plaintiff and defense witnesses and contrasted their credibility.

"Mr. Blankenship doesn't care about miners or their safety or other independent third parties," Fawcett concluded. "He cares about one thing, profits. There are only six people in the whole world that can stop Massey from doing this and can send a message to Massey: this isn't the way you do business."

When it was Stanley's turn, he said, "We understand how Don Blankenship's mind works. He is a predator. He goes and he looks for opportunities. He is always negotiating. He is always looking for the next opportunity."

Stanley's words were full of righteous anger, but he spoke so softly that everyone except the jurors strained to hear. Even they had to keep rapt attention, or Stanley's words would be lost in the hum of the air conditioner. He had purposefully chosen this intimate tone, which forced the spectators to focus solely on him. But it maddened those who could not quite grasp his words, including his own colleagues.

Fawcett and Stanley made powerful statements, but their remarks sounded like little more than preambles. They reiterated their central contention: not only had Massey gone about destroying Harman but Blankenship had personally, malevolently directed it. Their most compelling closing arguments would come the following day, just before the case went to the jury.

"I don't want you making up your mind yet," Hoke admonished the jury as he dismissed them for the day. "Like *The Tonight Show,* there is more to come."

28

On the following morning, the first day of August and the twenty-ninth day of trial, the courtroom was at least two-thirds full, and there was a restless energy in the air. The spectators included Dave's father, who had again driven down from Pittsburgh. Fawcett's companion, Kathleen Trow, was not going to miss the closing arguments, so she too had made the trip. The jury was excited that, after nearly seven weeks, their ordeal was ending. As Hoke addressed the lawyers, the jurors were talking so loudly in the jury room that their voices risked overwhelming anything going on in the courtroom. It was already hot and the air conditioner was moaning, and as the crowd kept entering it moaned still louder. After Hoke warned the spectators to be quiet, the jurors filed in.

Ramey would be making the defense's closing argument. It was an unusual choice, since the jury was more familiar with Woods, but Ramey had made the defense's opening statement. At the beginning of the trial, Ramey had condemned Caperton as a failure who sought in the courtroom what he could not win in life. The defense lawyer's words had been so extreme that they might have moved some jurors to pity Caperton. But they'd presumably delighted Blankenship, who'd attended the opening arguments.

Blankenship did not appear for the closing arguments, but Ramey took his strategy even further: never back off from your enemy, keep hitting harder and harder. Ramey began by exploiting the jury's misery and blaming the plaintiffs for the trial's length. "We think the trial should not have taken as long as it did," Ramey said, looking directly at the jurors. "We certainly tried everything we could do to move it along, but we believe that one reason this case has gone so long is the plaintiffs want to convince you, well, we have been in trial for seven weeks. You have got to award big damages; otherwise, what has all of this been about?"

Ramey did not mention that the defense had complained when Hoke had shortened the trial by limiting the questioning of witnesses. If Ramey and his colleagues had gotten their way, the trial likely would have gone on even longer.

Ramey portrayed Caperton's life as a dark comedy, one of an inept man failing upward. Ramey said when Harman was about ready to collapse into bankruptcy, Caperton "used Massey's declaration of force majeure to force Massey to bail him out of the hole that he dug for himself with no help from Massey."

"We all know that just because someone files a lawsuit doesn't mean they should win," Ramey said. "There is some lawyer out in California suing to take God out of the Pledge of Allegiance. Does anybody believe he should win?"

Even after seven weeks, Caperton still found it painful to listen to the defense attorneys attacking him. "His hope was he could take money out of Harman, put it into these companies so that even if Harman failed, he could still maintain that comfortable lifestyle," Ramey said.

During the trial, Fawcett and Stanley would have leapt up and objected, reminding the jury that Caperton could hardly steal from himself and that he was personally responsible for many of Harman's debts. But lawyers had more leeway in their closing arguments, and Hoke had warned the teams not to interrupt each other. And so the two lawyers remained seated, seething as they waited for their turn to make unchallenged statements.

Ramey was setting out some powerful arguments, but it was so hot in the courtroom that it was hard to tell if the jurors were concentrating or merely imagining the moment when all of this would end. The defense attorney roamed in front of them, making eye contact whenever he could, but he could not be sure how he was doing.

"Can I get you some water, ma'am?" Ramey asked one juror who looked ready to pass out from heat exhaustion. "It is very hot in here today, and I have two and a half hours because [the plaintiffs] have two and a half hours. I want you all to know that if any of you feel uncomfortable at any point, let me know, and we can take a break."

Ramey continued, ridiculing Caperton and Cook's projections that in 1998 Harman would have made a dramatic turnaround. "Things are going to get different," Ramey said. "Sow's Ear, Incorporated, is going to become Silk Purse, Incorporated."

As Ramey spoke, more spectators silently entered and found places in the crowded room. "Proverbs, chapter 27, verse 1, says, 'Boast not thyself of tomorrow, for thou knowest not what a day shall bring forth,'" Ramey noted, aware that you could never go wrong quoting scripture in Boone County, West Virginia. "We don't know what tomorrow will bring, what misfortunes we may suffer, but that is what they are trying to do. That is how a sow's ear becomes a silk purse."

Ramey moved on to persuade jurors from other demographics: "It is sort of like being a NASCAR driver, never won a race, in the Daytona 500, one lap to go with twenty laps down. He has got twenty-three cars ahead of him. They want you to believe that lightning is going to strike all those twenty-three cars, that somehow they are going to bring it in. They are going to change, and all of a sudden they are going to start making a profit."

For those who preferred other sports, Ramey offered this: "Or like a basketball team that has never won a game all season. They are going to win the conference championship and win the NCAA tournament."

And now, for those who cared about family—a group that could include just about everyone—he said, "I think we have all seen families that buy the house beyond their means, buy cars beyond their means. They have other expenses beyond their means. They have a child, perhaps two. The pressures grow. There are fights over money. What happens to a lot of those families? Those families grow apart, and those children suffer the scars of those broken marriages because the family was living beyond its means.

"This family, the Harman family, wasn't Ozzie and Harriet Nelson. It wasn't the Huxtables," Ramey said. He paused. "It was more like Ozzy and Sharon Osbourne."

Whatever the jury may have thought of Caperton, they knew he wasn't like the British heavy metal musician, the self-anointed "prince of darkness" who had bitten the head off a bat onstage. Nor was the private, sedate Kathy anything like the rocker's wife, who had exposed her family's life on the TV reality show *The Osbournes.*

Kathy had sat there while the defense had declared that her husband was a virtual thief, but comparing him to Ozzy Osbourne was too much. She stood up and departed as quietly and unobtrusively as she could, but almost every eye in the courtroom was on her, fully aware of why she was leaving. Ramey went on expanding his analogy, describing a dysfunctional family with "a lazy brother," "a mistress," and "old Harman" with "a gambling problem." Then the defense attorney compared Hugh Caperton to Scarlett O'Hara in *Gone with the Wind,* "simply living on borrowed time."

After an hour and a half of Ramey's attack, Hoke called a five-minute break. The courtroom was now so full that the judge instructed the spectators that they would have to file back in through the metal detector. "The clerk's office doesn't keep handbags [for you]," he said. "That's because if you leave your handbag in the clerk's office and then come back and the pistol wasn't there, you would be upset. Now, that is more than a joke because I have been shot at in the courtroom by a lady with a handgun in a handbag."

After the break, Ramey rose again to complete the defense's closing arguments. In the entire two and a half hours that Ramey spoke, he never addressed whether Massey had falsely declared force majeure with the intention of destroying Caperton, why Massey had purchased a narrow band of coal around the Harman mine, or why at the final minute Massey had refused to close the deal that was Hugh Caperton's last hope. Ramey later had no apologies for what he did this day. He was proud of the defense's strategy, and he believed that everything he said and did was professional and merited.

"Now, there is an old saying among lawyers that if the facts are against you, pound the law," Ramey told the jury. "If the law is against you, pound the facts. If both the facts and the law are against you, pound the pavement. After I sit down and I can't say any more, you are going to see some more pavement pounding."

Ramey concluded, focusing on his own personal discomfort: "I want to thank you so much for your attention today. It is very hot in here. You could imagine how I feel having to stand up here and go through this and go through all the evidence in the case."

When Ramey returned to the defense's table, Caperton hurried out of the courtroom to find his wife perched on the steps. He sat next to Kathy, hugged her, and assured her that Fawcett and Stanley would be speaking now and that everything would be all right.

29

Fawcett had been preparing his closing statement for months, and he'd thought he would revel in this moment. But as he stood before the jury for the final time, it felt nothing like that. Ramey's words had hurt him, and he did not know quite how to respond. What do you do when the opposing attorney compares your client to Ozzy Osbourne and quotes biblical passages that purport to show his corruption? Fawcett was not a quick study, and he could not improvise a new attack on all that Ramey had said.

"I have pledged to myself that I would keep my temper at this stage of the proceeding," Fawcett said. "Certain statements have me extremely angry and have my client extremely angry, but I am not going to pound the table or stomp my feet."

Fawcett knew that if he lost his temper, he would lose control, but he could not let Ramey's tirade go unchallenged.

"In Mr. Ancil Ramey's opening statement, he made statements that had nothing to do with this case," Fawcett said. "It had everything to do with demonizing and digging up dirt on Mr. Caperton. Don't talk about the conduct, but blame the victim: Mr. Caperton made no sacrifices. Mr. Caperton didn't care about Harman. Mr. Caperton was a failure. Mr. Caperton was living beyond his means.

"What is this, a gambling problem, a lazy brother or mistress? Can we make this any more personal and vindictive? Can Massey possibly do more to Mr. Caperton? Can they call him any worse names than what they have called him?"

Fawcett took a breath. "Now, ladies and gentlemen, this is a very, very simple case," he said. "The existence of a contractual relationship . . ." He paused, rummaging through his papers. "I am not having my luck today, because I can't find anything."

Fawcett was organized and disciplined, and it was unlike him not to have his documents in order. Stanley sensed that his colleague was near exhaustion after all these weeks. Stanley had at least gone home for the Fourth of July weekend, but Fawcett had stayed at the Hampton Inn; he had worked for more than a month and a half largely without interruption. He'd spoken strong words but seemed distracted, disconnected from the jury, unable to dispel Ramey's closing. Stanley hoped that Fawcett would collect himself before the jury decided that something was wrong.

Fawcett found the missing document and forged ahead, holding his hands high and folding his fingers, one by one, as he ran down what he called Massey's top ten acts of interference and fraud. He unintentionally ended with his middle finger raised high in the air, and he jerked his arm down in embarrassment when some in the courtroom chuckled.

"The damages [Harman incurred from the force majeure] were never disputed," he noted, beginning to wrap up. "We say it is $29 million. This is Mr. Caperton's and Harman's day in court, and what you do will affect him for the rest of his life and the Harman companies'."

"Let's wind it up," Hoke interjected.

"Thank you," Fawcett said, and he sat down, cut short before the end of his long presentation.

When Stanley stood up to make the plaintiffs' final argument in what was left of their two and a half hours, he did not blame his friend and co-counsel for having fallen short. But Fawcett had unintentionally placed an even greater burden on him. Regardless of Fawcett's performance, this would have been the peak moment in Stanley's thirteen-year law career. He had never been in a courtroom with so many spectators, who included his parents, the Sylvester women, court employees and townspeople, and many Massey miners. As Stanley gazed around the auditorium, his eyes fell on Caperton, to whom he gave a wink and a confident smile.

Stanley waited until the restless spectators quieted themselves. He waited until the eyes of every member of the jury locked onto him with anticipation. He waited until Hoke looked down on him with a quizzical, disbelieving stare, as if to ask, Why aren't you speaking? He waited until some people thought that he was tongue-tied, struck dumb by the sheer magnitude of what he faced.

And then he made a fist, lifted it, and pounded it on the table in front of the jury.

The sound jolted the room, and Stanley waited until it was quiet again. Once again he pounded his fist, the sound rising to the highest reaches of the balcony.

And then he waited before he hammered his fist a third time.

KABLAM!!!

Stanley turned toward the seated Ramey and pointed his finger. "I don't want you to walk out of his courtroom disappointed," Stanley said.

"Thank you," Ramey replied, taken aback.

At the end of his closing, Ramey had quoted a saying among lawyers: if both the facts and the law are against you, pound the pavement. Then he'd said, "After I sit down and I can't say any more, you are going to see some more pavement pounding." In pounding the table, Stanley had done a reasonable approximation of what Ramey had said the plaintiffs' lawyers would do, energizing the courtroom.

"If Hugh Caperton can't stop Don Blankenship, what chance does any other person have?" Stanley asked. "The only thing that is missing from me pounding on that table is Massey wishes it was *its* fist."

Stanley turned and walked to the plaintiffs' table and put his hand on Caperton's shoulder. "And he wishes *this* man was under it."

"We aren't asking you to take God out of the Pledge of Allegiance," Stanley noted, referring to Ramey's final argument. "We *are* asking you to put the fear of God into Don Blankenship. We *are* asking you to tell King Don that this is America, not his private monopoly board, and no man is above the law. They didn't tell you that Don Blankenship was pounding on the table at the November 26 meeting," he said, referring to the day before Thanksgiving in 1997. "Assassins don't make noise."

It was a risky strategy, asking these six citizens of Boone County to render a verdict that would be seen as directly confronting the most powerful business leader in the region. Blankenship was a vengeful man who had already warned the jurors to what lengths he would go if the residents fostered an atmosphere hostile to Massey.

"The mistake Don Blankenship made," Stanley declared, "was thinking that Hugh Caperton was just going to roll over and die."

Stanley turned once again toward Caperton and pointed at him. "*This* man has a massive mortgage. He is not sitting free and clear at home. He is sitting with the weight of the world on his shoulders, with creditors lined up from here to Richmond, Virginia, wanting a piece of him."

"And *that*," Stanley said, waving toward the defense attorneys, "is Massey." Blankenship had chosen not to be here in person today, but if he had been, Stanley would have waved instead toward the Massey chairman. "It is because of Massey [that the defense lawyers] didn't come in here and explain why what they did was not fraud," Stanley said. He argued that Massey's attorneys did not even try to defend Massey's acts of interference and fraud, because they had no defense.

Unlike Fawcett, Stanley had no trouble mocking Ramey's arguments. "I can't get over the last statement Mr. Ramey said to you," Stanley told the jury. "'You can imagine how I feel standing up here and talking with you for two and a half hours.'

"How do you think *he* feels," Stanley said, nodding toward Caperton, "after five years and nothing but an uncertain future waiting?

"We have placed our faith and our trust in your hands, and we are confident that you will act on that faith and that trust with your hearts and with your minds. Based upon the evidence that you have heard in this courtroom, you now know the truth. Thank you."

30

"Ladies and gentlemen, that concludes the rebuttal arguments of the plaintiffs," Hoke told the jury. In his black gown, Hoke had suffered more from the heat than had anyone else, and he was glad everything but the verdict was finally over. "Now it is time for you to go in. We will be sending in lunch and the exhibits."

While the jury began its deliberations, Hoke oversaw the last housekeeping moments of the trial. Ramey inundated Hoke with an encyclopedic list of objections about the judge's voluminous instructions to the jury. The defense had niggling complaints about most of the specific instructions and made further arguments about how the verdict form was inadequate and misleading. Hoke knew that Ramey was throwing in everything he could to justify an appeal to the Supreme Court of Appeals of West Virginia.

These objections at least distracted the lawyers from the tension of awaiting the jury's verdict. When the defense finished placing its complaint into the record and the court finally emptied out, the Capertons joined the lawyers at Freda's, a hole-in-the-wall down the block, for a final lunch. The restaurant fried everything but the silverware. Caperton's and Fawcett's stomachs were rumbling, and they could not even think of eating.

All through the trial, Fawcett and Stanley had been confident that they were winning, but as they waited that confidence waned. They knew that the sharpest jury in the world could find some reason to vote against you. Or they could award you 10 percent of what you deserved and think they were doing you a favor. Or maybe there'd be one holdout who loved Massey Energy, creating a hung jury.

Stanley, however, was convinced that even though Fawcett might have come up short in his closing, their team had made a powerful case and they deserved to win.

After lunch, Fawcett made his way to the basement hallway of the courthouse, where he found a bench on which to lie down. It was as cool as a grotto and seemed a world away from the courtroom above. An occasional person walked by and, noting the dormant form on the bench, assumed that Fawcett was asleep. Although he was exhausted and his eyes were closed, he was vividly awake, thinking about everything that had gone on during the four years he had been fighting *Caperton*.

The Johnny Cash song "I've Been Everywhere" kept floating through his mind, providing a theme for his reflections. And he had been everywhere, taking depositions and attending hearings. He had been to Richmond, Virginia. He had been to Big Stone Gap, Virginia. He had been to Louisville, Kentucky. He had been to Charleston, West Virginia. He had been to Abington, Virginia. And he had been all the way to Sioux City, Iowa, in the dead of a midwestern winter to depose Harman's previous owners.

Fawcett's father had already left, after telling his son that he had spent too many hours of his life waiting for juries' verdicts. Dave understood and kept thinking about his father's legal philosophy: you did your best and moved on. Dave had never been much good at that, but for the first time in his life he understood. He felt right and good. He kept thinking of the jurors. He had looked into their eyes and was convinced that they'd gotten it and would do what was right. But you could never be sure. Whatever they decided, Dave knew he had done his best, and he thought that now, after more than four years of preparation and nearly seven weeks of trial, he was ready to move on.

While Fawcett reflected on everything that had gone on, Devine busied himself packing up boxes of legal documents and putting them in the trunk of his car. As Hugh and Kathy Caperton wandered around the courthouse and its environs, they came upon the paralegal, the only one involved who was even pretending to be doing any work.

Caperton knew what he was asking these six jurors to do and how extraordinary it was. He understood the risk he was asking them to take. As he sat talking with Kathy in the courthouse corridor, he badly wanted this to be over. He wanted his life back, whatever was left of it.

After about five hours of deliberation, the bailiff announced that there was a verdict.

It took only a few minutes for the lawyers to rush back to their seats in the courtroom. Before the jury was brought in, Judge Hoke called a side-bar discussion, in which he told the lawyers that the jurors had requested that they be allowed to exit through the back door after the verdict was read. Whom did the jurors hope to avoid? everyone wondered. That only heightened the tension.

In the courtroom, Caperton reached out for Fawcett's hand, and all of the plaintiffs' lawyers took each other's hands, a long link along the table. Hoke read the jury's decision from the lengthy verdict form. Yes, Massey had tortiously interfered with the contract. Yes, Massey had made fraudulent misrepresentations in its dealing with Caperton and Harman. Yes, the Harman plaintiffs deserved $29,696,000 in compensatory damage. Yes, the Harman plaintiffs deserved $3,000,000 in consequential damages. Yes, Massey had tortiously interfered with Caperton personally. Yes, Massey had fraudulently concealed from Caperton. Yes, Caperton deserved $3,417,406 in compensatory damages. Yes, Caperton deserved $425,000 in consequential damages. Yes, Caperton deserved $7,500,000 in general damages. Yes, the Harman plaintiffs deserved $2,000,000 in punitive damages and Caperton deserved $4,000,000.

For Caperton and his lawyers, it was all a magnificent blur, and they did not even try then to tabulate the total amount. Hoke looked over at the jurors and saw that several of them were crying. He would say later that he believed they had made the right decisions but he was surprised at the verdict's amount.

"Let's all be upstanding for the jury, please," Hoke said, asking everyone to rise as the jury left for the final time. "Mr. Bailiff, if you will escort the jury to their vehicles and off the lot. Thank you so much for your service."

Massey's lawyers, some of the jurors would later say, had misunderstood them. "They treated us as if we were kind of stupid, that we were going to fall for their antics," reflected juror Barbara Jewett. "In closing arguments they referred to Caperton almost like he was a prostitute, something to do with money. That irritated me a lot. If they had a case, they should have presented it and not just these antics."

As everyone trooped out of the courthouse, Fawcett dropped down onto the grass, rolled around, and laughed. For the second time today, Stanley was surprised by his friend's behavior. First the closing statement, and now this, a public display unlike any Fawcett had made in his life. For seven weeks he had spent almost every night at the Hampton Inn obsessed with *Caperton,* away from his children and his significant other. The verdict was not just a financial triumph but a repudiation of Massey and the way the company operated and fought its enemies.

As Fawcett lay there, punch-drunk and giddy, jurors walked past. He knew he was not supposed to talk to them, but he had to say something. "You did the right thing!" he shouted.

Then the group went back over to Freda's, where, for the first time, they started figuring out just how much they had won. "Fifty million!" someone said. "Fifty million!" And indeed, the amount totaled $50,038,406.

Fawcett jumped up and started banging on the walls, hooting and high-fiving anyone within reach. He was sure that the case was finally over, having taken more than four years—two more than he had originally told Caperton it would take. He was sure that Massey wouldn't appeal to the liberal Supreme Court of Appeals of West Virginia, where the company would lose and then have to pay the 10 percent yearly interest that would accrue during the interim, adding a good $5 to $10 million.

Caperton cried in joy and relief, hugging and kissing his wife. His optimism was the bedrock of his character, and he'd always known, even in these last few months when he'd feared that his electricity was going to be turned off, that he would prevail. He'd just never imagined that it would take so long to win justice, or that justice in this instance would equal $15,342,406 to him personally.

Stanley cried, too. It was one of the greatest moments of his life, but he disagreed with Fawcett. Blankenship would never walk away. Stanley said, "Dave, treasure this moment. Treasure it always, because nobody will ever be able to take this feeling away from you. But they will try. I am telling you. They will try."

Fawcett shouted and wailed a few more times. He banged his hand on a metal sign in the back of the bar and hooted like a cowboy. Then he grew almost frightened. "Whoa, we're in Massey country," he thought. "We better get the hell out of here." He corralled the other celebrants and said that it was time to leave. Everyone was invited to his hotel room, thirty miles north, for an evening of celebration. Within minutes everyone was gone, out in their cars, heading away from the golden-domed courthouse.

At the party at the Hampton Inn, music was blaring and people were flying high. Fawcett jumped up onto the bed, held up a bottle of Jack Daniel's, and screamed, "Here's to kickin' ass . . . and Johnny Cash!"

Many times in the years that followed Fawcett looked back on that day and asked himself how he could have been so wrong in thinking everything was over.

PART FOUR

AUGUST 5, 2002

31

In early August 2002, after the verdict was revealed, Blankenship wrote a letter to the thousands of Massey employees. "Dear Massey members," it began. "The verdict is a frightening result. It is worse than the infamous McDonald's coffee spill verdict. It will damage Massey, but it will also damage all of West Virginia and play a role in further impoverishing the children of our state."

The only way the verdict could hurt West Virginia's children was if an angry Blankenship carried through on his threat to have Massey leave the state or trim its operations there. Massey could easily pay the $50 million. His company was constantly being sued or hit with fines for environmental damages; that was the cost of doing business in a litigious society.

But this was personal. Blankenship was willing to spend whatever was necessary to have the judgment overturned on appeal and get even. "The winners were rude to Massey witnesses throughout the trial," the letter continued. "They made the ultimate obscene gestures and addressed Stan Suboleski with the 'F' word."

In his letter, Blankenship reminded the Massey "members" about their colleagues who had been shot and beaten up by union militants, and all the misleading stories the media had put out about Massey. "This verdict has kept me awake and concerned me more than all those issues," Blankenship wrote.

Blankenship would appeal, but he was not just going to hand this case over to appellate attorneys and let them do their tepid legal thing. He would fight not only a fraudulent verdict but an insult to him, his company, and all that he believed he had done for West Virginia.

The Massey chairman was infuriated at his defense lawyers, and some of his anger was not without justification. When, in Caperton's Virginia trial, the losing Massey subsidiaries had appealed to the Supreme Court of Virginia, the petition had not been signed by a Virginia lawyer, as is mandated; on that technicality, the court had refused even to hear the case. Because the appeal was dismissed, Massey was forced to pay the Virginia verdict in the weeks following the Madison verdict.

It was one measure of Blankenship's fury over losing cases against Harman in Virginia and West Virginia courtrooms that he not only fired Wyatt, Tarrant & Combs, the Kentucky law firm that had defended both cases, he also had Massey sue the law firm for incompetence. In the end, one of the the lawyers who tried the case, Jeff Woods, says that the malpractice suit against his firm was "resolved and dismissed."

The $6 million Virginia verdict had risen, with interest, to $7.2 million. After Buchanan Ingersoll and the local counsels took their cuts, there was enough money to give the creditors a taste of what they were owed, bankroll the ongoing legal expenses, and pay Caperton the $265,000 he was due for spending four years handling all the business details in closing down the bankrupt operation.

Caperton was relieved, but he owed so much money to the IRS, the Grundy National Bank, and others that he could hardly begin to pay back any but his immediate creditors. A hedge fund approached Caperton, offering him $1 million in exchange for $2 million when he got his Boone County trial money. The interest rate was extreme, but it gave Caperton a chance to pay off many of his debts and to refurbish the house in appropriate style. He saw no reason to downscale when his lawyers had told him that in a year or two he would almost certainly be a wealthy man. And if for some outlandish, unthinkable reason he never did get his payoff from *Caperton*, he would not have to pay the hedge fund back its money.

As soon as Caperton got the hedge-fund money, he sent off several hundred thousand dollars to the IRS. He had hardly cleared things with the feds when he started getting new dunning letters, hitting him up for taxes he owed on the $1 million he had just received. The interest and penalties were constantly mounting but, he reminded himself, he would soon be well-off.

Everything involving *Caperton,* however, was complicated and endlessly prolonged, and getting Hugh's money proved no different. Blankenship had vowed to fight the verdict with all his money and might, and the Massey lawyers immediately began to throw up innumerable legal obstacles to delay the finalization of the verdict. They filed a large number of post-trial briefs to Hoke, in which they objected to almost everything that had gone on in his courtroom, from fundamental issues of the trial to the most obscure legalistic points.

As Fawcett went back to Pittsburgh and accepted the congratulations of his colleagues in the firm, he faced another kind of legal challenge. His divorce proceedings were nearly finalized, and his three children were with his ex-wife. Fawcett wanted joint custody, but she fought him in court.

Before making his decision, the family court judge asked Fawcett and his former wife to see a psychologist, who would make a recommendation regarding custody arrangements. Fawcett felt it was important that the children have equal time with him. He did not want to behave like his father and grandfather, who'd seldom told their children they loved them and had treated their sons as if whatever they did was not quite good enough.

Fawcett hated to discuss the intimate details of his private life. It was a measure of how much he wanted his children that he was even willing to talk to the therapist. As good a trial attorney as he was, he was a lousy lawyer for himself. He was angry at the whole process, which opened up for scrutiny the most intimate human concerns, and he acted arrogant, superior to the entire business. That was not what he truly felt, but that was what he projected.

Fawcett told the psychologist that he worried that his wife was still having problems and there could be an accident. The psychologist, suspecting that these apprehensions were a disingenuous attempt to get custody, asked him, "So you were so concerned, yet you traveled for work for seven weeks?"

Fawcett tried to explain how important the Boone Country trial had been and why he had not returned very often to see his children. He told the therapist all that he had done for his kids when he had been there.

"Do you think you're Superman?" the psychologist asked.

Fawcett was incensed. He thought that this psychologist was judging him harshly for having done the best he could, the only way he'd known how. Fawcett stood up defiantly and raised his voice.

"Yes, I *had* to be Superman," he pleaded, near tears, further hurting his case. He had been given no credit for the perilous year and a half when he had managed to run the house while his wife was gone or incapable. He felt he had saved his children, and now his commitment to them was being questioned. The psychologist recommended that Fawcett have his kids no more than every other weekend. "Show that you care and the recommendation may change," he lectured.

Fawcett knew that it was because of his weeks in West Virginia that he could not live even half-time with his three children. Everyone involved with *Caperton* had paid, but Fawcett was the only one who had lost a measure of his children.

Fawcett and Stanley believed that Hoke had done a superb job of managing the courtroom during the long, difficult trial. They had faith that he would continue his exemplary service by making short work of the many Massey briefs and objections. In their experience, it should take the judge no more than a few months to deal with all the minor legal issues and finalize the case so it could move beyond his court. At that point, Massey would appeal. Unlike most states, there were no intermediate appellate courts in West Virginia, and when Massey appealed it would be directly to the Supreme Court of Appeals of West Virginia.

Hoke had never dealt with lawyers that so inundated him with paperwork. They were able attorneys, and it took him time and thought to reply to each one of their complaints. And what was the point? He would finish reading one set of briefs, and there would be another set coming in the door.

With all the activity on the civil and criminal docket that Hoke had to handle on a daily basis—arraignments, sentencings, marriages, property disputes, landlord and tenant complaints, and estate administration—it was hard for him to find the hours necessary to consider the exhaustive arguments and research the multitude of issues that the par-

ties had submitted about *Caperton*. Hoke was a quick and sound decision maker on many matters, but after the seven-week trial he let *Caperton*
slide.

Hoke did not realize that the Massey attorneys were playing him,
drawing everything out so long and so well that the very nature of justice
was challenged. Years afterward, as he reflected on what had gone on,
Hoke said that he believed he had been used. "Anytime I made a decision
on whatever matter was in front of me at the time, the lawyers submitted
more stuff," he reflected. "I did not connect the dots at the time. Subsequently, when I looked back, I said 'Oh, my goodness, this is what's happened.'"

Hoke was complicit in a different snafu, which was just as damaging.
The lightning that struck near the Boone County Courthouse on July 19,
2002, during Blankenship's testimony, had destroyed one morning's
record, but the rest of the trial had been properly recorded. Yet months
after completion of the trial, court reporter Meadows had still not produced a workable record of the rest of the seven-week-long trial. Meadows was a longtime employee whom Hoke admired. He did little or
nothing to prod her or, if she was incapable, to find someone else to produce a trial record.

Although Fawcett and Stanley had all kinds of suspicions about how
the dark hand of Massey lay behind the delay, there was apparently
nothing conspiratorial about Meadows's extraordinary lassitude. Her
failure may have been merely a psychological block. Whatever the reasons, when justice is not timely, it often is not justice at all, and the endless delay had severe consequences to the plaintiffs' case.

32

Massey had not yet appealed to the Supreme Court of Appeals of West Virginia, but everyone involved in *Caperton* knew that it would do so, and that one day the plaintiff and defense lawyers would meet again in Charleston. The Supreme Court of Appeals of West Virginia was one of the most progressive courts in the nation, and Massey's prospects did not look good. The court was highly supportive of plaintiffs who had received jury verdicts against corporations and of anyone and anything that appeared to elevate the downtrodden and the oppressed. *Caperton* may have been a fight between businesses, a big one and a small one, but three of the five justices would likely be more attuned to Hugh Caperton and the plight of the displaced UMW workforce than to Massey.

But there was an undercurrent of change that would dramatically affect the court. The transformation had begun back in 1996, when three new Democratic justices won elections. The biggest vote getter, Larry V. Starcher, was a longtime circuit judge in the northern tier of the state and a lifelong progressive. Starcher had a white beard and a provocative, devilish air. He consoled court employees, hiring those who thought his way, watching out for those he deemed his friends while advancing his own progressive agenda. Unlike the other justices, he gave regular staff parties. At Christmas, he held a special event for staff families where he dressed up as Santa Claus.

His liberalism was not just words. He volunteered for Habitat for

Humanity, using his considerable carpentry skills to build homes. His clerk Tom Rodd had gone to prison as a draft resister during the Vietnam War. Starcher wanted to be someone court employees came to with their problems. He had a long tradition of concern for the advancement of minorities.

The second-highest vote getter, also elected to a twelve-year term, was Elliott "Spike" Maynard, a longtime Mingo County circuit judge and Blankenship's old friend from back in the days of the 1984–85 UMW strike. In West Virginia, you pretty much had to be a Democrat to win an election, and so Maynard called himself one, though he was more conservative than many Republicans. The third new judge, Robin Jean Davis, had also been elected as a progressive, but as the lowest vote getter to a four-year unexpired term.

Starcher assumed that he would be closely allied with Davis. The forty-year-old Davis was a political generation younger than the fifty-four-year-old Starcher and the other court members. Davis and her husband, Scott Segal, arguably the most successful trial lawyer in the state, were the capital's most celebrated power couple. While he made tens of millions of dollars taking on contingency cases, she was one of the capital's top divorce lawyers. When she decided to run for the state supreme court, she loaned her campaign $216,737.

The justice lived behind tall gates with Segal in a twenty-thousand-square-foot house that may have been the largest private residence in the state. "Because I represent working men and women, I wanted to do something special for them," Segal says. "This house was built entirely by unions whose members I have represented in personal injury cases. It is an architectural and union masterpiece that unions and our family could be proud of." On weekends the couple frequently flew in their private jet with their adopted son, Oliver, their chef, and Oliver's nanny to their vacation home in Colorado.

Starcher had good reason to think that he and Davis would work together. Before announcing for office, Davis contributed $1,000 to Starcher's campaign. Her husband also contributed $1,000 while other attorneys in their small firm gave $4,000. Both justices had won with the endorsement of the UMW and the help of other labor unions and trial lawyers. They appeared destined to vote together most of the time as part of the court's 4–1 progressive majority.

And Starcher believed Davis owed him big-time. As a circuit judge in Monongalia County, Starcher had overseen twenty thousand cases in which people had claimed lung disease, cancer, and other ailments because of their exposure to asbestos. Starcher had been so forceful in pushing these cases to trial that the insurance companies agreed to settlements they might not have made otherwise.

No one benefited as much from this as did Davis's husband, whom she had met when they were both students at the West Virginia University College of Law. "I'm told by folks in the asbestos fraternity business that Scott Segal made probably ten to twelve million dollars in my courtroom," says Starcher. "But some lawyers say that's not true. He made fifteen to twenty million dollars." Segal says he did make millions, but he did so not only in Starcher's courtroom but in two others as well, giving the young personal injury attorney a lucrative head start.

Davis and Starcher took their new positions with the utmost seriousness. He projected an open, affable manner on the bench, while she was humorless and serious. She appeared, as *Charleston Daily Mail* reporter Chris Stirewalt expressed it, "like a teacher instructing an eighth-grade class."

Unlike her fellow freshmen justices, Maynard and Starcher, who had decades of experience as circuit judges, Davis had never faced many of the issues that came before the court. But she was a hard worker, and she immediately set out to develop the necessary expertise. Starcher figured that he could mentor Davis, and he aggressively pursued a collegial, professional relationship with her. Davis soon learned that her older colleague was not so much a conversationalist as a monologuist. He overwhelmed her, as he did almost everyone else, with his bubbling, enthusiastic manner.

Starcher knew that his liberal colleagues Warren McGraw and Joseph P. Albright stood firmly with him. And he knew where Maynard stood, too—to the far right. As for Davis, Starcher believed that she belonged right there with him, beside McGraw and Albright.

Starcher looked at everything that passed his way on the court and asked whether it helped the poor, the needy, or the vulnerable. If he concluded that it did, he sought a legitimate legal way to advance that issue.

Starcher himself had grown up poor in an old farmhouse outside Spencer, in the central part of the state. When he was thirteen, he and two of his friends exploded several mailboxes with cherry bombs. Starcher's father whipped his son regularly with a belt that raised welts on Larry's back. This time, Mr. Starcher thought it better to send the boy off to the reformatory than to put him on probation, but his teachers argued that Larry had promise and should be given another chance.

That was the defining experience of Starcher's young life. As a circuit judge, he believed that when it came to youthful offenders, the penal system in the state was little better than a machine for churning out adult criminals. He did whatever he could to keep young people from getting criminal records. He saw youthful offenders before court or afterward, giving them chances few other judges would have, trying to get them to see straight, rarely putting their names in the court record. Starcher fancied himself a kind of "social worker with clout," practicing what he called "people-oriented justice."

In the Supreme Court of Appeals of West Virginia, the position of chief justice rotates among the five judges. Davis was replacing another justice, and she had hardly arrived when she was sitting in that seat. It was there that Davis and Starcher had their first public disagreement. Throughout his entire career, Starcher had promoted minorities in government, and he'd become the justice that the few African-Americans working for the court could go to for advice. He was delighted when, in the fall of 1997, the court appointed a young black man, Rodney Teal, as the supreme court clerk. Teal had a number of difficulties on the job; a year later, he resigned, stating that the court was "tearing itself apart, and I knew it was going to get worse before it got better." Starcher and Davis were subsequently overheard having a loud argument, focused, in part, apparently on the issue of racism.

"I'm almost certain that if Judge Starcher was pegging something as racism, he wasn't making it up," reflected Teal several years later. "While I suspected in my individual case that I was treated differently for reasons that may have been because of my race, I never had any proof. I don't know if Robin had a problem with me that had anything to do with my race, but I didn't like her. She could have been blue."

The animus among the justices spilled over into the halls and the corridors. Between 1997 and 2000, the first three years that Davis and Starcher were on the court, fifty-one of the approximately one hundred employees of the Supreme Court of Appeals of West Virginia left their positions.

Starcher came to despise almost everything about Davis. "She is the least compassionate human I have ever known," Starcher says now, looking back on those days. "I have no love for her, that's for sure."

"She's no Loretta Lynn," he adds, referring to the country music star. "Where her daddy was a coal miner in those days, they were making fifty thousand to sixty thousand a year, her mother was a school principal, and she was an only, privileged child who went to a private school."

Davis made less of her modest roots than did Starcher, though, like him, she grew up in a tiny community, Van, outside Madison, where the *Caperton* trial took place. Her mother drove up to Charleston to get an education to become a school principal. Davis was brought up to believe that she could do anything.

Davis insisted that in the court everything be on paper. She was cryptically quiet in the judges' discussions. This irritated Starcher, who felt that it masked her insecurities and her inability to match wits with him in debate. As hard as he tried to make his points to her, he believed, she would not listen.

"He would practically jump over the table shouting at her," says Steven D. Canterbury, the court's administrative director. "And she never, ever yelled back or lost her cool. She would say sometimes, 'I've had enough of this.' She would flush and simply walk out."

Starcher did many generous things personally and professionally, but he had a habit of making outrageous, over-the-top statements that undermined whatever he was trying to accomplish. One day in the judge's conference room, his irritation boiled over.

"I get so tired of your bullshit, Robin," he said.

"If you cuss at me again, I'm going to file a complaint," Davis warned. From then on, Starcher watched his mouth. But Davis's revenge would be both slow and excruciating.

Davis, meanwhile, became increasingly friendly with Maynard. The justice was fifty-three when he won election to the Supreme Court of Appeals of West Virginia. From a relatively early age, he had a thick head of white hair, which conferred an uncommon maturity and suggested the charm of a country gentleman. The lifelong bachelor was known as a ladies' man.

Davis found a rapport with the conservative Maynard that she did not enjoy with their three progressive colleagues. Davis's votes no longer reliably favored the liberal coalition that had helped elect her. But even without Davis, there was a clear 3–2 progressive majority on the court, and Fawcett and Stanley had every reason to believe that they would win in the state supreme court, just perhaps not with the margin they had anticipated. A strong record had been made to support each of the claims presented to the jury, and the verdict, they believed, was fully justified.

In 2003, Davis and Maynard signed a dissent that attacked the majority justices for crippling "not just the financial well-being of a few companies doing business in West Virginia, but also scarce West Virginia jobs." The two justices seemed to be suggesting that their three liberal colleagues were in cahoots with the trial lawyers and their anti-business lawsuits.

Despite Maynard's lifelong, pro-business voting pattern, he began voting in favor of almost every measure that had Davis's husband's name on it. In twelve of the thirteen cases involving Segal's clients that came before the court between 2005 and 2007, Maynard voted for Segal's side; in the other case, he was part of a unanimous decision against him.

In one case, *Tawney v. Columbia Natural Resources*, Segal represented lessees who claimed that they had been underpaid for their natural gas reserves. Maynard wrote the majority opinion in an unusual pretrial appeal that cleared the way for the case to proceed to a jury trial in a lower court and came close to directing a finding of liability and a liberal measure of damages. The court ultimately awarded $405 million to the plaintiffs, with more than $120 million of that amount presumably going to Segal and his colleagues on the case.

Starcher was suspicious that Davis had struck a deal with Maynard, trading his votes in her husband's cases for her vote in matters important to Maynard. "What people tend to do is to look at one track record and say he gets special treatment," says Segal. "I could look at another track record and say I'm the teacher's pet because I get bashed over my head in close cases that maybe a less likely lawyer would have won. It's all these people trying to inoculate their failures or bad results by pointing their fingers at someone else."

Conservatives considered the liberal West Virginia court a symbol of everything wrong with the American judicial system, hijacked by arrogant, overreaching justices pushing a big-government, anti-business agenda that they could not achieve in the legislatures of America. In their eyes, one of the biggest villains was Justice McGraw, who voted for workers in 88 percent of workers' compensation claims and, they believed, acted as though he were a working-class hero as he did so.

A story in the July 21, 2003, issue of *Forbes*, whose cover bore the image of a judge with a bull's-eye on his back, reported that the United States Chamber of Commerce had spent $100 million over three years waging what the magazine called a "secret war on judges" to create pro-business courts all across America. The chamber and its money had defeated liberal incumbents in twenty-one of twenty-four elections, the article said, replacing them with business-oriented, conservative justices; in the next 2004 election, Justice McGraw would be one of their targets. The article became a must-read in the judicial community, and McGraw thought that the cover image was meant to represent *him*, Warren McGraw, the people's candidate.

McGraw had a problem right at home on the court with two of his colleagues, who had both personal and ideological reasons to help oust him and welcome in a more conservative justice. Steve White of the Affiliated Construction Trades Foundation told the *Charleston Daily Mail* that "people like Spike Maynard and Robin Davis are gunning for Warren McGraw because he represents small business and workers, while they represent big businesses." If McGraw were to be defeated and replaced by a conservative, not only would the court move to the right, but Davis would become the court's swing vote, like Anthony Kennedy and, before him, Sandra Day O'Connor on the U.S. Supreme Court. Davis would thus be the court's most powerful member, wooed by her fellow judges as she largely defined the future of justice in West Virginia.

What conservatives needed was a way to defeat McGraw, whose reelection seemed almost automatic. His brother Darrell was state attorney general, and no family in the state was more adept at getting its members elected. Warren was a lifelong politician who, in his thirty-four-year career in government, had served in the House of Delegates, in the state senate, as the state senate president, and on a county school board; he had been a prosecuting attorney, a justice of the state supreme court, and chief justice of the state supreme court. He had also failed in a run for governor. McGraw knew that he was considered a shoe-in in the 2004 election, but he was still nervous.

Judicial election campaigns had always been rather sedate, bringing the decorum of the courtroom into the political arena. But with the massive influx of campaign money had come an equally massive influx of negativity. The money worked most effectively when it bought television and other media ads that attacked specific opinions on issues sensitive to voters.

West Virginian voters were overwhelmingly liberal in believing that the government should provide the crucial safety netting beneath their lives but overwhelmingly conservative on such social topics as abortion and gay rights. McGraw's opponents needed an issue that would so upset the socially conservative voters that they would flush him from the court forever.

33

As Fawcett and Stanley pondered how they could expedite *Caperton*, they paid little attention to the Supreme Court of Appeals of West Virginia election. McGraw was demolishing a challenger in the Democratic primary before taking on Brent D. Benjamin, an obscure, forty-eight-year-old corporate attorney, in the general election. No Republican had been elected to the court since 1928, and this neophyte politician was unlikely to reverse the pattern.

The two Pittsburgh lawyers at least read about the judicial elections, but they knew nothing about an obscure matter that was before the Supreme Court of Appeals of West Virginia in March 2004 that would play a crucial role in their own case. Just as the judicial election was gearing up, the court was deciding whether to grant probation to twenty-two-year-old Tony D. Arbaugh Jr. He had served six years of a fifteen-to-thirty-five-year sentence for one count of sexual assault, which, he claimed, he'd committed when he was thirteen years old; the prosecutors said he was fourteen years old.

Tony had been born in remote, rural Pendleton County, West Virginia, the oldest of five children, in an encampment of half a dozen decrepit modular shanties known as Big Run. From the age of seven, he had been sexually abused by three adults, including two relatives and a close family friend. They would first get him high on marijuana, then begin sexual "play" with him. One of those who abused him was an elementary school teacher of his, a highly regarded member of the local gentry. His mother repeatedly let her dealer sexually mistreat Tony's younger half brother, Brian, in exchange for drugs. Brought up in this atmosphere, Tony, at the age of ten, started fondling Brian, which is a common result of childhood sexual abuse.

Tony and his four younger siblings often went to school dirty and hungry. From an early age, they used drugs and alcohol. Sometimes when they had been made to party all night, they fell asleep at their desks. It was not until Tony was fourteen, in April 1996, that child welfare authorities concluded that Mrs. Arbaugh was an unfit mother and took Tony and Brian off to a children's shelter.

A few weeks later, Tony and Brian escaped back to Big Run. The authorities caught Brian, but Tony was quicker.

For seven months Arbaugh scurried between a tent he'd pitched in the deep woods, cabins he broke into, and relatives' homes, until one morning in February 1997, when the police found him sleeping at his grandparents' house. He bolted out the back window and would have escaped by jumping into the river, but as he ran an officer pointed a gun at his head and told him to raise his hands. The officer put the fifteen-year-old in handcuffs and tossed him into the squad car.

Brian had offhandedly told the social workers that his older brother had sexual contact with him, not thinking that Tony had done anything out of the norm and hardly imagining that Tony would be punished. As the policemen drove Tony to the station, they berated him for the abuse. This was the first time that Tony had ever heard that what he had done was wrong—and since he wasn't doing it anymore, he could not understand why the officers were so upset.

"The last time I had any kind of [sexual] relationship with my brother was when I was thirteen," says Arbaugh. "I heard that if you did what we were doing it meant you were gay, and I didn't want that, and it was the time anyway that I got interested in girls.

"They said that when I ran, the only reason I took my brother with me was so that I could do those things to him. I done never did none of that to him then. I was through with all that. I done matured. I was with women. But they got me to say that I done did it."

Arbaugh's young lawyer, Jeffrey Roth, was appalled at what he saw happening to Tony, but he did not know what he could do. The authorities in Pendleton County were obsessed with the hidden world of sexual abuse, so common in the region. They were cleaning out Big Run, arresting at least ten young people roughly Arbaugh's age, trying them as adults for sex and drug charges, and shipping them off to long terms in prison. No one asked whether it was appropriate to punish young teenagers severely for having exhibited behavior that, for the most part, they'd learned from their parents.

Roth did not like the idea of Arbaugh pleading guilty without a trial, but he knew how the jury would respond to what Tony had done. No part of the state was more conservative and tougher on this sort of crime. Local defense attorneys lamented that in any kind of criminal case, if the judge wanted a guilty verdict in an hour, the bailiff brought the jury coffee and doughnuts as they began their deliberations. If the judge wanted a guilty verdict in half an hour, he gave them nothing. Roth was not about to go to trial.

Arbaugh could barely read and write, and he had only a vague idea of what was happening to him. He had never heard the term "plea bargain," but when the prosecutors talked about him pleading guilty to one count of sexual assault as a fourteen-year-old adult, he thought that sounded pretty good. As he saw it, that meant he was copping a plea to having done the bad things once, and what could they do to you for that? He did not understand that for that one count he could be sentenced, as he was in September 1997, to fifteen to thirty-five years in prison.

The authorities first sent Tony to the Chestnut Ridge Center in Morgantown, which treated adolescents for addiction and psychiatric illness. If he successfully completed the program, he would be reevaluated. His sentence might be lessened, or he could even be offered probation.

Tony began a journey toward self-understanding. Not only did he study for his high school equivalency in the locked-down facility but he had daily individual and group therapy. He first worked with Terry Sigley, a psychologist who headed the program, and when she left he was seen by the new head, Gary McDaniel, a clinical social worker.

"Tony is a gentle, good soul," says Sigley. "He was trying to work his way through this."

"He was the most motivated kid I've ever worked with," says McDaniel. "He grew leaps and bounds in the program."

Arbaugh struggled to grasp these alien concepts of what was considered right and wrong. In those years at Big Run, he and his relatives had played at sexuality the way other children their age went out to play tag or ride bicycles. He had sexual experiences with two of his sisters, another brother, two nephews, two peers, and two cousins.

With each disclosure, so painfully evoked, came greater awareness. One day Brian came to visit, and in front of the therapist, Tony apologized to his half brother for what he had done.

"That was part of me growing, I done had to do that," Arbaugh reflected years later. "It done opened my eyes to everyone. I didn't know how wrong it was, how I hurt my brother, how dysfunctional my family was, how behind that was. It showed me everything. That's where I learned what most people would call morality. Everything I know about how a person should act, I learned there."

Arbaugh came to embrace the idea of enjoying a sexual life with a woman his own age, getting married one day, and having kids. In August 1998, after a year in Chestnut Ridge, the seventeen-year-old Arbaugh graduated from the facility. Before he left, the therapists performed a series of tests that showed that he was not aroused by children. Their report declared that he was at "very low risk" of ever again engaging in the kinds of sexual conduct with underage boys and girls that had brought him there. They judged him at "moderate risk," however, of relapsing with drugs and alcohol, especially when tense or under stress. The therapists believed that this would remain a challenge for Arbaugh until the day he died.

Arbaugh was next moved to a therapeutic residential program for teenage males that was located two hundred miles from Big Run. He did fine in the group home until he went back to Big Run on a weekend release. When he returned to the facility, he tested positive for marijuana. That got him transferred to a correctional center for young adult inmates, where he was incarcerated for a year before being released on five years' probation.

Arbaugh's attorney, Roth, begged his client not to return to Big Run—where, he sensed, Arbaugh would not survive. But Big Run was all Tony knew. He got an apartment in Petersburg, in Grant County, near Big Run, where he could walk to his night-shift job icing chickens at a Perdue plant. He did okay for the first few weeks, but he met a girl and then started skipping work and smoking pot. He had not been out for four months before he was picked up and sent back to prison.

A year and a half later, in April 2002, the twenty-year-old Arbaugh was back before Judge Donald H. Cookman, seeking another shot at probation. Arbaugh's new attorney, Amanda See, had gone to great lengths with Wheeling's Youth Services System to set up a rehabilitation program for him in the northern tip of the state, far from Big Run. See told the court that the program "doesn't usually take offenders of this nature, but they are willing to stick their necks [out] and waive that rule." Cookman said that although he was "very sympathetic to the situation," he denied reconsideration.

Ten months later, in February 2003, Arbaugh had a woman who worked in the prison laundry smuggle marijuana into the Northern Regional Jail and Correctional Facility for him. When he was caught, Arbaugh pleaded guilty to a felony. He was sentenced to four months in prison, to run concurrently with his present sentence.

It was not a smart thing to have done just as his lawyers were appealing his case to the Supreme Court of Appeals of West Virginia. It seemed unlikely that he would get probation—and even more unlikely that his life would soon intersect with that of Don Blankenship.

34

When Starcher read Arbaugh's appeal for probation, he felt sorry for Tony. In his years on the circuit court, Starcher had seen all kinds of young men and women like Arbaugh destroyed by what he considered a twisted system that prized vengeance and subjugation over justice. If Starcher had been Arbaugh's judge when he was first convicted, at fifteen, he would not have permitted the youth to be tried as an adult, with the attendant risk of decades in prison.

As Starcher leafed through the document, he knew this was just the kind of obscure matter—involving someone with no money or power—to which several of his fellow justices would give only cursory attention. Starcher felt that helping people such as Tony Arbaugh was one of the reasons he was here. He knew that most West Virginians saw the mark of Cain on Arbaugh's forehead—even though between 85 and 95 percent of juvenile sex offenders are never again arrested for sexual crimes, and Arbaugh had done nothing to suggest that he would be rearrested for a similar crime.

Starcher could not give Arbaugh back the six years he had lost within the state penal system, but maybe he could give him a new chance. The justice was an engine of persistence, and he went to his two progressive colleagues Albright and McGraw and persuaded them to vote with him and grant Arbaugh probation.

Starcher did not bother to court the other two justices. He knew that

Maynard would inevitably vote against Arbaugh's probation. The conservative former Mingo County circuit judge almost never voted in favor of anything that might help a convict. Starcher respected Maynard neither as a man nor as a judge, but he despised Davis, and he would not ask her for anything. If she voted no, her vote, in the minority, would not matter anyway, and would be just another indication of her betrayal of the progressives who had supported her election to the court.

Starcher was so sure of himself that he sometimes underestimated his enemies. In this instance, Davis indeed intended to join Maynard in opposing Arbaugh's probation, but she had more power than her single vote. In the Supreme Court of Appeals of West Virginia, the justices rotate writing the majority opinions. It does not matter whether they agree or disagree with their colleagues, and on *State of West Virginia v. Arbaugh, Jr.,* Davis said it was her turn. Although she did not agree with a word of it, she wrote the majority opinion affirming what Albright, McGraw, and Starcher had voted.

Starcher assumed that Davis and Maynard did not care about the likes of Tony Arbaugh, but in her way Davis was as concerned with the case as Starcher was. The majority opinion was a perfunctory, routinely written twelve-page document that found probation suitable, while Davis's dissent, which she also penned, ran a more keenly argued nineteen pages.

The most controversial part of the majority decision was a passage in which Davis said that Arbaugh "would be employed as a janitor at a local Catholic high school." It was not necessary to go into such detail, but she did. The court records to which Davis had access actually showed that Arbaugh was going to be employed not by the school but by Youth Services' Offender Job Skills Development Program, where he would "provide janitorial services under the supervision of a Marist brother." He would be overseen by members of the Catholic order. Although the details were not spelled out in the majority opinion, Arbaugh would be cleaning the school in the evenings, when no children were present.

In her dissent, Davis claimed that "the majority eviscerates the law to effectuate its own personal view of a proper outcome in this case. . . . The majority would be well to remember that 'accumulation of power in the same departments . . . is the "very definition of tyranny."'" Davis also condemned the idea of freeing a man who had "repeatedly raped his younger half-brother."

In all the courtrooms in which Arbaugh's case had been heard and in the entire voluminous public record, this was only the second time anyone had called Arbaugh a rapist. The first occasion was in the state's brief to the supreme court, which attempted to justify Judge Cookman's refusal to grant Arbaugh probation.

Davis also wrote that Arbaugh had "sexually assaulted a number of other victims ranging in age from four to thirteen, including two brothers, two sisters, two peers, two nephews, and two cousins." That was true, but Arbaugh had told this to his therapist in what he'd been told was the protected sanctuary of therapy. That he had opened himself up with such honesty was one of the reasons his therapist thought he would never offend again. All of that became part of Arbaugh's record, but none of it was to have become public. The state's mentioning of it in its appeal was a terrible abuse of his rights to privacy.

Starcher was so upset by Davis's dissent—challenging the legal integrity of her fellow justices—that he wrote his own concurring opinion. "I wish to express my amazement and displeasure with the personal attacks that the author of the dissent has made upon the articulation of the facts and law," he noted. "I am not happy with the gratuitous license that the author of the dissent took in the dissent."

Albright, McGraw, and Starcher later told the press that they either did not see the passage in Davis's majority opinion about Arbaugh's working in a school or did not understand it. That may have been true, but their lack of diligent concern had left McGraw vulnerable to assault by his enemies.

When Arbaugh was released from prison and arrived in Wheeling, in April 2004, he looked more like a teenager than a twenty-two-year-old ex-con who had spent six years in the prison system. Just under six feet tall, he had a moon-shaped, unlined face. Maybe he was not smart, he told himself, but he knew right from wrong. He was not smoking dope or boozing any longer; he was attending Alcoholics Anonymous.

When Arbaugh first arrived in Wheeling, he worked evenings as a janitor at a Catholic school. "Rod Lee [of Youth Services] always took me there," Arbaugh recalls. "The kids weren't there at night. I vacuumed and mopped classrooms and then did the bathrooms." After a few weeks, he moved on to a better job in construction and from there to unloading fruit and vegetable trucks at night.

Arbaugh spent his first few months at Spirit House, a residence for men who had drug and alcohol problems. Art Kerns, who was helping to run Spirit House, had never before worked with a registered sex offender. He investigated Arbaugh's past and concluded that "a terrible injustice had been done to Tony." He became so comfortable around Arbaugh that he left him alone with his young son. Arbaugh brought his girlfriend from back in Pendleton County and asked one of his new friends, Rod Lee, what he thought of her. "He was on the right path," Lee says.

As Arbaugh walked to work each evening, he surely appeared to be on the right path, but he had no idea that some of the most powerful people in the state were talking about him as they planned a campaign— that they were, in essence, going to use his story to bring down McGraw.

35

Blankenship disdained the compromised, compromising Republican establishment almost as much as he despised the inbred, entrenched Democrats. But in the early months of 2004, he also knew that he had to play the game of politics to advance Massey's fortunes in the state. His lawyers had kept *Caperton* boxed up in the Boone County court system, and almost inevitably the case would reach the Supreme Court of Appeals of West Virginia well after the election. The Massey chairman knew that if McGraw lost and was replaced by a conservative, Massey might have the votes on the court to overturn the *Caperton* verdict.

Blankenship wanted to do something to change the state, and he believed that nothing would change it quicker and better than defeating McGraw and replacing him with an ardent conservative. The vote of his old friend Spike Maynard was already solid. If Davis continued her journey to the right, the election of the Republican candidate Brent Benjamin would turn the court into a pro-business, conservative body.

A conservative such as Benjamin undoubtedly would vote Massey's way not only in *Caperton* but in any number of suits involving the corporation that would be heard in the next few years. The justice would likely vote a pure pro-business slate that would help transform the state.

In mid-July 2004, Blankenship set up a meeting with a young right-wing political consultant, Gregory Alan Thomas. The two, both libertarians, hit it off immediately. Thomas thought that the state was ready to abandon its corrupt Democratic traditions and move toward the furthest right reaches of the Republican Party, and that Blankenship was the instrument that could help it do that.

That transition had begun in the 2000 presidential campaign, when the coal industry and the Republicans had pilloried Vice President Al Gore as an environmentalist dupe who planned to shut down the industry in what the conservative *Charleston Daily Mail* called his "fossil-fuelless vision of the future." The state, with a huge majority of registered Democrats and historically as liberal as Massachusetts, denied Gore the five electoral votes that would have made him president, giving George W. Bush what White House staffers called "basically a coal-fired victory." The head of the West Virginia Coal Association boasted about a "payback" as the new administration loosened restrictions on mountaintop removal, opposed regulatory controls on carbon dioxide emissions, and engaged in a new kind of loosened regulatory regimen. The coal industry faced the bright prospects of business as usual, and the state Republican party saw a future in which it was no longer in a minority.

Thomas may have been the most creative and original political consultant in the state. He was undoubtedly the most negative. He brought a new viciousness into West Virginia politics and took no greater pleasure than in publicizing Democratic misdeeds and contortions.

Blankenship talked about his vision of a new West Virginia, a land of unfettered liberty where Massey could mine coal without the onerous constraints of excessive regulation and the outrageous lawsuits of greedy trial lawyers. Everything was timing. If McGraw could be replaced by a true conservative, Blankenship reasoned, the new majority on the court would help build this new world. Blankenship was too shrewd to talk to Thomas or anyone else about electing Benjamin so that he could overturn *Caperton*. If he was caught saying that, his efforts would be wasted—for the newly elected justice might be forced to recuse himself.

Blankenship told Thomas that he was willing to contribute $1 million to defeat McGraw and that the young consultant should work out a plan for how that money should be spent. Thomas went off for several days to prepare.

When Thomas presented his plan to Blankenship, it was for $2 million, not the $1 million the Massey chairman had said he was willing to spend. The youthful political consultant knew that money equaled votes, and he told Blankenship $2 million was the bare minimum. Blankenship told Thomas that he expected the consultant might hit him up for even more money before they were finished.

"You're probably right," Thomas said, believing that only a bombardment of attack ads could dislodge an established Democrat from the court.

Early on in the planning, Benjamin drove down to southwestern West Virginia and across the border into Kentucky to meet Blankenship in his workplace. The modest offices had a small conference room, where Blankenship installed his guest. Blankenship was a talker, not a listener, and so was Benjamin. Blankenship wanted to tell the candidate his concerns and how he thought the justice system should change, but Benjamin started pontificating and would not stop. At one point Blankenship stood up and walked into the next room to get a document from his secretary, and Benjamin just kept on talking. Blankenship told Adam Liptak of the *New York Times* that he said to Benjamin, "I don't know who you are, but if you go around talking to business people about raising money, you need to do more listening than you do talking. I've hardly been able to find out anything about you, but I don't like McGraw."

Despite having no rapport with the foolishly garrulous Benjamin, Blankenship agreed to spend at least $2 million defeating McGraw and electing the Republican. Thomas set up a meeting for Blankenship with attorney George Carenbauer in a conference room at the Charleston law firm of Steptoe & Johnson, where Ancil Ramey was also a partner. Blankenship told Carenbauer that he was going to try to defeat McGraw. He was seeking the lawyer's advice about how he could spend his money to do that.

Although a Democrat who had once headed the state party, Carenbauer thought that McGraw symbolized all that was wrong with West Virginia's judicial system. The lawyer welcomed the opportunity to help defeat his fellow Democrat. Carenbauer investigated the possibilities before suggesting that Blankenship set up a 527 organization, a tax-exempt, nonprofit advocacy group. Carenbauer explained how with a 527, Blankenship could not sponsor ads supporting Benjamin, but he could spend whatever he wanted to attack McGraw. The 527 was, in effect, a machine built to spew out negative ads, just what Thomas would have wanted to do anyway. The classification would allow Blankenship to use somebody else's name as a front and remain anonymous until a couple weeks before the November election, when his contributions would have to be made public.

The 527 rules also required a cordon between the Benjamin and Blankenship camps. The Massey chairman could not talk to Benjamin or his staff members, and if the candidate or one of his advisers called him, Carenbauer said, he should immediately slam down the phone.

Blankenship agreed to the 527. When Massey had lost the $50 million verdict in Boone County, Blankenship had written to his employees that the jury's decision was "play[ing] a role in further impoverishing the children of our state." That image stayed with him, and he named his new 527 organization "And for the Sake of the Kids."

Thomas brought to Blankenship's attention the Tony Arbaugh opinion in the Supreme Court of Appeals of West Virginia. It was the perfect device to enrage voters from Bluefield to Wheeling. Blankenship not only gave his money but also acted as a hands-on political operative with a sense of what would work to destroy McGraw and elect Benjamin.

The Massey chairman wrote ads and helped to choose where they would be placed and when the overwhelming onslaught would begin. "Letting a child rapist go free? To work in our schools?" one of the TV spots asked rhetorically. "That's radical Supreme Court Justice Warren McGraw." These were as venomous a series of ads as had ever been run statewide, yet they were legally impregnable. Everything was based on Davis's dissent and what she had written in the majority opinion about Arbaugh's working in a school. Using the two court documents as legal grounds, Carenbauer approved each one of the ads.

Arbaugh's duplex apartment in Wheeling, West Virginia, was the best place he had ever lived. He felt safe and happy up here, in the state's northern panhandle, hours away from all the temptations of life in Big Run.

Early one September morning Tony was walking downtown when he looked up and saw a billboard. There, 150 feet above the ground, was his mug shot and these words, visible a block away: "JUDGE WARREN MCGRAW LET THIS CHILD RAPIST OUT." He wished he could get up there and take it down, but of course he could not. Instead, he hastened away, trying to escape what he had just seen. But soon, above the highway, he saw another billboard, with another mug shot, and another accusation of "CHILD RAPIST." As he looked up, he knew that his rehabilitation and any attempt at a decent life were ruined.

Arbaugh went back home and, in tears, called his longtime lawyer Roth. "Jeff, this is awful," Arbaugh said. "I can't live here anymore."

Arbaugh was now the central figure in one of the largest targeted political advertising campaigns in state history. His face was on signs all across the state, in newspaper and television ads, his name repeated all over the radio. Arbaugh told Roth that he could no longer live in Wheeling. By his terms of probation, Arbaugh had to stay in West Virginia but there was nowhere in the state he could go to escape the images and accusations.

The media campaign had begun so suddenly and so overwhelmingly that it was only a day or so before everywhere Arbaugh went people knew who he was. Whenever he walked down the street, mothers grabbed their children and hustled them inside. Whenever he went out to play a pickup game of basketball in the school yard, the other young men turned away. Whenever he went to Alcoholics Anonymous, people left the meeting. Wherever he went, police officers watched him.

Arbaugh did not know why anybody would do this to him. He did not know Blankenship or Benjamin, Carenbauer or Thomas. He just knew that that wasn't the true Tony up there. That was somebody who had his name, somebody he had never really been. He had thought he would be okay this time when he got out and he would have a good life, but now he didn't know what to do.

36

McGraw was thunderstruck. He had been running the race as if he were the preordained winner, having won election after election against hapless Republicans who didn't have a chance. He had refused to debate Benjamin and was not about to risk giving interviews to unreliable, troublesome reporters. Now, wherever he went, there were these ads accusing him of freeing a rapist.

It was not just Blankenship's operation but also the official Benjamin campaign that was running the Arbaugh ads. The candidate's spokesperson told the *New York Times* that "everything in Brent Benjamin's campaign ad that dealt with the Arbaugh case was taken directly from the court record."

"Have you victimized Tony Arbaugh by using this case as your central theme to win the election?" asked a member of the editorial board of the Beckley *Register-Herald*.

"No," Benjamin replied. The polls showed that Benjamin was becoming a true challenger. McGraw's next chance to talk to a large audience came a few days later at the annual UMW Labor Day rally in Racine. The headliner was Massachusetts senator John Kerry, the Democratic candidate for president, but there was plenty of room on the platform for every prominent Democratic politician in the state. Among the other speakers was Cecil Roberts, the UMW president. Roberts had long since become part of the Washington political establishment, but when he returned to speak in West Virginia, he became a rip-roaring populist. He did not so much speak as yelp, with a high-pitched voice that sounded like a hound dog in heat. The words may have been lost in the crazed presentation, but Roberts pleased almost everyone except McGraw, who had the misfortune of following him.

McGraw had come prepared for this Democratic audience in a red, white, and blue shirt sprinkled with stars that could not decide whether it was a bowling shirt, a referee's jersey, or an American flag. He had a judicious stump speech in his pocket that his friend Starcher had helped him write, but that would not do after the UMW president had revved the crowd up to the point where they would have marched on the Bastille.

"There are people who continue to find a reason to attack honest, hardworking Christian people here in West Virginia, trying to make us look ugly; they follow us around trying to take ugly pictures and do ugly things," McGraw yelled, pointing his finger in rhythm like an orchestra conductor, motioning out in the crowd where a Benjamin videographer was filming the speech.

McGraw denies today that he was suggesting that his opponent was not a Christian, but he seemed to be playing into the atavistic prejudices of the region. The Republican candidate's surname sounded Jewish, but like McGraw he was Methodist, as Jewish as Shirley Temple.

"My Republican opponent and his Republican money are all out to destroy democracy and the freedom that we Democrats try to enjoy," McGraw said as he continued pacing across the stage. "No doubt somewhere in this crowd, look beside you, people are taking pictures to make me look ugly and use on television. They follow us everywhere we go, looking for ugliness."

McGraw went on to blame Republicans for the fact that women had the right to abortions, that there was no prayer in schools, and that in some states homosexuals could marry. His words made no sense and were wildly patronizing toward the West Virginians whose votes he courted. They played into a dying nativism that shamed the state and its people. But that didn't stop him from raging on. He condemned "the people of New York and Washington," who in the midst of all their other presumably degenerate pursuits had found time to be responsible for the anti-McGraw ads.

Although Senator Kerry did not try to outhowl McGraw and Roberts,

as a presidential candidate, he still won almost all of the immediate publicity. Benjamin's operatives, however, took in McGraw's speech and
heard the sweet sounds of the candidate's self-destruction. Both Benjamin and Blankenship began producing television and radio ads that
were little more than excerpts of what became known as "the rant in
Racine." Just as with the Arbaugh ads, there were such shrewd and effective media buys between the two camps that it was almost as if they were
coordinating their operations, though they denied this.

Blankenship devised the idea of buying a half hour of television time
and using robocalls to build an audience to watch the entire rant, inter-
spersed with the Arbaugh ads and other attacks on the Democratic candidate. By this point, in mid-September, most voters had learned that
McGraw had purportedly unleashed a child rapist upon the innocent
state, and here he was again, this so-called judge, in a loutish tirade that
cast more shame on West Virginia.

In the midst of all this, Fawcett got a disconcerting call from Berthold. "Ads are all over the TV," Berthold reported, "running 'round the
clock."

"Well, an unknown Republican isn't going to have a chance in West
Virginia," Fawcett said.

"I don't know about that," Berthold said. "Moms and dads, especially
the coal miners, are sitting down to dinner, seeing these ads, and saying,
'I don't know who I'm voting for, but I'm sure as hell not voting for
McGraw.'"

For the first time, Fawcett feared that they might lose a crucial vote
on the Supreme Court of Appeals of West Virginia.

No one watched the Arbaugh ads and the rant in Racine with more
shock than the state's trial lawyers, who feared that this media assault
might change the fundamental nature of the court. It was almost incon-
ceivable to them that McGraw might lose to a rotund Republican novice,
but the polls were frightening.

This election was not about ideas, not good versus evil, not liberalism
versus conservatism. It was about money and power. If Benjamin won
the election, he would be beholden to Blankenship and his contributions. If McGraw won, he would be beholden to certain trial lawyers in
an even more pernicious way.

The trial lawyers had their own 527 organization, which raised about

$2 million for the primary and the general election. By funneling the money through another entity, they were able to keep the names of the biggest contributors secret. By the way the trial lawyers' organization filed its election report, it appears that two or three major donors may have given at least $500,000 apiece. If McGraw won, these lawyers would have had every reason to privately tell him of their extraordinary generosity, a memory that would likely be in his mind every time one of his benefactors came before the court.

As for Tony Arbaugh, he could not understand why no one stood up for him. Nobody talked about how he hadn't relapsed. Nobody mentioned that he was not a predator but a childhood survivor of pedophilia, and that he displayed no signs of pedophilia himself. And yet he understood that the people who could stick up for him—people whose organizations were trying to help folks in Wheeling—feared that they might get drawn into this battle and be destroyed.

When a producer from West Virginia Public Broadcasting invited Tony onto its magazine show, *Outlook,* he agreed. He appeared on the program along with his half brother Brian. Tony had grown a reddish-brown goatee and mustache and was heftier than Brian.

Brian was a slight, soft-spoken young man whose mere presence on the program said much in Tony's defense. His picture was not on billboards. He could have walked away from public scrutiny. He was sending his own picture across the state, standing witness for his brother, showing how much he loved him.

"Warren McGraw and Brent Benjamin are not the focus of this heated race," the narrator said at the beginning of the program. "Most of the attention has been on Tony Arbaugh."

"When did you become an abuser?" the show's producer asked Tony.

"Around eight or nine," Tony said.

"With your brother?" the producer asked haltingly.

"I'd say so," Tony said.

"I don't think the right word was 'offending,'" Brian said. "I don't feel I was offended or abused by him. I mean, we done things. I wasn't offended or abused. A lot of things have been exaggerated. My understanding was that this was just part of life. I don't think we even knew that we were doing things we shouldn't have been doing."

"Do you think anybody would have ever heard about you if it wasn't for the decision that referred to a plan for you to work in a local high school?" the producer asked Tony.

"I honestly don't know," Tony said. "I wouldn't have done anything to bring it up, but apparently this guy has nothing from his life that he can say he can offer. So he has to take my mistakes and use it as his ammo. They want to talk about what I've done. But they're pretty much doing the same thing, but it's not sexual. They're ruining someone's life to help themselves."

McGraw's progressive colleagues on the court were stunned by what they saw happening and how their vote on Tony Arbaugh was being used to destroy their friend. Starcher had a shock of repulsion when he realized how Davis had played the issue, writing both the majority opinion and the dissent. In early October, Starcher charged in the *Charleston Gazette* that Davis had "used the decision to set her colleagues up for a political fall." He was accusing her of inserting herself into the election campaign to defeat McGraw, an abuse of power.

In mid-October 2004, the Blankenship-funded 527 had to file its election report, and the Massey chairman's involvement in the campaign became public knowledge. Stanley and Fawcett were stunned. Even in their most paranoid moments, they had never imagined that Blankenship would so transparently undertake such an extravagant effort to elect a justice who would likely vote Massey's way. They also assumed that the newspaper reports of Blankenship's spending would turn voters against his candidate but, as Fawcett would say later, TV trumps newspaper headlines like rock crushes scissors. They'd assumed that they were outthinking and outworking Blankenship, and now they realized that he had devised a way to try to win in the Supreme Court of Appeals of West Virginia that they had not even thought possible. Caperton was so worried that he sent the trial lawyers' 527 organization a check for $5,000, an enormous amount for him. Fawcett and Stanley sent checks, too, as did several lawyers at their firms.

It was not only Caperton's lawyers who saw a connection between the campaign contributions and the lawsuit. "Massey's got a $50 million lawsuit that they lost down in Boone County," McGraw campaign manager Andy Gallagher told a camera crew making a documentary, *The Last Campaign*. "The case was done very well, so they've [the plaintiffs] got a pretty airtight appeal. Their [Blankenship and Massey's] notion is to knock Warren McGraw off the court in hopes that they can get the three–two vote the other way."

Blankenship outspent the trial lawyers and had much meaner attack ads. In the last weeks of the campaign, he raised the ante even higher, broadcasting the vicious Arbaugh ads and the pathetic rant in Racine so frequently and widely that they seemed to take over the airwaves. On Election Day, Benjamin won: 377,123 votes to 329,991. To ensure that victory, Blankenship had spent over $3 million, or 60 percent of the campaign's expenses, in indirect and direct donations.

That night, November 2, 2004, Fawcett and Kathleen Trow drove to Stanley's Pittsburgh home to monitor the West Virginia election results. Fawcett and Stanley doubted Benjamin could pull it off, but after midnight, when it became clear that McGraw had been overwhelmed by Blankenship's money, the two lawyers cursed themselves for not figuring out Blankenship's secret involvement, though there'd have been little they could have done. Now, they knew, they faced an even more emboldened Blankenship, the architect of this extraordinary victory.

At the Benjamin victory party that Tuesday evening at the Capitol Roasters coffee shop in Charleston, Blankenship made his first public appearance at any event involving the Republican candidate. "Nice to meet you, Dan," said Benjamin's wife, Janice, misremembering the Massey chairman's first name. In his victory speech, the newly elected justice did not thank the man whose money had been the single most crucial factor in his election.

"I can tell you I am not bought by anybody," Benjamin insisted to reporters. Blankenship left the Benjamin bash to go to a nearby hotel bar, where he met up with his buddy Democratic justice Maynard, celebrating the election of his new Republican colleague.

On many later occasions, Benjamin professed that he had not asked Blankenship for money. That seemed unlikely, but no one could authoritatively challenge that assertion until 2009, when the *New York Times* ran Liptak's interview with Blankenship, in which he discussed meeting with Benjamin at the beginning of the campaign to discuss finances.

In the aftermath of the election, Benjamin did his best to create distance between himself and his benefactor. The justice acted as if the Massey chairman had been the one running the negative ads, when the two men had both used Arbaugh to destroy McGraw.

Many in the Blankenship camp thought that in refusing to acknowledge their efforts, Benjamin was both disingenuous and ungrateful. But Blankenship's supporters also understood Benjamin was shrewd to distance himself, as one day he would be asked to vote on *Caperton* and other suits involving Massey.

In 2007, Benjamin told the National Press Club in Washington that "no independent expenditure group ever gets people to vote for you. They don't win elections." He was proud to say that he had voted against Massey several times, though he did not mention that he had done so in majority decisions when his was not the crucial vote.

As Benjamin saw it, Blankenship's massive spending was of no consequence. But every time the justice voted in favor of Massey, many people would see him as a corrupt Blankenship puppet.

37

Blankenship now had far less to fear if, despite all his efforts, the *Caperton* case reached the Supreme Court of Appeals of West Virginia. And this was only the beginning of Blankenship's attempt to reconstruct the court in his image. Benjamin had hardly won when Blankenship began targeting Starcher for defeat in the 2008 election, saying next time he would spend $4 million.

Meanwhile, in the quiet, isolated corridors of the Supreme Court of Appeals of West Virginia, Davis had gotten rid of one of her enemies, replacing him with a sweetly tempered gentleman with whom she could work. She had provided the template used to destroy McGraw. In so doing, she had also set up Tony Arbaugh for a destruction far more fundamental and far-reaching than McGraw's.

Arbaugh was the greatest loser in the November 2004 race. His lawyers had sued the school district for its role in allowing a teacher to abuse Arbaugh sexually, and in the midst of the campaign, he'd received a check for $200,000, his cut of the $500,000 settlement. It would have been a lot more, but when his attorneys saw what was happening to Arbaugh, they thought they had better take what they could before Tony did something that would destroy the settlement discussions.

The lawyers wanted Arbaugh to let them set up an account that would allot him a fixed amount of money every month; the rest would be invested, providing income. But Arbaugh said no. He wanted to buy several homes in Wheeling, fix them up, and earn a living by renting them out. He had already zeroed in on a couple of places, but he was almost too trusting, and everybody stood ready to take advantage.

When Arbaugh got his big check, at the height of all the trouble, he gave up on his plans. He did not care about much of anything. He bought a truck for Art Kerns, back at Spirit House, and he purchased vehicles for some of his relatives. When they wrecked them, he bought them new ones. He went to New York to sightsee and to Atlantic City to gamble.

"I'm feeling scared, alone, threatened," Arbaugh said. "That's why I started carrying a gun. I felt it was me or them. Then I wanted to kill myself, thinking I was as bad as they said. I'm giving my money away because, in my mind, I'm throwing it away to let them know it didn't matter. I buy cars, clothes. It was scary. I did drugs, but even the high wasn't fun. And I know I'm messing up. I sneak back home to be with my family because I love them."

In February 2005, when Arbaugh's money was about gone, he was stopped by police officers near his home in Pendleton County. In his car, they found a .357 Magnum handgun as well as marijuana and methamphetamine. When he was released on bond, he fled north to Wheeling, skipping bail and the hearing.

His friends in Wheeling were glad to see him, but they knew that the police were after him. They were afraid that if he went back to Pendleton County, as he surely would, the police would shoot and kill him and few down there would grieve. So for what they considered his own good, they told the police where Arbaugh was going to be, and when he showed up at Rod Lee's house with a couple of teenage women in his car four patrol cars converged.

Arbaugh returned to serve out his fifteen-to-thirty-five-year sentence at Huttonsville Correctional Center, about fifty miles from his birthplace in Big Run. He remains there today, hoping to be paroled in 2015, at the age of thirty-three.

PART FIVE

JANUARY 13, 2005

38

In January 2005, nearly two and a half years after the jury's verdict, Hoke had still not signed off on *Caperton*. Fawcett had proposed that he and Berthold go down to Hoke's courtroom and sit there, day after day, until the judge issued a decision finalizing the case. But the Charleston attorney appeared regularly before Hoke, and he was not about to provoke him. Stanley, too, was opposed to the plan: he had such a high opinion of Hoke's conduct in the trial that he couldn't bring himself to blame the judge.

Although it was clearly not the case, Fawcett also became suspicious that perhaps someone had paid the court reporter to delay preparing a transcript. How else could the years of delay be explained? The delay had given Blankenship time to elect a supreme court justice to his liking and to engage in more of the same apparent misconduct that juries in Virginia and West Virginia had repudiated. Blankenship had admitted during the Boone County trial that when he had contemplated declaring force majeure against Harman, he'd considered the likely legal costs if Caperton sued him. Blankenship's concern with the bottom line was not just a business cliché but an immensely shrewd understanding of the costs of doing business. When he engaged in wildly provocative business practices, he knew Massey might be sued, and he neatly factored that into his calculations.

———

Fawcett saw that confrontational approach firsthand when, on January 13, 2005, he drove to Wheeling, where Blankenship and Benjamin had destroyed Arbaugh's chances at a semblance of a normal life. Fawcett had scheduled a meeting there with James G. Bradley, the CEO of Wheeling-Pitt, one of the last major steelmakers in the Northeast.

Fawcett walked into the company's modest office building, where Bradley and his entire executive team sat in a conference room around a large wooden table. The walls were lined with black-and-white photos of the company's various plants and mills.

"This guy is the Michael Jordan of suing Massey," said Bradley, fifty-nine, introducing Fawcett to the other Wheeling-Pitt executives, who were there to decide what to do about their own battle with Massey. Bradley described what had been happening, and why he thought he might need Fawcett's services. As he had when he'd first met Caperton, Fawcett said little, occasionally writing notes on a yellow legal pad.

Fawcett had such a deep understanding of how Blankenship and Massey worked that he could have finished many of Bradley's sentences. Wheeling-Pitt had a long-term contract that required one of Massey's subsidiaries to meet all of the steel company's yearly needs for metallurgical coal, for which Wheeling-Pitt paid nearly $30 million annually. Wheeling-Pitt used the coal to make coke, which, along with iron ore, is one of the two main ingredients for producing steel. The company made coke by heating metallurgical coal in special airless ovens at temperatures up to thirty-six hundred degrees Fahrenheit. In the past few years, as the price of metallurgical coal had more than doubled, fewer coal cars had been arriving at the Wheeling-Pitt plant in Follansbee, West Virginia. In the first months of 2004, the plant was sometimes getting only 20 percent of its requirements.

To justify its failures to deliver the stipulated coal, Massey sent an array of letters. The company offered various excuses: Poor geological conditions. Limited production. A flood. Inability to find and hire new miners. A mine fire. No coal cars from the railroad.

Bradley tried everything to get the coal he needed. He called Blankenship and wrote him letters, but nothing worked. So in June 2004, he decided to go see him.

"I'd been listening to all these excuses that were offered up," Bradley told Fawcett. "And so finally, I thought I needed to go talk to Blankenship myself. I just felt like Blankenship is head of a public company, and there are certain standards, and I'm going to sit down and talk face to face with this guy. I was kind of encouraged because he didn't hide from us. He was willing to talk."

Bradley and three of his colleagues drove to the Ohio County Airport, outside Wheeling, where a Massey jet was waiting. The plane flew to Charleston, where a Massey helicopter lifted the men southwest over the Appalachian Mountains, the verdant landscape slashed with the brown remnants of mountaintop removal.

"We're going to take you and show you what the chairman is building," the copilot said as the chopper buzzed over the land, then hovered above a mountaintop outside Williamson. Bradley looked down and saw, on a narrow plateau at the top of the mountain, a tall building that was nearing completion. "The chairman's bedroom is up there on the top floor," the copilot shouted over the engine. "That's the only bedroom. And you should see the marble for the floors. They went down to Brazil to get it."

The helicopter finally zoomed off in another direction. Bradley had no idea where the pilot was flying them, but he was taking his passengers to one of Blankenship's two luxury cabins in the hills of southeastern Kentucky. Blankenship stood at the landing pad to greet his guests. Then he gave them a tour that included a view of the riding stables and a large gym. The house had an upscale, rustic look, courtesy of Ethan Allen. Blankenship led them into the living room, where a bear rug lay in front of an enormous fireplace.

"I asked him how many employees he had," Bradley related. "He said he had one person full-time to take care of the horses, and he had a chef, and one other person. But the more he talked and showed us around, the madder and madder I got. You can imagine."

Bradley was ready to start talking about the future of his company, but Blankenship sat his guests down in front of an enormous screen and showed them two videos. The first was titled *Who Is Don Blankenship?* and was a tribute to the greatness of the Massey chairman. The second concerned his stock-car-driving son. Only then did Blankenship take his visitors to the dining room, where his executive chef had prepared a lavish luncheon.

As he had when telling Caperton that he had no friends, the Massey chairman seemed to be not so much showing off as reaching for human contact. Bradley was a fun-loving fisherman, a devoted father of six, and a grandfather of seven, and Blankenship appeared to like being with him.

Bradley was generally seen as a reserved problem solver, but he had a temper when he thought he was being mistreated. Blankenship was pointing at a Persian rug when the Wheeling-Pitt CEO exploded: "You're fucking us up, Don. Okay? You're not paying attention to your business. You're down here doing whatever the fuck you do, and you're not paying attention to the coal-mining business, at least as it relates to Wheeling-Pitt Steel.

"Do you fucking understand what you're doing to us?" Bradley added. "It's not like delivering bread to some goddamn grocery store. We shut down our coke ovens, and we're fucked. We can't use 'em anymore. You understand what you're doing to us? Huh?"

"I'm sorry," Blankenship said, seemingly untroubled by Bradley's cursing. "But you know we just can't get enough coal miners."

"Are you kidding me?" Bradley said. "There's unemployed workers everywhere. What are you doing to get 'em?"

"Well, we're flying a plane over Myrtle Beach, with a banner saying we need miners and a phone number," Blankenship said. As the Massey CEO spoke, he was smacking his lips, which Bradley found strange and disconcerting.

"You gotta be shitting me," Bradley said. "That's the dumbest thing I've ever heard. Why do you think people lying on the beach in South Carolina would go to work in a coal mine? People on vacation have a job. They don't go down there looking for work."

"What can we do?" Blankenship shrugged, chewing away on his lips. "We can't get the miners, and we can't get the coal cars."

Bradley figured that if Blankenship did not have the miners, he needed fewer coal cars, and he might have one of those problems but not both.

"I'll do whatever I can do to make sure that you have the coal you need," Blankenship said finally. "You're never gonna run out of coal."

Bradley thought he had gotten everything he needed out of the meeting. He wanted to jump back into the helicopter and get back home to share the news with everyone.

In Wheeling, Bradley told his staff that in a few days coal cars would start arriving to keep the plant operating at maximum capacity. But month after month, the coal shortages grew even worse, until, in January 2005, Massey's subsidiary hit Wheeling-Pitt with a force majeure letter, saying it was unable to deliver the full amount the contract required each month because of circumstances beyond its control. This was the first of twenty-five such letters the company would send.

Fawcett saw that Bradley was anguished. Bradley had rescued Wheeling-Pitt from bankruptcy twice, and he feared that everything he had fought for would be destroyed. Like Caperton, Bradley was concerned not just about himself but with Wheeling-Pitt's three thousand employees. Unlike Caperton, Bradley was not yet ready to sue. He was like someone contemplating a serious operation, putting it off while looking frantically for some other answer.

"I still think if somehow I can get through to these guys, they'll understand," Bradley told Fawcett. "We just got to let them know how vulnerable we are, what they are doing to us."

Fawcett thought this was crazy. He had seen Blankenship straight on. He knew what the man was, and nothing was going to change him.

"That's not going to matter at all," Fawcett said. "Massey looks for people in vulnerable positions to take advantage of. You can do all the explaining you want about how it could ruin your business and put people out of work, how you're going to be screwed. I assure you, you tell him you're weak, it's going to hurt you."

"How can you know that for sure?" one of the other executives asked.

"I know because I've been there. You guys all know about *Caperton*. Okay? Caperton went to Blankenship and said, 'Hey, let's close this deal to sell you my company because I'm running out of money.' It was a very foolish thing to say. That was the end for him. Blankenship will have no hesitancy putting an end to your company, too."

"But we just want our coal," one of the other executives said. "That's all we want." The steelmaker probably could have purchased metallurgical coal on the spot market, but it would have been so expensive that it would have wiped out any profits before they even began making steel.

"Look, I'd like you to get your coal," Fawcett said. "But I know these guys. A suit is going to be the only way to get what you want."

This was the first time Fawcett had pitched a client by saying that they would have to sue. Potential clients hated to hear that, and Fawcett saw litigation as a last resort. But not with Massey.

As Fawcett investigated the case, he found that Massey was also shorting other American steelmakers and shipping their coal to buyers paying higher prices, mostly on the export market. These larger, more powerful companies wronged by Massey were not contemplating suing. They knew of Massey's scorched-earth tactics and feared they would be cut off completely. Wheeling-Pitt had no choice, even if Bradley didn't quite yet realize it. The steelmaker had to either sue or sink back into a third and final bankruptcy.

A few weeks after meeting with Fawcett, Bradley called him and asked him to take the case and go ahead with the lawsuit. They talked briefly about a contingency arrangement. Fawcett knew that Bradley would be reluctant to give Buchanan Ingersoll the standard 40 percent of any award, plus expenses. With everything Fawcett already knew about Massey, he was convinced that any jury would find Massey's excuses bogus and might award Wheeling-Pitt tens of millions of dollars. That money would be needed to keep three thousand employees at work. Fawcett decided that instead of pushing for a contingency agreement, he would take the case at his standard rate of $500 an hour.

In April 2005, Fawcett filed *Wheeling Pittsburgh Steel Corporation and Mountain State Carbon v. Central West Virginia Energy Company and Massey Energy Company.* The lawyer brought to the case everything he had learned about Blankenship and Massey over the past seven years, and he felt confident that he would win even without Stanley, who worked for a different law firm and was not considered to be part of this case. Fawcett knew that the Blankenship he would be facing this time was the uncrowned king of the coal fields, a far more formidable figure now than when Fawcett had first deposed him, in September 1998.

As much as Fawcett cared about winning, he was happier than he had been in many years. In May 2005 he married Kathleen Trow. He persuaded her to give up her profession and devote herself to their five children, and he tried this time around to be the kind of husband and father he had not been before.

39

It was not until March 2005, two and a half years after the end of the *Caperton* trial, that Hoke filed his final order, but the proceedings still lacked a complete transcript, and without it Massey could not begin its appeal to the Supreme Court of Appeals of West Virginia. When Fawcett and Stanley talked, they shared their frustration: they had no means to force the court reporter to produce a finished document.

Bringing Blankenship to justice had long since become the focus of Fawcett's and Stanley's lives. Fawcett was preparing to take Wheeling-Pitt to trial, but Stanley was sitting on his hands. Hearing Fawcett talk about the case, Stanley felt a tingle of jealousy. He desperately wanted another shot at Blankenship. Yet nine months after Hoke filed his final order, there was still no transcript, and Stanley thought all he could do was wait for the court reporter to finish a job she should have completed two years ago.

Stanley was in his office on January 19, 2006, when he heard that there had been a fire in the Aracoma mine, outside Logan, West Virginia, and that two miners were missing. One of Stanley's brothers had been a federal mine inspector, and Stanley was convinced that the fire had been caused by safety code violations. "I bet you anything it's a Massey mine," Stanley told his Reed Smith partner Tarek Abdalla.

Stanley tried to work, but he kept checking the news on the Internet. It turned out that the Aracoma mine was indeed a Massey subsidiary.

An hour passed with no news of the miners' whereabouts. "They'll never find them, not alive," he told Abdalla. "They've killed those boys." Stanley kept watching the news until he learned that Don "Rizzle" Bragg and Ellery "Elvis" Hatfield had perished in the blaze.

Over the previous five years, eleven other miners had died at Massey subsidiaries. In every case, federal regulators had found that safety violations had contributed to the accidents. Stanley knew enough about mining to be convinced Bragg and Hatfield would still be alive if Massey had not made grievous errors.

Stanley's father had worked in Aracoma as a young man, and Stanley felt it was his destiny to represent the Aracoma widows. As passionately and idealistically as he cared about becoming a part of this, there was a practical benefit to his participation: the case would likely bring dollars into Reed Smith, which was awaiting a *Caperton* payoff that might still be several years off.

Stanley figured that there were lawyers in West Virginia already knocking on the widows' doors, trying to sign them up, and that his chances of getting one of them as his client in a wrongful death suit were almost zero. Along with coal, personal injury law was one of the region's few lucrative industries, the source of fortunes. The highways were lined with lawyers' billboards. The television and radio airwaves were full of ads boasting of attorneys' abilities to get tremendous judgments for their clients. When they signed on new clients, lawyers talked of their close connections with local judges and politicians.

Some lawyers had scouts who lived up in the most remote hollows and moved in whenever anybody died or lost a limb in an accident. They showed up at funeral homes boasting that they were a fourth cousin and crying loudly at the services. They befriended rural mail carriers and store owners, knowing that a referral could lead them to a big contingency case.

And whenever an attorney got a case, he or she followed the script. When you filed a suit, you jumped up and down, bemoaning the inexcusable tragedy. Then you settled for the amount that everyone knew an arm, a leg, or a life was worth, and you moved on, taking your 40 percent plus expenses, usually without the nuisance of a lengthy trial.

There was another unspoken rule: a case must never go to one of those fancy out-of-state attorneys who were always coming down to scoop up easy treasure. If some ingrate from Pittsburgh or Richmond did keep a local lawyer from his rightful contingency prize, the judge could make the case maddeningly difficult for the big talker from a far-away land. That way the outsider learned that the West Virginia legal system thrived on what was known as "home cooking," the favored diet all across the state.

Frustrated that he was a player whose number was never called, Stanley kept watch on *Caperton*. In March 2006, Stanley read a story in the *Pittsburgh Post-Gazette* that mentioned that attorney Tonya Hatfield was representing Elvis Hatfield's widow, Freda; Tonya bore no family relation to either the deceased or his wife. Stanley decided he would phone Tonya and offer to join the Aracoma wrongful death case. No other lawyer at Reed Smith would ever have called a small-time lawyer hoping to hitch on to a contingency case. But despite his years at the corporate firm, Stanley still had the soul of a hustling, living-on-the-edge trial lawyer working with just a couple of partners out of an office in a shabby part of town. His instincts told him that Hatfield might not realize it but she was in trouble. Stanley sensed that she lacked the resources and the stamina to fight Blankenship. So he left a message on her answering machine.

Hatfield, then thirty-seven, worked as a sole practitioner in the Mingo County town of Gilbert, population 417. She trusted people and took them at their word—an admirable trait for a human being but a potentially disastrous one for a lawyer. Hatfield was not part of the old boys' legal and political network that ruled Mingo County. In her eleven years of practicing, she had seen how certain judges and lawyers worked together to mete out justice, which the powerful and the well connected always seemed to escape. It was one futile fight after another with the coal-controlled political system and what she called the "yellow-bellied bloodsuckers" who did their bidding. A tall, handsome woman, she was physically hard to ignore. She scrambled along in her hardscrabble way, handling small suits and claims, the stuff the big boys would hardly touch. She had never taken on a big personal injury case and was not high on the list of those you would ask to represent you in what promised to be one of the biggest cases of the year.

One of Freda Hatfield's relatives—and one of the few people she truly trusted—was a minister. He had performed the marriage ceremony for Tonya and her own coal-miner husband, Roger, and had recommended her to Freda, saying that Tonya was a good person with whom she would feel comfortable. Freda was a mountain woman who had never traveled far beyond her hollow. Right after the fatal fire, she was approached by lawyers and their representatives, who tried to bowl her over with their promises. Tonya's father, now retired, had been a miner, too, and it was a relief for Freda to talk to another woman, one who spoke her language.

In early February 2006, Tonya went out to visit Freda in the mobile home where she had lived with Elvis, her second husband, in Long Branch, a hollow outside Gilbert. A thin macadam road snaked up the mountainside. If you were an outsider driving up there, you might be coming to attend services at the little white church, or heading just beyond, to where drug dealers and sex workers plied their trade.

Tonya had been brought up in a modular home too, but it was a double-wide. Freda's was a single trailer, fifty feet long by fourteen feet wide. Tonya was far closer in circumstances to Freda than she was to most of the lawyers she argued against in court. Tonya had gone to tuition-free Berea College, a celebrated Kentucky institution that provides first-class educations to those primarily from low-income Appalachian families. She hadn't strayed from her roots.

When Tonya had been ready to get married, she hadn't sought out someone who would take her away from this place; she'd married a man like her father, a miner who worked above the ground, in mountaintop removal. Tonya was no fan of strip-mining, but she loved Roger's strength. He was strong, brawny, honest, and self-reliant, a model of Appalachian virtue before the coal companies and the dole arrived.

As Tonya looked across Freda's narrow trailer, she saw that Freda had filled the place with pictures, bowls, vases, and candles. These were sold at "home interior" parties, where you ordered from one of your neighbors.

Freda had been in a troubled marriage. Elvis, then her next-door neighbor, was also unhappily married. Freda and Elvis began seeing each other and, as soon as their divorces were finalized, were married on her birthday, March 7, 1997. They didn't want to keep living next to Elvis's ex-wife and their kids, but they didn't have enough money to move. Freda worked at McDonald's for a while, and Elvis took whatever job he could until he got hired at Aracoma, and then they finally had decent money.

Freda could not stop crying. With Elvis, she said, she'd had everything that mattered in life. Now she had nothing.

"We got to talking just before," Freda told Tonya. "Elvis said, 'I'm gonna die in Aracoma. I'm telling you, I'm gonna die.'

"I told him, 'You don't do this to me, Elvis, don't talk this silly talk.'

"He said, 'It ain't silly talk, and when it happens, I want you to get outta here. You hear me. You take what money they give you, and you get yourself a new trailer, and you put it somewhere else.'"

Freda signed a contingency contract that promised Tonya a third of any settlement, less than the 40 percent most lawyers would have charged. They tried to keep it quiet, but within hours Tonya's phone rang with calls from lawyers wanting part of the action.

Massey made a couple of offers to settle, so small that Tonya believed they said less about the case than about how the company's lawyers viewed this small-town female attorney. Despite that, Tonya believed that she was still the right person to handle this case, or at least half of the right team. She was the supportive friend and adviser Freda needed, but she would be taking on Blankenship, and she wanted a powerful lawyer at her side. She knew that Stanley had helped win a $50 million verdict against Massey. She figured he wouldn't be afraid to sue Blankenship. And so she returned his phone call.

"Would you have any interest in meeting with me to see if I can be of assistance on the case?" Stanley asked. It was the first indication of Reed Smith's clout that the firm flew Tonya up to Pittsburgh in April 2006, where she met Stanley in person and decided that she wanted to work with him.

Tonya might have brought in another attorney to negotiate an agreement with Stanley, but she trusted him. Tonya and Stanley agreed verbally to split the contingency fee; a contract was never drawn up, and money was never an issue between them.

40

Stanley was excited that he, just like Fawcett, had his own Massey case, and when Fawcett and Stanley talked, they shared stories of their new suits. *Wheeling-Pitt* was moving along toward a trial, while Stanley was working on Aracoma with Tonya Hatfield. Fawcett and Stanley also talked of the continuing struggles over *Caperton.*

The Massey lawyers still hoped that they could have the case dismissed before it reached the state supreme court—but even if it did get to Charleston, with Benjamin now seated the company's chances for a reversal had drastically improved. In June 2006, when—after nearly four years—the court reporter still had not produced a trial transcript, Massey filed a federal lawsuit against her in which it argued that the verdict should be thrown out and the case tried again.

When Massey filed its suit, the Pittsburgh attorneys knew that they had to do something dramatic. Stanley tracked down the transcribing machine's manufacturer, in Louisiana, and had the court reporter's damaged machine shipped down to it. The company repaired the hard drive, capturing material that had been lost. Reed Smith paid a new court reporter to transcribe the seven-week-long trial. The document still lacked a crucial portion of Stanley's cross-examination of Blankenship just before the lightning struck, but Massey's appeal could go forward.

In late August 2006, Hoke certified the trial transcript that Stanley had delivered to the court, basically nullifying Massey's suit against the court reporter. In October, Massey filed its petition to have *Caperton* heard by the Supreme Court of Appeals of West Virginia, more than four years after the Boone County verdict.

The month before, Stanley had driven down to Logan for a meeting with officials from the governor's office investigating the fire at Aracoma. Also present was Delorice Bragg, the widow of Rizzle Bragg, who had also died in the fire. Delorice had milky skin and a mane of brown hair. She had the most sweetly beguiling voice and a shyness that masked her strength of spirit. She had been married to Rizzle five years at the time of the fire.

Bragg, who had been working at the mine for only two years, was a decade younger than Elvis Hatfield, who had helped show him the way. Rizzle and Elvis were roof bolters and had performed a crucial job in the mine. As the coal was clawed out, the two friends came in right behind with a hydraulic lift and metal struts to support the ceiling and protect the miners from cave-ins. Rizzle and Elvis were an amiable, joking duo, but they did good work and they earned good money, $20 an hour, plus overtime. The other miners talked about them as if they were almost twins, always together, always in a good mood.

The two men shared something else. They had both married women who had come out of desperate marriages. Delorice Bragg was fifteen when she married her first husband and gave birth to her son Billy, followed seven years later by a second son, Ricky Dale. Delorice left her spouse to raise her two boys by herself. She brought up two boys largely alone while studying to become a nurse and then working at Logan General Hospital.

Delorice did not have the money to get her own place, so she lived with her ex-husband's family, including his first cousin Rizzle. She had grown up in a house not fifty yards from his, and their lifelong friendship slowly turned into love. They married and moved out to a little house of their own. They both had jobs that paid enough to let them make payments on two new SUVs. They had no children of their own, but Rizzle was a devoted father to Delorice's two boys. Billy was twenty years old, working on a strip mine, but twelve-year-old Ricky Dale was still at home.

Delorice knew nothing about mining except what her husband told her. She knew nothing about Massey or Blankenship, nothing about any of it. Sometimes Rizzle would talk about conditions in the mine and say, "Somebody's going to get hurt over that." For Rizzle it was just a job, a way to earn enough money to have a decent life. He shrugged off the danger. Delorice had the same attitude. She had seen so much hurt and pain that she figured there wasn't much you could do.

When the ambulances brought car accident victims into Logan General on her nursing shift, Delorice did not sit around bemoaning why someone had been driving so fast or had knocked down his sixth Bud before getting behind the wheel. You could not determine when the Lord was coming to get you. You'd just better make sure you were ready.

On Rizzle's thirty-third birthday, January 18, 2006, Delorice gave her husband a set of keys and led him to the garage. There sat a four-foot-tall two-piece Craftsman, the Rolls-Royce of tool chests. He spent hours fitting each of the many drawers with the special liner material Delorice had also bought him.

The next day Rizzle got up quietly, trying not to wake Delorice after her overnight shift at the hospital. Around noon, he made himself a couple of sandwiches, tossed in two Mountain Dews and snack cakes, and went back to the bedroom to kiss his sleeping wife good-bye before heading off to the second shift, which would keep him away until 12:30 or 1:00 A.M., when Delorice would still be at work.

Delorice woke up after her husband left and fiddled around the house for much of the afternoon, until it was time to drive to work. She was at the hospital at around 6:30 P.M. when Rizzle's mother called, asking, "Have you heard anything about a fire in Rizzle's mine?"

Delorice knew there were lots of men in the mine, and although she worried about her husband, she figured that if anybody would be okay it would be Rizzle. Then she started getting more phone calls, and she learned that two men were missing and that he was one of them. She hardly remembers the next few days, in which she waited for word of his fate: the vigil in the church near the mine, the glare of the media descending on what had been a good and simple life, and then the news that Rizzle and Elvis had been found dead.

In the days afterward, Delorice became certain that something terribly wrong had led to her husband's death. The personal injury lawyers laid siege upon Delorice, too, calling her, writing her, saying whatever they thought would get her to sign her name to their ready contract. They patronized her as a naïve, uneducated woman who desperately needed their help. She may not have had a law degree from WVU, as most of them did, though she did have a bachelor's in nursing. She also had what she considered an even higher education: in sheer survival. She knew she was savvier than any of them imagined, and she saw right through the lot of them.

Delorice understood that only an outside lawyer would dare to do what had to be done: to go after what had killed her Rizzle. She told no one what she intended to do. She played a meek, quiet woman. And she set out to learn everything she could about a world she'd never thought she would enter.

Delorice was amazed at all that Massey would do to get her to settle. Blankenship called and not only offered his condolences but invited Delorice and her sons to fly to Pittsburgh to watch the Pittsburgh Steelers from the team owner's box. Knowing that Billy and Ricky Dale would love that, she said yes. She also knew what Blankenship was up to, and it wasn't generous; it was cheap.

Stanley had already been talking to Tonya about representing Delorice. "You know, kiddo," Stanley said, using the nickname he almost always called Tonya, "it would be better if I represented Delorice Bragg, too. That's the only sure way to guarantee that we get the resources from Reed Smith to do the job the way it has to be done."

At the family-update meeting with representatives of the various investigating teams, Tonya introduced Stanley to Delorice. He gave her his card and said, "If you want to talk, give me a call."

A few days later, Delorice called Stanley in Pittsburgh. She asked him some questions and wanted to know if he would be willing to meet with her. "How about I drive to Logan this week?" Stanley asked. "I can meet you at the Chief Logan Lodge. Would that work?"

Delorice agreed.

Stanley drove down to Logan, population 1,779, and stopped outside town at the state-owned Chief Logan Lodge and Conference Center. He arrived early and was sitting in the conference room when Delorice walked in. As he stood to greet her, he spilled his coffee all over the table. He cringed, embarrassed that he had begun this first meeting so ineptly, but Delorice found it refreshing. Here, she decided, was a real human being.

"I want you to understand this, Delorice," Stanley said. "If we do this, I'm not just going after Aracoma and Massey. I'm going after Don. You understand. I'm going after him individually as hard as I can. And I'm going after Uncle Sam."

That was what Bragg wanted to hear. She knew that she had found the right man. Stanley believed that the federal Mine Safety and Health Administration inspectors had failed miserably at Aracoma, and, although he did not yet have legal proof, he suspected they had been bribed. Even if they had not been paid off, the federal government still deserved to be brought to justice for their failures, and he vowed to file a potentially groundbreaking suit against MSHA.

After six years of fighting Massey and Blankenship, Stanley saw how it all fit together: the destruction of Harman, the threat to Wheeling-Pitt, and the deaths of Rizzle and Elvis. To him, it was a stunning disregard for the individual human life and an obsession with profit at any cost. Stanley believed that two men had died at Aracoma because of Massey and Blankenship, and the lawyer wanted desperately to fight and win this case.

"I think we can do this, Bruce," Bragg said. "I really do."

As Stanley left the meeting that afternoon, he was thrilled to be representing both Delorice and Freda. It meant that Reed Smith would give him everything he needed. And there was something else. He cared about Caperton, but this was different. Two men had died, and their deaths must not go unpunished. It had taken courage for Delorice and Freda, instead of just settling, to agree to confront Massey, Blankenship, and the federal government. "I've got the armor of the widows around me," Stanley told himself. "These people cannot touch me. None of their trickery. None of their crap is going to be able to stop me now."

Freda was almost overwhelmed by the death and the lawsuit and how everything had changed, but Delorice wanted to bring Blankenship to justice as much as Stanley did. In that struggle, she was growing and learning and becoming strong and bold. Delorice treated the case as the one positive challenge in a life she would now spend alone. It pained her that some of her late husband's relatives were making claims against

Rizzle's estate, saying they deserved some of the money. But she put that out of her mind as she steeled herself for the days ahead.

"Don and Elvis were just two guys who got up and went to work in a horrible environment because it's what they had to do to take care of their families," Stanley reflected several years later. "And that these people took their lives wasn't enough for [Massey]. Now [Massey] wanted to take the widows' dignity . . . to take whatever little bit else they had and treat them like someone's fucking commodity, like you're a fungible good. Take your goddamn insurance settlement and your health coverage and be fucking happy. Get out of our lives."

Stanley invited Delorice and Freda to every deposition and schooled them in the legal technicalities of the case. Stanley had learned that as with Caperton, when you kept your clients informed, they were better clients, better witnesses, and you had a better chance of winning.

When Stanley came home late, as he usually did, his wife, Debbie, and his daughters, Laura and Emily, were almost always already there. They were a close family, and most nights, around the kitchen counter, Stanley talked of Blankenship and Massey and the continuing struggle. He never exercised and did nothing to relax except lift a few drinks. His family worried that this obsession might cause a stroke or a heart attack. But nothing slowed his pace. He went into his home office after dinner and was often up in the middle of the night, sitting in front of the computer. He acted as if he were the only person who could stop Blankenship.

Wherever the Stanleys went and whatever they did, Blankenship traveled with them. His wife and daughters were proud of Stanley and his struggle, but after all these years and all this work, had he even begun to bring Blankenship down? Why didn't Caperton have even a cent of his money? What had Stanley truly achieved, and who was paying the price?

41

Nothing was going to push Blankenship from his perch. He scanned the horizon for enemies, and if you looked at him askance, he would teach you a lesson. If he sued you, he might not win but he would send you a message you would not forget. And if you sued Massey, you might end up like Hugh Caperton, endlessly adrift on the legal seas.

Blankenship sued the *Charleston Gazette* for defamation for reprinting an inaccurate 2004 AP story. The following year, he sued Democratic governor Joe Manchin for allegedly attacking him personally and threatening his business life when Blankenship fought to defeat a $5.5 billion pension bond issue. Neither suit got anywhere, but they tempered the *Gazette*'s coverage of Blankenship for many months and likely made other potential opponents wary of attacking him.

Blankenship's public stature continued to rise not simply because of his high-profile role in state politics and the continued expansion of Massey but because he was the king of a dying empire that made him seem larger than he was. Coal is a finite resource, and after 130 years of mining in high Appalachia the biggest and most easily mined seams in the region were gone. The fuel is more environmentally harmful than natural gas, and the longtime marriage between the coal and electric industries was threatened as power companies turned to other sources.

Blankenship and his cohorts made it a scary business to live in West Virginia and dare to suggest that the state could no longer be so dependent on coal for economic growth. Not a single major politician in the state directly faced the realities of a declining coal industry and a future in which, if the state's leaders did not wake up, the historic coal fields would be nothing but wastelands of the lost and the left behind. Politicians knew if they offered even the mildest criticism, the coal industry would immediately vilify them as traitors and look for ambitious candidates to challenge them. There were no easy solutions and no technical magic wand that could place mini–Silicon Valleys, for instance, up mountain hollows—but no one was asking the questions that had to be asked.

Blankenship acted as if his world would go on unchanged forever. He lived alone in his house in Sprigg, above the modest trailer where his estranged daughter, a mail carrier, lived. (In 2009, after his former wife died, Blankenship made up with his daughter and built her a great house on the hilltop next to his home.)

When Blankenship wasn't in Sprigg, he often stayed at a palace of a house on a mountaintop outside Williamson that he used primarily for entertaining, or he was off at one of his cabins in Kentucky, or riding somewhere in his big bus, in which he was driven to stock-car races to watch his son compete.

Outside the coal industry, there was so little work in southern West Virginia that people took jobs that would go unfilled in much of America. Blankenship had a maid, Deborah May, who took care of all his different homes and the bus. In November 2005, May quit. In her four and a half years on the job, Blankenship had given her one thirty-cent raise and was paying her $8.86 an hour. When she complained, he wrote to her, "Financially I know things must be difficult for you. At the same time you'd be lucky to find one person in all WV & K [West Virginia and Kentucky] that earns more for the job you have than you earn."

The maid had often fallen short in following through on the ten-page list of duties he had given her, and Blankenship regularly pointed out her failings. "Got a message from Mr. B for not having an empty hanger in his closet to hang his coat on," May wrote in a note to herself in July 2005. "So he in turn rips the whole tie and belt rack off the fucken [sic] wall literally destroying it. His remark was that the reason he tore it off was maybe this would help me remember to leave hangers out for him in the future. He acts like a fucken 3 year old."

Blankenship felt that the maid did not understand all that he was up against. "I've had three dogs stolen in 9 days, mines robbed, people complain incessantly, all of them want more money, none of them do what their [sic] asked," the Massey chairman wrote May in a scribbled note on a fax, replying to her complaints.

In the weeks before May left, she had a hard time concentrating on her job. Blankenship had assigned her also to take care of his new German police attack dog, and it was just too much. She desperately needed a raise so she could get medical insurance for her daughter. She was so anxious that she went to a nurse-practitioner, who prescribed antidepressants. Her medical consultant concluded that "her symptoms appear to be stress related. It is my medical opinion that she is temporarily unable to work pending medication adjustment and reevaluation."

Unemployment compensation is easy to get in Mingo County, but when this disgruntled former employee of Blankenship's applied, strangely enough, she was turned down. She decided to appeal, and her case eventually reached the Supreme Court of Appeals of West Virginia.

May had kept careful notes, and she laid out a devastating account of all the abuses she had suffered. This was the first time this side of Blankenship had ever been publicly displayed. Justices Davis and Maynard felt the matter should be kept quiet, while Justices Starcher and Albright wanted the public to know everything Blankenship was accused of doing. Davis and Maynard were willing to vote to give May her unemployment money as long as the court's opinion contained none of the ugly details. "That's okay," Starcher said, poking Albright in the ribs. "That's good."

The two justices waited until the court filed the majority opinion before submitting their concurring opinion:

On two different occasions, Mr. Blankenship physically grabbed Ms. May. Once, while trying to stock the coach bus after a last minute notice to do so, Mr. Blankenship grabbed her arm, pulled her towards him, and told her to leave the bus. Ms. May found that treatment to be embarrassing since many of Mr. Blankenship's guests were on the bus when the incident occurred. On another occasion, Mr. Blankenship sent her to McDonald's to purchase breakfast for him and his interior decorator. Ms. May placed the order, accepted the food and returned to the Blankenship home. As she unpacked the food, Mr. Blankenship discovered that McDonald's filled the order incorrectly; Mr. Blankenship started slinging the food and he grabbed Ms. May's wrist, telling her "Any time I want you to do exactly what I tell you to do and nothing more and nothing less."

Such conduct by an employer is reminiscent of slavery and is an affront to common decency.

May had so much to do in part because Blankenship was so often home. For a man of Blankenship's wealth and status, he did not enjoy much of the world beyond the Appalachian hills. He flew to Las Vegas to gamble sometimes, and he regularly visited the Greenbrier Resort in White Sulphur Springs, West Virginia, but he rarely ventured beyond familiar places.

In early July 2006, Blankenship took what for him was a highly unusual trip, flying to Monte Carlo with Della Cline, a Williamson lawyer with whom he'd had developed a relationship. There, in southern France and Monaco, Blankenship met up with one of the reasons he was optimistic about his chances in *Caperton:* his longtime friend Justice Maynard, whom he had known for more than two decades.

Maynard had been a judge most of his adult life, and he surely knew that he could be severely criticized or even sanctioned for socializing with a man whose company had an important case coming before the state supreme court. In most states, Blankenship could be prosecuted if there was proof that he'd offered an appellate judge anything of value during a pending appeal by Blankenship's company.

Maynard, age sixty-three, was traveling with forty-two-year-old Brenda Magann, a paralegal in the magistrate division at the Supreme Court of Appeals of West Virginia. The couple was staying a few miles up the coast, in Nice.

The foursome saw each other at least three days in a row. The two men and their companions had a number of lunches and dinners at restaurants along the French Riviera, toasting each other with flutes of champagne that cost more than entire meals at most West Virginia restaurants.

Upon her return to Charleston, Magann told two close friends at the court, forty-four-year-old Sheila Crider and forty-five-year-old Debbie Henley, about her trip. Magann and Crider, who is African-American,

worked next to each other in the magistrate's division under Pancho
Morris, an African-American lawyer of Jamaican heritage. Henley
worked in a different department, but to many in the court the three
single women seemed inseparable, often gossiping about their lives and
jobs.

Magann often bemoaned how cheap Maynard was, but on this trip,
Blankenship had made up for that. He'd bought her a designer purse and
had given her money to gamble with. "She opens the purse, and she's got
this huge wad of money from her winnings," recalls Crider. "She said she
tried to give it back to him and he goes, 'No, just keep it.'"

One day Magann called Crider over to her computer. "Sheila, look at
these pictures," Magann said, showing her photos of the European trip
that Maynard had e-mailed to her. Crider was stunned. Here was Justice
Maynard and Don Blankenship sitting at a café, high above the Mediterranean Sea, with wineglasses before them. And here was the happy foursome in Monaco, at the famous Grand Casino, the Prince's Palace, and
Port Hercule.

Crider figured that Magann had no idea that these photos could be
Maynard's political suicide. Crider hurried over to Henley's desk. "Debbie, have you seen the pictures?" Crider asked.

"No," Henley said.

"You need to go and talk to Brenda and look at the photos."

Henley went to talk to Magann, and Crider went back to her computer. After a long time, Crider looked up to see Magann standing over
her workstation holding a computer disk in her hands.

"What's that?" Crider asked, looking up.

"A copy of the pictures."

"Are you serious?" Crider said, shaking her head.

"Yeah, this is so your job will always be protected," said Magann, who,
after her conversation with Henley, had realized the photos' significance.
"In case anything would ever happen to me or if your job would ever be
in jeopardy, you'll always be protected with these."

As nervous as Magann was about the photos, she had not jettisoned
her sense of humor. Her nickname for Maynard was Leroy, after the
balding skirt chaser featured in *The Lockhorns,* a popular single-panel
cartoon. She'd titled the CD "Leroy's Greatest Hits."

Crider was happy to have her copy. Like most of the handful of minority employees there, she was close to Starcher, and now that Davis, Maynard, and Benjamin largely controlled the court, she'd grown worried about her job. Nobody who worked at the court had tenure, and she thought it made sense to hold on to those photos until a day when she might need them.

Before *Caperton* could reach the Supreme Court of Appeals of West Virginia, Blankenship also wanted to get rid of Starcher's vote, and he did so without the nuisance and expense of an election campaign. Blankenship must have known what would set Starcher off, and in the fall of 2005 he provoked the justice to verbal excess, just as he had provoked the striking miners to physical violence in 1985. In response to a speech Blankenship had given at West Virginia University, in which he'd attacked Starcher and vowed to drive him out of office, the justice called the Massey chairman "a clown," "stupid," and "an outsider."

Blankenship's provocation worked brilliantly: how could anyone now imagine that Starcher could objectively rule on Massey cases? Blankenship had likely gotten rid of a second liberal judge without spending a dollar of campaign money. But Starcher refused to recuse himself systematically in cases involving Massey, and in August 2006 the coal giant sued in federal court, citing the WVU comments by Starcher and charging that the justice had such "a strong personal bias" against Massey and Blankenship that he had no business hearing cases involving the company.

Benjamin was just as adamant as Starcher about not recusing himself in Massey cases. When Caperton's attorneys filed an unsuccessful motion to disqualify Benjamin, the justice said that the motion was nothing but "surmise, conjecture and political rhetoric." The legal system allowed a justice to decide for himself if he should recuse, and Benjamin was not about to do so.

In the autumn of 2006, Starcher's role was dramatically diminished in a procedural vote that enhanced the power of the conservative bloc on the court. In the West Virginia court, the chief justice appoints lower court judges to take the place of recused supreme court justices. Since there are only five justices on the state court, not nine as on the United States Supreme Court, that one justice's vote takes on even higher importance. By naming either a circuit or a retired judge who will most likely vote his or her way, the chief justice in essence has two votes. This is such an extraordinary power that for almost thirty years the position of chief justice rotated annually from judge to judge, in a firm, recognized pattern. Nothing was written down about that and nothing had to be, for it was such a crucial part of the fairness of the court that it was unthinkable that anyone would change it.

When the five justices met in early October 2006, it appeared that Davis, Maynard, and Benjamin had already gotten together to decide what they were going to do with Starcher, whose public utterances against Blankenship, Benjamin, and Davis rankled them. Less than a week earlier, Starcher had given an interview to the *New York Times* in which he'd said, "It makes me want to puke to see massive amounts of out-of-state money come in and buy a seat on our court. Now we have one justice who was bought by Don Blankenship." The comment hardly endeared Starcher to Benjamin, whom Starcher considered "the biggest name-dropper I've ever met, just a chubby kid who wants to be liked."

"Robin has done such a great job as chief justice, and she has these women's programs that she needs to work on for another year," Starcher recalls Maynard having said of Davis. "So we're going to let her be the chief for another year."

"It's not that you've done anything wrong," Benjamin said, looking at Starcher. "Robin needs to do this."

In other circumstances, Starcher would have raged at them. But he knew that he and Albright were outnumbered, and he figured that, if he must, he would wait a year and then take his turn as chief justice.

"In that case, I'll be chief justice in 2008," Starcher said.

"Oh, no, Larry," said Maynard, who would be running for reelection that year and was next in line after Starcher to be chief justice. "Two thousand eight is *my* year."

"We're not trying to cut you out," Benjamin said, following the political rule of saying precisely the opposite of what you mean.

"You *are* trying to cut me out," said Starcher.

As Starcher left the conference room that day, he realized that he and Albright would now largely be bystanders, repeatedly outvoted and ignored, and there was nothing he could do. "I think that Benjamin and Maynard got together and said, 'By God, Starcher can't be the chief justice,'" Starcher reflects. "And then I think Davis bought into it to help protect her husband, the high-powered plaintiffs' lawyer. They were determined that Larry Starcher was not going to be picking any judges."

Court administrator Steve Canterbury watched the drama of Starcher's downfall approvingly. Canterbury had managed Maynard's 1996 campaign, and he'd come into the court with Maynard as his champion. Although Canterbury says he hardly knows Blankenship, in a November 2004 *Charleston Gazette* profile of the Massey chairman, Canterbury is quoted as an intimate: "If he's your friend, my God he's your friend. But you don't want him as your enemy, because he's just as tenacious."

Canterbury despised Starcher and had for years watched with frustration as his influence spread. Under the new power triad, anyone friendly with the progressive Starcher feared that Canterbury would boot them from their nontenured jobs. Starcher had made a point of helping minorities, and most of the few African-American employees felt especially vulnerable. "It used to be a good place to work," says Crider. "Everybody got along well. Everybody worked together. Then it became backbiting."

It was even worse for the African-American attorney Pancho Morris, who had arrived, through Starcher's efforts, in early 2004 to oversee the magistrate courts. "When Benjamin was elected, the tables turned, and our lives became a living hell," says Morris. "At one point, Steve [Canterbury] said to me, 'Look, the problem here is Starcher. You need to stay away from Starcher.' I couldn't go and talk to him because I was seen as a spy for Starcher. It was bad."

The infighting spilled into the courtroom. "The terms 'conservative' and 'liberal' are not helpful to describe what went on," says Tom Rodd, Starcher's longtime law clerk. "It was about power. To solidify the three votes, there was an understanding. Benjamin was the third vote. He didn't engage in the trading, but he was going to be pro-business. For the other two, principles didn't matter. It was an exchange."

The new court was very much to Maynard's liking. In August 2007, he announced that he was running for reelection in 2008. It was early to announce, but he was hoping to scare off challengers. At his side stood his friend and colleague Robin Davis. Canon 5 of West Virginia's Code of Judicial Conduct states that a judge or judicial candidate "shall refrain from inappropriate political activity" and shall not "publicly endorse or publicly oppose another candidate for public office," but that did not prevent the justice from giving her colleague her public blessing.

When Maynard campaigned he played the centrist Democrat, but to his friend and traveling companion Blankenship he played a conservative slightly to the right of U.S. representative Ron Paul of Texas. Unbeknownst to almost anyone, the two old friends were in frequent communication, discussing political and other matters. In October Maynard e-mailed the Massey chairman a link to an opinion piece in the conservative *Charleston Daily Mail* saying, "Conservatives are buoyed by the possibility in '08 of further shifting the court to their side, regardless of the party affiliation of the candidates."

Fawcett and Stanley figured that the Supreme Court of Appeals of West Virginia would hear *Caperton* well before the 2008 election, so at least they would not have to worry about more new justices brought into the court by Blankenship's money. They worked preparing their *Caperton* briefs for the state supreme court, but they also spent hundreds of hours planning for trial in their separate cases involving Massey.

While fighting Blankenship separately, they remained in close contact. Fawcett would call his friend when he returned from taking a deposition, to report on the newest evidence of Massey's misconduct toward Wheeling-Pitt; Stanley would call with updates on his progress in the Aracoma case. "Wait till you hear this fuckin' one," Stanley would say, and then he'd tell his friend of some new piece of evidence he believed showed Massey management's callous disregard of safety. They may have been on different pathways, but Fawcett and Stanley had not gone separate ways. They were as committed to *Caperton* as they had ever been, and they knew that eventually they would be arguing the case together before the Supreme Court of Appeals of West Virginia.

42

On May 31, 2007, Fawcett made his opening statement in *Wheeling-Pitt v. Massey* in a courthouse along the Ohio River in Wellsburg, West Virginia, three miles south of Wheeling-Pitt's coke plant. He argued that by not delivering the contracted coal to the steelmaker, Massey's subsidiary had violated its agreement.

Beyond that Fawcett charged that Massey had purposefully defrauded Wheeling-Pitt when Blankenship had reassured James Bradley that Massey would never let Wheeling-Pitt run out of coal. The Massey chairman had said that while at the same time directing sales to higher-paying export customers. This was doubly harmful to Wheeling-Pitt, for coke ovens must be kept constantly fired. They simply cannot be shut down or put on a low burn. In the end, because Massey had failed to deliver the mandated coal, Wheeling-Pitt had run so short that the company's coke batteries had been damaged, and the steelmaker had nearly been driven out of business.

Unlike on the opening day in the *Caperton* trial, Blankenship was not in the courtroom, but he was nonetheless the central figure in the case. Fawcett argued that Blankenship had understood the vulnerability of Wheeling-Pitt, one of Massey's oldest and best customers, yet had disregarded his loyalties and legal obligations in exchange for maximizing Massey's gain. It was as though Blankenship had done a cost-benefit analysis, figuring that the profits from stiffing the vulnerable steelmaker and selling the coal elsewhere far outweighed the cost of paying lawyers to defend Massey's action.

Fawcett's primary adversary was Charleston attorney William Henry Jernigan. The formal, white-haired Jernigan looked like Hollywood's version of a seasoned corporate lawyer. The presiding judge, Martin J. Gaughan, was an austere, cautious jurist, nothing like Hoke.

As Fawcett looked out at the jury and gave his opening statement, his words were familiar to him from the Boone County courthouse five years earlier. But he felt them no less than he had the first time he'd spoken them. "This is a case about a broken promise," Fawcett began. "It's about corporate greed and, actually, the greed of a couple people at the top running a big powerful corporation. Thirdly, it's about dishonesty."

How many times had Fawcett said that in his battle against Blankenship? How many times had he stood before a jury and accused Massey and Blankenship of fraudulent deception? How many times had he accused Blankenship of being a corporate bully and acting as though he and his company were above the law?

"When the price of coal went up," Fawcett told this jury, "Don Blankenship had Massey's coal salesmen going around the world entering into new contracts at much higher prices, knowing full well that it could not produce enough coal to fulfill all the coal promised in the various contracts. And guess who got shorted to a much greater degree than anyone else? Wheeling-Pitt."

In the defense's opening statement, Jernigan said that Massey's subsidiary coal sales company had followed its contract with Wheeling-Pitt to the letter. When unforeseen circumstances had prevented the company from delivering all the agreed-upon coal, Massey had appropriately notified the steel manufacturer that it was invoking the force majeure clause.

"This is not a case about some grand and complex scheme hatched by Mr. Blankenship but, rather, a case where we are trying to get Wheeling-Pitt to live up to the terms of its agreement that they made with us," Jernigan said, blaming the steelmaker for the problems.

Two plaintiff witnesses brought the case back to the human realities. The first was James Bradley, the former Wheeling-Pitt CEO. Bradley talked about his visit to Blankenship's luxury cabin and how the company suffered when Massey restricted its coal shipments.

"You know, this may sound kind of corny," Bradley said, "but I struggled with this company for a long time, through some pretty dire circumstances, and I think this situation was wrong. It hurt us at the time and should be corrected. That's why I'm here."

Fawcett had subpoenaed Blankenship to testify for the plaintiffs. The Massey chairman was by far the most consequential witness in the trial, the one person who knew exactly what Massey executives had done, why they had done it, and how they had done it. No one else had anything close to all that understanding.

On the first day Blankenship testified, Stanley was in the courtroom. Fawcett was so focused on the case that Stanley did not even know if his colleague realized he was there. As Stanley listened and watched, Fawcett performed at a level Stanley had never seen him reach. He was on his own here without Stanley standing beside him, and he was playing both the role that was natural to him and the role that was natural to Stanley.

Fawcett addressed the jury in a way he had not during the Boone County trial. The lawyer had not lost his technical proficiency, but there was a humanity in him and a rich empathy that the jury could not help but feel. And Stanley thought, not without pride, that during those seven weeks together in the Madison courtroom, Fawcett had learned something from Stanley, and the way he worked a jury. "It's like I'm up there," Stanley thought.

When Fawcett examined Blankenship, it was the fifth time he had stood before the Massey chairman either in a courtroom or at a deposition. He knew Blankenship's strengths and his failings as a witness, and he looked at the CEO the way he would look at anyone with whom he had previously interacted. But Blankenship acted as if he were seeing Fawcett for the first time.

In all Fawcett's previous encounters with Blankenship, the Massey chairman had used defiant words—few witnesses would have spoken as boldly. On those occasions, his lawyers had probably prepared him otherwise, but once he got on the witness stand he usually said precisely what he wanted to.

Today, Blankenship was different. He was the most detail-oriented of business executives, yet he seemingly could not remember whether Massey had filled the far more lucrative export orders at a higher rate than what it had supplied Wheeling-Pitt under its long-term contract. It was not "no" any longer; it was a deferential "I don't think so." It wasn't "yes"; it was "we may have."

Blankenship tried to distance himself from owning up to any intimate knowledge of what had occurred. Fawcett, however, showed that in 2004, when Massey had claimed it had to declare force majeure because of unprecedented mining problems, its costs had risen only 5 percent, while profits had increased 15 percent. In another of its force majeure letters, Massey had blamed labor shortages. Rob Devine had discovered e-mails in which Massey's human resources director had asked the Massey chairman about giving a 3 percent raise to all employees, and Blankenship had scribbled back curtly, "We will not chase these rates. Looks like turnover will continue."

The next morning in his cross-examination, Jernigan had the Massey CEO detail the difficulties of running the giant coal company and why it was sadly inevitable that Massey could not deliver all the contracted coal to Wheeling-Pitt. For everything Fawcett had found wrong or fraudulent, Blankenship had an excuse and a reason. Blankenship did a compelling job of defending Massey, and when Jernigan finished with his final question, the judge called for a lunch break. After they returned, Fawcett would have a few minutes more to complete his cross-examination.

By any estimation, Fawcett had done an excellent job of presenting the plaintiff's case, but he was so self-critical that he began fretting that Blankenship's testimony had changed everything. If he had faulted others the way he faulted himself, he would have been an impossible nag. As it was, he was so down on himself that, with almost panicked resolve, he decided he had to do something dramatic to regain the upper hand.

Fawcett had prepared each question of his cross-examination with precision, lining them up one after another. But those queries had all been used, and he didn't know where to go. He wasn't like Stanley, who enjoyed improvising, throwing out whatever he felt might work. When Fawcett started to improvise, without having had time to think his presentation through, as he had in his closing arguments in Boone County, it could all fall apart, a sloppy mess on the courtroom floor.

Fawcett's mind kept returning to several new documents Devine had come up with at the last minute that seemed to show, indisputably, how Massey had intentionally shorted Wheeling-Pitt to make more money elsewhere. Devine had been pestering him to use them, but something had warned him away. He had not expected to present them in the courtroom, and he had not gone over the memos the way he usually did. If he relied on them now, he was convinced, they might backfire.

Devine leaned over and said, "Use it!" Fawcett listened, but he was worried that Blankenship would be ready with another excuse, perhaps knowing something Fawcett didn't. With great uncertainty, Fawcett placed into the record a document that showed that when the company opened a new mine in 2005, instead of shipping the metallurgical coal to fulfill its contract with a desperate Wheeling-Pitt, Massey signed a new contract to sell the mineral to United States Steel for $84 a ton, about double what Wheeling-Pitt would have paid.

Fawcett had long since learned to read Blankenship's face and the gestures that showed when he was anxious. The instant the memo appeared upon the screen, Blankenship began nervously smacking his lips. Fawcett asked the soft-spoken Massey chairman to move the mike nearer, which amplified the smacking sound throughout the courtroom. Then he placed another document into the record and asked another question.

"In February of 2005, according to this document, what percentage of coal were you delivering to Wheeling-Pitt, compared to what was being requested?"

"According to that document, twenty-two percent of what was requested," Blankenship said, his lips sounding like a loud, dripping faucet in an echo chamber.

"And in March of 2005?" Fawcett asked.

"Thirty-one percent."

"How does it help to make the orders when you open a new mine and it has coal that would perfectly meet Wheeling-Pitt's specifications, and you don't sell it to Wheeling-Pitt, but you sell it to another on a new contract at a much higher price?" Fawcett asked, his voice rising. "How does that help you to meet orders?"

Blankenship looked up, his mouth moving vigorously, his voice as quiet as always: "Well, it helps you to make orders to have orders for all of your accounts, and we don't know what all the circumstances were at that time."

"Did you ever think of maybe telling U.S. Steel or the foreign steel companies, 'You know, we'd love to sell you coal, but I've got a contract with a fellow West Virginia corporation, and they're relying on me to fulfill it, and we've been shorting the heck out of them, and, therefore, I can't enter the contract?'" Fawcett said. "Did you ever think of saying that?"

"I think that would have been a terrible mistake because we were doing what we could do to make all the orders," Blankenship said.

Blankenship had no real answers. It was a devastating finale to his testimony, one that the jury would likely remember.

43

In his opening statement, Fawcett had constrained his anger at Blankenship. He had a long, complicated story to tell, and he did not want his emotions to overwhelm it. That story had been told, and now, on July 2, 2007, the final day of the monthlong trial, as he prepared to give his closing statement, he believed the moment had come to fully condemn the man.

"When you deliberate," he told the jury, "think not just about Massey's revenues and how they grew. And don't just think about how Massey enormously increased its profit margins by selling coal on the export market. And don't just think about how callously Massey treated Wheeling-Pitt.

"But think about this: think about what it would take to deter Don Blankenship, who does a cost-benefit decision on every major decision he makes in his life in running Massey. What would it take to make him take care to treat customers with special care and not be tempted to cheat in the future?

"If you enter a judgment that's less than what Massey gained by its conduct, what do you think the cost-benefit analysis will show? Was it worth it to cheat?"

Stanley sat in the back of the courtroom. Fawcett was making some of the same arguments he had made in the Boone County courtroom, but they were more passionately spoken and more direct, and Stanley could tell that they resonated with the jury.

Joseph G. Nogay, the local counsel, rose to begin the defense's closing statement. Like Ramey in the *Caperton* trial, Nogay had played a role with limited visibility. Unlike Ramey, Nogay was a veteran trial attorney. His job was to assert the West Virginia virtues of the defendants and to denigrate the plaintiff's Pittsburgh counsel. His problem was that over the days of the trial, Fawcett had developed a relationship with the jury of the sort that more personable lawyers like Stanley often achieved.

"I have to tell you a secret," Nogay said, leaning toward the jury. "I pray every morning when I come to trial. What I pray is that I have wisdom. I pray the judge has wisdom, and I pray you all have wisdom." Then he paused and looked at Fawcett before continuing. "I haven't gotten around to praying for Mr. Fawcett yet; that's my sin, and I'm sorry for my sin."

Nogay seemed to enjoy his sin. "I don't know Mr. Fawcett," the defense attorney added. "I know his firm. It's one of the biggest firms in Pittsburgh, maybe one of the biggest firms in the country. There's lawyers back there from Pittsburgh that you don't even know about back there."

As Nogay luridly described it, Pittsburgh was teeming with attorneys ready at any moment to exploit the Mountain State. And when a lawyer like Fawcett arrived in West Virginia, what did he find in the Massey men he was attacking in court but the very spirit of the state. "Let me tell you something, they're hardworking guys," Nogay said, referring to Massey's executive team. "There's not one guy that has a slick lawyer degree. There's not one guy that has an MBA from some prestigious university. They are hardworking West Virginia people. They went to school in West Virginia. [Chief operating officer] Chris Adkins blew out his knee, and his dad says, 'You're not coming home. Quit school. You're going back to the mines and work.' And I understand that. These guys worked their way up. They're not liars."

Although Nogay did not intend it, he sounded almost patronizing to the jury, and his attempt at wooing them with his folksy anecdotes did not work. In the end, the jury awarded Wheeling-Pitt $220 million, including a whopping $100 million in punitive damages, a mark of how outrageous the jury considered Massey's conduct. The amount was one of the highest verdicts rendered in a United States courtroom that year.

Fawcett didn't roll on the grass. He celebrated quietly with his new wife, and pledged to himself that he would do everything humanly possible to make sure that, this time, Massey would end up paying the damages it owed. The front-page headline in the *Pittsburgh Post-Gazette*—"Verdict Gives Lift to Struggling Steelmaker"—gave him great pride, but no assurance that Massey would do anything but appeal and cause endless delays.

Massey was so optimistic about an appeal that its fourth-quarter 2007 financial statement estimated that the Wheeling-Pitt verdict would end up costing the company only $16 million, most of that presumably legal expenses. Fawcett told the *Pittsburgh Post-Gazette* that he suspected Blankenship was "flaunting what he perceives to be his 'inside track'" at the Supreme Court of Appeals of West Virginia.

Blankenship further showed his absolute disregard for the jury's verdict when, in early 2008, Massey again started shorting Wheeling-Pitt's coal as prices began rising again. As Blankenship must have expected, Fawcett filed a new suit against Massey.

PART SIX

OCTOBER 10, 2007

44

When Fawcett and Stanley walked into the courtroom of the Supreme Court of Appeals of West Virginia on October 10, 2007, to argue *Caperton*, Fawcett was coming off his resounding victory three months earlier in *Wheeling-Pitt*, while Stanley was still a year away from going to trial in his Aracoma widows' case. It had been over five years since the Boone County verdict.

The West Virginia high court is one of the most impressive public rooms in the state. At the front of the thirty-foot-high chamber, visible to lawyers and spectators, is a quotation from Thomas Jefferson: "The true foundation of republican government is the equal right of every citizen in his person and property and in their management." The justices look out onto the far wall, which bears a line from Lincoln's second inaugural address: "Firmness in the right, as God gives us to see the right."

This morning's hearing would determine if the court would uphold the *Caperton* verdict, which, with five years of interest, had reached $70 million. As Stanley and Fawcett looked up at the five justices hearing the case, their gaze met what they considered many unfriendly eyes. The two lawyers had already written off Benjamin's vote. They believed that he had fought their recusal plea so he could rule in favor of the benefactor whose money had largely elected him. As for Maynard, a vote against *Caperton* would reaffirm his conservative ideology and his longtime friendship with Blankenship. Fawcett and Stanley figured him as certain a pro-Massey vote as Benjamin. The two *Caperton* attorneys were equally convinced, however, that Starcher and Albright would vote their way. The key vote, they believed, was Chief Justice Davis, and as they settled into their seats beneath the high judicial bench, it was she whom they wanted primarily to address.

The *Caperton* legal team this morning included local counsel Robert Berthold, who was supposed to be a conduit into the inner workings of the legal and political system in the capital. Joining the lawyers in the courtroom were Hugh and Kathy Caperton.

To argue Massey's case today, the coal company brought in D. C. Offutt Jr., a Huntington, West Virginia, attorney. The lawyer's seventy-one-page brief to the court was an encyclopedic assault on almost everything that had gone on in Hoke's courtroom.

"With the court's permission, I'll address res judicata and some other major issues," Offutt began. Res judicata is to a civil suit what double jeopardy is to a murder trial. The concept dictates that a plaintiff cannot hop from jurisdiction to jurisdiction, state to state, filing and refiling a case until the desired verdict is achieved. Caperton's company had had its victory in Virginia; he could not go running over to West Virginia to assert the same claims all over again.

"And then if the justices have any questions, I'll be happy to respond to them," Offutt said.

"In addition to res judicata, I would like for you to address the forum selection clause [in the contract between Harman and Wellmore], please," Davis said.

"Okay, I will," Offutt said. "That's one of the ones I intended to."

Fawcett and Stanley were startled to hear Davis mention the forum selection clause as if it were a defining issue in the appeal. The contract between Caperton's company and Wellmore/United required that legal matters be settled in Virginia, so that's where Fawcett had filed the contract dispute. But he had chosen to file the broader tort suit in West Virginia, where Caperton lived, where his company had its headquarters, and where Massey did most of its business.

Forum selection was such a settled issue that the massive Massey appellate brief brought up the question of whether the Boone County suit should have been filed in West Virginia in only one sentence. Having read the Massey brief, Fawcett and Stanley were convinced that Offutt had originally had no intention of talking about forum selection. He could not have anticipated that Davis would ask about the issue, and yet he appeared incredibly well prepared. Fawcett and Stanley were concerned that someone could have tipped him off. The two Pittsburgh attorneys had come ready to respond to the defendant's brief, and now they would have to scramble to answer questions they'd had no reason to believe they would be asked.

During the Boone County trial, Ramey had spent much of his time building issues that could be used in an appeal. He had ignored Hoke's rule limiting the time of cross-examination, and the judge had responded by invoking a sanction allowing the plaintiffs to bring in Massey's past financial condition. That had hurt the defense, but today, half a decade later, Ramey was sitting in the back of the courtroom, watching the fruition of all his efforts.

"I've tried cases for twenty-nine years, and I've never had that kind of limitation," Offutt said of Hoke's time constraints. "I think it's grossly unfair, because it permitted the plaintiff basically to present opinions in a very quick fashion, and then severely restrict the ability of the defense to explore those opinions."

The lawyer was doing what any appellate attorney would have done: questioning how a lower-court judge had handled the trial. Like doctors, journalists, and other professionals, judges are protective of one another. It was a tricky matter just how far criticism should go. Hoke knew these justices. Sometimes, amid a high-court recusal, he would fill the absent seat. What's more, he had gone to law school with Davis, and they were personal friends.

Massey's appellate lawyer risked creating sympathy for the justices' colleague. But Offutt seemed to question Hoke's every action. The attorney mentioned Hoke's instructions to the jury. The defense attorneys, Offutt argued, "never had an opportunity to try to mold or shape those instructions in any way but were stuck with what Hoke decided he was going to give." Offutt said that Hoke "admonished counsel not to make any objections during the closing or he was going to sanction counsel if he thought any objection improper. Therefore, he discouraged counsel from making any kind of objection during the closing argument."

Fawcett rose to defend the lower court verdict. Before he could say a word, Maynard stood up and exited the courtroom through the curtains behind the bench, apparently unwilling even to listen to the arguments presented by Blankenship's enemies.

Fawcett was happy that Offutt had made res judicata the most important issue in his oral argument, and he had not been surprised by anything the Massey appellate attorney had said about the issue in his presentation to the court. Fawcett had already dealt with res judicata extensively in debates with defense attorney Jeff Woods before the beginning of Boone County *Caperton* trial, and he was ready to drive it away once again.

"The doctrine of res judicata does not apply to preclude our tort claims," Fawcett said. "I tried the Virginia case. And in the Virginia case, you had different parties. You had different issues. You had way, way different evidence, and you had different remedies."

"Justice Davis, you had asked a question about the forum selection provision," Fawcett said, although he had not come prepared to deal with that issue. "And I'd like to address that briefly if I may."

Fawcett made the crucial point that in the Virginia trial the defendant had not been Massey but the coal giant's subsidiary Wellmore/United, whereas Massey was the defendant in West Virginia. What the two trials had in common was that they had both found the defendants guilty of either breaching or interfering with Harman's lifeblood, its coal supply agreement. And here the twice-guilty party was claiming it had a right to invoke a clause in a contract that it had run through a shredder.

"It was their tortious activity that destroyed that contract, destroyed the business of Harman," Fawcett said. "And then for them to come in and say, Oh, well, we have the right to invoke the benefit in that contract just doesn't make sense, and it is far outside of existing law relative to that matter."

Fawcett went on to defend Hoke, thereby defending the jury's verdict. "The statements that have been made here and in the briefs appear very clearly to create the picture that Hoke let things get out of control, that this was a kangaroo court, a debacle," the lawyer said. "You know, this was a seven-week trial. And you can pick any day of the transcript, and what you'll see is a well-run trial. You'll see great hard work by Hoke,

deliberation at every turn, on every objection, and well-reasoned decisions. And I think it is also very telling—"

"I would like for you to address for one minute, please," Davis interrupted, "the different areas in the transcript where Hoke took over cross-
examination of the witnesses. And based upon my review of the record in
this case, there were pages and pages and pages of cross-examination by
Hoke with regard to the experts."

By acknowledging that she had personally reviewed those records,
Davis was raising the stakes dramatically, placing her credibility and the
credibility of the Supreme Court of Appeals of West Virginia at risk.
Fawcett had been in the Boone County courtroom during the entire
trial, and he knew that what Davis was saying was simply not true.

Davis had a reputation for coming to court well prepared, but it would
have taken her several days to read the voluminous transcript. Her clerk
or someone close to the case may have pointed out to her Hoke's soliloquy over the wrecking ball analogy, after which she merely extrapolated,
assuming that he had intervened with witness after witness. But whatever the reason, she was averring something that had not happened.

"With due respect, that's not my recollection," Fawcett said. "My recollection is in the course of this seven-week trial, the questions that he
asked were very limited." The appellate court rules did not allow Fawcett
to halt the proceedings and examine the trial record, but the transcript
shows that Hoke asked questions to five expert witnesses. These were
almost all short, deferential exchanges that, if anything, increased the
expert witnesses' credibility with the jury. Only in the wrecking ball colloquy did Hoke truly take over interviewing a witness.

"I think the question is whether the judge engaged in rehabilitating
witnesses," Albright said, asking whether Hoke had used his questions
to make the witnesses sound more credible. The liberal judge had not
read the transcript, and he believed that Davis knew what the lengthy
document contained. Davis's and Offutt's distorted recounting of the
Boone County proceedings made it difficult for the judges to comprehend what had actually occurred.

If Fawcett was to seek justice in this courtroom, he could not let
untruths stand as part of the court record. He could have confronted
Davis directly, but he had never been good with unpredictable situations

like this. Davis was the chief justice of the Supreme Court of Appeals of West Virginia, the most powerful judge he had ever addressed, and he simply could not bring himself to confront her.

When Stanley's turn came, he said, "My understanding of what Hoke was attempting to do was to clarify the nature of the opinions of those experts. And I thought he was doing that simply in the context not of rehabilitating the witnesses but, rather, making sure it was clear the nature of the opinions that were being rendered."

Stanley was trying to justify Hoke's conduct, but he, too, seemed to accept what Davis had said and, like Fawcett, didn't challenge the chief justice's assertions. Stanley fancied that there was nobody who could intimidate him and that he would unfailingly challenge the mighty with their wrongs, but not this morning. For Stanley and Fawcett to confront Davis for inaccurately relating what had transpired in the court was to go somewhere from which there was no coming back. It was to conclude that they had lost her vote and there was no reason to do anything but to stand up to her in the boldest, most unyielding terms and, in so doing, render themselves virtual outcasts in the West Virginia legal system.

As soon as Stanley sat down, the curtain behind the justices opened, and Maynard returned to his seat.

45

When the Caperton contingent left the courtroom that day, they were quiet except for Kathy Caperton. "We've lost!" she said.

"It's not that simple," Berthold said. "You can't judge by Davis's questions."

"I'm a woman, and I understand women, and I'm telling you that Davis had already made up her mind before she walked in that room. It's all over."

The next day, October 11, the five justices met privately in their conference room to discuss the case and vote. Even if they were merely going to rubber-stamp their ideological positions, the majority still had to choose the grounds they would use to justify their decision. Chief Justice Davis took her place at the head of the table. The other justices sat according to seniority, with Starcher on her right, followed by Albright. On the other side sat Maynard, who had presumably heard only Massey's side of the arguments. Next to him sat Benjamin, the most junior justice.

"Our next case is *Caperton v. Massey*," Davis said, as Starcher remembers.

"Well, I guess we all know how we're going to vote on this case," Maynard said. "We don't need to talk about it."

"What?" Starcher said. "We're not going to talk about this case after it's been argued?"

"Well, everybody knows how we're going to vote," Maynard said.

"Maybe we do, and maybe we don't," Starcher said.

"Well, I'm ready to vote," Benjamin said.

"Looks like we're just going to vote," Albright said, more to Starcher than to the other justices.

And then the five justices each announced their votes, without discussing the grounds for their decisions. Davis, Maynard, and Benjamin voted to overturn the Boone County verdict. Starcher and Albright dissented. Davis said that she would write the majority opinion.

That evening Starcher wrote in his diary, "We decided the now $75 million Massey Energy case in less than 60 seconds. (HONEST!) The Massey case obviously was pre-decided by the 'evil three.' Benjamin and Maynard are buddies with Don Blankenship and Robin kisses their butts to keep them 'with her husband' on his cases. The 'good ole boy' system rules the day."

As the chief justice, Davis got to decide when the court's opinions would be posted on its website, and she decided to keep the *Caperton* decision secret for many weeks.

Starcher was upset by the vote and felt that life on the court was no fun anymore. He was sixty-five years old. His wife, Becky, feared that if he ran for reelection in 2008, the stress of the vicious attacks Blankenship would inevitably wage might kill him. He did not want anyone to say that Larry Starcher had run away from a fight; better to play the good husband following an even higher authority and use that as an excuse to retire at the end of his twelve-year term.

Starcher was a big fan of the West Virginia University football team, and on October 20, 2007, he drove to Milan Puskar Stadium in Morgantown to watch the Mountaineers take on Mississippi State. He showed up early at a hospitality tent. Starcher was glad-handing his way through the partying fans when he came upon Debbie Henley. She had worked for him for a short while when his secretary was out sick and had become one of those employees for whom he watched out.

Henley had come to the event with her friend Brenda Magann. Starcher had never met Magann at the court, and he was interested to see what Maynard's lover looked like. After Magann walked away, Starcher and Henley started talking about Maynard. Henley said that

Maynard and Magann had broken up. Then she mentioned the trip her friend had taken to Europe with the justice and said there were pictures that included shots of the twosome with their companions Blankenship and Cline.

While Starcher watched West Virginia wallop Mississippi State 38 to 13, he kept thinking about those pictures and what he could do about them. He told only a few close associates, those who shared his disdain for Maynard and Blankenship. But soon rumors about the trip—and about the existence of photos proving it—spread into the highest levels of state politics.

Meanwhile, the Supreme Court of Appeals of West Virginia still hadn't posted its *Caperton* decision. The court usually took a few weeks before revealing its opinions. But in the third week of November, after seven weeks without an announcement, Caperton and his attorneys were incredibly anxious. They would have been even more nervous if they had known that Davis's husband, Scott Segal, had just hosted a fund-raiser at their mansion on Quarry Ridge that had raised more than $100,000 for Maynard's 2008 reelection campaign.

One night Stanley called his friend and co-counsel Fawcett.

"If they're going to kill us, when do you think they'll do it?" asked Stanley, though he already had his answer.

"They're not going to want anybody to see this shit go down," Fawcett said.

"You got it," Stanley said. "If they're going to kill us, it'll be the day before Thanksgiving." Obscured by the holiday, the decision would then get the least media play and popular attention. The next time Stanley talked to Caperton, he told him, too, that he thought a negative verdict would likely come down the day before Thanksgiving.

That day had a special meaning for Caperton; it was ten years before on such a Wednesday that Blankenship had come to his office in Beckley and this whole business had begun. Caperton did not think much of Stanley's prediction, but when Wednesday arrived and there was still no word from the court, he became even more nervous. If the court did not rule his way, he had no idea what he would do. At least he wouldn't have to pay back the $1 million to the hedge fund, but he had hundreds of thousands of dollars in other debts and no prospect of a job that would give him the money to begin to repay those obligations.

That afternoon Fawcett was at work in his office, though most of the other Buchanan Ingersoll lawyers had left for the long holiday weekend. At 3:10, his secretary buzzed him.

"It's Rory Perry," she said, announcing the clerk of the Supreme Court of Appeals of West Virginia.

"Fuck," Fawcett said, remembering Stanley's prediction.

"I just wanted to give you a call to let you know that a decision has been rendered in the *Caperton* case," Perry said. According to court protocol, Perry did not announce the decision but told Fawcett that he would now fax the opinion.

As Fawcett walked down the hall to the fax machine, he could hear the document arriving, page after page. By the time he stood over the fax, the decision was sitting there: sixty-four pages, twice the length of most opinions, with thirty-seven footnotes. He grabbed the pages, turned to the last one, and saw the only thing that mattered: reversed.

Fawcett immediately called Stanley, who was driving to his parents' home in southern West Virginia for Thanksgiving. As soon as Stanley saw Fawcett's name pop up on his BlackBerry's caller ID, he knew the result.

There was not much to be said, and the two men had only a short conversation, in which Fawcett could not face talking about the details of the lengthy decision. Stanley represented Caperton personally and it was now his duty to call his client.

"Hugh," Stanley said. "We got the supreme court opinion."

That was all the lawyer needed to say.

"Oh, God," Caperton said.

"I'm sorry, man, I'm sorry. I really don't know what to say. I'm so sorry."

"Nothing to be sorry about," Caperton said.

"I guess we're going to have to go back for a new trial," Stanley said.

"Are you kidding?" Caperton asked.

"Yeah, I guess we'll just have to go back and do it all over again."

"All over again?" Caperton sighed. "How can we do that?"

"I don't know all that yet, Hugh," Stanley said. "I just know that's what we're gonna have to do."

When Caperton hung up, he walked into his home's enclosed porch and sat down on a sofa and started to cry. Kathy, who had overheard his side of the conversation, was crying, too. Usually, he was great at consoling his wife, but not this time. For at least an hour, Caperton sat despondently on the back porch, trying to gear himself up to do the whole thing again. Then Fawcett called.

"We're done, finished," Fawcett said.

"Yeah, I know," Caperton said with a shrug.

"No, I mean it. The court killed it for good. Can't retry it."

"That can't be," Caperton insisted. "Bruce said we're going to have to refile and start all over again."

"Bruce called you before we read the whole decision," Fawcett said.

Fawcett went on to explain how they had initially thought that the court had ruled in such a way that the plaintiffs could try the case again. That was what the justices usually did. In this instance, the court had taken the unusual step of dismissing the case with prejudice. That meant the case could not be retried.

"That means we can't do anything else," Fawcett explained. "Unless we could get the United States Supreme Court to look at it, which is probably impossible, it's over."

Caperton hung up, went back onto the porch, and threw a table across the room. He tried to give his family a good Thanksgiving, but a dark future loomed before him. He was such an optimist that he had never spent much thought on what he might do if he lost; now he knew that he had to start thinking of some way to begin a new life and to provide for his little family.

In the next few days, Fawcett and Stanley pored over the court opinion. "At the outset, we wish to make perfectly clear that the facts of this case demonstrate that Massey's conduct warranted the type of judgment in this case," Davis wrote. "However, no matter how sympathetic the facts are, or how egregious the conduct, we simply cannot compromise the law in order to reach a result that clearly appears to be justified."

This was the same argument Davis had made in her dissent in the Arbaugh case. Once again, she played the role of a principled, stalwart defender of the law who would not go beyond its well-defined parameters even to render the noblest of results. She tried to show in indisputable logic why Hoke should not have allowed the trial to take place in West Virginia when the contract between Harman and Wellmore/

United mandated that legal proceedings occur in Virginia. She went on to say that Hoke also should have thrown the case out because Caperton had had his day in Virginia and had no right, because of res judicata, to seek a second hearing.

As he read and reread Davis's opinion, Fawcett couldn't help admiring the shrewd and sophisticated way she had gone about rejecting the Boone County verdict. It was not just that she had chosen reasons that would end the case forever but that she had done it with a surface logic that would seem to preempt any criticism. Only those with a deep understanding of West Virginia law would see that Davis had summarily discarded the state's law on forum selection by, in effect, adding eight new points of law and a new test to determine the proper venue and had then applied the whole jerry-built mechanism retroactively.

In his dissent, Albright criticized Davis and her "'consolation prize' language," which expressed dismay at what Massey had done to Caperton's company and then concluded that, alas, the law required that the injustice be allowed to stand. Albright wrote that Davis arrived at her conclusions about forum selection "by adopting by judicial fiat 'new law' not previously found in West Virginia's jurisprudence and applying that 'new law' at every turn in the manner most likely to yield the result of overturning the jury's verdict." He argued that the chief justice came to her conclusions about res judicata only by engaging in a "convoluted discussion of claims, causes of action and remedies to hide the fact that it molds the law to attain the desired result, without recourse to the historical differences between contract and tort actions."

"The point is that the majority went out of its way to make findings that fit its intended result rather than the justice of the cause," Albright concluded, putting that sentence in boldface.

In their years of struggle, Caperton's legal team had worked brilliantly together. On the rare occasions when they'd disagreed, they'd rigorously masked even the slightest internal dissension. But now it all spilled out. Fawcett was angry at Berthold for having known so little about the court. Stanley was disheartened that Fawcett had not stood up to Davis, although he himself had not done any better. The lawyers did not confront each other, but there were tensions.

"As this went on, you could feel the anger inside each one of us," Fawcett reflected several years later. "We tried to maintain respect, but you couldn't justify what was happening. I couldn't say to Hugh, 'Oh well, this kind of thing happens.' And Bruce had no explanation, either. It was taken away from us before our eyes, something that we had worked for and had prevailed."

Caperton was more distraught than his lawyers, who at least had careers and other cases and other trials. As Caperton saw it, he had nothing, and he welcomed any chance to do anything other than sit in front of his computer in his bare office, trying to figure out what to do.

On the first day of December 2007, Caperton hauled a ladder out of the garage and put it up against the wall of his house. He loved tinkering around the house, and the task gave him something to focus on besides his gnawing worries.

He strapped a leaf blower onto his back, worked his way up the rungs of the ladder, and got to work clearing leaves from the gutters. After only a few moments, the pads beneath the ladder began sliding, and he fell twenty feet to the ground, the machine strapped to his back. As he lay there, the machine still blowing, he knew that he had broken his back.

The police interrupted the town Christmas parade so that the ambulance carrying Caperton could get through. At Beckley's Raleigh General Hospital, he was wheeled in for a CAT scan.

"Mrs. Caperton," the radiologist said, "your husband has a broken back and a broken foot. His right foot is broken in eight places, and his left foot is badly strained. But he has a problem beyond today's accident. He has a tumor on his kidney." Before probing the growth for cancer, however, the doctors wanted to wait until Caperton's bones healed.

Caperton spent four days in intensive care, drifting in and out of consciousness. After ten days, he was released to a home hospital bed, where he lay immobile, a cast on one foot and medical boots on both feet. That gave him plenty of time to ponder what he would do if the diagnosis turned out to be cancer. Who would hire him then? How could he feed his family?

46

After the Supreme Court of Appeals of West Virginia's ruling, the managing partners at Buchanan Ingersoll and Reed Smith left it up to Fawcett and Stanley to decide what to do. *Caperton* had cost the two law firms around $7 million, and with the definitive results in the Supreme Court of Appeals of West Virginia, no one would have faulted Fawcett and Stanley for walking away. Instead, they set out with renewed energy and passion to find some way to win their case.

The first thing they did was to craft a petition asking the Supreme Court of Appeals of West Virginia for a rehearing. The petition asserted that the chief justice had unconstitutionally rewritten West Virginia laws and had "applied these new and unforeseeable statements of law retroactively to the Appellees." They knew their chances were infinitesimal, but they were making the larger point that they were still pounding on the courtroom door and would not be going away. Fawcett and Stanley tried to keep Caperton informed about what they were doing, but between the fog of pain and all the drugs he was taking, their updates faded into confused memories and dreams.

When the Charleston court refused to rehear *Caperton,* Fawcett and Stanley knew that their only chance of forcing the Supreme Court of Appeals of West Virginia to rehear the case was to have the United States Supreme Court hear it—where they would argue that Benjamin should have recused himself. But the Supreme Court took less than

1 percent of the petitions it received, and the duo's chances were no better than if they had been in West Virginia. Even if *Caperton* was heard by the nine justices and the court ruled that Benjamin should have recused himself, that would mean not that they had won but only that they would be going back to the Charleston court to be heard—presumably by two of the justices who had voted against them and a third judge brought in to replace Benjamin.

Fawcett took the lead in finding an appellate attorney who could raise the odds of being heard before the United States Supreme Court. He set his sights on Theodore Olson, knowing that the Washington lawyer had great cachet with the high court. He believed the leading conservative appellate attorney in America could win over the four of the nine justices who were his friends and ideological colleagues, and he would have a chance of winning 9–0.

Neither of the Pittsburgh lawyers was likely to have much of a political rapport with Olson, who had represented George W. Bush before the Supreme Court in the 2000 contested presidential election. Stanley believed that Olson had given America the worst president in a hundred years. Fawcett considered Olson an uncompromising right-winger who wanted not only to attack liberals but also to stomp out what was left of the moderate wing of the Republican Party, of which Fawcett was a proud member. Fawcett was so disenchanted with the direction his party had taken under Bush and with right-leaning local politicians that in early 2008 he registered as a Democrat, so that he could vote for Barack Obama in the Pennsylvania presidential primary, a turnaround that was mentioned in the *Pittsburgh Post-Gazette*.

Olson not only was the leading conservative attorney in the capital but, indeed, relished lashing out at Democrats. In 2006, before a wildly appreciative audience at the annual gathering of the right-wing Federalist Society, Olson said that the House of Representatives could amuse itself by "searching for any sign of movement in Speaker [elect] Pelosi's forehead," while senators could take pleasure observing "the expressionless, Pelosi-like forehead of Senator Clinton."

Olson's clients were primarily corporations, and now Fawcett would be asking him to take a case in which he would likely be more inclined to argue in favor of Blankenship's right to make limitless campaign contributions. Fawcett sensed that despite his public persona, Olson was more of a lawyer than an ideologue, and he felt that Olson's commitment to the justice system would trump the political overtones of the case.

Fawcett e-mailed Olson on December 13, 2007, asking if he would become involved. Though inundated by such requests, Olson looked at this one with a certain interest. Although his liberal detractors would question this characterization, Olson did in fact consider himself a fierce defender of a fair, neutral judiciary. As more and more campaign money descended on judicial races, the question had to be asked whether that money so tainted a recipient like Benjamin that he could not possibly render what a fair-minded person would consider unbiased justice. That was the constitutional issue that intrigued Olson: whether Benjamin had violated Caperton's rights to due process and a fair trial by not recusing himself.

The Supreme Court did not like to intrude in recusal questions. The last time it had done so was in 1984, and Olson had made the winning arguments. He had represented Aetna in *Aetna Life Insurance Co. v. Lavoie*. The issue was whether Alabama Supreme Court Justice Eric Embry should have recused himself in a case involving Aetna, since he had filed two personal cases against the insurance giant. The Supreme Court found that Aetna's rights had been abridged, and Embry was wrong.

Having nearly been nominated to the U.S. Supreme Court, Olson had deep insights into the minds of the justices and how they decided what cases to take. He knew that one day they would have to deal with the issue of recusal and large campaign contributions. Although he believed that Caperton's rights to due process had been violated, everything he knew about the court told him that they would not find *Caperton* the appropriate case to deal with such a crucial issue.

Olson's associate Amir Tayrani dealt with requests like Fawcett's e-mail. Tayrani made time to peruse the material and draw some conclusions. He did not even reach the point of considering the issues involved, for he was convinced that there was no chance of getting the case to the U.S. Supreme Court. The reality, he thought, was that "the opinion was about state law or contract issues and the U.S. Supreme Court doesn't have jurisdiction to review those issues."

On January 9, 2008, Tayrani called Fawcett with an unequivocal no, but Fawcett took it as a maybe, and he kept e-mailing Tayrani, trying to get him intrigued. Fawcett could not comprehend how the Supreme Court could pass on the case. It was not an issue of liberal versus conservative politics. If a judge was free to receive large campaign contributions from a litigant during a case and still hear the case, our entire legal system was in peril.

47

Despite their perfect record of rejection by the Supreme Court of Appeals of West Virginia, on January 4, 2008, Stanley filed a motion seeking to nullify Maynard's vote in *Caperton* and send the case back for a rehearing. He argued that the justice had had an affirmative duty to disclose his relationship with Blankenship, but he had not done so. Everyone in politics and the law in the state knew that the two men were close, but nobody did anything about it or dared to confront the justice.

Stanley had heard rumors that Maynard and Blankenship had vacationed in Europe together and that, upon their return, they had dined together. The idea of the two men going abroad together was so far-fetched that Stanley did not mention it in the motion. He did throw in a charge that the two friends had shared a meal three months before the court hearing, though, he admitted, he'd been "unable to independently verify" it. The story—and the entire motion—showed just how little hope remained. But at least they were taking some sort of action, and Fawcett e-mailed Tayrani, telling him what they had done.

Starcher watched Stanley's futile attempts to get Maynard to come clean with appalled fascination. Starcher was infuriated by the continued dismantling of everything he had cared for and fought for at the Supreme Court of Appeals of West Virginia. He was angry at Davis and Benjamin, but he directed most of his wrath at Maynard, who he considered an arrogant, corrupt servant of the most powerful business interests in the state.

Starcher could not stand the idea of Maynard's unchallenged ascendency in the court. His elevation to chief justice in January 2008 so offended Starcher that he refused to sit for the annual court photo. "Not only am I doing it just to p—— him off," Starcher wrote in his diary, showing a discretion in written prose that he did not usually exhibit in speech, "but I also have a fear that I might end up seeing the new Court photo in some of his election materials."

Starcher was further angered by Massey's troublesome lawsuit demanding that he recuse himself in all Massey-connected issues. On January 8, 2008, he wrote in his diary that he had decided that if "the evil three [Davis, Maynard, and Benjamin] plan to 'sell me down the river,'" he would "introduce the other side of Blankenship's case—his relationship to other members of the Court."

Starcher set out, in one last, great populist crusade, to destroy Maynard. He was sure that the story about the photos was true. He knew that several of the court employees had the disks, but they would not give them up, and nobody else who could help him would talk. If Starcher did not find them soon, his opportunity would vanish.

The court was now rife with suspicion and fear. Magann had lost her protector when she'd broken up with Maynard. Starcher had heard that Blankenship had called Magann and warned her in ominous tones not to show the photos to anyone. Henley was even more fearful. She knew that she had something that could change the whole nature of the Supreme Court of Appeals of West Virginia. The potential power of those photos had begun to unnerve her. It was a scary thing, having the photos and not knowing what people would do to get hold of them.

On Wednesday, January 9, 2008, as Stanley headed back to Pittsburgh from a long day in Logan attending a meeting with the Aracoma widows, his phone rang. A voice he knew well and whose identity he has never revealed said that a package he would want to see had been delivered to a law office in Charleston a few minutes earlier and asked when he could stop by to get it.

Stanley turned around and drove to downtown Charleston, where a plain brown envelope sat on a desk. Though he could be wildly impulsive and might have torn it open, he realized that the package could contain evidence of a crime. He lifted the envelope with a handkerchief, so that he wouldn't smudge any fingerprints, dropped it into his briefcase, and got back on the road to Pittsburgh. There, he locked it within a safe at Reed Smith.

Stanley decided to retain the services of a former U.S. attorney, who, in turn, hired two retired federal investigators. It was not until Friday morning, two days after Stanley retrieved the parcel, that Stanley and Abdalla met with the three men at Reed Smith's offices. Stanley brought in a videographer and a court reporter to record the opening of the envelope.

As Stanley and Abdalla looked on, the agents began to process the evidence systematically. The lead investigator gently worked open the flap, careful not to tear it. With gloved hands, he reached in and pulled out a computer disk. For the first time, Stanley thought that this might be the evidence he'd heard about of a Blankenship-Maynard rendezvous. The investigator inserted the disk into a computer and began a slide show. Within moments, Stanley saw what he'd thought he would never be able to prove: Maynard and Blankenship playing tourists in an exotic location. One photo showed the two sitting with champagne glasses at a café high above the ocean. Another one showed the men with two decidedly younger women at their sides. This was the smoking gun, and Stanley could virtually sniff the acrid stench. As the multiple images came out of the printer, he and Abdalla smiled broadly.

The dates stamped on the thirty-four photos revealed that they had been taken on July 3, 4, and 5, 2006. Still, Stanley worried that he was being played, and that perhaps the images had been doctored by someone working for Blankenship, someone trying to nail Stanley for falsifying evidence. So he and Abdalla retained a computer forensic expert, who established beyond any doubt that the photos had not been altered and that they had been taken in Monaco and France on the dates indicated.

As a lawyer, Stanley was an officer of the court, and he knew that it was his duty to surrender the original disk to law enforcement officers. Because of their suggestion that Blankenship had possibly bribed Maynard by paying any expenses of the Mediterranean trip, the photos required the involvement of the U.S. attorney in Charleston.

Stanley had the investigators seal the evidence and lock it inside Reed Smith's safe until an FBI agent could collect it. But he first made copies that he could use to file a motion at the Supreme Court of Appeals of West Virginia and give to certain journalists.

Caperton, meanwhile, was driving home from Ohio, where he had seen a cancer specialist at the renowned Cleveland Clinic. The doctor had said that his kidney tumor was malignant and would have to be removed but that surgery would likely eradicate the cancer.

Caperton had thought that the Supreme Court of Appeals of West Virginia's dismissal of *Caperton* was the worst thing that had ever happened to him. But the health problems that had begun almost immediately afterward had put everything in a different perspective. This was literally life or death, and he did not have the option of getting morbid or feeling sorry for himself. He played his usual upbeat self, pumping up Kathy as he drove, wishing he did not have to endure the three-hundred-mile trip in a full body brace, both feet in casts.

Then the phone rang. It was Stanley, who had a lilt in his voice that Caperton had not heard for weeks. "Got some news for you, brother," Stanley said. "You're not gonna believe this, but I'm sitting here looking at what I think are pictures of Don and Spike and their girlfriends. We gottta verify it, but looks like they're off in Europe vacationing a couple summers ago."

"Oh, my God!" Caperton said. The pain he had been suffering had been so bad that he had not been able to follow what Stanley and Fawcett were doing. But he had heard the rumors about the photos and realized that this could send *Caperton* back to the Charleston court, where this time it most certainly would be affirmed.

Stanley next called Fawcett, and they discussed how to proceed. The Supreme Court of Appeals of West Virginia had not yet acted on Stanley's motion to have Maynard recuse himself. Thus, over the weekend Stanley and Fawcett worked on a supplemental amended motion to have Maynard's vote in *Caperton* thrown out, forcing a rehearing with another justice taking Maynard's seat.

That was not all the two lawyers did that weekend. For years Stanley and Fawcett had been cultivating national media outlets, seeking coverage of what they considered a case worthy of attention. They had an intuitive sense that in order to get justice, they needed to involve journalists. As early as March 2001, Fawcett had written a five-page, single-spaced letter to a *Wall Street Journal* reporter. Nothing had come of that or any of their other attempts to woo journalists outside the state, but the two lawyers had kept trying anyway.

Like Olson, the national media considered *Caperton* a local story, unworthy of their or the country's attention. For years the media had refused to hitch themselves to the case, but by now the two lawyers had built a roster of media contacts who knew them and had reason to trust what they were saying. In pitching the story this weekend they put their case at the center, saying that they were filing the photos with the Charleston court in an attempt to have Maynard recuse himself and the case reheard. That way *Caperton* became as much a part of the story as the photos themselves.

In Pittsburgh, Fawcett tracked down Len Boselovic, a *Pittsburgh Post-Gazette* reporter, then drove to his home that Saturday to tell him the story. Boselovic had written about *Wheeling-Pitt* but never about *Caperton*. Fawcett's voice shook as he talked to the reporter, who thought the lawyer was playacting. But just as Fawcett was beginning to tell his tale, his cell phone rang. It was Adam Liptak of the *New York Times,* returning his call.

Stanley worked all weekend and stayed up late into the night on Sunday, trading drafts with Fawcett and putting the final touches on his supplemental motion for recusal. Stanley rose early Monday morning to make the four-hour trek to Charleston. He had decided that the photos showing the duo's female companions should be filed under seal. He did not want to be accused of ruining their reputations, although as a former journalist he also knew that the mystery of who had traveled with Blankenship and Maynard would keep the story going a few extra days. Fawcett thought the strategy was brilliant, but he still worried something would go wrong.

That Monday Stanley had scarcely filed the supplemental motion with the court clerk when the news reverberated through the building. "We had a staff meeting at 1:30," Starcher noted in his diary. "We were interrupted before 2:00 by one of Rory's (Court Clerk) clerks—she brought me copies of an Amended Recusal (of Maynard) Motion along with 34 photos (of the Monte Carlo Maynard-Blankenship vacation). What an explosion! The rest of the afternoon was spent chatting, looking at the materials given to me, calling others and anticipating what will happen next. Maynard was in his office all afternoon powwowing with people."

The next morning, January 15, 2008, Liptak's story appeared in the front section of the *Times,* accompanied by a photo of the two happy friends in Monte Carlo, smiling for the camera with empty champagne flutes lined up before them, a picture that could have run in the paper's travel section. "A justice of the Supreme Court of Appeals of West Virginia and a powerful coal-company executive met in Monte Carlo in the summer of 2006, sharing several meals even as the executive's companies were appealing a $50 million jury verdict against them to the court," the article began.

Liptak's story was the national media's first mention of the case, and the *Times'* imprimatur bestowed importance. That same day, Boselovic's story ran on the front page of the *Post-Gazette.* In Charleston, Stanley had talked to the AP's Lawrence Messina, who was also talking surreptitiously to Starcher. Messina's story went out from Charleston on the national wire. For years, the *Charleston Gazette's* Paul Nyden had fought a lonely struggle to expose Massey's conduct. Stanley had known and admired Nyden for a long time, and when he told the reporter the news, he could barely contain his excitement and delight. Nyden's story ran on the front page of the Charleston paper.

When Blankenship got back from Europe, he told a close associate that he had not liked Europe much. And now he had to deal with this. Blankenship and Maynard responded the day after the front-page news stories. "I don't know if it's totally a coincidence," Blankenship said. "I know that we didn't travel together, we didn't vacation together." His friend concurred. "The suggestion that I have done something improper is nonsense," Maynard told the *Charleston Gazette.*

Maynard had initially indicated his intention not to recuse. But with all the negative publicity, his reelection was no longer a sure thing, and he decided to remove himself to try to get the focus off him. "I have no doubt in my mind and firmly believe I have been and would be impartial in this case," Maynard averred. A few days later, only nine days after the photos publicly surfaced, the state supreme court voted 5–0 to rehear *Caperton,* setting a date in March 2008.

Stanley and Fawcett believed that this was not just about Maynard but concerned what they considered the institutional corruption of the court. They felt that the moment had come when not only would *Caperton* be honestly and fairly reviewed but the venality of the court would be exposed. Starcher thought the same thing. The justice wrote what he called in his diary a "bomb letter" to Canterbury, asking the court administrator to investigate the Maynard scandal. Canterbury refused to probe his mentor, saying that it was not in the court administrator's jurisdiction, and although FBI agents talked to Crider, she felt they were less than aggressive in asking questions about the court itself.

Facing continued questions about his conduct, Maynard showed AP reporter Messina copies of credit card records that, he claimed, proved that he, not Blankenship, had paid for his flight and hotel room. There remained serious questions about other costs of the trip and the whole relationship between the two old friends.

A serious investigation could have resulted in criminal prosecution of Blankenship, if it was found that he had given something of value to a judge during a pending matter. It could also have cast doubt on the relationship between Davis and Maynard, raising the question of whether her vote in *Caperton* was little more than part of a trade-off for Maynard's past favors. If federal prosecutors with the power of subpoena didn't step in, no one would ever know if these allegations had merit.

In early February 2008, Starcher attended a court meeting to decide what the justices' role would be in investigating one of their own. "We surmised that the four of them (Maynard, Davis, Benjamin, and Canterbury) had certainly talked and 'had a plan,'" Starcher wrote in his diary. "The result was that we [the court] decided to do nothing."

It was not just Starcher who was upset. For the first time, Americans in other places took notice and were equally disdainful of the West Virginia justice system. In April 2008, Dorothy Samuels, of the *New York Times* editorial board, wrote a scathing column berating the "decidedly farcical flavor" in the way the state supreme court was handling *Caperton*. Despite the dishonor dumped on the state, no political leader in West Virginia condemned what had gone on or called for an investigation of Maynard and Blankenship's travels together in Europe while *Caperton* was pending before the justices. The West Virginia State Bar, which supposedly stood for justice, remained on the sidelines, making no comment about a subject that dealt with the very integrity of the judicial system.

Blankenship's libel suit against the *Charleston Gazette* had been thrown out, but for months the state's premier paper backed off from its generally aggressive reporting about Massey and its chairman. Most of the other local journalists did no investigative reporting. Messina was an exception, and under the state's Freedom of Information Act, the AP sued the Supreme Court of Appeals of West Virginia for access to the e-mails Maynard had sent Blankenship from the court's computers. Maynard had been foolish not to communicate with a personal e-mail account from his home computer or personal phone, and the AP was successful in obtaining many e-mails that confirmed the close personal and political relationship.

The *West Virginia Record,* sponsored by the state's chamber of commerce, also sent Freedom of Information requests to the court, seeking to learn not whether Blankenship had bribed Maynard but whether Starcher was "'directing' the media coverage (ABC News, *Wall Street Journal,* etc.) from his office."

"I sure hope that the U.S. Attorney's office moves on this matter," Starcher wrote in his diary on February 5, 2008. "Otherwise Maynard wins." Starcher had been a judge for most of his career, and he knew that the authorities were extremely cautious in how they investigated political corruption. Sometimes indictments never happened, for reasons that had nothing to do with the strength or weakness of the potential case. There was nothing more sensitive for law enforcement than investigating judges; if not done prudently, it might be seen as an attempt to intimidate. That was far from the situation here, and it appeared that no one in government wanted to look too closely at the Charleston court.

The interim United States attorney for the Southern District of West Virginia was Charles T. Miller. One of his assistants was R. Booth Goodwin II, who came from a prominent West Virginia family of lawyers and judges. His wife, Amy Shuler Goodwin, was Maynard's campaign spokeswoman, giving Fawcett and Stanley reason to fear that the federal prosecutors would not pursue the case with vigor.

48

On January 29, 2008, John Grisham appeared on the *Today* show to discuss his new novel, *The Appeal,* which would soon be a number one best seller. The book tells a fictional story of a chemical company that, while appealing a $41 million judgment against it, spends millions to elect a state supreme court justice, who votes to overturn the decision. Host Matt Lauer asked if the plot was far-fetched. "It's already happened," Grisham said. "It happened a few years ago in West Virginia."

Fawcett knew that the novel could never be entered into evidence. But the book did prove the public's interest in the issue and offered yet another compelling reason for the Supreme Court to hear the case. After the program, Fawcett called Tayrani and once again implored him to give Fawcett and Stanley the chance to pitch *Caperton* in person.

"There's lots of stuff you don't know about," Fawcett said. "Can you give us an hour to tell Ted and you some of the background?"

Olson could have spent half his life listening to futile pitches from out-of-town lawyers desperate to hawk their cases. But the media interest in this case had become extraordinary, and Tayrani thought enough of Fawcett's earnestness to once again discuss *Caperton* with Olson. Though Olson was convinced that nothing was going to change his mind, he granted Fawcett and Stanley the professional courtesy of meeting with them in Washington.

On February 6, 2008, Fawcett and Stanley flew from Pittsburgh to Washington through a storm that bounced the small regional jet around. It was the worst flight of their lives, and they were nervous and unsettled even after the plane landed at National Airport.

Stanley was a drinker, but he outdid himself this evening at the hotel bar, downing one cocktail after another. Fawcett had once been a heavy drinker, too. Sitting for hours with Stanley, he renewed his acquaintance, although he could not quite keep up with his thirsty friend. The next morning Stanley was raring to make the pitch, while Fawcett nursed a horrendous hangover.

As a taxi drove them to Gibson, Dunn & Crutcher, Fawcett and Stanley were convinced that, after their ten-year fight, this was the moment that would certify *Caperton* as a historic case, justifying all they had endured. The two lawyers believed that if they could only look Olson in the eye, he would find himself unable to deny them. They had planned every minute of their one-hour appointment.

The Pittsburgh lawyers had never met Olson before, and when Tayrani came out to the reception area and led them into a conference room, they did not know that the Washington attorney usually greeted guests of even modest importance in his large corner office. There they'd see the portrait of Ronald Reagan that the president had signed with "heartfelt thanks" and the white quills symbolizing each of Olson's appearances before the Supreme Court. Olson's office managed a homey warmth unusual for Washington, but the modern, hard-surfaced conference room was the characterless sort found in law offices everywhere.

When Olson eventually walked into the gathering, he had hardly said hello before he was saying good-bye. Apologizing, he explained that he was on his way to the annual luncheon of GOPAC, a powerful Republican 527 organization, where he was to give a speech supporting Senator John McCain's presidential candidacy. Olson could spare the Pittsburgh lawyers only fifteen minutes of his time.

Fawcett nervously rushed through the obligatory pleasantries. "We had quite a time getting here," he said. "We were on the flight from Pittsburgh. It was crazy with the weather, up and down, back and forth. We dropped a couple hundred feet at one point and started thinking about Don Blankenship, and how happy he would be to see our plane go down."

As soon as Fawcett said the words "plane go down," he remembered how Olson's wife had died. He did not want to call attention to his gaffe by apologizing, and he tried to forge ahead, distracted and disconcerted. Stanley realized that Fawcett thought he had made a grievous faux pas and quickly stepped in to rescue his partner. Fawcett collected himself, and before long he had retaken command of the meeting. He showed Olson and Tayrani West Virginia newspaper articles whose front-page headlines screamed the importance of *Caperton,* and documents detailing the millions of dollars Blankenship had poured into Benjamin's campaign.

"This is a fascinating, important case," Olson said. "It's wrong what happened, but I don't see the legal hook that makes it a federal case. Look at your own briefs trying to get Benjamin to recuse himself. It's almost all state laws and state issues. I may be wrong, but I just don't think the court would agree to hear this case."

"But it's a federal issue," Fawcett insisted.

"Of course it is," Olson said. "In the past ten years, all three times the court has been asked to hear cases involving judges receiving large campaign contributions, the court has refused to hear the matter. The issue is percolating up. It's going to happen. But not now, I don't think, not with *Caperton.*"

"It's the perfect case," Stanley said. "Where could you have a more extreme example of everything that's wrong?"

"You're right," Olson said. "And you know what, it's so extreme and so challenging to the fundamental concepts of justice that if the justices ever heard the case, I'm convinced they would find overwhelmingly in your favor. The problem is getting there, and the justices want cases that come to them with the imprimatur of importance. I'm sorry to say this, but I think they'll see *Caperton* as a business dispute between coal companies in a state that people here hardly notice. *Caperton* just doesn't matter to most people. That may not be right or fair, but that's the way it is."

Fawcett and Stanley tried to rebut Olson, but within minutes he was gone. They were left to persuade Tayrani, whose youth, they thought, underscored how Olson regarded their case and all of West Virginia—whose borders lay little more than an hour's drive from the capital.

The two had hardly gotten back to Pittsburgh before Fawcett received an e-mail from Tayrani saying that Olson would not be taking the case. Fawcett interpreted Olson's second rejection as another maybe. He would not give up, and he wanted no other lawyer.

While Fawcett continued trying to woo Olson, he and Stanley had a chance to win *Caperton* without even going before the United States Supreme Court. In March 2008 they returned to the Supreme Court of Appeals of West Virginia. The lawyers counted on once again winning Albright's and Starcher's votes. They figured that the third, and deciding, vote would probably come from the judge appointed to replace Maynard.

But before the court date, that arithmetic changed. Starcher's intemperate public attacks on Blankenship had destroyed his credibility as a neutral jurist in cases involving Massey.

"When I referred to Blankenship as a buffoon, I knew that would most likely result in a recusal motion," Starcher reflected several years later. "I perceived him as a rich, spoiled bully, and I took some pleasure kicking him in the teeth the way I saw him kicking people in the teeth. I probably should have known better. People who know me well enough say, 'That's Starcher being Starcher.'"

Starcher understood that both West Virginia's and the American Bar Association's codes of judicial conduct stated that a "judge shall disqualify himself or herself in any proceeding in which the judge's impartiality might be reasonably questioned." The standard was what a fair-minded layperson would conclude about the judge's impartiality when presented with the crucial facts. And any fair-minded person would have concluded that when the name Massey was called, both Benjamin and Starcher should head for the door.

As much as Starcher despised Blankenship, he realized that if he didn't want to add to the bad name judges were getting from this case, he had no choice but to recuse himself. He believed that Benjamin should disqualify himself, too. Starcher felt he could not go to the colleague he had publicly rebuked and privately ask him to recuse himself. Instead, he tried to shame him in public, likely making Benjamin even more determined to vote a second time on *Caperton*.

Starcher wrote a recusal document that went on for eight pages without once acknowledging the conduct that had forced him to remove himself. "The pernicious effects of Mr. Blankenship's bestowal of his personal wealth and friendship have created a cancer in the affairs of the Court," Starcher wrote. "And I have seen that cancer grow and grow, in ways that I may not fully disclose at this time. At this point, I believe that my stepping aside in the instant case *might* be a step in treating that cancer—but only if others as well rise to the challenge. If they do not, then I shudder to think of the cynicism and disgust that the lawyers, judges and citizens of this wonderful State will feel about our justice system."

The five justices continued to wear their black robes and to act with studied dignity, but the Supreme Court of Appeals of West Virginia was a bickering, ludicrously dysfunctional institution in which the Mad Hatter would have fit right in as chief justice. As it was, Maynard *was* the chief justice, but since he had recused himself in *Caperton,* Benjamin was the acting chief justice—though according to the ABA standards he should have recused himself as well.

Here was an *Alice in Wonderland* moment: Benjamin, whose own credibility in the case had been challenged unsuccessfully by Caperton's lawyers, had the extraordinary power to appoint two temporary justices to take Maynard's and Starcher's places. If Benjamin chose those who thought the way he thought, he'd have three votes and be a one-man majority. To replace Maynard Benjamin appointed conservative pro-coal Judge Fred L. Fox. To replace Starcher he appointed Circuit Judge Donald H. Cookman, who had sentenced the fifteen-year-old Arbaugh to fifteen to thirty-five years in prison.

The rehearing centered on forum selection and res judicata, the fulcrum points of Justice Davis's first opinion. Davis asked Massey's attorney, "Mr. Offutt, have you done any research with regard to cases around the country applying the forum selection clause to nonsignatory parties to a contract?" Caperton had signed the contract with Wellmore as head of Harman Coal, not as an individual, and Davis was asking whether he could nonetheless be held to the provisions that all legal disputes had to be settled in Virginia.

"I have, Your Honor," said Offutt.

When it came Fawcett's turn to make his arguments, Davis took on a more adversarial tone.

"Do you agree that the majority of the courts in this country say that a forum selection clause can, in fact, be applied to nonsignatories to a contract?" Davis asked.

"No, I don't. . . . I don't know for certain," Fawcett said, stuttering. "But certainly our argument, Your Honor—"

Fawcett always prepared overwhelmingly for his court appearances, and this was a question he should have expected. But he did not have an answer, and he was not quick enough to deflect the question.

"Is it?" Davis interrupted. "Did you do the research?"

"Yes, yes," Fawcett said.

"But you don't know for sure?"

Stanley cringed. When Fawcett was on, there was no better attorney in a courtroom, but when he had to come up with a quick, unexpected response, he often got into trouble. He had not done well in part of his crucial closing in the Boone County trial. He had faltered with Olson. He had stumbled his first time before Davis, and now he was doing it again.

Stanley was upset with Davis for having patronized Fawcett. When Davis tried to do the same thing to him, he rolled over the top of her voice, refusing to let her overwhelm him. Nor did he allow the arguments to descend into a morass of technical minutiae. He wanted to remind Davis that in writing the majority opinion, she had admitted that Massey's conduct was wrong and despite that had turned her back on the jury's verdict: "We suggest respectfully that after the hard work done by this jury, and after this court's own unanimous conclusion that the jury's verdict was justified and well founded and a fair result, that to yank the rug out from under these cases and impose any other result than that which the trial court came to would be unjust."

When the lawyers and the Capertons walked out of the courtroom that day, Fawcett and Stanley believed that the decision had been made even before the justices had entered the chambers and the hearing had been nothing but a shadow play.

In April 2008, the court announced its opinion. Once again, the justices voted 3–2 to overturn the lower court, with Davis, Benjamin, and Fox constituting the majority. Albright and Cookman noted in their dissent that Davis had applied the same "indefensible legal grounds" while this time "strangely omitting the clearly correct assertion in the original majority opinion that 'Massey's conduct warranted the type of judgment rendered in this case.'"

"West Virginia seemed like a closed society," Fawcett says. "The press and people were afraid. I saw firsthand what it meant to have a chilling effect. The *Charleston Gazette* was muzzled. The West Virginia lawyers should have been marching like the lawyers in Pakistan"—he was referring to the mass protest movement the previous year—"but they were afraid to speak out. I would get these calls from lawyers saying, 'Did you hear that? This is what happened.' At first I thought, 'Wow, this is really interesting and exciting.' But eventually I would say, 'Don't call me again unless you have some evidence or you're willing to go on the record and say this, because what you're doing doesn't help us.'"

49

Fawcett had been talking to Madeleine Sauer, a producer at ABC News, about a possible story. In early March 2008, he flew to New York City to be interviewed by Brian Ross, the network's chief investigative correspondent.

Later that month, Ross and Sauer flew down to Charleston to interview Starcher. The justice sat alone in the courtroom, from which he would soon be retiring, for an hour-long interview with Ross. "He [Blankenship] bought himself a seat on the supreme court," Starcher told Ross and the camera. "That bothered me, and it still bothers me."

A few days after Starcher's interview, ABC associate producer Asa Eslocker, then twenty-seven, drove to southern West Virginia to shoot some footage for Ross's piece. ABC could not get Blankenship to agree to an interview, and Eslocker decided to approach him, uninvited, at his office in Belfry, Kentucky. Eslocker's great-grandfather had died in a coal mine two hours from Belfry, and the young producer felt a special affinity to the story. He started waiting for Blankenship at about 6:00 A.M. Several hours later, when Blankenship's black Cadillac coupe rolled into the parking lot, Eslocker drove in after him. As Blankenship walked toward the modest offices, wearing his usual black sports coat, the ABC producer strode toward the executive, his camera running.

"Mr. Blankenship, ABC News," Eslocker said, from a good twenty feet away. Getting no response, he spoke again: "How are you doing, Mr. Blankenship? ABC News."

Blankenship turned and started walking rapidly toward Eslocker. "If you're going to start taking pictures of me, you're liable to get shot," Blankenship said. "Who are ya?"

"How are you doing, Mr. Blankenship? ABC News," Eslocker repeated. Blankenship moved closer, raising his hand before the lens of the camera, grabbing at the lens finder, trying to rip it away.

"Don't touch my camera," Eslocker said. "Let go of me, sir. Let go of me. I've got a couple questions for you. Why do you feel you have to intimidate the courts?"

"You're trying to cause trouble this morning," Blankenship said, straining Eslocker's shirt collar as he reached for the reporter's throat.

"No, sir, I'm just asking a couple questions."

A burly man came out of the office, backed Eslocker against his car, and said, "It's time for you to go, buddy."

"Yes, sir," Eslocker said.

The footage of Blankenship grabbing at the camera accompanied an April 8, 2008, *ABC World News* story on the West Virginia court scandal that also ran later that evening on *Nightline*. Despite the visual evidence, Blankenship and his supporters contended that Eslocker had first taunted Blankenship and then shoved his camera up close to his face.

Although ABC did not have an interview with Blankenship, one of its reporters talked to Maynard's former mistress Brenda Magann, who claimed that she had no idea who had paid for the Riviera meals, since she was typically in the ladies' room when the checks came. The *Nightline* piece won an Emmy, and Blankenship became one of the best known, most infamous business leaders in America. The footage would be replayed in the coming years whenever Blankenship and Massey made the national news.

The day after the ABC story aired, Fawcett called Olson again. The Washington attorney had seen the ABC story, which demonstrated once again that *Caperton* was no longer an obscure case, unknown outside West Virginia. Now, with all the media play, Olson took Fawcett's call, and Fawcett had the audacity to tell Olson that the case would help Olson further his own reputation. And for the first time, Olson seemed interested.

There remained the issue of money. Tayrani explained that whenever Olson took a case to the Supreme Court, he charged between $1 million and $2 million, plus a bonus if he won. Fawcett had no up-front money, and he tried to get Tayrani to agree to take the case on contingency. Fawcett kept going to the managing partners at Buchanan Ingersoll, getting them to give up larger percentages of their cut of contingency money. Every time Fawcett came back, Tayrani would say, "That certainly makes it more interesting," but it was never quite interesting enough. Fawcett thought he could sweeten the offer if he could find some cash. He asked Cecil Roberts, the president of the UMW, to release the $250,000 that had been frozen in the bankrupt Harman's account for the union's retirement fund. Roberts agreed, putting the union money at risk.

When Fawcett hung up after talking to the union leader, he shook his head and said to himself, "Holy shit, the fucking union is paying Olson. He'd fucking die."

He quickly added, "That's why we're not telling him." Just because you're honest doesn't mean you have to be a fool.

On May 2, 2008, Olson and Tayrani called Fawcett to tell him that they were on board. Fawcett and Stanley knew that they still faced prohibitive odds against the Supreme Court's taking the case. But they also knew that their attorney probably had the best record of getting cases to the court—and of winning.

Fawcett called Caperton, whose Cleveland Clinic surgery had rid him of his cancer. He was as excited as his lawyers and grew even more so later that month, when Maynard lost his court seat in the Democratic primary in a rout. He finished a distant third, behind the two winners, former justice Margaret L. Workman and Starcher's friend Menis E. Ketchum.

Ketchum had used the notorious vacation photos of Blankenship and Maynard in campaign ads attacking Maynard. One of Maynard's other opponents had sent voters across the state negative mailers made to look like vacation postcards. The cards featured a photo of Blankenship and Maynard in Monaco, topped with cursive script that said, "Wish you were here!"

———

Meanwhile, Caperton had begun to receive e-mails from a person who called himself Bo Rumpole. This so-called Rumpole had a website where he described himself as "a lawyer seeking change on the Supreme Court of Appeals of West Virginia," but no one knew who he was. Caperton worried initially that Rumpole was peddling misinformation. But as the months went by, it became clear that Rumpole had an almost perfect ability to predict what was going to take place, as well as details of what had supposedly happened in the recent past.

"When Massey's appeal of your case got filed at the Court, Davis had her law clerks pull the briefs and record and start researching the case," Rumpole e-mailed Caperton on May 16, 2008. "That never happens. Justices never pay attention to a case until after the appeal is granted. But she was paying attention to your case from day one. When a petition for appeal is granted and the case placed on the Court's docket, before the case is argued, the chief justice randomly assigns all of the cases to the five justices in alphabetical order by last name. Davis was the chief justice and, what a surprise, your case was 'randomly' assigned to her."

Rumpole also claimed to have information from his own inside source on how the court had voted a second time to reject *Caperton*. "Davis was obviously keen to prove her first opinion was right," Rumpole wrote in the lengthy e-mail. "It didn't matter what arguments were made; she knew she was right and wasn't going to accept any argument that she was mistaken. When Davis circulated her draft [of the opinion], Cookman wanted some time to draft a decent dissent with Albright, so that they could see if Benjamin and/or Fox would be swayed by the dissent's reasoning. Davis apparently said no and scheduled the opinion conference to vote yes-or-no on her opinion without Cookman having time to talk to Fox. She rammed her opinion through so she could get it released before anyone had a chance to change their vote."

Rumpole made the same kinds of accusations about Davis's alleged deal making with Maynard that Stanley and Fawcett were hearing but could not verify. "As for Davis, she's a real disappointment," Rumpole continued. "I just can't figure out why she's so willing to compromise her integrity to make deals with Maynard. At least, I think she's made deals with him. Basically, she helps out Maynard and looks like a 'balanced' justice who will vote for and against plaintiffs; and in return Maynard votes to support anything Scott Segal does."

A 2002 *Wall Street Journal* article noted that Segal "finds suggestions that his law firm benefits from his wife's rulings 'tremendously offensive,' adding that 'my wife hands down a lot of opinions I do not agree with.'"

The national publicity had persuaded Olson to take the case, but he remained unconvinced that the United States Supreme Court justices would hear it. He believed that the court would conclude that *Caperton* involved no clear federal issue.

Olson delegated the writing of the *Caperton* petition to Tayrani. In a few short years, the writing of Supreme Court briefs had become the thirty-one-year-old Yale Law School grad's specialty. They resembled scientific papers in their precise language and noting of previous cases.

Tayrani was assisted by lawyers from Reed Smith and Buchanan Ingersoll. The firms were among the top three in Pittsburgh, usually in competition with each other for clients and territory. Yet several of the finest attorneys at the two firms thought the appeal so important and respected Fawcett and Stanley so much that they came together for the task.

Tayrani, who spoke the justices' language, took these ideas and worked them into a final brief. It was a powerful document, deeply researched and well argued, in places reading more like a criminal indictment of Blankenship than a civil brief.

The brief argued that *Caperton* "affords the Court an ideal opportunity both to clarify the circumstances in which due process mandates recusal and to restore the public's waning confidence in state judicial systems in the face of the increasingly significant role of campaign contributions in state judicial elections." It declared that "between 1999 and 2006, candidates seeking seats on state supreme courts raised more than $157 million, which is nearly double the amount raised by candidates in the four previous election cycles."

The synergy between the press and Caperton's lawyers was evident in the brief, which cited several newspaper articles, including those by the *Times*' Liptak and the *Gazette*'s Nyden.

Tayrani and his coauthors had written a strong petition, but they could not disguise one weakness: the list of previous cases used to evoke the court record in West Virginia, and to show why the U.S. Supreme Court had jurisdiction and should therefore hear the case, was woefully thin. There was little case history or precedent to justify the Supreme Court's delving into a state court matter that bar associations and state legislatures could fix. That was precisely what Olson had feared all along.

50

Olson and Tayrani felt it was crucial that their petition be accompanied by several supportive friend-of-the-court, or amicus, briefs, which are filed to supplement the parties' arguments and to give their cases more credibility. Despite the apparent unlikelihood of the justices hearing the case, *Caperton* won extraordinary support across America's legal and business communities, measured best by the quality and number of amicus briefs at this early stage.

This didn't just happen naturally. A small group of legal activists, including Professor James Sample of Hofstra University, an attorney with the Brennan Center for Justice, which is associated with New York University School of Law, went out and sought supportive briefs. The Brennan Center had long condemned the pernicious impact of money on judicial elections, and Sample thought *Caperton* offered the ideal opportunity for reform. "This issue had a pedigree that was all on the left," says Sample. "When Olson and Tayrani got in, that was in some ways the tipping point."

The American Bar Association, the professional voice of more than four hundred thousand lawyers, had written the code of conduct that Benjamin had violated. Yet the ABA was reluctant to file an amicus brief when there was so little chance that the court would hear the appeal. At the urging of Sample and his colleagues, the leadership at the ABA changed its mind. The ABA document argued that when a judge's impartiality was questioned, so was the very integrity of the American justice system: "The appearance of impropriety is not dispelled by a judge's belief in his or her impartiality. Where a judge's decision to remain on a case has been met with widespread public disagreement, the negative effects on the courts have been real and immediate."

Another amicus brief came from the Committee for Economic Development (CED), an organization that comprises the heads of America's largest corporations, including Walmart and Intel. Opposed to the intrusion of government into broad areas of American life, the CED might well have supported campaign laws that allowed corporations and business leaders to spend unlimited amounts to elect conservative justices. What worried these executives was the destructive pattern of massive donations, which could come from unions as easily as from trade associations. In its friend-of-the-court brief, the CED told the justices that when enormous campaign contributions "create the perception that legal outcomes can be purchased, economic actors will lose confidence in the judicial system, markets will operate less efficiently, and American enterprise will suffer accordingly."

Olson thought the entire package was about as strong as it could be, but he still did not like his chances. He discussed *Caperton* with an old friend, a judge on the U.S. Court of Appeals, who said, "They'll never take your case. They'll never take it. Not a chance, Ted. And if they do, you're going to lose."

Olson and Tayrani's papers, officially called a petition for writ of certiorari, were filed on July 2, 2008. The Massey lawyers had the right to read the appellate brief and reply, and with the Supreme Court in summer recess they took their time.

Before the Massey respondents filed their brief in opposition to cert, a bizarre development changed the course of the case.

Benjamin was the central figure in Olson and Tayrani's U.S. Supreme Court appeal. The West Virginia justice never imagined that he would be at the focal point of a possibly historic case in the United States Supreme Court in which he was pilloried for his conduct in Charleston. Benjamin decided he was not going to sit back quietly and take this assault on his integrity. On July 28, 2008, the justice filed a fifty-seven-page concurring opinion to the State Supreme Court of West Virginia decision in *Caperton*. The document filled no clear legal purpose and changed nothing in the state court's ruling, but it was Benjamin's bold attempt to enter the dialogue in Washington. Benjamin clearly hoped his words would be read by the nine justices of the United States Supreme Court and would play a role in their decision about whether to hear *Caperton*.

Olson and Tayrani read Benjamin's opinion with elation. By citing many federal cases, he ordained them for inclusion in the official record of the West Virginia case. For months, Olson had feared that the court might conclude that the case lacked a federal legal hook. And here this overwrought, angry judge had given them a gift for the ages. By the time they finished reading Benjamin's opinion, the two attorneys were convinced that the United States Supreme Court would hear their case.

Benjamin took an extreme position in defending himself. He preached and he postured, presenting himself as untainted by bias, a champion of true justice whose motives and actions could not be questioned. He maintained that no judge need recuse himself unless he had a "'direct, personal, substantial [or] pecuniary interest' in the outcome of the case."

Benjamin did not mention the ads pillorying McGraw for freeing Arbaugh, which had been the crucial element in electing the justice to office. Instead, he insisted that he had won because of his "campaign's message of fairness, stability and predictability in decision-making and the need for judges to exercise civility, integrity and personal professionalism."

Benjamin showered the pages with legal references. He seemed not to understand that the seemingly interminable brief—in which one single-spaced "footnote" went on for four pages—would squander the nine justices' time. He sought to ingratiate himself with his presumed brethren, quoting Justice Scalia extensively, squeezing in a mention of an essay Justice Ruth Ginsburg had written, and concluding with a line of appreciation for Justice Stephen Breyer's "note of caution" in a lower-court opinion.

For Olson and Tayrani, the brief's timing was exquisite. The Massey lawyers had not yet replied to the original brief, and on August 16, 2008, Tayrani zapped off a supplementary brief to the Supreme Court, attaching Benjamin's concurring opinion.

In his supplemental brief, Tayrani took only five pages to make his points. He paraded a list of federal cases the West Virginia judge had invoked, then went on to suggest that in refusing to admit even to the possibility of bias, Benjamin was a superb example of why the Supreme Court should act. Tayrani concluded, "This Court's review is necessary to restore public confidence in state courts inundated by staggering financial contributions to judges who insist on deciding their financial supporters' cases in the absence of evidentiary proof of actual bias."

The Massey lawyers did not submit their brief in opposition to cert until September 16, 2008. In it, they questioned whether the Supreme Court had jurisdiction over a state matter. Then they raised a larger, more ominous concern: if the justices acted precipitously, they might well face a barrage of First Amendment challenges and further legal problems about the vague nature of recusal standards. Beyond that, they said, *Caperton* was the wrong case at the wrong time. The Massey lawyers argued that "it would be unwarranted and at least premature for the Court to enter this area of traditional state concern, wielding the blunt instrument of a federal due process ruling."

In early October 2008, at their weekly conference, the Supreme Court justices discussed whether they should hear *Caperton*. Such matters were usually quickly decided—it took only four votes to grant a hearing—but they came to no decision and tabled the matter until the next week's hearing. They did the same thing for four weeks in a row.

Olson did not know what went on inside the justices' chambers, but he sensed that the nine judges realized that *Caperton* was a case that could dramatically change how judges were elected, and some of them were reluctant to step into the fray. Fawcett and Stanley were beside themselves with anxiousness.

Professor Sample, at the Brennan Center, was almost as apprehensive as the two Pittsburgh lawyers. He had been working for judicial reform for years, and he thought *Caperton* was the device that would push the Supreme Court to limit campaign spending in judicial elections. He feared that the justices were about to take the easy, expedient way out and not hear the case. Sample made an urgent visit to Dorothy Samuels at the *New York Times*. Like Sample, Samuels deplored the way she believed money polluted the justice system.

On Wednesday, November 12, 2008, the *Times* printed an unsigned editorial written by Samuels, titled "Tainted Justice." Some editorials are written to sway voters. Others push for political action. This one issued a rare direct challenge to the nine justices of the United States Supreme

Court. The implication was that if the Supreme Court could not hear a case about campaign contributions and the possibility of judicial corruption, that raised a question about the court itself and whether it was willing to face such a crucial issue forthrightly.

Samuels wrote, "For some reason, the court seems reluctant to add the case to the docket for the current term. Since the term began, the Massey case has been on the agenda at four meetings where the justices considered new cases. It will be on the agenda again at a meeting on Friday. Surely there must be the requisite four votes on the Supreme Court for taking the case."

In all probability, no one will ever know if the editorial of the most powerful paper in America affected the court's decision to hear *Caperton*. What was likely, however, was that if the justices did not decide that Friday to hear the case they never would.

51

O n November 10, 2008, two days before the *New York Times* editorial
appeared, and two years and ten months after Bragg and Hatfield died at
Aracoma, Stanley rose before Judge Roger L. Perry in the Logan County
Courthouse to make his opening statement in *Bragg and Hatfield v.
Aracoma, Massey and Blankenship*. The lawyer had kept his promise to
Delorice Bragg that he would file claims against not only the parent
company, Massey, and its Aracoma subsidiary but against Blankenship
personally.

Before speaking a word, Stanley looked over at Delorice Bragg and
Freda Hatfield, who sat at the plaintiffs' table. They were nervously awaiting their turn on the witness stand and a confrontation with the defense
lawyers. That would not come until after Stanley had argued that Blankenship's obsession with profits had killed their husbands. Blankenship
was not in the courtroom this morning, but he would be the star witness.

"Don Israel 'Rizzle' Bragg, thirty-three, of Accoville, went to be with
the Lord Thursday, January 19th, 2006, from the Aracoma Coal Company's Alma mine at Melville," Stanley began, speaking in the accent
and idiom of the land of his childhood, which he amplified—not to pan-
der to the jury but to emphasize his kinship with the culture and people
of the coal fields.

"Born January 18th, 1973, at Man, he was the son of Joyce Imes of
Accoville and Donald Nunley of Kistler," Stanley continued. "Preced-

ing him in death was paternal grandparents, James O., Sr., and Barbara Atkinson Bragg; his maternal grandparents, Matthew and Florence Nunley; one niece, Leah Grace Adkins, and two uncles, Joe Bragg and Charles Richmond."

As Stanley spoke, the jury and everyone in the courtroom looked not at the lawyer but at a sequence of photos on a screen, candid snapshots of an exuberant, joyful man and his life. When Stanley finished talking about Bragg, he spoke in equal length and detail about Hatfield's life, and there were photos of him that showed him, like his mine buddy, beaming with happiness.

Stanley did not say that he was reading Bragg's and Hatfield's obituaries from the *Logan Banner,* but almost everyone in the courtroom knew that he was. As he called out the men's names and those of their many relatives, it seemed he was tolling the mourning bells again. He had not prepared the widows for this, and they sobbed. Tonya sat next to Delorice and Freda, holding their hands, crying along with them.

Stanley told the jury that Blankenship had created not a company but a machine devoted to profits at any cost, even death. The lawyer intended to show that the Massey chairman cared nothing about an employee, whether a novice miner or the highest-ranking executive. If they could not deliver what Blankenship told them to deliver in the way he told them to deliver it, they were gone. The CEO mouthed the platitudes of safety, but he pushed his employees so mercilessly that they had little time to abide by federally mandated safety procedures, without which, sooner or later, miners would die. Stanley created a brutal and terrifying image of the company that dominated the lives and livelihoods of coal country.

Stanley described the longwall machine as the essential creature of the Aracoma mine, far more valuable to Massey than miners such as Rizzle and Elvis, who served it. The longwall is a massive device that moves a thousand feet across a seam face, clawing out a three-foot swath of coal at a time. These machines are so expensive that there were only four of them in the more than fifty Massey mines. Blankenship insisted that he receive production reports every two hours, faxed to his office during the day and to his house at night. Aracoma's Alma Mine No. 1 produced more than two million tons of coal a year. The operation was extremely capital-intensive, and on the shift in which Bragg and Hatfield died only twenty-seven men were working in the mine.

"The evidence is going to show that Massey invested as much as $80 million cash in this longwall operation, and that by the time of this fire, this operation wasn't making money," Stanley said. "We believe the evidence is going to show that a tremendous amount of pressure was placed on mine management from the highest levels of Massey to force them to mine coal at the expense of fundamental safety in the mine."

Since there were two sets of defendants—the corporate defendants and Blankenship personally—their representatives here comprised two sets of highly touted defense lawyers. To fight the formidable group, Stanley had brought a strong team to Logan, including two young attorneys, Alicia Schmitt and Will Sheridan, paralegal Mary Beth Alexander, and tech specialist John Worobij, who had made the video displays for the trial.

Stanley showed the jury a series of photos documenting the fire: the seared-away mine support, the burned belt, the carbon monoxide warning system that should have been with the victims' mining crew but was absent from their section, the mini-train the men took to try to escape, and Elvis's lunch box.

"We're going to ask you to find that Don Blankenship intentionally or recklessly committed outrageous conduct, which caused severe emotional distress to the plaintiffs," Stanley concluded. "We're going to ask you to be patient with us, and we're going to ask you to do justice."

When Charleston attorney Niall A. Paul made the opening statement for the two corporate defendants, Aracoma and Massey, he was fighting against not just Stanley's passionate attack but the government's own version of what had happened. The federal Mine Safety and Health Administration (MSHA), the state Office of Miners' Health, Safety and Training, and Governor Joe Manchin's independent task force had all done lengthy, serious investigations into the deaths, and they had all made similar conclusions. In its report, MSHA stated baldly that "the fire would not have resulted in the two fatalities" if mine management had not recklessly disregarded safety rules. Although the reports were the most devastating critique of management in the contemporary annals of the industry, they did not probe whether the Massey corporate culture, with its obsession over maximizing profit, had led to the deaths. That was a matter Stanley intended to address in this courtroom.

"I'm not standing here in front of you saying that no mistakes were made," began Paul, who kept referring to Bragg by the diminutive "Donnie," which his friends and family had never called him. "Mistakes were made; poor decisions were made. There's no question that things could have been done better. And in hindsight, things certainly could have been done differently and perhaps in a way that could have saved Mr. Bragg and Mr. Hatfield."

Paul then suggested to the jury that Bragg and Hatfield were complicit in their own deaths. "What we know beyond any doubt is that Aracoma provided all twelve [miners] with a secure secondary escape way, and trained them on how to get to it, and trained them to use it," Paul said. "We will prove to you that putting [a self-contained self-rescuer] on and getting to a safe airway is what saved ten out of twelve. But the issue is nobody at Aracoma knew the [two] men weren't going to follow their training."

As Paul sat down, Blankenship's personal attorney Thomas V. Flaherty stood to present his client's defense. Stanley had met the Charleston lawyer in 2002 just before the Boone County trial, when he'd handled the failed mediation in *Caperton*. As soon as Flaherty began to speak, Stanley knew that this was no longer the judicious mediator he had come to respect that day in the West Virginia capital.

Flaherty tried to distance Blankenship from the company's disaster. He told the jury that Massey was "a lot like real parents because real parents can try their best to tell the children how they should do their job, but they can't make them do everything." Then he compared Blankenship to another corporate leader whose product the jurors would recognize. "That CEO at McDonald's is no different than Don Blankenship at Massey Energy," Flaherty said. "That person sets policy. Maybe he tells them, 'This is how a Big Mac is going to be fixed,' so that when you get a Big Mac here or you get one in Kentucky, it's going to taste the same."

Flaherty acknowledged that Blankenship was an outspoken man, but he described his brutal candor as a mark of sincere concern. "He is not one to pussyfoot around with language and soft-pedal something," Flaherty said. "But he is a man that has done more for safety in the coalmining industry than anybody. He does not belong in this case."

After the day in court, Stanley, Tonya, and the rest of the team headed over to a conference room in the offices of a Logan attorney. Each member of the team focused on a task. Tonya had never been around lawyers who worked this way, and at times she distracted them with her comments and suggestions. There was no time for this, and Stanley had to explain to the others that Tonya was trying to help and that they would just have to deal with her as she was. Hatfield had a richly empathetic understanding of the two widows and was making her own contribution to the trial. She accepted whatever Stanley wanted her to do. He had not yet told her if she would be examining any of the witnesses.

There was almost nowhere left to eat or to shop in the town, which, like the coal economy around it, was slowly dying. When a business closed, whether the Capitol Movie Theater, the City Florist, or the G. C. Murphy dime store, no one bothered taking down the store's name or putting a rental sign in the windows. The places sat there frozen in their moment, year after year growing more coated with coal dust from the trains that rumbled through the center of town.

As soon as the legal team finished its work, everyone drove out of town to the Chief Logan Lodge. Stanley had eaten nothing during the day and had a big dinner before heading to his room to prepare for a few more hours. As consumed as he was with the trial, he kept thinking about the United States Supreme Court and how unlikely it was, after more than a month, that the justices would agree to hear *Caperton*. He knew nothing about the *New York Times* editorial in the works and what impact it might or might not have.

The following morning Stanley called his first witness, a longtime mine inspector with the West Virginia Office of Miners' Health, Safety and Training. Ernest Eugene White had worked with federal MSHA officials investigating the fire, and Stanley asked him to play the PowerPoint presentation his agency had used when it had presented its report. That way the jury could hear a narrative account of the fire based on about a hundred interviews and a detailed examination of the mine.

White said that at about 5:15 P.M. on January 19, 2006, several miners tried to use extinguishers to put out a small fire deep in the mine caused by a misaligned belt. The flames kept rising, reaching up to six feet. The miners attempted to attach a red fire hose to a water valve, but the threads were incompatible and they threw it aside.

Deeper in the mine, alerted to the fire more than half an hour after it started, foreman Michael Plumley ordered the dozen miners who reported to him, including Bragg and Hatfield, to jump onto a mini-train and ride away from the blaze. The twelve men joked as the vehicle moved through a tunnel, but they then smelled a burning odor and found themselves traveling through a light smoky haze. In an instant, they were enveloped in smoke and could not even see their hands.

In the blackness, the miners placed the mouthpieces of their self-rescuer devices between their lips and started breathing a nauseating, burning chemical mixture designed to provide each of them an hour's worth of oxygen. Feeling their way along the coal ribs, they managed to exit through one of the small safety doors that separated the various sections of the mine so that fire theoretically could not spread through the entire mine. They entered into a secondary escapeway with clear air.

Once Plumley moved through the escapeway, he realized that Bragg and Hatfield were missing. Several of the men opened the safety door from which they had just exited and shouted out into the dark smoke, but no one responded.

Over the next few hours, rescuers were hampered because of a number of serious failings in mandated protections. Not only was the communications system faulty, but the mine's air system had been reversed, feeding the fire, and the mine maps were inaccurate. It was not until the next day that the flames had been quelled enough to allow a thorough search for the two men.

"At approximately 2:47 P.M., Mr. Bragg was located," White said. "At approximately 3:20 P.M., Mr. Hatfield was located. At approximately 3:34 P.M., command center orders all mine rescue teams to stop exploring, monitor fire area, and wait further instructions. And that is the conclusion of the PowerPoint presentation. Thank you."

In his rebuttal, Paul tried to minimize the importance of the mining violations and to get the jury thinking again about Bragg's and Hatfield's possible complicity in their own deaths.

"And so some of the men stayed together, putting their hands on the rib or putting their hands on each other, and then found the man door, correct?" Paul asked.

"Correct," White said.

"And again the terrible tragedy of Mr. Bragg and Mr. Hatfield not finding the man door?" the defense lawyer asked in his final question.

"Correct," White said.

Stanley next called a series of witnesses who were working as managers during the mine fire, starting with Bryan Scott Cabell, who oversaw the belt system. He was a crucial witness because all three investigations had concluded that the fire was caused by the friction created by malfunctioning belts.

"Mr. Cabell, were you the gentleman who discovered the fire on the 19th?" asked Stanley.

"Upon the advice of my attorney, I exercise my Fifth Amendment rights to refuse to answer that question and any questions related in any way to my work at the Aracoma Alma Mine and the January 19th mine fire," Cabell said.

Stanley then called Jeffrey Brian Perry, the belt coordinator; Kenneth Williams, the chief engineer; Fred Horton, the second-shift foreman; Lawrence Lester, the mine superintendent; Dustin Dotson, the shift superintendent; and Gary Douglas Goff, the general manager of the Aracoma Coal Company. They all invoked the Fifth Amendment. Several even refused to say what their positions had been at Aracoma.

These men had not cooperated with investigations into the fire, either, and at every juncture had refused to speak about what had happened that day. Stanley had known that they would all take the Fifth, but he wanted to march each of the uncooperative men in front of the jury. He was hoping, as the Massey men came forward, one after another, that it would make the jurors think that some of these men and others might be criminally indicted and possibly spend time in prison for their behavior that day.

Stanley called two miners who had been on the mini-train and did not invoke the Fifth Amendment. One of them was electrician Harold "Mike" Shulls. He described in detail what he had gone through that day. When the miners were donning their self-rescuers, Shulls said, he heard people yelling, "Oh God, oh God, oh God" and Hatfield shouting, "How do you put this thing on?"

"I have one more question, Mike," Stanley asked. "Were Don Bragg and Elvis Hatfield good men?"

"Yes. Yes, they were," said Shulls. "They were hard workers. They were, you know, like brothers to us."

52

On Thursday, November 13, 2008, Stanley looked out on the court-room and saw Caperton sitting there. It meant something to Stanley that Hugh had made the drive from Glade Springs to show his support. Hugh was healthy now, but that meant only that he was ready once again to face all the anxieties and uncertainties of *Caperton*. All of his life had become waiting, and this time he was waiting for the United States Supreme Court to decide whether to hear his case.

Stanley called several miners to the stand. The first, Brandon Conley, watched over the thousands of feet of belt that carried the coal out of the mine. He testified that when he'd learned there was a fire, he'd been especially concerned: only a few weeks before, on December 23, 2007, he had reported a nonfatal fire in the same location.

"I went and immediately grabbed a roll of fire hose and went down to the fire valve, and the fire hose and the fire valve, it wouldn't connect properly," Conley said of that event. "And that's when I tried to strip it out to get it to work. And then when I turned the water on, there was no pressure."

Conley testified that he told the second-shift foreman, Fred Horton, about the dangerous situation. He also told the belt coordinator, Jeff Perry. The problem had to be fixed and fixed immediately, but like the others, Conley said, Perry did not seem to care. "He was in the mine office, and I had went in and I had told him what had happened on

December 23rd," Conley said. "And the way I got it, he just didn't even, you know, like he didn't even acknowledge. Like he wasn't worried."

The next witness, Charles Bradley Justice, the head of the Southern Coalfield Mine Rescue Association, had led the rescue efforts; his team had found the two bodies. It had been a sad business, and the defense did not want Justice to testify.

Paul called for a sidebar with the judge. "The basic argument, Your Honor," the defense attorney said, "is that it's not relevant or probative of any portion of the plaintiffs' case to have someone testify who can only testify about the conditions of the mine nearly a day after Mr. Hatfield and Mr. Bragg perished."

Stanley answered, "Mr. Justice is the man who found Don Bragg's body. There have been allegations about Mr. Bragg panicking. This witness found him in the mine and is capable of testifying about the status of his SCSR unit on his body at the time. Now, I can't think of anything more probative."

Judge Perry let Justice tell his story. The mine rescue chief said that extinguishing the blaze took longer than it should have because so many mandatory safety measures were not in place. When the flames were finally controlled, the team came upon Bragg's body, facedown in a fetal position.

The Massey lawyer had suggested that Bragg bore a certain responsibility for his death because he had not followed through on what he had learned in disaster-prevention training, but Justice gave evidence that the miner had done everything right. Crucial to that was the self-contained rescuer, or SCSR oxygen inhaler. Justice testified that he had found Bragg wearing his SCSR with the mouthpiece in place. He was also wearing a hard hat with a light, nose clips, and goggles. "The only thing exposed was his cheeks," Justice said.

The next witness, Jonah Francis Rose, had been working during the second shift. Stanley asked Rose to describe what he'd faced in the mine that day. "When I got engulfed in smoke, it hit so fast," Rose said. "I went to my knees. I got my rescuer off [my belt]. I couldn't get the top off of it, and I started hitting it. I started hitting it against the floor. I got it open, got it on, but it was hard to try to breathe when you got the smoke and everything that's making you gag."

Stanley wanted the jury to understand how terrifying it must have been for all of the men, and how the SCSRs were extremely unpleasant to use.

"Could you describe the sensation of breathing [through] that rescuer for the jury?" Stanley asked.

"Like drinking gasoline. The way that the smoke engulfed or basically got me, I wasn't expecting it to hit like that. It's not a little bit here or a little bit there; you had, you know, the smoke there, but you could still see. When the smoke, it engulfed me; it engulfed me all at once. It took my air; it took my vision, and you try to breathe to get it on, and you can't breathe."

"Do you think it's fair to say that there was a panic situation at the time?" Stanley asked.

"Very. You make your peace with God."

Stanley had decided that the last coal miner he would call to testify would be John Brown. He had been in the mine on the day of the fire, though not on the crew with Rizzle and Elvis. He had a different but powerful tale to tell, and Stanley relished having him speak.

Brown was so emotionally distraught, however, that Stanley worried he might self-destruct on the witness stand. Since the fire, the thin, wiry miner had often been unable to sit still for very long. His eyes twitched back and forth, as if searching for some new menace. He had nonetheless sat outside the courtroom for the first days of the trial. He'd broken out in hives as he'd waited to relive his days in the mine.

Stanley decided to have Tonya examine the witness. It was a risk many lawyers would not have taken: she had a disconcerting habit of turning the most modest question into a soliloquy. But Stanley believed in Tonya. Beyond that, there was a whole team of women sitting with him, and so far he had been the only one to examine witnesses. That might not play well with the women on the jury. In preparation, he had worked with Hatfield for hours, trying to purge the lawyer of her verbose style, coaching her to ask concise, direct questions and then get out of the way.

Tonya knew that she did not have Stanley's nimble legal mind and knowledge, but she knew, too, that she had something to give. Stanley had gotten Tonya to temper her garrulousness, but it was still Tonya Hatfield up there, not some citified lawyer.

"Your Honor, John Brown wears a pacemaker," Hatfield said. "He suffers from nauseousness and gets dizzy, and sometimes he passes out, sometimes even throws up, and it comes up unexpectedly. There's a garbage can there at the witness chair; he's been made aware of that. But he may need a break during his testimony."

Tonya had already gone on for far longer than Stanley had advised her to, but she spoke as a woman who cared about this man and addressed him as a friend. Once she settled down, she asked Brown one pointed, specific question after another. He trusted her as much as she trusted him, and his answers were as good and strong as the questions.

Brown, forty-four at the time of the trial, had been a carpet installer for most of his adult life, earning no more than about $5.50 an hour, spending much of his time on his knees. Five years before the fire, he had gone into the mines to make a decent living.

Brown worked on the longwall as a utility man. He described the gigantic machine with awe, how its two shearers ripped out three feet of coal at a time. It made one pass along a sheet of coal, then turned back and made a second. On and on the shearers moved, not stopping even when the shifts changed.

One day when the shearer was down, Blankenship's second-in-command, Massey COO Chris Adkins, called the phone at the longwall. "He said, 'What the hell is wrong?'" Brown told the jury. "'Why in the hell aren't we running coal?'

"I said, 'Buddy, the shearer is down, and I don't know; I'm fifteen hundred foot away from them, and I'm telling you what they tell me from the face, and that's all I can do.' And he just kept a-cussing and swearing at me, and then he hung up. Just a good ass chewing, that's all it was to me, for something that I didn't have no control over."

The longwall operation stopped for an extended period only when a seam had been fully excavated. The crew then relocated the giant machine, which generally took about two weeks. The previous summer, the relocation had taken thirty-three days, and Brown worked thirty-two of them, fifteen hours a day, in the nonunion mine. In the old UMW days, no miner would have worked that many hours or that many days straight. And if the bosses had tried to subject the men to the unsafe and often onerous conditions the men faced in Aracoma, the miners would have walked out and shut the place down.

Hatfield asked Brown what it had been like during those days moving the longwall.

"It was real muddy," Brown said. "And it was bad, top rock falling real bad."

"What kind of conditions are you exposed to when you're going through this process?"

"Lots of mud and water," Brown said. "Some of it's deep water, and then some of it's not so bad, but usually it's up to your knees."

Hatfield was an emotional woman, and she might have milked the drama out of this, but she knew that she'd do better by keeping it straight and simple.

"Does it ever get any deeper than that?" she asked.

"Yes," Brown said. "I've been in water days at a time up to my waist or further."

"Is that something [when the water is deep] that you're in a hurry to get done?" asked Hatfield.

"Well, they try to rush us, but you can do only what you can do, you know," Brown said. "You never did get a chance to rest or nothing, but just to come back to the next fifteen-hour shift to work."

"Who set your hours and told you you had to work that long?" asked Hatfield.

"The outside bosses," Brown said.

Hatfield asked Brown about half a dozen federally mandatory fire drills that had been officially recorded the previous year. Brown said that in his nearly five years in the mine, he had never witnessed any drills, adding that they slowed production and were considered an unnecessary nuisance.

"Did you ever discuss these records with your bosses?" Hatfield asked.

"They would just tell us that you went through this and that, and then blink an eye and say 'okay' and then just sign it and go off," said Brown.

A murmur rustled through the courtroom.

"They would say you went through this or that and then wink an eye?" Hatfield asked.

"And say, 'If anybody asks, you tell them that you went through it.' But none of them had taken place."

Brown left the mine the day of the fire and never returned. He could never quite understand what had happened or why, but he was not the same. He had cold sweats. He threw up when he hadn't even eaten. He couldn't sleep. He went to doctors, and they prescribed twenty-one different medicines, but none of it did much good. He never heard a word from his employer; no one asked if he was coming back or how he was doing. He heard from his fellow miners that the men who been working with Rizzle and Elvis had gotten a big legal team, including Scott Segal, to handle their case. Brown had not been with Rizzle and Elvis near the fire, and the lawyers said they did not want his case. That's when he'd talked to Tonya, and she'd agreed to file a suit on his behalf, charging that the emotional stress of the fire had devastated his life.

The defense knew it had to impugn Brown's powerful testimony, but in questioning him the lawyers spoke as if they knew nothing about the coal fields and how life was lived there. They wanted the jurors to think that Brown was lying when he said that his supervisors had falsified records of safety drills. But the jurors were from Logan County, and they would have no trouble believing that Massey was capable of falsifying records or taking other illegal actions. In recent years, Logan's mayor, magistrate, police chief, county clerk, and county sheriff had all been convicted of election corruption.

"Who did you tell about that?" asked James S. Crockett, one of the two corporate defense lawyers, referring to the fake reports.

"There was nobody to tell," Brown said.

"You never saw a mine inspector in that coal mine?" the defense lawyer asked.

"Yes, I could have told the mine inspector, but then I'd of lost my job," Brown said.

"Could you have called the police?" Crockett asked.

"Then I'd of lost my job," Brown said.

"You're sure that the law allows people that do that to fire you?" the lawyer asked.

"It's either do your job, or we can find somebody to replace you," Brown said.

Brown feared that he would fail to handle the defense attorneys' questioning well and that they would back him down. Hatfield and Stanley had the same worries, but his answers rang true.

Crockett then turned to Brown's long consecutive workdays, mentioning a detail that the witness hadn't: he had been compensated for his time, $18.50 an hour plus overtime.

"I'm not telling you that it wasn't tiring, because even lawyers sometimes have to work fifteen hours a day for thirty days in a row," Crockett said, comparing his situation with Brown's. "And it wears you out. But that [money] is the silver lining for that type of work, isn't it?"

"Yes, but it's four miles underground," Brown said. "You know what I'm saying? I've been tired; you're in mud and water up to your knees and running around."

After Brown stepped down, Judge Perry dismissed the jury for the day, and the lawyers discussed their plans for the next day with the judge. Stanley intended to play Blankenship's full four-and-a-half-hour video deposition, after which he would call a series of damages experts. The defense attorneys knew what Blankenship had said in the deposition, and they strenuously objected to the video.

"Mr. Blankenship is prepared to be here tomorrow and testify live," Flaherty said. "It doesn't make any sense to me to play a video if someone is sitting here live."

So far in the trial, Blankenship had not even entered the courtroom. Stanley was convinced that after reviewing Blankenship's video deposition, the defense had decided that it would do far better having Blankenship testify in person. "I want the opportunity to play what I consider are direct admissions by Don Blankenship," Stanley said. "If they want to, they can swear him on the stand and have him refute it, that's fine."

When the judge left the courtroom before deciding the matter, Stanley was irate. For several months, he had been planning to use the full video deposition, and he believed he had every legal right to do so. He turned to Flaherty and pointed his finger at him. "This is bullshit, Tom!" Stanley said. "If the judge tells me no, you better have Blankenship here tomorrow, ready to testify!"

"Get your goddamned finger out of my face!" Flaherty said and started parading around the room, berating Stanley.

Fifteen minutes later, Judge Perry returned to the courtroom. "I'm going to allow Mr. Stanley to proceed in the way that he wants to," the judge said, looking at Flaherty, "and you can deal with it."

53

The trial resumed on the morning of Friday, November 14, 2008. As the lights dimmed for Blankenship's video deposition, the back doors of the courtroom opened, and the Massey chairman walked into the courtroom. He wore a blue suit coat and an open blue dress shirt. His hair and mustache were atypically dark, as if they'd been dyed. He'd been less successful with the bald patch that ran down the middle of his scalp, today managing only a comb-over. His jowls were heavier and his double chin had grown so thick that his neck was hardly visible.

During the first two days of the trial, Flaherty had attempted to show the jury that Blankenship was not personally responsible for the fire at Aracoma. "He is a man that has done more for safety in the coal mining industry than anybody," Flaherty had said. "He does not belong in this case." Flaherty implied that only Stanley's vindictiveness had dragged his client into this courtroom. Today Stanley hoped to bind the Massey chairman to the mine's operations and unsafe working conditions, for the first time holding the man personally accountable for Massey's worst conduct.

As Stanley stood to introduce the long video, he could have been Blankenship's younger brother. Over the years their resemblance had gotten even stronger, so it was almost eerie to see the two men in the same courtroom. Like Blankenship, Stanley had a small mustache, jowls, and a serious expression. Stanley seemed almost to be mimicking Blankenship, talking in little more than a whisper only a bit louder than the chairman's. It was as if the two of them were speaking their own private language.

In the deposition, which had been taken in July 2008 at the Chief Logan Lodge, Stanley led Blankenship through fifty-three documents—most of them memos the Massey chairman had written or answered as he'd sat in his office—that revealed just how Blankenship managed the company.

On camera, Stanley politely pushed Blankenship to confirm that the documents were valid and that he had indeed written the words on these papers. Meticulously and relentlessly, just as Fawcett would have done it, Stanley detailed Blankenship's inner business world, giving him no opportunity to explain or justify his words. As the video deposition played, a second screen exhibited the individual documents.

When the defense attorney objected to something Stanley was reading, the judge called for a sidebar with the lawyers. Blankenship turned 180 degrees and stared at Delorice. She stared back at him until he turned away.

"Did you see what he did?" Freda asked Delorice.

"Yeah," Delorice said. "He doesn't scare me."

The memos showed that Blankenship was frustrated by what he considered inept Massey executives. The company had made a profit in only one quarter in three years, and he was convinced that "the great majority of our problems are management at the group president level."

"Believe it or not, we still have Group Presidents looking for reasons to cut off coal trucks and not ship coal," Blankenship faxed the top executives in February 2004. "We've run out of ways to say this, but the company is being destroyed by people that get in the way of our shipments. They have to get out of the way."

A day later Blankenship faxed the group presidents again, further clarifying his message. "It's indescribable how discouraging it is to still have individuals who will not try to make their Plan," he wrote. "These memos, I'm certain sound sort of crazy to many of you. But we are literally destroying every opportunity that we have because we have no urgency, no membership, no understanding of the basic purpose and no willingness to communicate or work hard at solving our problems."

In October 2005, Blankenship warned that if the executive team did not pick up production, "we're getting ready to do what we have to do to eliminate problem mines." If Blankenship did that, the executives at the targeted mines would likely lose their jobs. The next day Blankenship's secretary faxed a memo to the mine superintendents underscoring what little faith Blankenship had in the group presidents. "If any of you have been asked by your group presidents or anyone else to do anything other than run coal, you need to ignore them and run coal. This memo is necessary only because we seem not to understand that the coal pays the bills."

The memo was the talk of the company. Blankenship seemed to be telling Massey mine superintendents that if their bosses wanted them to spend time on matters other than mining, they should ignore them. He appeared to be saying what his enemies had long asserted: at Massey, safety was secondary to production. When Blankenship received feedback that said some might think he wasn't concerned about safety, he grew furious. "I would question the membership of anyone who thought that I consider safety to be a secondary responsibility," he faxed his managers.

The judge called a short break, and Blankenship left the courtroom and did not return. Stanley found that strange. He had little time to ponder the disappearance, because the jury soon filed back in. Stanley played the rest of the video deposition, in which he asked the Massey chairman about conditions at Aracoma in the days just before the accident.

At the time, the belts that carried coal out of the mine were down so often that on January 13, 2006, six days before the fatal fire, Blankenship sent one of his top troubleshooters, Linton Stump, to investigate. Stump notified Blankenship that the "belt strings were wrapped around both sides of tail roller bearings, causing heat to build up and melt grease inside the bearing."

"Were you operating under the assumption after you got this [report] back that all was otherwise well with the belts and bearings at Aracoma?" Stanley asked.

"I was operating under the impression that it had been brought to large enough attention that it would be okay," Blankenship said.

Blankenship had sent his troubleshooter to the mine because of the production delays, but the belts posed a significant safety threat and, indeed, were the cause of the fatal fire. "The two-hour reports that you got, were they indicating production during that time period with a lot of belt shutdowns, belts down, belts off?" Stanley asked.

"It would have been, yes, I mean the mine was performing poorly," Blankenship said. "The two-hour reports would have reflected those same problems, yes."

On the day of the fire, Blankenship's time-study experts were inside the mine observing the longwall operation, determining how they could accelerate production. A series of reports from the experts in the mine to Blankenship, faxed to him every two hours, appeared on the court-room screen. When Blankenship learned in one of the reports that the operation was down and probably would not be up until the next day, he faxed Aracoma president Sid Young: "What does this mean? Please advise particulars verbally ASAP."

That was Blankenship's last communication before the fire.

"Did the Aracoma mine in your estimation fall below Massey's stan-dard?" Stanley asked.

"Yes," Blankenship said.

"It did?" Stanley asked.

"Well, obviously on the tragedy it fell below our standards, yes. I don't know that any mine lives up to our standards."

And there the video ended.

"I was the snake charmer," Stanley said later. "I had him coming out of the basket and showing his true colors for four and a half hours. I'm not nitpicking. I'm not cherry-picking. I wanted everyone to know what the fuck he was."

As Stanley left the courtroom late that afternoon, he saw that he had many messages on his phone, including several calls from Fawcett, whom he called back first.

"They're taking the case, Bruce," Fawcett said. "We're going to the Supreme Court!"

"Good God, now I know why Blankenship left the courtroom today and never came back," said Stanley, feeling richly vindicated. "He didn't want to come and see me sitting there gloating."

At nine that evening, a mediator called Stanley in his hotel room, saying that the defense lawyers in the Aracoma case wanted to talk settlement. The next morning, for the first time in all the years that Stanley had been dealing with Massey, he engaged in serious settlement negotiations with the company's lawyers. Delorice, Freda, and Tonya sat beside Stanley while Massey's lawyers and insurance representatives kept raising their offer.

The plaintiffs' decision to consider settling was not easy. Freda had been exhausted by the week-long trial and even more by the prospect of testifying. Bruce and Tonya had assured Freda that she could survive anything the Massey lawyers threw at her, but she did not know how much more she could take.

Delorice did not want to settle, but she saw that Freda had little more to give. Tonya wanted to let the jury decide. So did Stanley, who could envision the jury awarding $100 million. But he represented the women, not himself, and, knowing how little most of the jurors had, he could also envision it deciding that $2 million was appropriately massive. What's more, he reminded his clients, after all these years, Caperton hadn't seen a cent of his $50 million verdict.

Massey had a $20 million insurance policy, and its offer soon reached a confidential amount that was life-changing by any definition— although ultimately, Delorice and Freda hardly changed their lives at all.

When Judge Perry dismissed the jurors, they were disappointed to hear of a settlement. They believed in the women and their case. They wanted their verdict to be registered in the annals of the law. And so they settled, too—for coming up to the widows and hugging them, saying how they grieved for their loss and were convinced that Massey was guilty.

Juror Ella Workman thought that in the courtroom the Massey chairman looked self-centered and was not concerned with the common man. She believed "he was more for the profit, not for the safety of his men and their concerns." Like Delorice, she was a nurse, and the men in her family had been coal miners. That last morning in court, Workman had kept staring at Blankenship. She felt he'd exhibited no remorse, no feelings for the women, never once looking over at Delorice and Freda with concern.

What settled it for juror Charlene St. Clair were the seven witnesses taking the Fifth Amendment. "I thought that was a poor thing," says St. Clair. "To me, that proved they had something to hide."

The widows hoped that Blankenship would now call for a company-wide safety evaluation and begin the reforms that were so necessary. But after the settlement, he went on a statewide radio show hosted by the outspoken conservative Hoppy Kercheval, one of the few media outlets where Blankenship felt comfortable.

"It's just a mistake, and people make mistakes," Blankenship said. "Nine of the eleven [miners] came out, even with the mistake. For whatever reason, the two that didn't either didn't get their masks on or panicked or whatever happened."

Freda and Delorice couldn't believe what they'd heard. "I've tried to understand him," Delorice said. "He lost his humanity. Once he got a taste for that power, nothing was going to stop him from going higher and higher. If I could give the settlement back and put him in jail, I would."

Stanley believed that the only way to stop Blankenship and to prevent further disasters was if he, along with the other executives managing Aracoma, were criminally indicted. The only thing that would affect Blankenship's behavior was a threatened loss of personal freedom, not civil suits or media criticism. Stanley knew that criminal indictments of mine-company executives were almost unheard-of in coal country, but he believed that it was time for a change. To begin that process, he took John Brown to the FBI, where the former miner repeated his claim of falsified safety drills. That led to criminal misdemeanor convictions, involving no prison time, for five Aracoma foremen.

The Aracoma Coal Company, as part of an agreement with the federal government, pleaded guilty to one count of willfully violating mandatory safety standards, resulting in death; nine counts of willfully violating mandatory safety standards; and one count of making an untrue statement to federal investigators. It paid a record amount for a mining accident, $2.5 million in criminal fines and $1.7 million in civil damages.

Stanley still considered this a pathetic excuse for justice. The year Bragg and Hatfield died, Blankenship personally earned an estimated $23 million. The $4.2 million in penalties to his company was paid by Massey and was less onerous to Blankenship than a traffic ticket. Worse than that, as part of the Aracoma plea agreement, no Massey employee or officer would be criminally indicted. Blankenship had no incentive to change the way Massey did business.

One of Stanley's brothers was a retired federal MSHA inspector, and

Bruce knew that world well. He believed that either Aracoma management had bribed the inspectors, the officials had been wildly incompetent, or management had prevented them from doing their jobs. Now, Stanley decided, it was also MSHA that he would hold to account, so that never again would its failures help cause anyone's death. That was why, on behalf of Freda and Delorice, Stanley filed a suit in April 2010 against the federal government for the mine inspectors' failures. He went ahead with what he knew would be a long, difficult struggle for a worthy goal. If the suit was successful, it would allow miners to sue the government when they were not protected as they should have been.

In the more immediate future, Stanley was excited that in a few months he and Fawcett would be going to Washington to sit beside Olson as the appellate attorney argued *Caperton* before the United States Supreme Court. In early December, Fawcett received some other good news from the United States Supreme Court. The justices had declined Massey's attempt to appeal *Wheeling-Pitt,* and the coal company would have no choice but to pay what had by then grown to be a judgment of $267 million.

But the money had come too late. Massey's conduct had wreaked such economic damage on the NASDAQ-listed company that it had become vulnerable to a takeover. Bradley had been pushed into retirement, and the company had ended up in the hands of new owners, who, a year later, sold it to Severstal, a Russian steelmaker. When the U.S. economy collapsed, in late 2008, Severstal kept the coke-making plant, but sold the steelmaking operations to another company, RG Steel, which ran them into the ground and then declared bankruptcy. By then, all of Wheeling-Pitt's steelmaking operations had been halted and most of its employees were out of work. To Bradley, it was "a sad ending to a proud American company whose roots date back to 1715." All that was left was the coke plant and Fawcett's second lawsuit against Massey on behalf of the shareholders.

At the Supreme Court of Appeals of West Virginia, *Caperton* had destroyed Maynard, humiliated Benjamin, and embarrassed Starcher, but Davis moved onward. The justice did have one worry, though. She wanted to fire the three women—Brenda Magann, Debbie Henley, and

Sheila Crider—because she believed they had leaked the photos that had disgraced her friend and colleague Maynard and ended his career in public life.

There were many who thought the whistleblowers should have been celebrated for calling attention to Maynard's grievous abuse of a justice's authority and none, other than Davis, who thought they should be fired. The court's new director of magistrate services, Janie L. Moore, was so troubled by Davis's attitude that she e-mailed administrative director Canterbury in February 2009. "For some reason, she [Davis] wants to get rid of Sheila, Brenda, and Debbie H.," Moore wrote. "Why, I do not no [sic]. I have been told she watches their comings and goings."

There may have been another victim of Davis's endeavor. Moore had been hired to replace Magann and Crider's supervisor, Pancho Morris. Like other court employees, he'd served in a nontenured position and had been fired for unstated causes. He contends today that Davis had wrongly suspected that he'd had something to do with releasing the European photos.

For unstated reasons, Canterbury also fired Crider, who had worked for the court for sixteen years. She insisted on an administrative hearing, which was held in January 2010. She acted as her own lawyer.

"I have an e-mail where you and Janie [Moore] also had a conversation that Justice Davis wanted me, Brenda [Magann], and Debbie [Henley] all fired," she told Canterbury.

"Justice Davis was very annoyed about the pictures and in an emotional moment she thought that it was time to clean house, I believe is what she said," Canterbury said. "I reminded her that that was not the solution."

Canterbury contends that Morris and Crider were fired for legitimate reasons, and points out that Magann and Henley are still with the court. Morris found a position as a public defender, earning $30,000 less than his previous salary, but after many months Crider was still out of work.

54

Throughout the month of February 2009, during the last four weeks before the Supreme Court arguments, Olson sat from early morning until late afternoon in a conference room, focused on nothing but *Caperton*. He took no phone calls, read no e-mails, and spoke only to Tayrani and Helen Voss, his longtime secretary.

Olson had a special reason for concern. It had taken five weekly conferences for four of the justices to agree to hear the case—so what were Olson's chances of getting five of them to vote his way? He worried that most of the justices did not like the arguments made in the petition for a hearing, in which the Pittsburgh lawyers had played such a significant role.

Tayrani helped Olson shape his arguments before he displayed them in front of half a dozen other Gibson, Dunn & Crutcher appellate attorneys in a rehearsal moot court. Many of these attorneys had appeared before the Supreme Court themselves. They disrupted Olson. They peppered him with questions. They cut him off. They belittled his arguments. They interrupted his every answer. Olson did two of these brutal sessions, each about two hours long—far longer and far more difficult than what he would likely face at the Supreme Court.

During one of these sessions, Caperton arrived at Olson's office to meet him for the first time. Caperton expected Olson to greet him in a polite, cursory way and then gently usher him out. Instead, Olson invited him to watch the moot session.

The attorneys grilled Olson in a constitutional legalese Caperton had never heard. He knew only that this was his life these men were discussing and that on their words hung his future and survival. He was proud that his name would be called in the highest court in the land, but how could his fate be fairly determined in such a strange, exotic language— especially when what he had suffered was due to basic corruption and greed?

Although Olson appeared to be consumed with his questioners, he noticed Caperton's discomfort. He called a break in the session and spent about twenty minutes explaining to Caperton the core concepts he was attempting to impart and the strategy he thought would have the best chance of winning a majority.

Caperton left Gibson, Dunn & Crutcher that day full of excitement. Back in 1998, Fawcett had said *Caperton* might take two years to win, and he had thought that ridiculously long. Now here he was, in 2009, with no job, few prospects, and nothing in his bank account. He'd always believed he would someday win. But he had never imagined that he, Hugh Caperton from Slab Fork, West Virginia, would have his case argued before the United States Supreme Court by one of the most famous and celebrated attorneys in America.

Tayrani and Sample, meanwhile, had sought an array of friend-of-the-court briefs. Now that the Supreme Court had agreed to hear *Caperton,* more powerful allies joined them, such as the Conference of Chief Justices, as well as twenty-seven individual former state justices and chief justices. The Massey team also presented amicus briefs, including the attorneys general of seven states, but nothing like the influential supporters that Tayrani, Sample, and others collected.

Fawcett and Stanley gave Olson and Tayrani whatever help they could, but now that the written briefs had been filed, the preparation for oral arguments lay with the two Washington lawyers.

A few days before the March arguments, Stanley called Tonya and talked about the upcoming hearing at the Supreme Court. When she hung up, she had the crazy idea to get herself up to D.C., to be there when Stanley appeared before the highest court in the land.

On March 2, 2009, the day before the Supreme Court hearing, a snowstorm threatened to close the West Virginia roads, but Tonya decided that she had to drive to Washington to see her friend. She grabbed some clothes and jumped into her car and pointed it north. She was in such a hurry that she forgot her winter boots, and the snow was already falling big-time—but boots or not, she was headed to the United States Supreme Court.

PART SEVEN

MARCH 3, 2009

55

At 9:30 A.M., half an hour before the clerk would call the Supreme Court to order on March 3, 2009, the courtroom was already full. Caperton was having a whispered conversation with the woman seated next to him, a Washington federal judge who had braved the freezing weather to hear the arguments in the case.

Fawcett's father sat looking out on the historic room, seated next to Claire Fawcett, his granddaughter, and Kathleen Fawcett, Dave's wife. A few rows back, Stanley's wife and daughters sat together. Fifteen-year-old Emily turned her head as the journalists walked silently to their seats at the side of the room. One of them was NPR's Nina Totenberg. Emily Stanley nudged her twenty-one-year-old sister, Laura; Emily could hardly believe that she was sitting only a few feet away from her hero. Hatfield sat on the other side of the room, finally warm, feeling the same sense of expectation as most of those there that morning.

At precisely 10:00, the nine justices appeared in unison from behind the long scarlet curtain. As Olson looked up, he was seeing not only justices, many of whom he had addressed in the court scores of times before, but friends. He had known Antonin Scalia, John Roberts, Clarence Thomas, and to a lesser extent Samuel Alito and Anthony Kennedy since the early 1980s, when he'd been an assistant attorney general in the Reagan administration and had traveled at the highest level of Washington political and legal society. He sat next to them at dinners. He joked with them. He argued politics. He did not go back so far with the other four justices (Stephen Breyer, Ruth Bader Ginsburg, David H. Souter, and John Paul Stevens), but they traveled in the same social and legal circles.

Every time Tayrani came to the court and sat down beside Olson, he was struck by how small and intimate the setting was; he felt he could almost reach out and touch the justices. In front of him, Tayrani kept a series of cards numbered from one to thirty. Each lawyer had a half hour to make his argument. Representing the petitioner, Olson went both first and last. Olson always saved five minutes for his final argument. There was a clock in the courtroom, but it was a violation of protocol to look up at the clock or down at one's watch. So Tayrani flashed a card as each minute ticked by, though Olson had developed such an acute sense of timing that he hardly needed the reminder.

Before hearing the arguments in the two cases before the court this morning, the justices swore in a group of attorneys from around the country, a rite of passage so that in the future they would be able to argue before the court. Stanley watched with pride, for one of the lawyers was Alicia Schmitt, his colleague at Reed Smith.

At 10:15, Chief Justice Roberts said, "We will hear argument first this morning in Case 08-22, *Caperton v. Massey Coal Company*. Mr. Olson."

Olson stood at the lectern before the nine justices. What he faced was a difficult, complicated task that he had to make seem simple, full of seamless arguments. He needed to speak deliberately and slowly while thinking incredibly quickly, never missing a beat or being thrown off. In his deep, resonant voice, he spoke his first sentence as if it were an epigram containing the essence of everything he would say this morning. He began with twelve words honed to what he considered perfection.

"A fair trial in a fair tribunal is a fundamental constitutional right."

Olson paused, letting the words resonate. Then he continued: "That means not only the absence of actual bias, but a guarantee against even the probability of an unfair tribunal. In short—"

"Who says?" interjected his friend Scalia. "Have we ever held that?"

To anyone who had never stepped inside this courtroom, Scalia might have seemed wildly impolite. But Scalia and his colleagues took pleasure in testing Olson. If the speaker at the lectern had arrived from Charleston or Pittsburgh to argue here for the first time, the justices might have tempered their questions, but not with Olson.

There was a larger reason why Justice Scalia reacted so quickly and fiercely. He lit out primarily against lawyers espousing liberal positions, and it was almost unthinkable that the man up there today doing just that was his good conservative friend Theodore Olson. It was almost as unlikely for Olson to argue this position in *Caperton* as it would be for him to join the Democratic Party.

Scalia believed that the government should stay out of people's lives. He was not about to set arbitrary standards for determining when judges should or should not hear a case. He opposed any recusal standard other than a judge's own judgment. Anything else was dangerous, unnecessary, and subject to the law of unintended consequences.

In 2004, Scalia had not recused himself from a Supreme Court case involving Vice President Dick Cheney—even though, after the court had agreed to hear the case, the justice had flown off on Air Force Two to go duck hunting with his White House friend.

"You have said that in the *Murchison* case and in a number of cases, Your Honor," Olson answered.

When Olson told Scalia, "You have said," he did not mean that the justice had personally rendered this opinion but that the court had. The 1955 *Murchison* case involved a Michigan judge who had indicted two witnesses for contempt in the secrecy of a one-person grand jury and then convicted and sentenced them without a public trial. The court ruled that the judge had violated the due process clause in Section 1 of the Fourteenth Amendment of the Constitution—precisely what Olson believed Benjamin had done by insisting on voting in *Caperton*.

The due process clause dictates that no state shall "deprive any person of life, liberty, or property, without due process of law; nor deny to any person within its jurisdiction the equal protection of the laws." Olson was arguing that when Benjamin had refused to recuse himself, Caperton had been denied the equal protection of the law.

Olson was speaking in a rarefied, compressed language fully understood primarily by lawyers and judges conversant in the court's history and opinions. The justices and attorneys had read all the briefs and other documents and spoke in a kind of shorthand.

"A guarantee against even—" Scalia began, referring to the probability of bias.

"Yes, the language of the *Murchison* case specifically says so," Olson said, anticipating the justice's thought and having the audacity to interrupt him. "The court said in that case, 'A fair trial in a fair tribunal is a basic requirement of due process. Our system of law has always endeavored to prevent even the possibility of unfairness.' And in that paragraph, the court goes on—"

"'Has always endeavored,'" Scalia said, his voice overwhelming Olson's, suggesting that just because a court sought to prevent unfairness did not mean that it always succeeded.

"Pardon?" Olson said.

"'Has always endeavored,'" Scalia repeated, as if to a listless schoolboy. "'Has always endeavored.'"

"Yes, but that's—" Olson began again, before Scalia once again asserted his prerogative to say what he wanted to say when he wanted to say it.

"And there are rules in the states that do endeavor to do that," Scalia said.

Scalia did not so much ask questions as assert answers. He had read the briefs, and he had made up his mind. He sat up there on the high bench not to learn but to instruct.

The justices tended to ask most of their questions to the lawyer with whose positions they disagreed. Olson could have guessed that it would be Scalia asking the first questions, followed by the less argumentative but almost equally conservative Chief Justice Roberts. The chief justice was more likely than Scalia to question, not debate Olson, and he did this morning, bringing up one of the dilemmas: how do you ascertain the probability of bias?

"If you've a fifty percent chance of bias, a ten percent chance?" Roberts queried. "Probable means more than fifty?"

"It's probable cause, Mr. Chief Justice," Olson said.

Olson was doing what he called "fouling the ball," deflecting the question away and then stepping back to the plate to hit away. Scalia came back, pitching a few curve balls that he hoped would prove unhittable. From the way the two justices were speaking, Olson had lost Roberts's and Scalia's votes even before he'd said his first word. This was a great intellectual squabble, but Olson had no time for a debate that would squander his limited time.

As Olson responded, he saw at least four of the other justices give him anticipatory looks, signaling their desire to ask questions, and he did his best to create just enough space so that another justice could slide into the dialogue.

Olson knew that on a Supreme Court evenly divided between liberals and conservatives, the key was Justice Kennedy, the one clear swing vote. Convince him, and you probably win. That dynamic seemed almost set in stone. Olson had no inkling that three years later, in the court's ruling on the Affordable Care Act, Roberts would be the swing vote for the progressive majority and Kennedy would vote with the conservative minority.

It was almost fourteen minutes into Olson's arguments when Justice Kennedy managed to insert himself into the colloquy with Scalia and Roberts. "You know, all of us know, that a ruling in your favor means that law could change drastically in states all across the country," he said. "Disqualification [of a judge] for bias will now become a part of the pretrial process. It doesn't seem to me that the standard you offer is specific enough."

In their brief, Tayrani and Olson had not suggested a dollar amount or a percentage of campaign funds that would require recusal. That was one of the fundamental problems with their argument, but they'd chosen to leave it vague rather than set forth a standard that would immediately be attacked. Kennedy's question suggested that he was looking for a way to vote to ensure that in situations such as Benjamin's, a judge would have to recuse himself. And so Olson's answer could be decisive.

"Well, there are several answers," Olson said. "The Conference of Chief Justices of all the states of the United States filed a brief in this case and said that we need a standard with respect to recusals for extraordinary campaign contributions. They also said that—"

"Was their standard the same as yours?" Scalia interjected, once again elbowing his way into the debate. "I mean, frankly, that's one of the problems in this case."

Fawcett and Stanley had no trouble following the arguments, and they both felt that Olson was handling the tough questions well. But Fawcett was growing increasingly upset. He had sought out Olson because he thought the conservative lawyer had a chance at winning all nine of the justices' votes. That wasn't going to happen. By their questions, Scalia and Roberts had signaled how they were going to vote. Fawcett believed that the issue transcended ideological lines, and it was devastating for him to hear the judges making points as if the hearing were just another political skirmish.

Each time Scalia and Roberts drew Olson into their debate, the appellate attorney tried to escape by taking the subject back to the world as it was, where money was overpowering judicial elections and challenging the integrity of the entire system.

Even when the high court deals with murder appeals, no blood-stained evidence appears in the courtroom, no guarded defendants, no teary-eyed victims, and devastating human topics sometimes became leather-bound abstractions. When Justice Ginsburg spoke, she brought *Caperton* back to the world outside the courtroom.

"You have a defendant in the ongoing litigation who is, in fact, a prime culprit from the point of view of the plaintiff," Ginsburg said. "That is, Blankenship, who made all these contributions, and is charged with driving Caperton out of business. So he is not simply the CEO of the company that's named as the defendant, but he is targeted as the perpetrator."

The Massey chairman may not have been in the courtroom this morning, but he was the central presence, and Justice Ginsburg acknowledged it.

Before Olson sat down, he took his arguments far from the coal fields of West Virginia. "The principle that we're articulating here is not new to the jurisprudence of the Western world that we come from," he said, looking up at the justices. "In the Magna Carta, the king promised, 'To no one will we sell justice.' And Blackstone repeated that and restated it: 'For injury done to every subject, he may take his remedy by the course of law and have justice freely without sale.'"

Olson's final four words—"justice freely without sale"—had also been obsessively crafted. He had met all the justices' attacks, and he had ended by suggesting that *Caperton* should be elevated to an honored place in the history of law and justice.

56

During the half hour Massey attorney Andrew L. Frey had before the court, it was the liberal justices who challenged his almost every assertion, though with more deference than Scalia had exhibited.

Frey argued that the Supreme Court had no business barging into the states' business. The individual state legislatures were already dealing with the problem, he said, by instituting campaign laws that limited contributions. It would be unnecessary, foolish, and dangerous to mandate any action. "I think this is a situation," Frey said, "where the states are dealing with it legislatively and . . . the court has recognized that this is . . . something that is meant to be dealt with through legislative or canons of judicial ethics or codes."

"Is it your position that the judge is elected just like a legislator is elected, and legislators all the time are beholden to interest groups?" Justice Ginsburg asked, not warming to the idea that her elected colleagues in the state courts were nothing more than politicians in black robes.

"Well, of course, I don't agree that Justice Benjamin was in the least beholden to anybody in this case," Frey replied. Like Olson, Frey responded by answering a question that had not been asked.

Then Justice Stevens weighed in.

"Mr. Frey, is it your position that the appearance of impropriety could never be strong enough to raise a constitutional issue?" he asked.

"Are you saying that appearances without any actual proof of bias could never be sufficient as a constitutional matter?"

"I think we are," Frey said. "We are saying that the due process clause does not exist to protect the integrity or reputation of the state judicial system."

"That's not an answer to my question," Stevens noted with a twinge of impatience.

"No, I don't think just appearance could *ever* raise the due process issue," Frey said. "The question is whether there is *actual* bias of a kind that is recognized as disqualifying. The court has recognized—"

Frey was a top appellate attorney from New York who had argued before the court many times, but he had made a novice's mistake. He had staked out a position far more absolutist than was necessary, and by contrast Olson's arguments seemed centrist and reasonable.

"We have never confronted a case as extreme as this before," Stevens replied. "This fits the standard that [the late justice] Potter Stewart articulated when he said, 'I know it when I see it.'"

Tonya laughed with the audience. She knew that Justice Stevens was referring to a celebrated phrase Justice Potter Stewart had used in 1964 in trying to define pornography. And so it was with the appearance of judicial bias: hard to delineate, but it existed nonetheless. Stevens had come closer to defining this issue than had any of his colleagues.

Justice Souter, then sixty-nine, was only a few weeks from announcing his retirement, and his questions focused on the broader role of the court in American life. He was particularly fond of a quotation from the late federal judge Richard Arnold, who had said of the American judiciary, "There has to be a safe place, and we have to be it." The Supreme Court of Appeals of West Virginia had proved that it was not a safe place, and the question was whether the United States Supreme Court could help make it safe once again.

"We have an appearance standard under the ABA canons, but I think it would be difficult to make a very convincing argument that that standard was effective in this case," Souter said.

"I think I would agree that reasonable people could have a different view one way or the other about whether there is an *appearance* of impropriety for Justice Benjamin," Frey said. Coming from Massey's attorney, that was an extraordinary admission. Stanley and Fawcett were astounded. A poll they had taken in West Virginia had revealed that to most people Benjamin appeared biased, and that perception risked tainting the votes of the entire Supreme Court of Appeals of West Virginia. If reasonable people thought Benjamin was biased, as even Massey's own attorney had suggested they might, then how reliable was any Supreme Court of Appeals of West Virginia opinion in which he had participated?

Frey took his full half hour making his argument, and then Olson stood for the final five minutes of his allotted time. He began by invoking the highest law of the land.

"The words 'due process' are in the Constitution, and that is what we're talking about today," Olson said. "This court has repeatedly said that due process means a fair trial in a fair tribunal."

Olson did not squander these last precious minutes attacking Frey or rebutting his arguments; instead, he attempted to raise the debate to a high level of legal philosophy and past judicial decision. When Olson had begun this morning, he'd hoped he might win all nine of the justices' votes, but from their questions they seemed to be leaning the way they usually did, four to the left and four to the right. If so, Kennedy was the key.

Scalia and Roberts forged back in, trying to reassert their positions. They had already rummaged through all their major points, and now Roberts fell upon a bizarre, unlikely example. "What about protective donations?" he asked. "You actually give not three million but a couple hundred thousand to somebody you don't want deciding your case."

It was a wildly imaginative idea: Don Blankenship, say, financing Starcher's reelection campaign so that the judge could not vote in cases involving Massey. "As this court has said," Olson replied, "you can't allow a litigant to try to game the system in that way."

In his last moments, Olson acknowledged two of the justices he considered safe votes. "I think I would go back to Justice Stevens's and Justice Breyer's question," he said. "This is a situation where there has to be some limits. We think there has to be some constitutional limit."

"Thank you, Counsel," Roberts said. "The case is submitted."

The lawyers had come into the building by a side door that led into the bowels of the structure but they left, like everyone else, through the front doors, spilling out onto the cold but sunlit steps, where in the early morning hours Hatfield had stood in the darkness. They were met by a gang of videographers and reporters.

Stanley looked down and saw Totenberg interviewing Frey. Olson stood nearby, surrounded by admirers, paying no attention to the media. "We got to move, Ted," Stanley urged. "You can shake hands afterward. You have to work the media now."

Olson thought that it had gone well, but he was not one to make pronouncements about the odds of winning. "This case is so complex that the court is unlikely to issue a ruling until early June," Olson told the reporters.

Every time Olson appeared before the Supreme Court, he gave a luncheon afterward for all those who had been involved in the case and their families. The festivities were held in a private room at Morton's steakhouse, downstairs from Olson's law offices. Stanley's two daughters, Laura and Emily, were there, as were Caperton's daughter, Preston, and spouses Lady Booth Olson, Kathy Caperton, Kathleen Fawcett, and Debbie Stanley. Fawcett's daughter Claire was there, as well as his father, the oldest person in the room. Sample had taken the train down from New York City to attend the hearing and the lunch.

Olson had hosted more than forty of these events, but this was the most emotional. "You know, Bruce and Dave, it's been quite something working with you," Olson said. "You represent the highest professional standard in the way you have fought for your clients. It is compelling, and I want you to know how much I admire what you are doing. And I appreciate that you came to me this with this important case."

"Yeah, well, next time you have a big litigation matter, refer it to me," Fawcett joked. "I'll try it."

PART EIGHT

JUNE 8, 2009

57

Olson was already preoccupied with his next case, which the court was scheduled to hear just three weeks later. In *Citizens United v. Federal Election Commission*, Olson would be arguing on behalf of Citizens United, challenging provisions in the McCain-Feingold campaign finance law that had prohibited the nonprofit corporation from running its partisan documentary *Hillary: The Movie* thirty days prior to the 2008 presidential primaries.

At the same time, Olson had another case that, like *Caperton*, appeared to betray his conservative principles. He had joined with the progressive attorney David Boies, his opponent in *Bush v. Gore*, in trying to overturn Proposition 8, California's voter-enacted ban on same-sex marriage, in the United States District Court for the Northern District of California.

The Supreme Court usually announced its decisions on Tuesdays or Wednesdays, but on Monday, June 8, 2009, the *Caperton* opinion appeared on the court's website. The court ruled that Benjamin had been wrong in not recusing himself. Justice Kennedy wrote the opinion for his four concurring colleagues, Stevens, Souter, Ginsburg, and Breyer.

"There is a serious risk of actual bias," Kennedy wrote, "when a person with a personal stake in a particular case had a significant and disproportionate influence in placing the judge on the case by raising funds or directing the judge's election campaign when the case was pending or imminent."

The court had come down 5–4, with Kennedy proving the expected swing vote. In his fourteen-page dissent, Roberts listed forty questions that he believed would now haunt an already overwhelmingly busy court system. "How much money is too much money?" he asked. "How long does the probability of bias last?" He predicted that the court would be deluged with "Caperton motions, each claiming title of 'most extreme' or 'most disproportionate.'"

Many of Roberts's assertions read as if they had been taken directly from Benjamin's concurring opinion. The chief justice claimed that "Blankenship's independent expenditures do not appear 'grossly disproportionate' compared to other such expenditures in this very election." In the general election, Blankenship had personally contributed $2,463,500 to And for the Sake of the Kids, plus $517,707 in individual expenditures to defeat the Democratic candidate. He'd also written letters to doctors and others soliciting money for Benjamin, and Massey executives and managers had contributed more than $50,000. On the other side, hundreds of trial lawyers and others had donated roughly $2 million to Consumers for Justice to support McGraw in the primary and general elections.

Roberts added that it was "far from clear that Blankenship's expenditures affected the outcome of this election," not even mentioning the ubiquitous ads calling Arbaugh a rapist freed by McGraw that had been so thoroughly covered in Tayrani's briefs. Instead, Roberts wrote that "many observers believed that Justice Benjamin's opponent doomed his candidacy by giving a well-publicized speech that made several curious allegations." McGraw's Labor Day speech had actually occurred only after voters had been inundated with the Arbaugh ads and initially was not publicized at all. Only through ads largely paid for by Blankenship did West Virginia voters learn about the "rant in Racine."

In his dissent, Scalia shared many of Roberts's doubts. "The facts relevant to adjudicating it will have to be litigated," the justice wrote. "Many billable hours will be spent in poring through volumes of campaign finance reports, and many more in contesting nonrecusal decisions through every available means."

There is no evidence that any of this has occurred since the decision.

"While the dissenters predicted, with certainty, that Caperton would open the litigation floodgates, in reality, it produced barely a trickle," says Professor Sample. "In the decision's aftermath, the floodgates predictions proved so wildly inaccurate, measured by the actual facts, that the dissenting opinions inadvertently end up providing a case study illustrating why courts decide cases based on an actual record, as opposed to on high dudgeon assertions about the future."

Olson was delighted by the *Caperton* victory, but *Citizens United v. Federal Election Commission* had taken a peculiar twist. The court asked that the case be argued a second time on a far broader basis, and so it was on September 9, 2009. In a 5–4 vote, based on the proposition that corporations are "people," the court ruled that corporations and unions deserved the same rights to First Amendment freedoms as individuals and should be allowed to spend whatever money they chose electing candidates to office. The result was the greatest onslaught of special-interest money in American political history. *Caperton* still stood, but it was a cordon sanitaire outside of which anything went. *Caperton* is not discussed with anything like the frequency of *Citizens United,* but the two decisions are legal bookends defining an issue that remains one of the most crucial concerns in American public life.

The Supreme Court decision did not affirm the jury's verdict in *Caperton* but merely sent the case back to the Supreme Court of West Virginia for a rehearing in which Benjamin would have to recuse himself. Hugh Caperton dreaded ever seeing Justice Davis again, but after this chastisement, he could not imagine the West Virginia Court again turning back *Caperton.*

Caperton's optimistic outlook on the future of his lawsuit was matched even by those disinclined to Pollyannaism. Caperton had run out of money, so with the Supreme Court's opinion in hand, he approached another hedge fund. Like the group that had loaned him the $1 million that he would have to repay only if he got the verdict money, this fund also wanted to double its money. Appellate lawyers with a rich knowledge of the law ran the fund and they had such confidence in a *Caperton* victory that they, too, loaned him $1 million, with the same terms. Caperton cashed the check and paid off some creditors, starting with the IRS, but he once again owed the federal government several hundred thousand dollars in new taxes. That hardly concerned him, because he was sure that within a few months he would finally be able to settle every one of his debts, including both hedge funds, and still be well off.

Not only financiers shared Caperton's optimism; the legal and journalistic communities did, too. "The case now goes back to West Virginia, which has a black eye for its handling of the case and much to prove," a June 2009 *Pittsburgh Post-Gazette* editorial noted.

Like seemingly everyone else, Fawcett and Stanley thought that the Supreme Court of Appeals of West Virginia justices would show appropriate deference to the opinion of the United States Supreme Court by affirming *Caperton* and putting it behind them. The case had become an embarrassment and a humiliation to the state. It had created some of the biggest national publicity West Virginia had received in years, most of it negative, furthering stereotyping the Appalachian highlands as a place of corruption, cruelty, and deal making, plus a lack of legal civility.

Fawcett and Stanley were not quite so optimistic when they started counting the votes on the state court. Starcher had retired. Albright had taken a leave in July 2008, when he'd been diagnosed with cancer, and the seventy-year-old jurist had died the following year. Benjamin was still on the court, but he had been forced to recuse himself. The only other member of the current court who had voted previously in *Caperton* was Acting Chief Justice Davis. Fawcett and Stanley could see the shrewd politician in Davis deciding that the smart thing to do was to act magnanimously and confirm *Caperton* without admitting that she had made a mistake. But they also feared that Davis might feel that she had to dismiss *Caperton* to defend her leadership of the court.

Davis might try to woo her colleagues to once again turn back *Caperton*, but Fawcett and Stanley figured that they had at least as good a shot at each of the other four votes. Newly sworn-in Democratic justice Ketchum had talked during his campaign about how poorly he thought the court had handled *Caperton*. He seemed the most certain pro-*Caperton* vote of all. Another of the new judges, Margaret Workman, was a moderate Democrat and a coal miner's daughter who had sat on the court before. She, too, seemed open-minded and fair and a likely pro-*Caperton* vote.

Governor Manchin had appointed retired supreme court justice

Thomas E. McHugh to replace the incapacitated Albright. McHugh had decided to run for office in 2010. Fawcett and Caperton did not know much about McHugh, but they would have been disheartened if they'd learned that as the court was deciding *Caperton,* Segal was planning a fund-raiser for him, at his and Davis's home, that would raise $146,000. To fill the fifth seat, Acting Chief Justice Davis appointed retired circuit judge James O. Holliday, who might feel a certain loyalty to Davis for choosing him for this lucrative, prestigious assignment.

Stanley's and Fawcett's hopes sank when Davis declared that they would not be allowed to submit a new brief. That document would have been filled with quotations from the United States Supreme Court and would have served as a further rebuke of her handling of the Charleston court's affairs.

When Fawcett and Stanley appeared before the court for the third time, on September 8, 2009, Massey attorney D. C. Offutt supported Justice Davis's reasons for having twice overturned the Boone County verdict. He argued that *Caperton* should again be rejected because of res judicata, trying the same case twice, and forum selection, having been wrongly filed in West Virginia. More than in any other case she had helped adjudicate in her thirteen years on the bench, *Caperton* would reflect on Davis's honor and reputation. She had twice written the majority opinion, and she had already decided she would write it for the third time, however she and her colleagues ruled. Yet this morning the justice sat back and asked no questions as Offutt spoke.

"Cancellation of that contract was deemed to be the triggering event that started Caperton and the Harman companies on this downward trend, resulting in their bankruptcy," Offutt said. "If you look at the West Virginia case, Mr. Fawcett, in his closing, said to the jury, 'This is a very simple case. It's the existence of a contractual relationship.' He told the jury that the essence of their case was this contractual relationship, and Caperton was a part of that case."

As Davis had done in the previous arguments before the court, Offutt incorrectly described what had happened in the Boone County courtroom, but this time Fawcett was prepared to respond. "This statement was made that I said in the closing that this was a simple case and related to the breach of a business relationship," Fawcett told the five justices. "I checked that, and in my closing argument, I held up my hands, my fingers, and I listed ten acts of interference that Massey engaged in over this year's period of time, and that's at pages twenty-four to twenty-seven of the July 31, 2002, trial transcript."

As Fawcett answered, he was startled by how unprepared several of the justices seemed, and he worried whether they were even capable of understanding his points. He had thought that after the United States Supreme Court's admonition, these judges would have had to rethink the original opinion that was so obviously tainted by the participation of Justices Benjamin and Maynard. Yet he wasn't sure what was happening this morning. Were these new judges honestly trying to rethink the court's two previous opinions or merely pretending to hear him out when they had already made up their minds?

Davis's most significant contribution during the session was alerting Fawcett that his time was running out. When Caperton and his lawyers left the courtroom that afternoon, they were guardedly optimistic except, once again, for Kathy Caperton. "Davis, I know that woman; I know her," Kathy said. "That was all a big front in there. She made up her mind years ago, and nothing will change it."

Caperton respected his wife's opinion, but this time he thought she was wrong. Then, six days later, he received an e-mail message from the mysterious Rumpole detailing the inner workings of the court. "My source says the latest arguments before the Supreme Court were nothing more than Kabuki Theater, all flash designed to keep everyone guessing where the votes will come down," Rumpole wrote on September 14, 2009. "If you can settle, do it before Davis has the latest draft of her opinion written. This time the opinion is likely to be unanimous unless Workman throws a bone to Berthold and dissents."

Whether or not one trusted Rumpole's e-mails, they did confirm the court's decay: here was someone within the court releasing confidential, privileged information that could conceivably lead to a mistrial. Rumpole had his own website, where he titillated Internet browsers with his inside information, but his name remained secret. Like everyone else, Caperton was not able to find out the identity of this mysterious person with his awesome knowledge of court goings-on. Fawcett and Stanley had no idea who he was, either.

Three days later, Rumpole e-mailed again: "Confirmed. Saw a copy of the courts 'decision conference' notes. Right now it is 4 to 1 to reverse [the Boone County verdict], the opinion to focus only on the forum selection issue. Sorry. . . . Get what you can and run."

On November 12, 2009, the Supreme Court of Appeals of West Virginia revealed that it had rejected *Caperton* a third time, not by another 3–2 margin but, as Rumpole had predicted, 4–1. During their presentation before the court, Fawcett and Stanley had hacked away at most of Davis's reasons for denying them. She was left in her lengthy, heavily footnoted opinion with just one legal reason for rejecting *Caperton*. That was forum selection, the argument she had made in the first hearing and now used to destroy *Caperton* thrice and for all.

"Kathy, they did it again," Caperton said as he stood in their kitchen. He did not cry or throw a table across the room. He felt so abused by the court that he had gone numb.

To Fawcett and Stanley, the 4–1 vote was not just a defeat but also an insult and an attempt to silence them. They believed that Davis and her colleagues had arrogantly dismissed not only them but the highest court in the land. They believed that Davis had lobbied her colleagues to obtain a vote decreeing that no one must ever again challenge the authority and judgment of her court in such an exaggerated, prolonged fashion.

Stanley and Fawcett found solace only in the opinion of the lone dissenter, Justice Workman. Little in her long career had suggested that she would do anything that would attach her to controversy. But the opinion Workman issued condemned what she considered the misguided judgment of colleagues she saw every day in court.

"Neither the sheer length of the majority's opinion, nor the large number of cases cited (but erroneously applied), nor even its expansive conclusory statements, can obfuscate its lack of sound legal reasoning and its result-driven approach," the opinion began.

Workman, unlike Davis and Benjamin, wrote in language not buttressed by footnotes and citations. "The majority has turned West Virginia jurisprudence on its ear," she wrote. "The majority not only deprives the plaintiffs of the substantial damages awarded to them by the rightful finders of fact, a Boone County jury, but also leaves them with no legal recourse by which to address Massey's extensive pattern of fraudulent conduct. It similarly eliminates any recovery for the plaintiffs' numerous creditors. Not least among those creditors are the Harman Companies' union miners, who lost their jobs as a result of Massey's fraudulent conduct, and the Harman Companies' hundreds of retirees, to whom the Harman Companies previously paid pensions and medical benefits."

Fawcett and Stanley knew that they would have to file the suit in Virginia and start again, and that was a daunting project. "It's like putting on a wet bathing suit," Stanley said. "Once you jump in the water, you're okay." That was a good line, and it played well every time he used it. But Stanley was a far more mercurial soul than Fawcett, and he sometimes had his doubts. People talked about civil suits sometimes as if they were tepid, academic affairs, but the emotions were enormous, and sometimes they almost ripped a person apart. He was a passionate man who cared greatly about whatever he was doing, but that way of living was exhausting and difficult and there was never any reprieve. He could never admit it, but he found it hard to get up for this case all over again.

PART NINE

APRIL 5, 2010

58

Blankenship had never stood at a higher, more secure place than he did in the early months of 2010. He had finally defeated *Caperton* for good in West Virginia, sending a message regarding what would happen to those who challenged him. He still was wildly controversial, but in certain conservative quarters he was highly esteemed, an honored presence. He was living next door to his once estranged daughter. He was proud to go off on his tour bus to watch his son race stock cars.

Blankenship could accept no criticism of the industry that had made him his fortune. No elected politician in the state dared to offend him or the rest of the coal establishment by standing up and saying that the economic, political, and social world dominated by the mineral would have to change. Blankenship condemned environmentalists as misguided fanatics bent on destroying the jobs of good West Virginians.

For years environmentalists had been arguing that nothing would reduce air pollution faster than reducing the number of coal-fired electric plants, but it was economics that eventually drove that transition. Natural gas prices had fallen so far that coal's share of electric production was down from a half to a third, except in West Virginia, where it was still 98 percent. The thicker, more easily accessible underground coal seams were gone, and about half the coal was now mined by expensive longwall machines and large mountaintop removal projects. Neither required the number of miners once used underground.

But Blankenship was as optimistic as ever about the future of Appalachian coal. Early in 2010, Massey's board rewarded its chairman by signing him to a new two-year contract with performance bonuses that could raise his earnings beyond anything he had been paid before. That was a good possibility, for he was once again in the mood to expand aggressively. In March, Massey acquired Cumberland Resources for $960 million, to help double its sales of metallurgical coal by Blankenship's goal of 2012. "The market is strong," Blankenship said, looking forward to a long future at Massey.

Not two weeks later, at 3:00 P.M. on April 5, 2010, the earth shook in Montcoal, West Virginia. The Upper Big Branch mine, a Massey subsidiary, had exploded. A thousand feet underground, the tracks that moved the coal cars from the face of the mine to the portal lay twisted like paper clips, and the mining machines were not even recognizable. Ambulances and fire trucks bracketed the mine, and worried wives, other relatives, and friends waited and prayed that their loved ones were still alive.

The following afternoon, Blankenship arrived at the disaster site and walked toward the people who were continuing their vigil. Surrounded by a dozen or more police officers, he confirmed that everyone deep below had died, twenty-nine of their husbands, fathers, brothers, and sons.

Some of the mourners yelled out that Blankenship cared more for money than he did for miners' lives. Others screamed that he was to blame and had blood on his hands. And when one miner threw a chair at him, the cops escorted Blankenship away.

Upper Big Branch was the disaster that Stanley, Fawcett, Caperton, Tonya Hatfield, Freda Hatfield, and Delorice Bragg had believed was inevitable as long as Blankenship operated on a pure cost-benefit basis. Since 1995, Upper Big Branch had been cited at least three thousand times for safety violations, including two citations on the day of the explosion. There had been several recent evacuations at the mine, and many of those who worked there had long feared a disaster. Miners tended not to complain, but for at least two months before the blast, U.S. Representative Nick Rahall had been hearing from miner constituents worried about methane levels at Upper Big Branch.

Stanley immediately saw the similarity between the explosion at Upper Big Branch and the fire at Aracoma. He worked the phones, talking to reporters, giving them memos and documents he had used in his

Massey trials. "What we're afraid of is that the same types of ugly conditions at Aracoma may resurface again at Upper Big Branch," Stanley
presciently told the *New York Times* in an interview on April 22, 2010.
"And that perhaps the lessons of Aracoma might not have been learned."

Massey executives had done their best to contain the bad publicity
on Aracoma, but Upper Big Branch was a problem of a whole different
magnitude, and the company would have to reach out beyond the largely
captive media where Blankenship felt comfortable. On April 26, 2010,
the day after a memorial service for the twenty-nine victims attended by
President Obama, Massey called a media conference at the Charleston
Civic Center. Next to Blankenship sat two board members, Stan Suboleski, the former chief operating officer and witness in the Boone County
trial, and Admiral Bobby Ray Inman, a former director of the National
Security Agency.

Blankenship spent very little time paying deference to the dead miners before he began defending his company's commitment to safety, saying that anyone who thought otherwise was flat-out wrong. The main
task now, he said, was not to point fingers and apportion blame but "to
make major improvements in correcting whatever allowed this explosion
to occur."

Suboleski was introduced not only as a retired top executive and
board member but as the former commissioner of the Federal Mine
Safety and Health Review Commission, appointed during the term of
President George W. Bush, who would not have won election without the
help of the coal industry. Suboleski nudged any blame toward the federal
MSHA inspectors. He said that despite Massey's objections, MSHA had
forced the company to install a complicated new ventilation system in
the mine. "I'm just stating the facts of the case," Suboleski said. "If I were
going to generalize, a complicated system is more difficult to administer
than a simple system."

Inman had come this morning to attack Blankenship's enemies. He
complained about reporters and others who had been spreading "this
big lie that we traded safety for profits." Referring presumably to Stanley, whom he didn't name, Inman said that those charges had been
launched by "a lawyer for a plaintiff in a suit against Massey."

59

A day after the Upper Big Branch disaster, as Stanley was moping around his office, he received a call from Kevin Thompson, a West Virginia trial lawyer. Thompson told him that he represented 650 plaintiffs whose water had been poisoned by a Massey subsidiary and he needed some help with the case. As Stanley listened, he was stunned at the magnitude of what had supposedly gone on, how enormous the damages would likely be, and what an opportunity it appeared to be to drive a stake into Massey and Blankenship. What made it all the more poignant and powerful was that Blankenship himself lived in one of the affected communities and would likely have known in personal detail everything that had gone on.

Thompson was a great storyteller, and he had Stanley mesmerized as he described how for more than two decades Rawl Sales had poisoned the water of hundreds of people living in and around Rawl, along the Tug Fork River, near Blankenship's home. The problem could be traced in some measure to the Clean Air Act of 1970, which established national air-quality standards. The act forced coal companies to produce cleaner-burning coal, which Massey and its competitors achieved by washing the raw coal with a mix of water and chemicals, including magnetite and, often, diesel fuel. The process stripped the worst of the contaminants but left a dangerously polluted liquid full of chemicals and heavy metals.

Massey and other companies most commonly disposed of this liquid, called slurry, in man-made lakes or impoundments, and coal country had become spotted with lifeless pools. This was the kind of liquid that had poured into popular Laurel Lake during the Boone County trial. In 1972, in one of the worst disasters in West Virginia history, a slurry dam broke, spilling 130 million gallons of polluted water down Buffalo Creek Valley, killing 118 people and destroying or damaging over one thousand homes.

Thompson explained how at the Rawl Sales operation in the early 1980s, Massey had discovered that it was far cheaper to inject the coal slurry into old mines than to build impoundment ponds. Starting at about the time Blankenship arrived at the company in 1980, Rawl Sales had allegedly dumped 1.4 billion gallons of black liquid into old mine shafts. This was seven times the amount of oil that leaked into the Gulf of Mexico during the 2010 BP oil spill.

Thompson explained to Stanley how the slurry had traveled through aquifers and seeped into the well water of people who lived near the preparation plants. Residents started getting sick and dying as their water turned various colors, from orange and red to brown and black.

The people living near Rawl Sales didn't at first know that Massey had injected the slurry into the abandoned mines. All they knew was that when they tried to cook a plate of beans, the beans turned black in the pot and scum rose to the top of the water. They resigned themselves to getting their water from a water truck the county had sent out. It was enough for drinking and cooking but not for showering or washing clothes.

Blankenship had another solution for himself. He ran a line from Matewan to his home to supply his family with that town's fresh, clean municipal water. He never once asked his neighbors how they were holding up.

Thompson was the public voice of the lawsuit, but over the years many people had been involved even before he took the case. In January 2004, the nonprofit Coal Impoundment Project held a training session in the community of Delbarton, a few miles from the affected communities. Many of those who showed up lived around Rawl and brought bottles of their discolored water.

Afterward, Professor Ben M. Stout III, of Wheeling Jesuit University, spent a number of days visiting the various homes and testing the water. Stout walked to a well shed with a teenager who had only one tooth and was proud to be getting dentures. "Ever do meth?" Stout asked, aware that the drug could have destroyed the boy's teeth. "No, never," he said. Stout's test results showed that the water was so contaminated with manganese that it would have eaten through anyone's teeth. When Stout showed the data to independent water-quality experts, they were stunned. "They said it was the worst water quality they had seen anywhere in the world," Stout says.

The professor figured that the young man's teeth were not the only part of his body the water had eaten; he might well have dementia by the time he was forty. "There were lots of times I went back to my hotel and just cried," Stout says.

By this point, the people in the affected communities had decided that they should get themselves a lawyer who would take the case on contingency. They interviewed several candidates, including attorneys from several big firms in northern cities. They also talked to Thompson, who worked by himself out of Williamson's Mountaineer Hotel, in three adjoining rooms that, strewn with documents, suggested the research archive of a mad alchemist. Several personal injury lawyers had offices along Williamson's main street. But none of them would have considered taking the case. It was too big, too difficult, too expensive, and too anti-coal. Beyond that, nobody had the courage, cash, and legal resources to challenge Massey.

Common sense would seem to dictate that if the people who lived around Rawl were going to sue Massey, they should choose a rich, large outside firm and not Thompson, who had little in the bank and few other resources. But Thompson was one of them, a West Virginia boy who had moved to New Orleans and come back here to fight. He was a persuasive speaker, and he could talk to the people in their own language, the way outside lawyers could not.

In February 2004, as soon as Thompson won the job, he called his wife. "Honey, the water is so bad that they're not gonna have any defense," he said. "We'll make twenty million dollars in six months."

Thompson didn't have any business cards, never advertised, and had an unlisted number. He not only lacked the money needed to get first-rate expert witnesses but was disorganized and undisciplined, unable to do sufficiently the incredibly onerous discovery work that would be an essential part of this case. Beyond that, he'd had little experience litigating, and this was a case that would challenge even the most experienced trial lawyer.

Without the resources to vet the hundreds of people who wanted to join the suit, Thompson accepted everybody who showed up at the Mountaineer Hotel and signed an affidavit. Donald K. Dillon, a retired Massey miner, signed his name. He had four tumors in his back and a cyst in his brain. Billy Sammons Jr., a disabled Massey truck driver, signed on. He, his wife, and their children had constant diarrhea and frequent high fevers. Another truck driver, James Anderson, signed. He was only forty-one years old but had heart problems and was losing his memory and concentration. Christina Doyle signed not only for herself but for her two children; her daughter had been born without a pituitary gland. Madonna McCoy, a housewife, signed her name. She had been told by her doctor that because of the contamination, her sixteen-year-old daughter would never be able to have children.

The word went out that if you had ever so much as sipped that dark water, you should sign up. There was a family that had moved to Ohio and driven back to West Virginia for Thanksgiving one year whose intellectually disabled son drank the water with his turkey and cranberry sauce. They signed him up. An elderly couple listed their grandkids as living with them, figuring that this way they could leave those poor kids with some blessings they'd never had. These people did not think they were doing wrong. That was the way things were done. As far as they saw it, there was plenty of money to go around for anyone who had the gumption to get to Williamson and sign up.

Thompson was battling not only Blankenship and Massey but the counsel Massey had hired, Jackson Kelly, a prosperous Charleston firm that was considered mercilessly tough. He was also fighting the political power structure of Mingo County, and it was as painful an education for him as it had been for Tonya Hatfield, thirty miles away in Gilbert.

In April 2009, Circuit Judge Michael Thornsbury attempted to settle the claims. He put the hundreds of plaintiffs in a non-air-conditioned gymnasium with the temperature pushing eighty and shuttled them over to the courthouse in groups. The judge dangled before the plaintiffs amounts between $5,000 and $30,000, with most on the lower end.

Thompson advised his clients not to go along, but Thornsbury was a powerful, intimidating figure; he told the plaintiffs that "very few have fared better at trial than they did at the settlement conference." Most of the plaintiffs had never seen such sums of money in their lives, and when the judge gave them no more than five or ten minutes to make up their minds, scores of them settled. One of those who did not go along, Larry Brown Jr., said that he "felt like an animal being lined up and pushed through the door."

That left Thompson with about 650 clients, the prospects of a big trial, and little money to pay for expert witnesses and other expenses. He admitted to Stanley that the Pittsburgh lawyer hadn't been his first choice for help. He had several close out-of-state lawyer friends. He'd gone to them and, in exchange for the money to keep him going a little longer, had cut them in on his potential take. But those funds had run out.

Thompson was broke, and he made it clear to Stanley that he did not see how he could go on much longer unless Reed Smith came in with its checkbook. He would cut the firm in for an appropriate amount of the final settlement, and everyone would be happy. Stanley, however, wasn't about to ask Reed Smith merely to bankroll Thompson's suit. Stanley did not have a passive bone in his body, and if he got involved he'd want to take the lead.

Stanley understood that if he walked into a courtroom alongside Thompson to face Massey's lawyers, he would carry all of Reed Smith's authority, knowledge, financial resources, and expertise with him. No longer would the Massey lawyers be the bullies in the room, pushing Thompson around. Stanley would intimidate right back.

"I don't know if we can help or not," Stanley said. "But why don't you come up here. We'll sit down and talk it through."

It was a measure of how seriously Stanley regarded the potential case that when Thompson arrived at Reed Smith's Pittsburgh offices, four of the firm's young associates were sitting there with Stanley for the meeting. The firm had 1,500 largely buttoned-down corporate lawyers around the world, and although Stanley was the odd man out, many young associates wanted to work with him on the unusual, exciting cases that came his way.

Stanley could tell immediately that Thompson was "at wit's and wallet's end." Yet everyone in the room thought it was a strong case. If the plaintiffs could prove that the deaths and illnesses had derived from the tainted water, there could be hundreds of millions of dollars in a settlement or jury verdict. But to forestall that, the defense attorneys were practicing the three most maddening maxims of defense: delay, divert, and complicate. "They're wicked, dude," said Stanley. "They get paid for wrestling you in the mud year after year after year." The good news was that the case was near trial, and Stanley would be able to come in for only a limited number of hours—and, of course, to Reed Smith only a small percentage of any eventual settlement.

Thompson had put everything he had in the world—his financial resources, his emotions, and his entire career—into this case. It was easy to see why he feared that a monolith like Reed Smith, now by some estimates the fifteenth-largest law firm in the world, might come in and overwhelm him, taking credit for what should have been his alone. For Stanley's part, he was not going to sit back and watch this case fail because it was handled ineptly or because Thompson was too drained to do what had to be done.

Stanley had to prepare a lengthy proposal. It was not until July 2010 that Stanley went to managing partner Gregory Jordan and got his approval for Reed Smith to take on the representation on a contingent-fee basis. By then, there was already an inevitable and natural tension between Stanley and Thompson.

60

Stanley went to court with Thompson for the first time in August 2010, but it was not until the following month that he drove the three hundred miles to Rawl, to meet with about a hundred of the plaintiffs. He picked up Thompson in Williamson, and together they headed over to the Rawl Church of God, which stood in Rawl at the top of the hollow.

The church's fifty-five-year-old pastor, Larry Brown, had been presiding here for more than thirty years. He had spent his youth working in mining, but his blood pressure and arthritis had gotten so bad that in 1989 he'd quit. He was on welfare until 1996, when he started receiving full disability. That had not stopped him from preaching.

In 1989, Massey had been strip-mining on the mountain above Brown's single-wide modular home, which sat beside the church. The miners were not aware that there were pockets of methane buried in the mountain, and when they set off an explosion to expose the underlying coal, the entire top of the mountain blew off, damaging homes all the way down the hollow. The blast smashed the church's windows and cracked its walls, and within days the water from Brown's deep well turned shades of red and black.

A number of those whose water turned bad wanted to sue Massey, and they came to Brown because his church was the one place large enough for a meeting. He was a man of God, not of politics, and he did not know what to do. On a terribly hot summer day, he got down on his knees. "Lord," he prayed, "what do you want me to do with this church? What do you want me to do with this lawsuit?"

And then, Brown says, he heard the Lord respond to his prayers: "Stand with the people." When he looked up, he saw nothing but blood everywhere he could see, and he was afraid. But the Lord had spoken.

Brown drove his four-wheeler to what was left of the mountaintop. He sat there, gazing down on the world below, then closed his eyes and prayed. The mountainsides were thick with green foliage, but when he opened his eyes he had another vision. He saw only white. He knew what he was being told, thinking, "Oh, Lord, now I see this, and I must stand for the people." Then Brown looked across the valley, and there stood Blankenship's house, high above all the other homes. He said to himself, "The king's gonna come off his mountain. He's gonna come off 'cause there's only one king, and that's Jesus."

When Brown came down from the mountain, he told the people that they could hold their meeting at his church, and that he would join them. There were about 120 families in his church, but once he stood up against Massey his flock started to leave. Some left because they worked for the company and thought they had better not risk offending their bosses. Some could not stand the smell that permeated the church because of the bad water. Others did not want their children around the chemicals; so few children attended Sunday school that Brown had to end the classes. And others simply thought a preacher should preach and leave politics to the politicians. Soon there were only fifty families, and then thirty, and by the time Stanley and Thompson arrived that evening there were no more than twenty families left in the church.

Before the meeting, Stanley talked to a number of the hundred or so people who had shown up for the meeting. "I'm from Breeden," he said.

"Oh, my gosh!" said a man pressing up to meet him. "Why, you're from the poor side." Breeden gave Stanley more credibility here than a Harvard law degree.

"Let's pray," Brown said to open the meeting. "Let's put our faith in God. God, bless these people who have come here this evening because we are in trouble. And, God, thank you for bringing these lawyers, Bruce and Kevin, to us. Bless them, too; bless all of us. Amen."

Stanley knew that the people before him had been fooled, misguided, cheated, and abused so many times that they could only half-believe a lawyer's promises. "Look, folks, this is what I'm doing," Stanley said, in the same quiet, hard-to-hear voice he used in the courtroom. "I don't want this to go to court. You understand? I want to get this settled and get you your money. But the only way to settle cases with Massey is to let them know you're gonna haul them to court and go to trial. You can't bluff it. You gotta be ready. That's when they settle."

When Stanley finished and moved slowly up the aisle, he was surrounded by people telling him their stories and thanking him for coming. He had done his best to inspire them, and it was clear that they felt comfortable with him in a way they did not with Thompson.

On the drive back down to Williamson, Stanley kept looking at Thompson and thinking how the other lawyer had been projecting his own discouragement onto the hundreds of plaintiffs. "You're the plaintiff, for Christ's sake," Stanley said. "We've got to start attacking Massey and not just let these fuckers have at you."

Stanley had hoped that the courts would view the plaintiffs' case as a class action suit, expediting a resolution. But the Supreme Court of Appeals of West Virginia rejected that idea and instead appointed three circuit judges—James Mazzone, John Hutchinson, and Jay Hoke—to oversee litigating the many cases.

Stanley had respected how Hoke had handled *Caperton* in the Boone County courtroom but had disdained how he had let Massey's lawyers delay the resolution of the verdict for four years. And he wondered if Hoke and the others would now sit back and let this overly complicated scenario collapse in more years of delay. Hoke was perfectly aware of the likely unpleasantness and intricacy of the suits, and he had agreed to participate only as a special favor to some of his colleagues at the state supreme court.

The judges decided that the case should be adjudicated in a series of trials that would involve seven plaintiffs at a time, representing seven different categories of illnesses and maladies: "cancer or renal failure; cognitive impairment such as attention-deficit disorder; colon or kidney problems; leukemia, spina bifida or pancreatitis; cysts, boils or internal ulcers; gallbladder problems; and chronic diarrhea, rashes or other so-called 'sentinel symptoms' of exposure to contaminated water." In each trial, if the jury determined that the plaintiffs' conditions were due to the water and Massey had caused the problem, there would be a second trial to determine damages. The multiple trials could spin on for years.

The judges asked Thompson and Stanley which plaintiffs' cases they thought should be heard first. Stanley knew this was a Fawcett moment, when you wanted to be prepared beforehand with your desired litigants and present them to the three judges in such a way that their claims would seem not only legitimate but inevitable. But that was not Thompson's way. Instead of making suggestions, he made excuses.

"Some of our clients are in jail," cried Thompson. "And lots of them live in Ohio now and other places, so it's hard to get them together."

One of the judges went on to insist that all the plaintiffs—no matter where they were—show up at a mediation hearing at the Charleston Civic Center. If the hearing accomplished nothing else, it would at least reduce the number of plaintiffs.

Some of these litigants were in their eighties. Some were in wheelchairs. Some were practically bedridden. Some had never been to Charleston in their lives. Some lived hundreds of miles away. And practically all of them had to be there or, in all likelihood, they would be dismissed from the case.

Stanley rented four tour buses, and early on the morning of November 15, 2010, hundreds of the plaintiffs set off for the capital. Most got to Charleston on their own, and when Stanley walked into the civic center, he was stunned to see that the auditorium was packed. It was obvious to Stanley that the chances of mediating a settlement amid this circus were minimal, but the judges had issued a challenge, and in getting almost everyone there Stanley and Thompson had met it. Looking out at row after row of those who had made the journey, Stanley knew that he would never again doubt the plaintiffs' resolve.

Stanley talked to as many of the plaintiffs as he could, including Donald Dillon, one of the plaintiffs' leaders. Dillon had all kinds of ailments including lesions, an enlarged prostate, and blood in his urine. He believed that his wife had died from the bad water, and today he wore a T-shirt bearing his wife's picture and the words "Sadly missed by the family."

Stanley was distressed to see the last person he expected to on this long day: the Honorable Robin J. Davis of the Supreme Court of Appeals of West Virginia. Since Davis was one of the justices who'd named the three-judge panel, she had a legitimate right to be here and to acknowledge the plaintiffs publicly. She stood up and briefly addressed the group, speaking in a droning monotone. She was reportedly considering running for the United States Senate, but even if she did not, her speech to the coal slurry litigants would help in her 2012 reelection campaign.

Stanley and Thompson had alerted the local media to the massive mediation, and camera crews and reporters from around the city had shown up. That evening, the story led the local news, and the next day it was on the front pages of the *Charleston Gazette* and the *Charleston Daily Mail,* with pictures of litigants displaying their bottles of discolored tap water. As Stanley looked at the news stories, he thought: "Those Jackson Kelly boys wanted a fight. And now they're getting one."

61

In the aftermath of Upper Big Branch, Blankenship and Massey faced a public relations crisis unlike anything they'd experienced before. Blankenship was finally forced into assuming a conciliatory manner that was not in his nature. He gave a statesmanlike address at the National Press Club, in Washington, D.C., on July 22, 2010, in which he condemned "knee-jerk political reactions" to mine deaths. He regularly lectured on Twitter ("We regret the national news is so inaccurate").

And then, on November 19, 2010, Blankenship called a press conference at Massey's regional headquarters in Julian, West Virginia, inviting a select list of leading national and state journalists, including those he despised. Blankenship never raised his voice as he condemned reporters for having attempted to blame Massey when they should have been looking at the failures of the federal regulators. The focus, he said, should be not on the "underdog" coal companies but "on the physics, the chemistry, the math, the science, to figure out what the source of the explosion was, rather than trying to point fingers."

In the two-and-a-half-hour marathon, Blankenship acted as if he stood above other men and other executives, that he was invincible. Blankenship's only strategy was to aggressively move forward. The only subject Blankenship declared off-limits was the possible sale of Massey. To his associates, he made the folksy analogy that you did not sell your truck when it was broken. At a time when the company's stock was down and the media were beating him up, he wanted to go out and acquire a new company and grow even bigger.

Immediately after the press conference, as the Massey board prepared to meet at the Greenbrier Resort in White Sulphur Springs, West Virginia, the *Wall Street Journal* reported that the board members "may clash with longtime Chief Executive Don Blankenship as they debate a possible sale of the coal company and some other options that would produce a leadership change." In dumping Blankenship, it appeared, they hoped to dump culpability.

Eight months after the twenty-nine deaths at Upper Big Branch, Blankenship left the company. In early December 2010, after thirty years at Massey, he announced his retirement. He left with $10.9 million in salary and assorted benefits, a $39 million retirement package, plus $14.4 million in accumulated perks and severance. The arrangement included five years of an office complete with a secretary, the company house where he had lived most of his adult life, $267,111 for payment of property taxes, an option to buy the land next door, a consulting contract worth $5,000 a month for two years, and a 1965 Chevy truck.

There was no public mourning among Massey's 5,800 employees, nor any editorials praising Blankenship's accomplishments. The most enthusiastic response came from Wall Street, where Massey stock rose $1.21, or 2.4 percent, per share.

Blankenship disappeared from public view, but everything Stanley and Fawcett knew about the man said that he was not gone for good. In some way, at some place, he would likely reconnect with the only world he knew, likely to assume some other major role in the coal industry.

Fawcett and Stanley knew that starting *Caperton* over again in Virginia would test their own resolve as well as tax their respective firms' willingness to continue financing the case, and they struggled with what to do. In the end, Buchanan Ingersoll decided that the law firm had sacrificed enough money and time fighting *Caperton* and they were moving on. Instead of joining them, Reed Smith took the extraordinary step of picking up the corporate suit as well, and Stanley went ahead and filed in Virginia in November 2010.

The crucial reason behind Buchanan Ingersoll's refusal to continue fighting *Caperton* became clear the following month when the firm's major client in the coal industry, Alpha Natural Resources, announced it had agreed to purchase Massey for $7.1 billion in cash and stock to close in June 2011. With all the legal problems inherited by the enlarged company, Buchanan Ingersoll anticipated a large increase in hourly billing, far more than Fawcett generated fighting Massey.

Fawcett was a highly regarded partner, but it would be both unethical and bad business to have him taking potshots at Alpha. If he had followed his father's philosophy, he would have shrugged the whole business off, walked away from his Massey cases, and gone on with things as they were, perhaps even using his expertise to defend Alpha in a suit or two. But that was not Fawcett.

Fawcett had anticipated spending his entire career at Buchanan Ingersoll, but in December 2010 Fawcett became a partner in Reed Smith, with Devine accompanying him as a legal assistant. Stanley had helped to bring Fawcett to his firm, where, in all likelihood, he himself would end his career as he'd begun it, a few doors down from his longtime friend and co-counsel. As part of signing on Fawcett, Reed Smith took over the full burden of financing Fawcett in the Harman corporate suit, while Stanley continued representing Caperton in the personal suit. The firm did not look askance at total costs that had reached well over $4 million.

62

In May 2011, Stanley was working on the coal slurry suit in his office, and down the hall Fawcett was busy on the second Wheeling-Pitt suit. Since the two lawyers remained closely involved in bringing down Blankenship, Stanley felt it was important for him to be in the audience to hear the report of Governor Manchin's task force investigating Upper Big Branch at a press conference at the Tamarack Arts Center, outside Beckley.

The governor had deputized J. Davitt McAteer, a former assistant secretary of labor for the Mine Safety and Health Administration, to head the investigation. Stanley knew many of the people involved writing the report, and he wanted to show that he believed they were all in this together.

Three detailed reports had followed Bragg's and Hatfield's deaths at Aracoma: one commissioned by the governor, one by state regulators, and one by the federal government. The tragedy at Upper Big Branch showed that in the aftermath of Aracoma nothing had changed—not Massey's behavior, not the region's coal culture, and not the political and legal power structure that ensured that those ultimately responsible for miners' deaths would escape punishment.

Stanley feared that this latest report would also change nothing. Stanley was friends not only with McAteer but with another of the report's contributors, Patrick C. McGinley, who'd been one of his teachers in law school. Stanley had talked with McGinley for hours, explaining how and why he thought the tragedy was the inevitable result of conduct that he and Fawcett had been chronicling for more than a decade. Stanley talked about Aracoma and the similarities to Upper Big Branch. He talked about what he and Fawcett had done in the courtroom to expose the culture of Massey and its architect, Don Blankenship.

Stanley was disappointed to learn that a coal slurry hearing in Wheeling that day would keep him from the media conference, and he asked Caperton to go in his place. If nothing else, Caperton reasoned, the event would get him away from his home office, where all he did was send out résumés and worry about the new suit in Virginia. He made the short drive to the arts center, which had been built by his cousin Gaston Caperton when he was governor.

Caperton had prepared a statement in case reporters wanted to talk to him, but as soon as he saw the twenty-nine victims' spouses and relatives exiting from their private meeting, he put the paper back in his pocket. He vowed that if any journalist approached, he would say he had no comment and walk away. His role here today, he realized, was the role that the women of Sylvester had played at the Boone County trial and he had played at the Aracoma trial: to sit in support and show that he and the victims were united against Blankenship.

As he sat waiting, Caperton could not help thinking of his own situation. He had creditors at his throat. He owed several hundred thousand dollars to the IRS. The Grundy National Bank was trying to enforce a judgment against his assets. State tax authorities were after him. Even if he had gotten a settlement, the first thing he would have had to do was to pay $4 million to the two hedge funds.

Caperton felt that his life was nothing but "pure hell" and the sheer unfairness of it was overwhelming. He had fought until the laws of the land had been changed and his name would rest forever on a historic opinion at the United States Supreme Court, but what did he have? Many of Massey's other victims had rightfully received settlements. Fawcett and Stanley had gotten new clients and prestige. He had gotten nothing but a haunted future with no seeming exit from his troubles.

Caperton felt that in fighting for a measure of justice, he had sacrificed almost everything. He had, in fact, gotten $2 million from the two hedge funds. That was enough money to maintain the illusion to the world that life was the way it had always been. It had not been enough money, however, so that he could pay his massive debts.

In challenging Blankenship, Caperton had acted with courage and resolve and without him the fight against the Massey chairman might never have begun or reached such a forceful level. But with the prickly pride that had sustained him in this endless legal battle, he had refused to seek out a new life somewhere else. Caperton had held off his creditors for years and not made the hard choices that, now that the money was running out, he might soon have to make.

Before the conference, Caperton read a copy of the report. One page listed the names and titles of eighteen Massey employees, beginning with Blankenship, who had taken the Fifth Amendment rather than testify about Upper Big Branch to the three sets of government-sanctioned investigators.

Caperton had attended a day of the Aracoma trial, and he had a good grasp of what had caused the fire that had killed Bragg and Hatfield. As he leafed through the report, he realized how similar the two incidents were. Just as at Aracoma, in the days before the explosion, there'd been miners at Upper Big Branch who'd said they were "just scared to death something bad is going to happen." Reading the report, he could see that Upper Big Branch was also a capital-intensive, longwall operation in which the miners were pushed unrelentingly to produce. There were the same problems with reversed ventilation, faulty water pumps, neck-deep water, and filthy conveyer belts.

The Upper Big Branch report found state and federal inspectors derelict, as they had been at Aracoma. In the mine, rock dusting, which prevents explosions, had been insufficient, but that lack had gone unnoted. So had the methane buildup, which had ignited the fireball that had roared two miles through the mine.

"Ultimately, all of the historic lessons so painfully learned as a result of the terrible loss of life during the first decade of the 20th century apparently were forgotten or ignored by the management at Upper Big Branch," the report said.

Caperton was fascinated by the report. He read: "Massey Energy Chairman and CEO Don Blankenship had a long history of wielding or attempting to wield influence in the state's seats of government." And then, as Caperton continued reading, he was startled to see his name and to read how Harman had been forced into bankruptcy. The report also named Delorice Bragg and Freda Hatfield and quoted federal authorities who blamed Massey for "reckless disregard" of safety rules in Elvis's and Rizzle's deaths.

The report described an outlaw company aided and abetted by the most powerful people in the state.

"If we are going to have a mining industry, we have to reform the way we do business, or our fellow citizens will suggest that we shouldn't be in this business at all," McAteer told the assembled journalists. "We can't continue to mine with the reckless disregard for the safety of our miners."

When Fawcett read the report back in his Pittsburgh office, he was impressed by the investigation's boldness. Unlike any previous official or semiofficial coal accident report—and likely spurred on by Stanley's vigorous public and private lobbying and all the media interest their fights together had generated—the document moved beyond the immediate explosion. It spoke about the Massey culture, which, as Fawcett saw it, had bankrupted such companies as Harman and Wheeling-Pitt, destroyed the environment, and killed its own employees and neighbors. The report also criticized the political climate in West Virginia, detailing how it supported Massey's behavior and was complicit in the Upper Big Branch tragedy.

When McAteer asked for questions, a reporter shouted out, "Massey has already put out a statement." The journalist read the Massey press release aloud. Instead of expressing sympathy to the families of the twenty-nine dead miners, it began by insisting that the explosion was an unfortunate, unforeseen natural act. "We believe that the explosion was caused by a massive inundation of methane-rich natural gas," the statement read. "Our experts feel confident that coal dust did not play an important role."

When Caperton left that day, he was glad he had come, but whenever he was around coal people, he had melancholy feelings about no longer being part of that world. Despite everything he had gone through, he still loved the coal industry and would have given up any prospect of a financial settlement if he could just start all over again without any debts and run a mine.

Caperton knew that he would do it right, not like Massey and Blankenship. It sickened him to hear that press release, to know that the culture of Massey and Blankenship was still alive—even the arrogant and cavalier way they dealt with their critics. They never said they were sorry. They never accepted any blame. And they walked bold and tall while he walked alone, trying to puzzle out some kind of future.

63

In the first months of 2011, Stanley became overwhelmingly frustrated with the coal slurry litigation's process. He had never in his career wished he hadn't signed on to a case, but he sometimes did now. He was discouraged by what he believed was a poor job Thompson had done preparing for trial. Beyond that, some of the plaintiffs had begun to complain about colitigants who, they felt, hadn't been harmed and would lessen the true victims' awards. That was something that could blow up publicly and destroy the case. Stanley feared that the case was in such bad shape that the judges might not even allow it to go before a jury.

Despite all of the effort needed to prepare for the coal slurry trial, Thompson had filed a separate class action lawsuit accusing a Massey coal-loading silo close to an elementary school of exposing schoolchildren to coal dust and creating environmental hazards. It was a complicated business and took Thompson away from the coal slurry suit, a fact about which the litigants endlessly chattered. Stanley was not surprised when, in March 2011, a jury returned a verdict in favor of Massey.

Many of the same expert witnesses would be testifying in the coal slurry litigation. Stanley had gotten into the suit too late to change the witness list or to hire new experts, so he was stuck with them. Even if they won with these witnesses, the cases were supposed to go ahead seven at a time, and Stanley realized that they could be fighting an unending series of battles. Some of the plaintiffs were so old and sick that they would probably die before they ever saw their day in court. Such, Stanley figured, was the price of justice in West Virginia.

Stanley had arranged to depose Blankenship in the water cases on June 2, 2011, at the Embassy Suites hotel in Charleston. Ever since the Upper Big Branch disaster, the media had intensified their attacks on Blankenship. Dana Milbank wrote in the *Washington Post,* "If Don Blankenship had any sense of shame, he'd crawl into a mine and hide." In the six months after leaving Massey, Blankenship had indeed gone missing. He was no longer living in Sprigg, and almost no one knew where he was. The deposition would mark Blankenship's first public appearance since his retirement.

Stanley and Thompson wanted Blankenship to make what they called "a perp walk" from the offices of his attorney Jackson Kelly, across the street from the hotel, into the deposition room. Thompson had alerted WCHS, the local ABC affiliate, and two of its camera crews would film Blankenship's every step.

At ten minutes to one, Blankenship, who had lost about twenty pounds and appeared as fit as he had in decades, emerged with his lawyer from the building that housed the law firm. When a crew approached, Blankenship refused to grant an interview, but the cameras trailed him as he and his attorney crossed the street. As they reached the curb, a second camera loomed up, boxing him in. Blankenship had learned his lesson after the ABC skirmish in Belfry. He politely stepped aside and kept on walking.

As Blankenship proceeded up the Embassy Suites driveway, a process server, who had been pretending to doze on a bench, thrust a document at him. Blankenship pressed his hands to his side, letting the summons flutter to the ground, the incident caught on video. The former CEO said nothing as his tongue licked at his lips.

Blankenship took the hotel elevator up to the meeting room where the deposition would occur. He could look down onto the atrium, where the West Virginia Association for Justice, the state trial lawyers' organization, was holding its annual convention.

The lawyers were having a meet and greet for notables, including one of the afternoon's speakers, Justice Davis. She worked the gathering just as she had the coal slurry plaintiffs' mediation seven months before. She had once been described by a sympathetic journalist as looking like an eighth-grade teacher. That was no longer the case. She wore a sleeveless black dress and designer pumps, and diamond studs shimmered in her ears. Most of the trial lawyers welcomed the chance for a few minutes of conversation with the formidable judge before whom they might one day have to appear.

All Davis had to do was look up and she would have seen the man for whose company she and her colleagues had saved a verdict that with interest had reached $76 million. Three times she had sought to end *Caperton* for good, and the third time, she thought, she had finally succeeded. But most likely one day Fawcett or Stanley, or both of them together, would stand before her at the Supreme Court of Appeals of West Virginia on some other matter involving Massey and Blankenship and take their chances once again.

When Blankenship walked into the room, three of the plaintiffs were sitting there, including Dillon, whose ailments took two pages to list. Blankenship looked at the men and said, "Good luck."

"It was more like, Get me if you can," says Dillon. "That's how I took it." The retired miner had worked for Massey in a number of operations and knew that the company dumped slurry into abandoned mines. He said that he'd turned down one job at a Massey preparation plant "because of the fact of them pumping slurry in there." He had worked for Rawl Sales for twelve and a half years. When all he'd needed was six months more to be fully vested in his pension plan, the company had let him go. "To me, Massey is greedy," Dillon says. "Massey destroys families."

It had taken this lawsuit and Thompson's shouting to get Mingo County to install pipes so the people could drink clean water, even if it cost them $60 a month when their well water had been free.

Dillon was seventy-three years old, and he figured he did not have much longer to live. His wife had died a terrible death, he believed, because of the water. His daughter was sick, and his son had health problems, too. Dillon wanted a measure of justice and money that might give his children and grandchildren a better life.

In 2002, during the Boone County trial, Blankenship had acknowledged that he'd employed a cost-benefit approach to every decision he made. Today, nearly a decade later, he used language in the deposition that was strikingly familiar. He admitted that "underground injection probably represents a cost savings" and that he had directed no research into the environmental consequences of injecting slurry into the mines.

Blankenship expressed little knowledge of the underground injection without an environmental permit that had first taken place in the early 1980s, when he started at Rawl Sales, and had continued as he'd risen to the top of the company. When the deposition was almost over, Stanley asked a question to show how employees were indoctrinated to do whatever Blankenship told them to do.

"The story I heard," Stanley said, "is a gentleman found himself at the desk for the first day [at Massey] and there sat a DAD'S coffee cup with a DAD'S root beer logo on it. And he asked, 'What's this for, DAD'S?' And they said, 'That means "Do as Don Says."' Is that true?"

"There is some truth to that," said Blankenship, unsmiling. "After giving a lot of directions that aren't followed, which oftentimes leads to bad results, you get where you want someone to follow the direction you're giving. It's a humorous way, if you will, to have a reminder just to have a cup sitting there. Just remember the DAD'S cup."

"Have you visited any of the folks in the Rawl or Sprigg area to discuss with them any of their problems?" Stanley asked next. The nearest of them lived only a few hundred yards from Blankenship's house.

"No, I haven't done that," Blankenship said. "I've talked to one or two of them when they run into me on the street."

"Have you discussed with any of them their health problems or any of the concerns that they have as a result of their exposure to the slurry?" Stanley asked.

"I wouldn't see any purpose," Blankenship said, as the five plaintiffs sat looking at him. "And I wouldn't be qualified to discuss it with them, and it would be outside the realm of what counsel would want me to do in these circumstances."

Stanley knew that Blankenship had said what his lawyer wanted him to say, and for the most part he had given nothing away. Stanley knew, too, that when the Jackson Kelly lawyers presented their defense, they would likely produce medical evidence showing the appalling health of people all through the region, not just in Rawl. And the defense lawyers would argue that there was little proof that the coal slurry had seeped into aquifers and run into well water a good distance away, and that well water in these parts was often poor anyway. As Stanley walked out of the Embassy Suites that afternoon, he knew that he was in for a tough fight in which what he considered victory and full justice was unlikely.

64

In mid-July 2011, two weeks before the Rawl coal slurry trials were set to begin, the panel of judges brought in two new judges to try to mediate a settlement. Thompson and Stanley went at it with the Massey attorneys all day long and well into the evening. At midnight the defense lawyers made their first real offer, and the two sides negotiated until four in the morning. They settled on $35 million, plus $5 million for medical monitoring to be divided among the 650 plaintiffs based on the severity of their conditions.

Thompson had sought far more money for the plaintiffs and for himself. The victims would be suffering for years to come, and he'd wanted Massey and the entire coal industry to understand that if they poisoned the environment of the people of West Virginia, they would pay a monumental price.

Stanley figured that if the plaintiffs could have proved their case in court, they might have merited hundreds of millions of dollars. But he had signed on too late. He hadn't had years to dig for incriminating documents, as he, Devine, and Fawcett would have done.

After the lawyers took their 33 percent fee, the proposed settlement would likely net several hundred thousand dollars for each of the most aggrieved plaintiffs and several thousand dollars for the least injured. Stanley considered the $35 million a misdemeanor fine for a felony criminal offense. But just as in the settlement of Delorice and Freda's case, he had to be realistic. As many as a hundred of the plaintiffs might not have legitimate claims. The defense attorneys could bring them into court, destroy them, and thus raise doubts about the rightful grievances. What's more, the Jackson Kelly lawyers would tear apart Thompson's expert witnesses, just as they had only a few months before.

In the end, the plaintiffs agreed to the settlement. Stanley and his team wound up working far more hours than he had originally planned, yet by the terms of the contract with Thompson, his firm would receive less payment than some of the expert witnesses. He believed that without him there would have been no settlement at all. That the plaintiffs would probably never know this was of no consequence to him.

65

In the summer of 2011, soon after Alpha Natural Resources finalized its purchase of Massey Energy, Caperton phoned Michael J. Quillen, the chairman of Alpha, to ask him if he wanted to sit down to try to settle *Caperton*. Caperton appreciated the work his lawyers had done, but he became irritated when Stanley blustered on about how Alpha was just another name for Massey. Caperton knew Quillen, who had founded Alpha in 2002 and played an important role in building it so quickly into such a major player.

Quillen was a coal man, like Hugh. Caperton thought it was just plain foolish to start mouthing off when Quillen might be ready to start talking settlement. And if Quillen did, Caperton believed, he would have to be the one up front, speaking coal man to coal man, possibly with a team of new lawyers who weren't so confoundedly anti-coal.

This wasn't just Caperton's over-the-top optimism speaking, either. When the Alpha executives had negotiated the purchase price, they had factored in the likely amounts they would have to pay out for Massey's many ongoing lawsuits. Caperton figured the new owner would want to put as many of these suits behind it as it could, and would be delighted to try to settle *Caperton*.

Quillen couldn't have been friendlier in his chat with Caperton, sharing all the industry gossip. Then he said that Alpha was overwhelmed with Massey's leftover legal cases and that it would address *Caperton* as soon as it could. Several months later, however, Alpha still had not offered to settle, so Caperton called again, and Quillen gave the same explanation. A few months later, Caperton called yet again and got the same response.

Caperton had still not found a job. He traveled to Pittsburgh to talk to a major construction company and called coal operations in South Africa and Australia. Coal companies did need salesmen, and he had the skills to be a good one. But he would not be able to sell to the biggest coal company in the region as long as he was suing it. He sent out hundreds of résumés, and he went to scores of interviews. Everybody was polite. Everybody praised him. But nobody would hire him.

In October 2011, Stanley and Devine drove to Clintwood, Virginia, for the first *Caperton* hearing in state court. There they met the Capertons. At fifty-six, Caperton was still handsome, but his hair was graying. Despite everything that had happened, he was as much a believer in the coal industry as he had been when he was the proud owner of the Harman mine. Even Alpha's refusal to negotiate with him had not changed his attitude.

The Capertons had long experience with how well Fawcett and Stanley worked together. They found it disconcerting that Fawcett, who was busy with another case, was not here. Stanley, meanwhile, was glad his friend had not driven down. Fawcett could do just one important task at a time, and as he prepared for one trial, he could not get ready to make a key argument in another. That's just the way Dave was, Stanley thought. He felt that Fawcett would have been so distracted that he would have been a hindrance.

As Stanley sat down at the plaintiffs' table with local counsel Thomas L. Pruitt and Caperton beside him, arrayed across from him was a formidable group of opposing attorneys from Kellogg, Huber, Hansen, Todd, Evans & Figel, a leading boutique Washington firm. They were led by forty-year-old Kevin B. Huff, a Columbia Law graduate who had clerked for Justice Scalia, and thirty-one-year-old Daniel G. Bird, a Yale Law School graduate who had edited the *Yale Law Journal*. Kathy Caperton thought that the youthful Huff appeared much like Fawcett when she had first met him, close to a decade and a half ago.

Judge Henry Vanover had a silver-white beard. The hefty judge looked down on the courtroom with a scowl and commanded the lawyers to proceed.

Caperton had become an orphan suit. In her three rejections, Justice Davis had said it didn't belong in her state. Now that the plaintiffs had come to Virginia, they feared that they wouldn't be wanted here, either.

Huff began arguing, in a tedious drone, that res judicata mandated that Caperton had no right for a second trial in Virginia, since the case had long since been resolved. Stanley recognized legal quality when he heard it, and he knew that this young lawyer was making a thorough presentation. He figured the Washington firm charged $1,000 an hour; including preparation, he estimated, he was listening to an argument costing a good $400,000. As counsel on a warmed-over contingency case, Stanley was hoping one day to be paid his $500 an hour, but he wasn't counting on having it on hand when it came time to finance his youngest daughter's college education.

Stanley knew that these Washington lawyers were doing whatever they could to keep *Caperton* from a jury, which would likely find Massey guilty of egregious conduct, as had juries in Virginia and West Virginia and even the Supreme Court of Appeals of West Virginia, in its first reversal.

Stanley's argument was far more emotional. While the defense attorneys spoke in a narrow, directed fashion to the judge, Stanley at times sounded as if he were speaking to a jury. Judges sometimes disliked this approach, but if the case was to be decided on passion and intensity, Stanley had clearly won.

As Stanley left the courtroom, he worried about their prospects. He thought there might have been a mistake in the complaint that would require them to amend. That was a serious matter in any legal proceeding, but he shrugged it off. Caperton, of course, thought it had gone well. And now, as always, they had to wait for the judge's decision.

In November 2011, Caperton finally found a job. He was hired by an Australian company, Mine Site Technologies, an innovator in underground communications, where he became director of eastern sales. As he traveled the territory, he reflected sometimes that Stanley and Fawcett stood at exalted positions in their careers, while he was starting over at an age when many men were thinking about retirement. He could not indulge in endless remorse or a litany of "What if?" and "Why did I?" He was competing against men half his age in a tough business, and his financial condition was still so dicey that every time he looked behind himself he saw the shadow of bankruptcy.

Professor Sample talks of the Capertons' "strength and resolve, which in all likelihood will never, ever personally benefit them, but will resonate for decades to come with the landmark principle of the case that bears their name. Hugh and Kathy have managed to stay married, and even to give of themselves to others in deeply personal ways, through positively biblical struggles ranging from health to finances to humiliations."

Hugh had stood up to an onslaught that would have broken most men, but the lawsuit had caused what he considered "unfathomable pain and suffering to me and my family." He wondered if his ordeal would ever end.

After all these years, Caperton was emotionally overwhelmed by the sheer unfairness of this struggle. He wanted to strike back at those who had wronged him or let him down, but he risked flailing out and damaging only himself.

66

In December 2011, an order arrived at Reed Smith's Pittsburgh office from Judge Vanover of the Virginia Circuit Court. It dismissed *Caperton* on the grounds of res judicata, saying that the plaintiffs had no business filing another suit in the Commonwealth of Virginia.

Fawcett and Stanley called Caperton and explained that they would be appealing to the Supreme Court of Virginia. The two attorneys believed that Vanover's arguments were flawed and that, if the Virginia supreme court heard their appeal, *Caperton* would likely once again go to trial. The Richmond court, however, was more conservative than its West Virginia counterpart, and the justices might not welcome the yellowing pages of a suit that had been wandering through Appalachia for almost a decade and a half. And if they did rule that *Caperton* could proceed, it might be several more years before the saga ended.

For Fawcett and Stanley, there was not even a moment of debating whether they should give up and move on in this case, which had reached close to $5 million in unpaid billing for Reed Smith and another $3 million for Buchanan Ingersoll. They immediately began to prepare their appeal. It was emotionally and intellectually an immensely difficult business. They had been at this for thirteen years now, and they had never for a moment been able to relax. On this occasion, they had to deal with a Caperton who worried that his two attorneys were no longer paying close attention to his case and had moved on to more exciting and more lucrative cases. Within the firm, they could express only the most exalted optimism, and not let any self-doubt creep into their voices.

That may have all been cheerleading, but when they sat down to begin the appeal, they knew that their opponents were some of the best young lawyers in Washington. They had to be at the top of their game. They objected vociferously to each detail of the documents that would be filed with the Virginia Supreme Court, sending a message that they would be fighting over every inch of ground.

Meanwhile, the government investigated the Upper Big Branch explosion with a vigor it had not shown after the Aracoma deaths of Bragg and Hatfield. A miner who had faked foreman's credentials and lied to investigators pleaded guilty and was sentenced to ten months in jail. The security chief was convicted and sentenced to three years in prison. The mine superintendent pleaded guilty and was sentenced to a maximum of five years in prison and a $250,000 fine for "conspiracy to defraud the United States." His plea suggested that he may have given evidence against his superiors, even possibly including his ultimate superior: Donald Blankenship.

Fawcett continued to fight the second Wheeling-Pitt case. It sickened him when people accused him of making a profession out of suing Massey and said that in his latest case he was overreaching. As Fawcett saw it, Blankenship was the one who had overreached, daring to attempt the same outrageous strategy that had already cost the company a $220 million verdict in the first trial. Moreover, those who said he was overreaching had not read the discovery materials from the coal company. Fawcett worried primarily not that he would lose in court but that the jury would come up with such an enormous verdict that it might be overturned upon appeal.

In June, Fawcett flew to Washington to depose Blankenship at the Reed Smith offices. Wearing a baseball cap, Blankenship slumped in, surrounded by a team of lawyers. He had gained back the weight he had lost and looked almost forlorn. He faced possible criminal indictment for the twenty-nine deaths at Upper Big Branch, and beyond the team of Alpha lawyers he had with him his own personal attorney.

It had been a long war, and as Fawcett set out to depose Blankenship in a conference room crowded with lawyers and videographers, he felt none of the personal animosity he once had. It was all so sad and unnecessary and such an awesome waste, but as Blankenship started answering questions, Fawcett could tell that the former Massey chairman had learned little. He was the same soft-spoken, belligerent presence he had been the first time Fawcett had deposed him in Richmond, almost fourteen years before.

In August, on the day before the trial was to begin in Wheeling, Alpha settled Fawcett's second Wheeling-Pitt case. Fawcett had been asking $32 million in compensatory damages plus punitive damages that could easily reach $100 million or more. The settlement was confidential, but it was enough to keep what was left of the beleaguered company going and secure scores of union jobs.

Fawcett had a profound sense of resolution. He took a week off and spent time with his wife, enjoying her company. Fourteen-year-old Daniel was the only child left at home, born just as Fawcett's struggles against Massey were beginning. Father and son went running together and did some backpacking. And on Saturday morning, as always, Fawcett took the talented musician to his cello lessons at Duquesne University. Fawcett was at peace in a way he had never been before, and he sensed that he was a fortunate man.

The Dave Fawcett of old would not have been so sanguine. For fourteen years he had struggled to bring Hugh Caperton a measure of justice. Where was Hugh now but driving alone on those narrow mountain roads, traveling from coal mine to coal mine, in a job he was happy to have. And from the legal struggle, he carried with him an endless legacy of anguish. Blankenship was living the good life in his new home in Tennessee while Tony Arbaugh served out his years in Huttonsville Correctional Center. The former Wheeling-Pitt's steel plants were mainly shuttered and so were the lives of the union men who had worked there.

None would dare call this justice, and once Fawcett would have found a way to blame himself. Young Fawcett had wanted to change the world. If there was nobility in this, there was also a measure of arrogance in the way he assumed it was his fault when he did not achieve what he considered a fair result. He saw life differently now, in some measure the way his father saw it. He saw that a man could do only his best, and he had done that. And he had paid his own steep price. Because of his obsession with *Caperton*, he had lost for two years the right to live half-time with his children. He had lost not only lucrative clients but his very law firm. He had fought as hard as a lawyer could fight, but it was time to move on now, to other battles and other wars.

As Fawcett looked back, he was most proud of the jury verdicts. He had presented complicated cases in three small American towns— Grundy, Virginia; Madison, West Virginia; and Wellsburg, West Virginia—hundreds of miles apart, to conservative, hardworking, independent-thinking jurors, people who were willing to keep an open mind and do what was right.

In every case, Massey had hired highly talented, fierce advocates from multiple law firms. In every case, these lawyers tried to delay and derail the cases before they got to a jury, and Massey's trial lawyers defended the coal company vigorously. They claimed that these were complex business disputes in which their client was not culpable. They put on long defenses and argued that money damages were not appropriate, but the jurors saw through them.

In each closing argument, Fawcett told them what he knew to be true: "You are now well qualified to decide this case." And, as his father had said to so many juries over the years, he added, "All we ask for—all anyone who comes into court can ask for—is that you do what is right and fair under the law."

Over the past few years, Fawcett had come to see that he was truly his father's son. He was thankful that his father had brought him up to adhere to high standards of conduct. He was proud of this, as a Fawcett man and his father's son. He saw now, as he hadn't as a young man, that his father did not care about living ethically merely to impress the world but because that was what a man was supposed to do.

All of Fawcett's life, no matter what he had done, no matter how high he'd reached, no matter how extraordinary the accolades, all his father focused upon was the integrity of the effort. Fawcett had bristled at that but in the last months of his life before Dave Fawcett Jr. died in May 2012, father and son expressed an open pride in each other. They came to recognize that what they might have seen as differences were immaterial, and what they shared was far greater and far more alike than they ever knew.

Fawcett was still very much "a cause kind of fellow," as his father had called him so many years ago. There was no greater satisfaction than fighting to right a wrong, and Dave felt empty when he did not have such a case. He had become involved with a pro bono case for the Innocence Project, trying to free a young man he believed had been falsely convicted to three life terms for an arson that had killed three Pittsburgh firefighters. The case did not consume him the way *Caperton* had, but it kept a flame burning.

In April 2012, just before the statute of limitations deadline, Stanley filed a suit against Blankenship and other Massey executives on behalf of the mother and siblings of Edward Dean Jones, one of the twenty-nine victims of Upper Big Branch. Rarely in a disaster did family members other than the surviving spouses and children receive compensation for their losses. Stanley believed that if he could only get before a panel of jurors, they would understand that attention must be paid to a mother's pain, a twin brother's grieving, and a sister's unrelieved sadness. It was such a quixotic quest that no other trial lawyer filed a similar suit for the families of any of the other twenty-eight victims.

Stanley figured this would be one of the greatest challenges of his professional life. He knew that the Massey/Alpha attorneys would fight with shrewdness and savvy at every junction. But Massey and Alpha had learned painfully that Stanley was neither a bluffer nor a man intimidated by the strength of their legal team. In August 2012 they came to Stanley and settled the suit. The amount was confidential, but whatever it was, it was an extraordinary, precedent-setting victory.

"Bruce, there is really no appropriate expression that could adequately thank you," Jones's sister, Judy Jones Peterson, e-mailed Stanley. "You believed in us. You validated our pain and loss. You fought for justice for my brother, and you continue the good fight against an industry that needs some heroes who step forward to hold them accountable. I never thought I would ever say that my association with a LAWYER would make me a better person, but you certainly managed that feat. Keep fighting for the right and making the world a better, safer place."

Stanley also persisted in his suit against the federal government for the failures of MSHA inspectors to protect Rizzle and Elvis at Aracoma. That case took on larger importance because, just as he'd predicted, none of the West Virginia attorneys representing the Upper Big Branch victims filed a similar suit. If in the end he won, West Virginia miners would be able to sue their government for its misconduct in a way they had never been able to do before. That could be monumental, and Stanley prepared diligently.

In May 2012, Stanley argued before a three-judge panel at the United States Court of Appeals for the Fourth Circuit in Richmond that Bragg and Hatfield should be able to sue the federal government because of the unconscionable misconduct of the MSHA safety regulators at Aracoma. Stanley hoped that the court would send the case back to the Supreme Court of Appeals of West Virginia for a full hearing.

In July, the Fourth Circuit returned the case to the Charleston court. The federal court was practically setting it up so that the West Virginia court would allow the case to go forward to hold MSHA partly responsible for the Aracoma mine fire. In October 2012, Stanley argued as much in the state capital. Stanley feared that the Charleston court might turn its back not just on the United States Court of Appeals but on the miners of West Virginia.

In February 2013 the court ruled 5–0 in an opinion written by Davis that "a safety inspector owes a duty of care to the employees whose safety the inspection is intended to secure." That may have been self-evident but it could prove one of the most important outcomes of the years of struggle against Massey.

Another man would have been in a hugely self-congratulatory mood over what he had achieved. That was not Bruce Stanley. Sometimes he would sit in front of his computer screen at three in the morning, despairing of everything he had done, considering it endlessly futile, some kind of cosmic joke.

The mountains of Stanley's youth had been disfigured; many West Virginians, including his own parents, had been displaced; and the region, despite having been the backbone of the Industrial Revolution, still ranked among the most impoverished in the nation. And then there was Blankenship. One of the things that had always bothered Stanley about Don Blankenship was how Don was a Mingo County boy and yet was capable of doing all that he had done to his own people. It was bad enough that West Virginia had always been set upon by outsiders, but to have one of your own, who could have done so much good, bring about so much harm was hard to take.

As the months went by, Blankenship continued to walk free and immensely wealthy, while the bodies of Rizzle, Elvis, the twenty-nine victims of Upper Big Branch, and some of Blankenship's neighbors lay in the ground. Stanley heard persistent rumors that the former Massey chairman could still face criminal charges for his role in the mine disaster. Stanley had been appalled at the feckless federal investigation after the Aracoma tragedy that had protected Blankenship and other Massey executives from criminal prosecution. The lawyer had placed much of the blame on the acting U.S. attorney in Charleston. But the new U.S. attorney in West Virginia, R. Booth Goodwin II, was going after one Blankenship subordinate after another, building a conspiracy case that appeared to be leading to the former Massey chairman.

Blankenship acted as if that was all behind him. He started a website where he described himself as "Don Blankenship: Competitionist" and set out to become leader of a movement to transform America. "I encourage like-minded Americans to join me on my journey to Save The Country and pursue real solutions to the problems that are threatening the prosperity of the United States that the politicians in Washington D.C. are unable or unwilling to address," he wrote, asking people to e-mail him. He tweeted: "Miners deserve the safest coal mine that truth and technology can give them. They aren't getting either today. We need to change that."

When Stanley saw all this, he wished he could have Fawcett's proud sense of fulfillment, but he was haunted by those deaths and by Blankenship walking bold and free. Stanley felt a sickening sense of irresolution and failure.

Then Stanley told himself that Blankenship had been forced out of Massey, and if not for all that Stanley had put in motion after Aracoma, Blankenship's reign probably would have survived the deaths of those twenty-nine miners. And then he reflected that *Caperton* had reached the United States Supreme Court and stopped wealthy individuals and powerful organizations from easily buying verdicts with contributions. And when he learned in October 2012 that the Virginia Supreme Court had agreed to hear *Caperton*, he knew that after more than fourteen years the struggle went on. He and Fawcett once again would argue that the case must not die in a barrage of legalisms, but live so that justice may be done.

And then Stanley thought of those with whom he had worked all these years in his struggle against Blankenship. Hugh Caperton had attempted to hold not only Blankenship and Massey accountable but the nation's entire court system. The widows not only had confronted Massey and Blankenship but were trying to hold the federal mine regulation system responsible for its myriad failures. Don Dillon and the other coal slurry litigants had not settled until they'd sent a message that corporate polluters were not immune from justice even in the farthest reaches of the coal fields. Stanley knew that he and Fawcett had stayed true to their idealistic beliefs as young lawyers, that they had held true to their clients no matter the price, and he felt good about that and knew that he had done right.

In the midst of it all, back when Stanley was at his most despairing, nineteen-year-old Laura Stanley returned home from college at WVU during a vacation break and showed her father a poem she had written about Stanley's struggle. He had thought about his daughter's poem many times since then. It said what had to be said and inspired him to never give up until he and Fawcett helped bring Blankenship to justice:

Devils slipping through the cracks,
Of courtroom floors and laws in books,
Filling up their piggy banks,
With proof from lives in which they took.

Vacationing on sweat and blood,
Of those they will not think of twice,
Sipping cocktails victoriously,
'Cause they're the men and we're the mice.

But judgment comes in many forms,
Though some may start out mild or vague
What a shame they don't recall
That it was the mice who brought the plague.

NOTES

PROLOGUE

4 *Harper's*: http://leamer.com/ecclesnosix.html.

PART ONE

11 Forty-year-old Hatfield wore: Interview, Tonya Hatfield.

13 Forty-three of those fifty-four cases: Interview, Amir Tayrani; *New York Times*, August 18, 2009.

14 revenues of $2 billion: *Charleston Gazette*, February 1, 2008.

14 "learned about, and struggled": http://www.donblankenship.com/about.html.

14 "What you have to accept": http://www.youtube.com/watch?v=S9lBWdK37VM.

15 "a frightening result": Memorandum, Don Blankenship to Massey Members, August 5, 2002.

15 In the eight years before: *Morning Edition*, NPR, March 3, 2009.

15 "impenetrable bulwark": http://press-pubs.uchicago.edu/founders/documents /v1ch14s50.html.

15 an average of $473,000: James Sample, *The New Politics of Judicial Elections, 2000–2009: Decade of Change* (New York: Brennan Center for Justice, 2010), p. 9.

15 Most likely, no individual: Interview, James Sample.

17 an interview Blankenship gave: *New York Times*, March 4, 2009; interview, off the record.

17 "flood of litigation": On Writ of Certiorari to the Supreme Court of Appeals of West Virginia, Brief for Respondents, *Caperton v. Massey*, Supreme Court of the United States, November 2009, p. 42 (http://brennan.3cdn.net/ 7b08a0af0f39d86b33_6jm6ibf6o.pdf).

17 Others credited the attorney's fourth wife: *USA Today,* August 29, 2011.

18 Olson to spend the next few hours: Interview, Theodore Olson.

19 "Blankenship may have": Interview, Dave Fawcett.

20 He boasted that: Author's discussion with Don Blankenship.

21 "Tonya! I can't believe": Interviews, Tonya Hatfield and Bruce Stanley.

22 "You know it's all the same": Interview, Bruce Stanley.

23 "more like a whale than a dolphin": Interview, Dave Fawcett.

26 "to have the honor": Interview, Theodore Olson.

27 Hatfield's predawn arrival: Interview, Tonya Hatfield.

27 "the beginning of the end": Interview, Dave Fawcett.

28 "in too many states, judicial": Quoted in "Judicial Independence: Remarks by Ohio Chief Justice Thomas J. Moyer," *Duquesne Law Review,* Fall 2010, p. 845.

28 The reporter gave a concise: Dave Fawcett, "On Harman: Prefatory Note from Counsel," *Duquesne Law Review,* Fall 2010, pp. 737–38.

29 "When Benjamin won": *All Things Considered,* NPR, March 3, 2009.

29 "I want to tell you something": Fawcett, "On Harman," p. 738.

PART TWO

34 In the midafternoons: Barbara Freese, *Coal: A Human History* (Cambridge, MA: Perseus, 2003), photo insert.

34 thin legs, devastated by rickets: Ibid., p. 83.

34 "chronic ennui": Ibid., p. 153.

35 "in the worst of the company-controlled": Quoted in John Alexander Williams, *Appalachia: A History* (Morgantown: West Virginia University Press, 2001), p. 259.

35 there were 130,457 miners: Figures courtesy of West Virginia Office of Miners' Health, Safety and Training.

36 produced 98 percent: *Coal Facts 2011* (Charleston, WV: West Virginia Coal Association, 2011), p. 20.

36 15,940 citizens each year: West Virginia Health Statistics Center, Statistical Brief No. 8 (http://www.wvdhhr.org/bph/oehp/hsc/briefs/eight/default.htm).

36 bought the closed Harman coal mine: Hugh Caperton owned a group of small companies, including the Harman Development Corporation, Harman Mining Corporation, and Sovereign Coal Sales, Inc. The Harman mine was the most important asset. It was at the center of the legal dispute between Caperton and Massey. In this book, these business entities will be referred to as "Harman" or the "Harman mine."

38 "acts of God, acts": Brief for Petitioners, *Caperton v. Massey,* Supreme Court of the United States, p. 4.

47 "A man wants to make a living": Interview, Dave Fawcett.

48 broke into a cold sweat: Interview, Dave Fawcett.

48 "bean counter": *Orange County Register,* April 11, 1993.

49 dismissed 12.8 percent of the employees: Ibid.

50 those children they could play with: Interviews, Eddie Croaff and Larry Croaff.

50 "you could only use": Donblankenship.com/about.html.

50 red from iron: *Charleston Daily Mail,* July 11, 2005.

50 Donnie, as everyone: Interview, Robin Croaff.

50 his hero, Willie Mays: Interviews, Eddie Croaff and Larry Croaff.

50 get the car up to 110: Interview, Eddie Croaff.

51 firing blasting caps: Interview, Darrell Ratliff.

51 CPA exam: Transcript of *Caperton v. Massey* in the Circuit Court of Boone County, West Virginia, July, 15, 2002, p. 10.

52 "I don't know anyone": *The Kingmaker,* West Virginia PBS documentary, Anna Sale, producer, 2005.

52 "closing down doors": Interview, Dave Fawcett.

53 "You'll have a real problem": Deposition of Donald L. Blankenship in *Harman v. Wellmore,* September 30, 1998, p. 165.

54 Fawcett and his legal assistant: Interviews, Dave Fawcett and Rob Devine.

55 "So you fellows came through": Interview, Jay Hoke.

57 "It's the way it was done": Ibid.

62 "Do I want to jump back": Interview, Bruce Stanley.

62 seventeen deputies had died: Rebecca J. Bailey, *Matewan Before the Massacre: Politics, Coal, and the Roots of Conflict in a West Virginia Mining Community* (Morgantown: West Virginia University Press, 2008), p. 186.

63 Bruce's two older brothers often: Interview, Joe Stanley.

66 "Let's talk about your coverage": Interviews, Bruce Stanley and Debbie Stanley.

66 up to $200 a week: *Williamson Daily News,* January 17, 1985.

66 bullet-shattered Zenith: *New York Times,* April 8, 2010.

66 armored personnel carrier: *Williamson Daily News,* April 24, 1985.

66 Blankenship walked out nonchalantly: *Williamson Daily News,* February 19, 1985.

66 his unpublished autobiography: Interview, off the record. See also *Charleston Daily Mail,* July 11, 2005.

67 "gotten too powerful": *Charleston Gazette,* March 31, 1985.

68 "wouldn't have expected": Interview, Patrick McGinley.

71 "I was raised in a house": Interview, Hugh Caperton.

72 Stanley asked himself: Interview, Bruce Stanley.

74 attempting to transform: Interview, Gregory Jordan.

75 He had to be intrigued: Ibid.

80 Stanley had seen Caperton: Interview, Bruce Stanley.

82 Berthold admired Flaherty's: Interview, Robert Berthold.

82 settle for around $25 million: Interviews, Bruce Stanley and Dave Fawcett. The two attorneys learned this much later.

83 But he sensed that Caperton: Interview, Dave Fawcett.

83 As Caperton sat: Interview, Hugh Caperton.

PART THREE

89 "*Voir dire* comes from a French word": Transcript of *Caperton v. Massey* in the Circuit Court of Boone County, West Virginia, May 30, 2002, p. 46.

90 "All of my kin": *Caperton v. Massey,* May 31, 2002, p. 171.

90 "Charlie Chan movie where Charlie": Interview, Jay Hoke.

91 Hoke knew Charleston-based: Ibid.

91 A hush fell: Interview, Bruce Stanley.

91 "What's the matter": Interview, Jay Hoke.

93 "The first part of the story is about people coming together": *Caperton v. Massey,* June 17, 2002, p. 130.

93 "Ladies and gentlemen, corporate greed": Ibid., p. 132.

94 "to inoculate the jury": Interview, Dave Fawcett.

94 "So, what is Mr. Caperton's case about?": *Caperton v. Massey,* June 17, 2002, p. 184.

95 "Massey crushed the deal": Ibid., p. 189.

95 "I represent Massey and its West Virginia": *Caperton v. Massey,* Ibid., p. 194.

96 "No company that Mr. Caperton has ever": Ibid., p. 204.

96 Caperton glared at Ramey: Interview, Hugh Caperton.

98 "Caperton knew from the beginning": *Caperton v. Massey,* June 17, 2002, p. 212.

99 "fundamental strategic mistake": Interview, Bruce Stanley.

99 "The opening by Mr. Ramey": *Caperton v. Massey,* June 17, 2002, p. 213.

99 "Ladies and gentlemen": *Caperton v. Massey,* June 17, 2002, p. 215.

101 "What are you doing, Henry?": Interview, Dave Fawcett.

102 even he thought this was going: Interview, Henry Cook.

102 "A person that gets on the list": *Caperton v. Massey,* June 19, 2002, p. 75.

103 "The question, Mr. Cook, was": *Caperton v. Massey,* June 21, 2002, p. 27.

103 "SG squared": Interview, Bruce Stanley.

106 "There's the fucking box!": Interview, Dave Fawcett.

110 He said that if he was crying: Interview, Ancil Ramey.

111 "I know that you guys": *Caperton v. Massey,* June 28, 2002, p. 8.

111 "Your Honor, we would ask": Ibid., p. 38.

112 "My co-counsel, who was watching": *Caperton v. Massey,* July 2, 2002, p. 12.

115 "Our objective was to retire": *Caperton v. Massey,* July 3, 2002, p. 99.

120 "Was there any discussion": *Caperton v. Massey,* July 8, 2002, p. 38.

124 "Thank God he": Interview, Dave Fawcett.

125 "Because I haven't been able to pay": *Caperton v. Massey,* July 20, 2002, p. 52.

125 "One of the things that happened to me": Ibid., p. 53.

127 "I'll fight them as long as": Ibid., p. 64.

129 "Thank you, Your Honor": Ibid., p. 75.

130 "The reason I'm doing this": Interview, Bruce Stanley.

130 "Harman *was* successful": *Caperton v. Massey,* July 11, 2002, p. 44.

130 "Yes, that's what I said": Ibid., p. 128.

131 "pruning a tree": Interview, Hugh Caperton.

131 "Isn't it a fact that you got": *Caperton v. Massey,* July 12, 2002, p. 61.

131 "Documents don't lie, do they?": Ibid., p. 62.

132 "Would it be fair to say": Ibid., p. 77.

133 "Let everybody understand": Ibid., p. 229.

135 "Subject to exceptions that I might determine": Ibid., p. 79.

135 General William Westmoreland's: *New York Times,* April 28, 2011.

135 Blankenship described how: *Caperton v. Massey,* July 15, 2002, p. 29.

135 initially had some interest: Ibid., p. 76.

135 "absent a reorganization": Ibid., p. 154.

136 "You can avoid": Ibid., p. 156.

136 Harman had $17,839,000 in assets: Ibid. These are the figures given in court, but the negative value would appear to be $11,161,103.

136 $22,000,000 of the liabilities: Ibid., p. 201.

136 $29,696,000 in damages: Ibid., p. 191.

137 $4,783,098 before he retired: *Caperton v. Massey,* July 16, 2002, p. 119.

137 "That comes to $866,350,000": Ibid., p. 143.

137 "Let's close the door": *Caperton. v. Massey,* July 17, 2002, p. 32.

137 "I think we're beyond the scope": Ibid., p. 38.

138 "I wouldn't have imposed this": Ibid., p. 47.

138 Massey's profits rose from $126 million: Ibid., p. 51.

141 "On the other hand, Don": Ibid., p. 109.

141 one of the worst safety records: *Wall Street Journal,* February 13, 2006.

141 spent more than twenty-five hundred hours: Interview, Rob Devine.

142 "No. We'll indicate minimum": Stan Suboleski to Don Blankenship, Drexel Short, August 1, 1997, Plaintiff's Exhibit No. 267, *Caperton v. Massey.*

143 "I had examined him": Interview, Dave Fawcett.

143 "The reply from my memo came back": *Caperton v. Massey,* July 17, 2002, p. 171.

144 "And what did you say?": Ibid., p. 205.

145 "You guys have been": Interview, Rob Devine.

145 "Why are you here?": Interview, Hugh Caperton.

146 "Your Honor, may we approach, please?": *Caperton v. Massey,* July 18, 2002, p. 46.

146 The roughly fifteen hundred employees: Ibid., p. 52.

147 "to deliver bad news": Ibid., p. 85.

147 "Don, do you have some ill will": Ibid., p. 109.

148 Massey removed the bluff: *Charleston Gazette,* February 8, 2003.

148 "We can't live like this!": Interview, Kathy Caperton.

149 "We both know a little something": *Caperton v. Massey,* July 18, 2002, p. 117.

150 "Mass protests by the union?": Ibid., p. 120.

151 "I don't recollect much of anything": Ibid., p. 131.

151 "No, you know Hugh is trying to": Ibid., p. 134.

152 "I think that if there's any CEO": Ibid., p. 126.

153 "We're unable to continue to invest": *Charleston Gazette,* July 20, 2001.

154 "small spills": Ibid.

154 as much as three inches: *Charleston Gazette,* July 21, 2002.

154 stripping out 870,000 tons: *Charleston Gazette,* July 20, 2002.

154 earnings fall from $203.4 million in 1999: Ibid.

155 "And, in fact, it would have threatened": *Caperton v. Massey,* July 19, 2002, p. 16.

155 "You're one of the two biggest assholes": Interview, Paul Nyden.

156 "Your Honor, we are very concerned": *Caperton v. Massey,* July 22, 2002, p. 5.

157 "sabotage": *Charleston Gazette,* July 28, 2002.

157 "observed children swimming": Ibid.

157 "I don't want to point": *Caperton v. Massey,* July 22, 2002, p. 7.

157 "I take that and note that for the record": Ibid., p. 9.

158 The thief had taken from Caperton's bulletin board: Interview, Hugh Caperton.

159 "How long of a drive": Interview, David Fawcett Jr.

159 "Good morning, Mr. Blankenship": *Caperton v. Massey,* July 22, 2002, p. 16.

159 "Do you have a wall or a fence": Ibid., p. 17.

160 "You could save the jury": Ibid., p. 30.

160 "But you did not read": Ibid., p. 56.

160 "Is it a practice of Massey?": Ibid., p. 76.

161 "not a hundred percent": Ibid., p. 88.

161 "I would say it is clear": Ibid., p. 134.

162 "Oh, man, I wish": *Caperton v. Massey,* July 29, 2002, p. 53.

162 The jurors had become boisterous: *Caperton v. Massey,* August 1, 2002, p. 6.

163 "That wasn't my husband": Interviews, Kathy Caperton and Hugh Caperton.

163 Let's assume that an individual": *Caperton v. Massey,* July 27, 2002, p. 153.

165 "That is the one reason I did it": Ibid., p. 270.

165 "concern with regard to the court's": Ibid., p. 275.

166 "Today I respectfully": *Charleston Gazette,* August 2, 2002.

166 weeks later much of Magic Island: *Charleston Gazette,* August 20, 2002.

167 "I have sat through all the evidence": *Caperton v. Massey,* July 31, 2002, p. 138.

168 "Nothing that I have said": Ibid., p. 175.

169 "I don't want you": *Caperton v. Massey,* July 31, 2002, p. 195.

170 two-thirds full: *Caperton v. Massey,* August 1, 2002, p. 6.

171 "We think the trial should not": Ibid., p. 12.

171 "We all know that just": Ibid., p. 14.

171 "Can I get you some water, ma'am?": Ibid., p. 24.

172 "Sow's Ear, Incorporated, is going": Ibid., p. 27.

172 "This family, the Harman family, wasn't Ozzie": Ibid., p. 31.

173 "simply living on borrowed time" : Ibid., p. 104.

173 "The clerk's office doesn't keep handbags": Ibid., p. 82.

173 everything he said and did: Interview, Ancil Ramey.

173 "Now, there is an old saying": *Caperton v. Massey,* August 1, 2002, p. 95.

175 "In Mr. Ancil Ramey's opening": Ibid., p. 126.

176 "Now, ladies and gentlemen, this is a very": Ibid., p. 124.

176 "The damages [Harman incurred . . .] were never": Ibid., p. 130.

176 "Thank you": Ibid., p. 131.

177 "If Hugh Caperton can't stop": Ibid., p. 132.

178 "And *that,*" Stanley said: Ibid., p. 137.

179 "Ladies and gentlemen, that concludes": Ibid., p. 140.

180 Fawcett made his way to the basement: Interview, Dave Fawcett.

180 Devine busied himself packing: Interview, Rob Devine.
181 As he sat talking: Interview, Hugh Caperton.
181 Hoke looked over: Interview, Jay Hoke.
181 He would say later that: Ibid.
181 "They treated us": Interview, Barbara Jewett.
182 Fawcett dropped down onto the grass: Interview, Dave Fawcett.
182 Caperton cried in joy: Interview, Hugh Caperton.
182 "Dave, treasure this moment": Interview, Bruce Stanley.
183 "Whoa, we're in Massey country": Interview, Dave Fawcett.

PART FOUR

187 "The verdict is a frightening result": Don Blankenship to Massey members, August 5, 2002.
188 losing Massey subsidiaries had appealed: *Charleston Gazette,* September 14, 2002.
188 Woods says that the malpractice suit: Interview, Jeff Woods.
190 "Show that you care": Interview, Dave Fawcett.
191 "Anytime I made a decision": Interview, Jay Hoke.
193 The third new judge: *Charleston Daily Mail,* November 6, 1996.
193 loaned her campaign $216,737: *Charleston Daily Mail,* December 6, 1996.
193 "Because I represent": Interview, Scott Segal.
193 their adopted son, Oliver: *Charleston Gazette,* September 6, 1998.
193 Before announcing for office: *Charleston Gazette,* January 22, 2008.
193 endorsement of the UMW: *Charleston Daily Mail,* March 23, 1996.
194 "I'm told by folks in the asbestos": Interview, Larry Starcher.
194 "like a teacher instructing": *Charleston Daily Mail,* October 30, 2002.
194 Starcher figured that he could mentor Davis: Interview, Larry Starcher.
194 Starcher himself had grown up: Larry Victor Starcher, "An Abbreviated Autobiography" (unpublished manuscript), pp. 3–4.
195 "tearing itself apart, and I knew": *Charleston Daily Mail,* June 19, 2000.
195 Starcher and Davis were subsequently overheard: *Charleston Gazette,* September 28, 1998.
195 "I'm almost certain that if Judge Starcher": Interview, Rodney Teal.
195 fifty-one of the approximately: *Charleston Daily Mail,* June 19, 2000.
196 "She's no Loretta Lynn": Interview, Larry Starcher.
196 "He would practically jump over the table": Interview, Steven Canterbury.
196 "If you cuss at me again": Interview, Larry Starcher.
197 "not just the financial well-being": *Charleston Daily Mail,* July 3, 2003.
197 In twelve of the thirteen cases: Justice Maynard voted favoring Segal's position in *State of West Virginia ex rel. Purdue Pharma, L.P. v. The Honorable N. Edward Eagloski,* No. 051692, November 5, 2005; *State ex rel. Independence Coal Co. v. Jay Hoke, Judge,* No. 071498, June 6, 2007; *State ex rel. Thomas Taylor et al. v. The Honorable David W. Nibert,* No. 062122, September 7, 2007; *In Re: Flood Litigation v. The Honorable John A. Hutchinson,* No.

060452, May 11, 2006; *Stump v. Chemtall*, No. 31766, May 31, 2005; *Tawney/CNR*, No. 32966, June 15, 2006; *Nationwide Lit*, No. 33175, November 30, 2006; *Stump v. Chemtall*, No. 33380, November 15, 2007; *Tawney/Columbia National Resources*, No. 32966, March 2, 2006; *Tawney/CNR*, No. 062307, September 21, 2006; *Nationwide Lit*, No. 062122, September 7, 2006; and *Southern WV Flood Litigation*, No. 72266, November 7, 2007. The justices voted unanimously against Segal in *Herbert J. Thomas Hospital*, No. 06144, June 28, 2006.

197 "What people tend to do": Interview, Scott Segal.

198 "secret war on judges": *Forbes*, July 21, 2003.

198 McGraw thought that the cover image: Interview, Warren McGraw.

198 "people like Spike Maynard": *Charleston Daily Mail*, July 3, 2003.

201 child welfare authorities concluded: Statement of Facts in Brief of the Appellant to the Supreme Court of Appeals of West Virginia, *State of West Virginia v. Tony Dean Arbaugh, Jr.*, p. 5.

201 Tony and Brian escaped: Interview, Tony Arbaugh Jr.

201 one morning in February 1997: Ibid.

201 This was the first time that Tony: Ibid.

201 "The last time I had": Ibid.

202 "Tony is a gentle, good soul": Interview, Terry Sigley.

202 "He was the most motivated kid": Interview, Gary McDaniel.

203 "That was part of me growing": Interview, Tony Arbaugh.

203 Arbaugh's attorney, Roth, begged: Interview, Jeffrey Roth.

204 "doesn't usually take offenders": *State of West Virginia v. Tony Dean Arbaugh, Jr.*, transcript of proceedings before Judge Donald H. Cookman, April 11, 2002, p. 3.

204 Arbaugh had a woman who: *State of West Virginia v. Tony Dean Arbaugh, Jr.*, Felony case no. 2003-F-24.

205 between 85 and 95 percent: Tony Arbaugh sent the author a highlighted copy of an article in the *Sunday Gazette-Mail* of January 8, 2012, that referenced these figures. They are well documented in academic literature. See, for instance, David Finkelhor, Richard Ormrod, and Mark Chaffin, "Juveniles Who Commit Sex Offenses Against Minors," *Juvenile Justice Bulletin*, December, 2009, https://www.ncjrs.gov/pdffiles1/ojjdp/227763.pdf.

205 he went to his two progressive: Interview, Larry Starcher.

206 "would be employed as a janitor": http://www.courtswv.gov/supreme-court/docs/spring2004/31326.htm.

206 "provide janitorial services": Community Rehabilitation Plan, Client: Tony Arbaugh, filed April 11, 2002; *State of West Virginia v. Tony Dean Arbaugh, Jr.*, transcript of proceedings before Honorable Donald H. Cookman, April 11, 2002, p. 9.

206 "the majority eviscerates the law": http://www.courtswv.gov/supreme-court/docs/spring2004/31326d.htm.

206 "repeatedly raped his younger half-brother": No. 31326, *State of West Virginia v. Tony Dean Arbaugh, Jr.*, J. Davis, dissenting, joined by Chief Justice Maynard, p. 6.

207 "I wish to express": No. 31326, *State of West Virginia v. Tony Dean Arbaugh, Jr.*, J. Starcher, concurring, in part, and dissenting, in part, filed March 31, 2004; http://www.courtswv.gov/supreme-court/docs/spring2004/31326c2.htm.

207 "Rod Lee [of Youth Services]": Letter from Tony Arbaugh to author, August 27, 2012.

208 "a terrible injustice had been done to Tony": Interview, Art Kerns.

208 "He was on the right path": Interview, Rod Lee.

210 "fossil-fuelless vision of the future": *Charleston Daily Mail*, October 2, 2000.

210 "basically a coal-fired victory": Freese, *Coal*, p. 194.

210 "payback": Ibid.

211 Benjamin started pontificating: Interview, off the record.

211 "I don't know who you are": *New York Times*, March 4, 2009.

211 Blankenship agreed: Interview, off the record.

212 "play[ing] a role": Don Blankenship to Massey members, August 5, 2002.

212 "Letting a child rapist": TNS Media Intelligence, "For the Sake of the Kids," television advertisement aired September 4, 2004.

214 "everything in Brent Benjamin's campaign": *New York Times*, October 24, 2004.

215 "There are people who": http://www.youtube.com/watch?v=TQ6nQaE2FM8.

215 McGraw denies: Interview, Warren McGraw.

216 which raised about $2 million: Brief for Respondents, *Caperton v. Massey*, Supreme Court of the United States, February 24, 2009, p. 4.

217 "Warren McGraw and Brent Benjamin are not": *Outlook*, West Virginia Public Broadcasting, October 14, 2004.

218 "used the decision to set her colleagues": *Charleston Gazette*, October 3, 2004.

218 "Massey's got a $50 million": *The Last Campaign*, documentary, Wayne Ewing, director, 2005.

219 60 percent: Reply Brief for Petitioners, *Caperton v. Massey*, Supreme Court of the United States, p. 5.

219 "Nice to meet you, Dan": Interview, off the record.

219 "I can tell you I am not bought by anybody": *Charleston Gazette*, November 3, 2004.

219 hotel bar: *Charleston Gazette*, November 3, 2004, and November 4, 2004.

219 where he met up with his buddy: *Charleston Gazette*, November 7, 2004.

220 "no independent expenditure group": Transcript of Forum on Judicial Advertising, National Press Club, May 23, 2007.

221 targeting Starcher for defeat: *Wall Street Journal*, February 13, 2006; *Charleston Gazette*, October 29, 2005.

221 would spend $4 million: *Charleston Daily Mail*, October 27, 2005.

222 "I'm feeling scared, alone, threatened": Interview, Tony Arbaugh Jr.

PART FIVE

226 Bradley described what had been happening: Interview, James Bradley.

226 In the first months of 2004: James Bradley examination, p. 948.

227 "I'd been listening to all": Ibid.; interview, James Bradley.

227 "We're going to take you and show you": James Bradley examination, p. 948.

228 "I'll do whatever I can do to make": Ibid.

229 This was the first time Fawcett: Interview, Dave Fawcett.

231 "I bet you anything it's a Massey mine": Interview, Bruce Stanley.

232 eleven other miners had died: *Charleston Gazette,* April 7, 2010.

233 In March 2006, Stanley read: *Pittsburgh Post-Gazette,* March 30, 2006.

234 Tonya went out to visit Freda: Ibid.

234 As Tonya looked across Freda's narrow trailer: Ibid.

236 Stanley tracked down the transcribing: Interview, Bruce Stanley.

237 Delorice Bragg was fifteen: Interview, Delorice Bragg.

238 Delorice gave her husband: Joby Warrick, "Into the Darkness: Deep in the Dangerous Mines of West Virginia, Thousands Willingly Risk Their Lives— for Coal, a Good Paycheck and Each Other," *Washington Post,* January 21, 2007.

238 2:30 P.M. shift, which would last: Examination under oath of Elmer Mayhorn Jr., Mine Safety and Health Administration, Coal Mine Safety and Health, February 10, 2006, p. 27.

238 "Have you heard anything": Jeff Goodell, "You Fight for What You've Got, Even If It's Only Worth a Dime," *Oprah,* July 2006.

239 "You know, kiddo": Interview, Tonya Hatfield.

240 "I think we can do this, Bruce": Interview, Delorice Bragg.

240 "I've got the armor of widows around me": Interview, Bruce Stanley.

241 "Don and Elvis were just two guys": Ibid.

242 defamation for reprinting: *Charleston Gazette,* June 16, 2005.

243 "Financially I know": Handwritten note on memo prepared by Deborah K. May, July 11, 2005, filed in *Deborah K. May v. West Virginia Bureau of Employment Programs,* Supreme Court of Appeals of West Virginia, Case No. 33703, January term, 2008.

243 "Got a message from Mr. B": Handwritten note, July 12, 2005, in ibid.

244 "I've had three dogs stolen": Don Blankenship to Deborah May, July 12, 2004, in ibid.

244 "her symptoms appear to be": From J. Timothy Kohari, DO, to "To Whom It May Concern," December 22, 2005, in ibid.

244 "That's okay": Interview, Larry Starcher.

244 "On two different occasions": *Deborah K. May v. Chair and Members, Board of Review; Commissioner, West Virginia Bureau of Employment Programs; and Mate Creek Security, Incorporated,* Supreme Court of Appeals of West Virginia, Justice Albright and Justice Starcher, concurring, June 17, 2008.

245 three days in a row: *New York Times,* January 15, 2008.

245 Magann told two close friends: Interview, Sheila Crider.

246 "She opens the purse": Ibid.

246 at the famous Grand Casino: Associated Press, January 25, 2008.

247 In response to a speech Blankenship: *Charleston Daily Mail,* November 1, 1995.

247 "surmise, conjecture and political rhetoric": *Charleston Daily Mail,* August 21, 2006.

248 "It makes me want to puke": *New York Times,* October 1, 2006.

248 "the biggest name-dropper": Interview, Larry Starcher.

248 "Robin has done such a great job": Ibid.

248 "You *are* trying": Ibid.

248 "I think that Benjamin": Ibid.

249 "If he's your friend": *Charleston Gazette,* November 7, 2004.

249 Canterbury despised Starcher: Interview, Steven Canterbury.

249 "It used to be a good place to work": Interview, Sheila Crider.

249 "When Benjamin was elected, the tables": Interview, Pancho Morris.

249 "The terms 'conservative' and 'liberal' are not helpful": Interview, Tom Rodd.

249 "shall refrain from": http://www.state.wv.us/wvsca/jic/codejc.htm#Canon 5.

250 In October Maynard e-mailed: From Elliot Maynard to Don Blankenship, October 5, 2007.

252 "This is a case about a broken promise": *Wheeling-Pitt v. Massey Energy,* Trial before the Honorable Martin J. Gaughan, May 31, 2007, p. 386.

252 "When the price of coal went up": Ibid., p. 408.

252 "This is not a case about some grand": Ibid., p. 450.

253 "You know, this may sound": Ibid., p. 996.

253 "It's like I'm up there": Interview, Bruce Stanley.

254 its costs had risen only 5 percent: *Wheeling-Pitt v. Massey Energy,* June 20, 2007, p. 3346.

254 "We will not chase these rates": Ibid., p. 3420.

255 to United States Steel for $84 a ton: *Wheeling-Pitt v. Massey Energy,* June 21, 2007, p. 3687.

255 "In February of 2005, according": Ibid., p. 3693.

255 "How does that help to": Ibid., p. 3694.

256 "I think that would have been": Ibid., p. 3696.

257 "When you deliberate": *Wheeling-Pitt v. Massey Energy,* July 2, 2007, p. 5467.

258 "I don't know Mr. Fawcett": Ibid., p. 5474.

258 "Let me tell you something": Ibid., p. 5485.

259 "flaunting what he perceives": *Pittsburgh Post-Gazette,* February 17, 2008.

PART SIX

263 "The true foundation of republican government": *The Supreme Court of Appeals of West Virginia,* state publication, March 2008, p. 20.

265 "I've tried cases for twenty-nine years": *Caperton v. Massey,* Supreme Court of Appeals of West Virginia, hearing October 15, 2007, transcript of audio-tape, p. 16.

265 "never had an opportunity": Ibid., p. 20.

266 Maynard stood up and exited: Interviews, Dave Fawcett, Bruce Stanley, Robert Berthold, and Kathy Caperton.

266 "The doctrine of res judicata": *Caperton v. Massey*, Supreme Court of West Virginia, hearing October 15, 2007, p. 21.

266 "It was their tortious": Ibid., p. 25.

267 "I would like for you to address": Ibid., p. 26.

268 "My understanding of what": Ibid., p. 37.

269 "We've lost!": Interview, Kathy Caperton.

269 "Our next case is *Caperton v. Massey*": Interview, Larry Starcher.

270 "We decided the now $75 million Massey": Personal diary of Larry Starcher.

270 he was interested to see: Interview, Larry Starcher.

271 raised more than $100,000 for Maynard's: *Charleston Gazette*, November 5, 2007.

272 "Fuck," Fawcett said: Interview, Dave Fawcett.

272 he knew the result: Interview, Bruce Stanley.

273 "At the outset, we wish": http://www.courtswv.gov/supreme-court/docs/fall 2007/33350.htm.

274 "'consolation prize' language": http://www.courtswv.gov/supreme-court/docs /fall2007/33350d.htm.

275 "As this went on, you could feel": Interview, Dave Fawcett.

275 As he lay there: Interview, Hugh Caperton.

276 "applied these new and unforeseeable": Petition for Rehearing of Appellee Hugh M. Caperton, Appeal No. 33350, p. 2.

277 "searching for any sign of movement": *Pittsburgh Post-Gazette*, November 20, 2006.

278 "the opinion was about state": Interview, Amir Tayrani.

280 "unable to independently verify": *Charleston Gazette*, January 10, 2008.

284 As early as March 2001, Fawcett had: Dave Fawcett to Dean Starkman, March 2, 2001.

284 Fawcett's voice shook: Interview, Len Boselovic.

284 "We had a staff meeting": Personal diary of Larry Starcher, January 14, 2008.

285 "A justice of the Supreme Court of Appeals": *New York Times*, January 15, 2008.

285 talking surreptitiously to Starcher: Personal diary of Larry Starcher, January 11, 2008.

285 told a close associate: Interview, off the record.

285 "I don't know if it's totally": *Charleston Gazette*, January 16, 2008.

285 "I have no doubt in my mind": *Charleston Daily Mail*, January 18, 2008.

285 state supreme court voted 5–0: *Charleston Gazette*, January 25, 2008.

286 "bomb letter": Personal diary of Larry Starcher, January 22, 2008.

286 FBI agents talked to Crider: Interview, Sheila Crider.

286 "We surmised that the four": Personal diary of Larry Starcher, February 5, 2008.

286 "decidedly farcical flavor": *New York Times*, April 15, 2008.

287 "'directing' the media": Chris Dickerson to Jennifer Bundy, April 14, 2008.

287 His wife, Amy Shuler Goodwin: *Charleston Daily Mail*, May 8, 2008.

288 "It's already happened": *Charleston Gazette,* January 30, 2008.

288 the professional courtesy of meeting: Interview, Theodore Olson.

289 "We had quite a time getting here": Interview, Dave Fawcett.

291 "When I referred to Blankenship": Interview, Larry Starcher.

291 "judge shall disqualify": Jeffrey W. Stempel, "Completing Caperton and Clarifying Common Sense Through Using the Right Standard for Constitutional Judicial Recusal," *Review of Litigation,* vol. 29, no. 2 (January 1, 2010), p. 269.

292 "The pernicious effects of Mr. Blankenship's": *West Virginia Record,* March 20, 2008.

292 Benjamin appointed conservative: *Williamson Daily News,* February 17, 2008.

292 "Mr. Offutt, have you done any research": Transcript of rehearing of *Caperton v. Massey* in Supreme Court of Appeals of West Virginia, March 12, 2008, p. 3.

292 "Do you agree that the majority": Ibid., p. 19.

293 "We suggest respectfully": Ibid., p. 32.

293 "indefensible legal grounds": http://www.courtswv.gov/supreme-court/docs/spring2008/33350d3.htm.

294 "West Virginia seemed like a closed society": Interview, Dave Fawcett.

295 "He [Blankenship] bought himself a seat on the supreme court": http://abc news.go.com/Nightline/video/wva-supreme-court-scandal-4612112.

295 Asa Eslocker, then twenty-seven: Interview, Asa Eslocker.

295 "Mr. Blankenship, ABC News": http://abcnews.go.com/Nightline/video/wva -supreme-court-scandal-4612112.

296 then shoved his camera: *Richmond Times-Dispatch,* April 4, 2008.

296 talked to Maynard's former mistrees: http://abcnews.go.com/Blotter/popup ?id=4582833.

297 "Holy shit, the fucking union": Interview, Dave Fawcett.

298 "When Massey's appeal": Bo Rumpole to Hugh Caperton, May 16, 2008.

298 "Davis was obviously keen": Bo Rumpole to Hugh Caperton, May 14, 2008.

298 "As for Davis, she's a real": Ibid.

299 "affords the Court an ideal": http://brennan.3cdn.net/f493e1e4053bc33660 _agm6b5ib9.pdf.

301 "This issue had a pedigree": Interview, James Sample.

302 "The appearance of impropriety": http://brennan.3cdn.net/3fdc25645e49e48980 _ezm6bnb5s.pdf.

302 "create the perception that legal outcomes": http://brennan.3cdn.net /2c21a25a061c25740f_dkm6bnptq.pdf.

302 "They'll never take your case": Interview, Theodore Olson.

303 "'direct, personal, substantial'": http://www.courtswv.gov/supreme-court/docs/spring2008/33350c4.htm.

304 "This Court's review is necessary": http://brennan.3cdn.net/5ad2b d9e69f3b3b8c3_p7m6bxcsr.pdf.

304 "it would be unwarranted": http://brennan.3cdn.net/90e5d22df01f870452 _gxm6bhhpg.pdf.

304 Sample made an urgent visit: Interview, James Sample.

304 This one issued a rare direct challenge: Interview, Dorothy Samuels.

305 "For some reason, the court seems": *New York Times,* November 12, 2008.

306 "Don Israel 'Rizzle' Bragg": *Bragg and Hatfield v. Aracoma, Massey and Blankenship,* Trial before Judge Roger L. Perry, November 10, 2008, p. 37.

307 there were only four of them: Ibid., p. 69.

307 only twenty-seven men: Davitt McAteer, Thomas N. Bethell, Celeste Monforton, Joseph W. Pavlovich, Deborah Roberts, and Beth Spence, "The Fire at Aracoma Alma Mine #1: A Preliminary Report to Governor Joe Manchin III," November 2006, p. 7.

308 "The evidence is going": *Bragg and Hatfield v. Aracoma and Massey,* November 10, 2008, p. 73.

308 "the fire would not have": *Report of Investigation Fatal Underground Coal Mine Fire,* U.S. Department of Labor Mine Safety and Health Administration, Aracoma Alma Mine #1, p. 41.

309 "I'm not standing here in front": *Bragg and Hatfield v. Aracoma and Massey,* November 10, 2008, p. 22.

309 "What we know beyond": Ibid., p. 86.

309 "a lot like real parents": Ibid., p. 109.

309 "That CEO at McDonald's": Ibid., p. 124.

310 Capitol Movie Theater: *New York Times,* January 14, 2007.

311 "At approximately 2:47 P.M., Mr. Bragg": *Bragg and Hatfield v. Aracoma, Massey and Blankenship,* November 12, 2008, p. 56.

311 "And so some of the men": Ibid., p. 63.

312 "Yes. Yes, they were": Ibid., p. 182.

313 "I went and immediately grabbed": *Bragg and Hatfield v. Aracoma, Massey and Blankenship,* November 13, 2008, p. 15.

314 "Mr. Justice is the man who": Ibid., p. 99.

314 "When I got engulfed in": Ibid., p. 131.

316 for most of his adult life: Interview, John Brown.

316 "He said, 'What the hell is wrong?'": *Bragg and Hatfield v. Aracoma, Massey and Blankenship,* November 12, 2008, p. 185.

317 "And say, 'If anybody asks'": Ibid., p. 183.

318 Logan's mayor, magistrate, police chief, county clerk: *New York Times,* January 14, 2007.

318 "Who did you tell": *Bragg and Hatfield v. Aracoma, Massey and Blankenship,* November 12, 2008, p. 186.

319 "I want the opportunity to play": Ibid., p. 202.

319 "This is bullshit, Tom!": Interview, Bruce Stanley.

320 "He is a man that has done": *Bragg and Hatfield v. Aracoma, Massey and Blankenship,* November 10, 2008, p. 233.

321 "Did you see what he did?": Interview, Delorice Bragg.

321 "the great majority of our problems": Memo from Don Blankenship to "Group Presidents," February 16, 2004.

321 "It's indescribable how discouraging": Memo from Don Blankenship to "Group Presidents," February 17, 2004.

322 "I would question the membership": Quoted in Deposition of Donald Leon Blankenship, July 11, 2008, p. 151.

322 "belt strings were wrapped around": Ibid., p. 168.

323 "It would have been, yes, I mean": Ibid., p. 174.

323 "What does this mean?" Memo from Don Blankenship to Sid Young, January 19, 2006, Deposition Exhibit No. 46.

324 "he was more for the profit": Interview, Ella Workman.

324 "I thought that was a poor thing": Interview, Charlene St. Clair.

325 "It's just a mistake, and people make mistakes": *Charleston Daily Mail*, November 21, 2008.

325 "I've tried to understand him": Interview, Delorice Bragg.

325 The Aracoma Coal Company: *Logan Banner*, October 12, 2010.

325 earned an estimated $23 million: *Pittsburgh Post-Gazette*, December 24, 2008.

326 "a sad ending to a proud": Interview, James Bradley.

327 "For some reason": E-mail from Janie Moore to Steven Canterbury, forwarded to Sheila Crider, February 26, 2009.

327 "I have an e-mail where you": Appeal of Sheila Y. Crider before the Honorable John L. Henning Jr., January 20, 2010, transcript, p. 76.

327 "Justice Davis was very annoyed": Ibid.

328 during the last four weeks: Interview, Theodore Olson.

328 Caperton arrived at Olson's office: Interview, Hugh Caperton.

PART SEVEN

333 Fifteen-year-old Emily turned: Interview, Emily Stanley.

333 He had known Antonin Scalia: Interview, Theodore Olson.

334 "A fair trial in a fair tribunal": http://brennan.3cdn.net/e17f15f7de93fa9a39_vqm6i6u9b.pdf.

336 "fouling the ball": Interview, Theodore Olson.

337 Fawcett was growing increasingly upset: Interview, Dave Fawcett.

342 "This case is so complex": *Charleston Gazette*, March 3, 2009.

PART EIGHT

345 "There is a serious risk of actual": http://graphics8.nytimes.com/packages/images/nytint/docs/supreme-court-opinion-caperton-v-a-t-massey-coal-co/original.pdf.

346 contributed $2,463,500 to: Brief for Petitioners, *Caperton v. Massey*, Supreme Court of the United States, p. 7.

346 roughly $2 million: *Charleston Gazette*, December 4, 2004.

346 "many observers believed": http://graphics8.nytimes.com/packages/images/

nytint/docs/supreme-court-opinion-caperton-v-a-t-massey-coal-co/original .pdf.

347 "While the dissenters predicted": Interview, James Sample.

348 "The case now goes": *Pittsburgh Post-Gazette,* June 11, 2009.

349 that would raise $146,000: *Charleston Gazette,* November 15, 2009.

350 As Fawcett answered: Interview, Dave Fawcett.

350 "My source says the latest": E-mail from Bo Rumpole to Hugh Caperton, September 14, 2009.

350 "Confirmed. Saw a copy": E-mail from Bo Rumpole to Hugh Caperton, September 17, 2009.

351 On November 12, 2009: http://www.courtswv.gov/supreme-court/docs/ fall2009/33350.htm.

351 "The majority has turned West Virginia": http://www.courtswv.gov/supreme -court/docs/fall2009/33350d.htm.

PART NINE

355 coal's share of electric production: *New York Times,* May 30, 2012. Figures also provided by the U.S. Energy Information Administration.

356 new two-year contract: *Charleston Daily Mail,* January 8, 2009.

356 In March, Massey acquired: *Charleston Daily Mail,* March 17, 2010.

356 "The market is strong": Associated Press, March 19, 2010.

356 lay twisted like paper clips: *New York Times,* April 9, 2010.

356 Some of the mourners: *New York Times,* April 7, 2010.

356 at least three thousand times: *Charleston Daily Mail,* April 6, 2010.

356 two citations on the day: *New York Times,* April 7, 2010.

356 several recent evacuations: *New York Times,* April 6, 2010.

356 Representative Nick Rahall had been: *Charleston Daily Mail,* April 8, 2010.

357 "What we're afraid of is that": *New York Times,* April 22, 2010.

357 "to make major improvements": *Pittsburgh Post-Gazette,* April 27, 2010.

357 "a lawyer for a plaintiff": Ibid.

358 poisoned by a Massey subsidiary: Interview, Kevin Thompson; research presented at Don Blankenship coal slurry deposition.

359 All they knew was that: Interview, Larry Brown.

360 "They said it was the worst": Interview, Ben Stout.

360 "Honey, the water is": Interview, Kevin Thompson.

361 four tumors in his back and a cyst: Deposition of Donald K. Dillon, *Halley v. Rawl Sales*, February 6, 2007.

361 constant diarrhea and frequent high fevers: Deposition of Billy Sammons Jr., *Brown v. Rawl*, April 12, 2005.

361 heart problems and was losing: Associated Press, May 1, 2009.

361 born without a pituitary gland: Ibid.

361 sixteen-year-old daughter would never: Ibid.

362 "felt like an animal being": *Charleston Gazette,* May 1, 2009.

363 "at wit's and wallet's end": Interview, Bruce Stanley.

364 He was on welfare until 1996: Deposition of Larry Brown in *Mingo County Coal Slurry Litigation,* April 12, 2005, p. 82.

365 "what do you want me to do": Interview, Larry Brown.

365 "Why, you're from the poor side": Interview, Bruce Stanley.

366 Hoke was perfectly aware: Interview, Jay Hoke.

366 "cancer or renal failure": *Williamson Daily News,* July 20, 2011.

367 Stanley was distressed to see: Interview, Bruce Stanley.

368 She was considering running: Interview, Paul Nyden.

369 "knee-jerk political reactions": *Washington Post,* July 25, 2010.

369 "We regret the national news": *Washington Post,* February 18, 2011.

369 "on the physics": NPR, November 20, 2010.

370 "may clash with longtime": *Wall Street Journal,* November 22, 2010.

370 He left with $10.9 million: *Wall Street Journal,* June 23, 2011; http://www.footnoted.com/wp-content/uploads/2011/06/topperks.doc.pdf.

374 "just scared to death something bad": "Upper Big Branch," Report to the Governor, Governor's Independent Investigation Panel, May 2011, p. 15, http://www.nttc.edu/programs&projects/minesafety/disasterinvestigations/upperbigbranch/UpperBigBranchReport.pdf.

374 "Ultimately, all of the historic lessons": Ibid., p. 55.

375 "If we are going to have": Audio of media conference, courtesy of Ken Ward Jr.

375 "Massey has already put": Ibid.

377 in March 2011: *Charleston Gazette,* March 26, 2011.

378 "If Don Blankenship had any": *Washington Post,* July 25, 2010.

379 "It was more like, Get me": Interview, Donald K. Dillon.

379 "because of the fact of them": Deposition of Donald K. Dillon, *Halley v. Rawl Sales,* February 6, 2007.

379 "To me, Massey is greedy": Ibid.

380 "underground injection probably represents": Deposition of Donald Blankenship in *Re: Mingo County Coal Slurry Litigation*, June 2, 2011, p. 114.

380 "The story I heard": Ibid., p. 224.

382 settled on $35 million: Associated Press, August 9, 2011.

384 Caperton phoned Michael J. Quillen: Interview, Hugh Caperton.

387 "strength and resolve": E-mail from James Sample to author, December 30, 2012.

387 "unfathomable pain": E-mail from Hugh Caperton to author, June 10, 2012.

389 maximum of five years in prison: http://www.justice.gov/usao/wvs/press_releases/March2012/attachments/032912May_plea_agreement.pdf.

392 Stanley filed a suit: Complaint, *Jones et al. v. Blankenship et al.* in the Circuit Court of Raleigh County, West Virginia, April 4, 2012.

393 "a safety inspector owes": *Delorice Bragg and Freda Hatfield v. United States of America*, Supreme Court of West Virginia, filed February 5, 2013.

394 "I encourage like-minded Americans": http://www.donblankenship.com/mail.html.

394 "Miners deserve the safest": *Charleston Gazette*, January 9, 2013.

BIBLIOGRAPHY

Andrews, Thomas G. *Killing for Coal: America's Deadliest Labor War.* Cambridge, MA: Harvard University Press, 2008.

Bailey, Rebecca J. *Matewan Before the Massacre: Politics, Coal, and the Roots of Conflict in a West Virginia Mining Community.* Morgantown: West Virginia University Press, 2008.

Biskupic, Joan. *American Original: The Life and Constitution of Supreme Court Justice Antonin Scalia.* New York: Sarah Crichton / Farrar, Straus and Giroux, 2009.

———. *Sandra Day O'Connor: How the First Woman on the Supreme Court Became Its Most Influential Justice.* New York: Ecco, 2005.

Casto, James E. *Southern West Virginia Coal Country.* Charleston, SC: Arcadia, 2004.

Caudill, Harry M. *Night Comes to the Cumberlands: A Biography of a Depressed Area.* Boston: Little, Brown, 1963.

Clark, Paul F. *The Miners' Fight for Democracy.* Ithaca: Cornell University Press, 1981.

Eller, Ronald D. *Miners, Millhands, and Mountaineers: Industrialization of the Appalachian South, 1880–1930.* Knoxville: University of Tennessee Press, 1982.

Freese, Barbara. *Coal: A Human History.* Cambridge, MA: Perseus, 2003.

Garbus, Martin. *Courting Disaster: The Supreme Court and the Unmaking of American Law.* New York: Times Books, 2002.

Goodell, Jeff. *Big Coal: The Dirty Secret Behind America's Energy Future.* Boston: Houghton Mifflin, 2005.

Reece, Erik. *Lost Mountain: A Year in the Vanishing Wilderness; Radical Strip Mining and the Devastation of Appalachia.* New York: Riverhead, 2006.

Shnayerson, Michael. *Coal River.* New York: Farrar, Straus and Giroux, 2008.

Stern, Gerald M. *The Buffalo Creek Disaster: The Story of the Survivors' Unprecedented Lawsuit.* New York: Random House, 1976.

Stewart, Bonnie E. *No. 9: The 1968 Farmington Mine Disaster.* Morgantown: West Virginia University Press, 2011.

Tams, William Purviance, and Ronald D. Eller. *The Smokeless Coal Fields of West Virginia: A Brief History.* Morgantown: West Virginia University Press, 2001.

Toobin, Jeffrey. *The Nine: Inside the Secret World of the Supreme Court.* New York: Doubleday, 2007.

Waller, Altina L. *Feud: Hatfields, McCoys, and Social Change in Appalachia, 1860–1900.* Chapel Hill: University of North Carolina Press, 1988.

Williams, John Alexander. *Appalachia: A History.* Morgantown: West Virginia University Press, 2001.

ACKNOWLEDGMENTS

In researching and writing *The Price of Justice*, I had help from all kinds of people in all kinds of ways. Any weaknesses and shortcomings are mine and nobody else's.

Without the endless support of Dave Fawcett and Bruce Stanley, this book would hardly exist. Hugh Caperton put up with questions that were at times intrusive. Tonya Hatfield was a wonderful guide to her West Virginia and Kentucky world, and she and her husband, Roger, were gracious hosts when I stayed with them. I also would like to give special thanks to Tony Arbaugh Jr. He is the forgotten victim of my book. Arbaugh is sitting in Huttonsville Correctional Center, where I visited him, and where, I am convinced, he does not belong.

My colleagues in journalism were supportive far beyond the measure of professional courtesy. Paul Nyden of the *Charleston Gazette*, Ian Urbina of the *New York Times*, and Michael Shnayerson of *Vanity Fair* gave me a journalist's most privileged asset: their lists of sources and phone numbers. Ken Ward Jr. of the *Charleston Gazette*, Len Boselovic of the *Pittsburgh Post-Gazette*, Dorothy Samuels and Adam Liptak of the *New York Times*, Shira Ovide of the *Wall Street Journal*, Brian Ross of ABC, Chris Dickerson of the *West Virginia Record*, Asa Eslocker and Madeleine Sauer formerly of ABC, Jeremy Keehn of *Harper's*, and Anna Schecter of NBC were all helpful. As always, organized-crime reporter Dan Moldea was there for me.

This is overwhelmingly a book of reporting, and I was fortunate in the many people who talked to me. I was fortunate, too, in the half a dozen individuals who supplied crucial material but chose to remain anonymous. This includes two persons close to Don Blankenship.

I tried to talk to Blankenship. Many times I asked him for an interview. On one occasion, at the Embassy Suites in Charleston, I asked him in person. He was gracious and polite, but he turned me down.

When I approached Justice Robin Davis of the Supreme Court of Appeals of West Virginia at the Charleston hotel that same day, she spun on her heels and walked away. I also attempted to interview Justice Brent Benjamin. He did not reply to my several requests. I must give a special acknowledgment to Justice Larry Starcher. He not only sat down with me in Morgantown for several interviews but gave me his private diaries for use in this book. I tried to interview the Massey defense lawyers. Ancil Ramey was the only one to talk to me extensively, although Jeff Woods gave a limited interview. I thank them both as well as Scott Segal for his thoughts.

Those who gave me interviews or provided other assistance include Professor Ben M. Stout III, Professor Pat McGinley, Professor James Sample, Tonya Hatfield, Roger Hatfield, James Bradley, Hugh Caperton, Sheila Crider, Steve Canterbury, Charlene St. Clair, Ella Workman, Deb Steinmeyer, Delorice Bragg, Kathleen Fawcett, Barbara Jewett, Rodney Teal, Johnny Brown, Rod Lee, Tony Arbaugh Jr., Sid Young, Debbie Stanley, Laura Stanley, Emily Stanley, Gregory Jordan, Thomas Rodd, David Kessler, Lonnie Owens, Mike Plante, Pat Condron, Dorothy Samuels, Asa Eslocker, Art Kerns, Gary McDaniel, Jeffrey Coleman, Vivian Stockman, Theodore Olson, Terry Sigley, Rod Devine, Tarek Abdalla, Judge Jay Hoke, Paul Nyden, Rob Devine, Jeffrey Roth, Robin Croaff, Eddie Croaff, Larry Croaff, Ancil Ramey, Matt O'Brien, the late Dave Fawcett Jr., Kathy Caperton, Judge Warren McGraw, Len Boselovic, Amir Tayrani, Alicia Schmitt, Darrell Ratliff, Joe Stanley, Carolyn van Zant, Larry Brown, Pancho Morris, Judge Tod J. Kaufman, Lary Garrett, Chris Dickerson, Don Dillon, and Kevin Thompson.

Bob Ickes was, at every stage, my first reader. His comments were always incisive, and his eye for detail and his ability to see the large picture were invaluable. I cannot thank him enough. I met my editor, Serena Jones, at Palm Beach International Airport, where I was signing books at the Paradies Shops. She came up to me, and we started chatting about publishing. She asked me about my next book and grasped completely what I wanted to do. She has never lost her enthusiasm for this project and has made notable contributions to its fruition. I was also extremely lucky in having Leslie Brandon at Holt handle the publicity.

Joy Harris has been my agent for most of my career and is an indispensable part of everything I do. Don Spencer has been doing a stellar job of transcribing my interviews for longer than either of us would like to acknowledge. The astute Ken Norwick has been my lawyer for decades.

A number of people read this book in manuscript, including my attorney brother, Robert, who had a unique perspective; my professor brother, Edward, who is always there for me; and my author colleagues Nigel Hamilton and Burton Hersh. My friend and intellectual sparring partner Dr. Heath King read the manuscript and other materials about Blankenship and provided his rich psychoanalytical insight. My Los Angeles friend and fellow book lover Raleigh Robinson made astute comments about an early draft and then later in the process read the pages again and topped herself in the usefulness of her criticism. My final manuscript reader was an old friend, the investigative journalist Kristina Rebelo, who read with the same focus and dedication she applies to her own work.

As always, my wife, Vesna Leamer, read endless drafts and was incredibly supportive. She took care of everything else in our lives and allowed me to work more than full-time on this project.

Several libraries and research institutions provided invaluable information. The West Virginia State Archives is a wonderful resource on everything West Virginian, and I spent about a week there. The Library of Congress, the District of Columbia Public Library, the Mandel Public Library of West Palm Beach, and the Palm Beach County Library were helpful, too.

With the exception of part of one day at the Boone County trial when a storm blew out the court reporter's transcription machine, the courtroom scenes in *The Price of Justice* are based on the voluminous court transcripts. While I have edited the lengthy courtroom dialogue, I have tried to be true to the letter and spirit of what was said.

One of my fondest memories of my research was the lunch I had with Dave Fawcett's father, the late Dave Fawcett Jr., at Pittsburgh's Duquesne Club. I am proud and happy to dedicate *The Price of Justice* to his memory.

INDEX

ABOUT THE AUTHOR

LAURENCE LEAMER is the bestselling author of fourteen books, including *The Kennedy Women* and *Madness Under the Royal Palms*. Leamer is an award-winning journalist whose work has appeared in *The New York Times Magazine, Harper's,* and *Playboy* and who has most recently written cover stories for *Newsweek*. He lives with his wife, Vesna, in Washington, D.C., and Palm Beach, Florida.